Medicine and the Behavioural Sciences:

an introduction for students of the health
and allied professions

To my family

Medicine and the Behavioural Sciences:

an introduction for students of the health and allied professions

Michael J. Pritchard

Department of Psychiatry
United Medical and Dental Schools
of Guy's and St Thomas's Hospitals
(University of London)

Edward Arnold

© M.J. Pritchard 1986

First published in Great Britain 1986 by
Edward Arnold (Publishers) Ltd, 41 Bedford Square, London WC1B 3DQ

Edward Arnold (Australia) Pty Ltd, 80 Waverley Road, Caulfield East, Victoria 3145, Australia

Edward Arnold, 3 East Read Street, Baltimore, Maryland 21202, U.S.A.

British Library Cataloguing in Publication Data

Pritchard, Michael J.
    Medicine and the behavioural sciences: an introduction for students of the health and allied professions.
    1. Social sciences   2. Psychology
    I. Title
    300′.2461   H61

    ISBN 0-7131-4498-X

Text set in 10/11 pt Times Compugraphic
by Colset Private Ltd, Singapore
Printed and bound in Great Britain by
J.W. Arrowsmith Ltd, Bristol

Preface

The necessity for those working in the health and other caring professions such as medicine, nursing, physiotherapy, occupational therapy, speech therapy, medical social work etc. to have an understanding of human behaviour, both individual and collective, is now well recognized and has been reflected in the introduction of the behavioural sciences, mainly psychology and sociology, into the curricula for students of these professions.

This book is written primarily for such students, though I hope it may also be of value to those, already qualified, whose earlier training was comparatively limited in this area. At the medical postgraduate level it may provide an introduction for trainees in general professional training – especially in such specialities as psychiatry, community medicine and general practice.

There are currently available a number of textbooks specifically for medical, nursing and other health students, devoted to the individual behavioural sciences of psychology and sociology. The approach I have attempted here – facilitated perhaps by single authorship – is to present the two subjects in an integrated fashion with comparisons and cross-referencing wherever appropriate. Such a presentation is, in many ways, easier to achieve within the framework of a book than in a series of lectures or seminars, so that it may prove helpful not only where the subjects are taught separately but even in combined courses.

Recognizing that students from a variety of health disciplines will have different degrees of familiarity with the traditional basic medical sciences and with medicine itself, I have tried to steer a path between, on the one hand, being too technical for some and, on the other hand, seeming patronizingly simplistic to others.

The fact that I am a clinician rather than a behavioural scientist calls for some comment and explanation. In medical education, as the behavioural sciences have become established alongside the more traditional basic medical sciences, their teaching has, quite properly, been taken over increasingly by behavioural scientists in the place of those doctors – such as psychiatrists, general practitioners and community medicine physicians – who largely pioneered their introduction. However, it was as one of those clinicians involved in such early teaching, and having long personal experience of the application of the behavioural sciences in clinical practice, that I was encouraged to write this book.

The question of clinical relevance is important to any consideration of the teaching of sciences basic to medicine but especially for those described as behavioural – in particular whether the content should be limited to those aspects with obvious applications to current medical practice. In my view such a restricted approach in relation to the behavioural sciences fails to provide the breadth of knowledge and understanding of people and their social environments necessary for those involved in the care of the sick. Furthermore it leaves no framework within which to comprehend and evaluate possible future clinical contributions from these sciences.

I have therefore attempted to give at least an outline account of the individual disciplines with something of their history, concepts and methodologies before proceeding to a systematic consideration of four basic and integrative psychosocial perspectives; analytic/reductionist, developmental, differential and interactional. Each of these approaches to the individual and to social groups is examined, together with references to clinical applications where appropriate. Finally, the last section is specifically concerned with the contribution of the behavioural sciences to an understanding of sick patients and their treatment. Although clinical aspects relate throughout to medicine as a whole, there is inevitably a particular concern with psychiatry since it is the branch of medicine dealing with disturbances of behaviour and experience.

Throughout, there are references to publications primarily in recognition of their authors' particular contributions to theory or practice – though these are necessarily selective and illustrative rather than comprehensive. Each chapter is followed by a list of suggestions for further reading.

I should like to make it clear that if the use of the masculine third person singular when referring to individuals is regarded as sexist, this was certainly not the intention and in each case 'he', 'his' etc. should be taken to mean 'he or she', or 'his or her' etc.

Finally, it is my hope that this book will help health students to acquire not only some knowledge of particular clinical applications of the behavioural sciences, but also a greater interest in and deeper understanding of people generally, whether sick or healthy.

London, 1986   Michael J. Pritchard

Acknowledgements

This book had its origin in the behavioural sciences course for pre-clinical students of St Thomas's Hospital Medical School in the teaching of which I participated for some years. This was a co-operative enterprise including clinicians, psychologists, sociologists and statisticians, and I am grateful to my fellow teachers for an experience that was for me both enjoyable and educational. More recently I am indebted to my colleague Phil Richardson, Senior Lecturer in Psychology for his helpful advice and encouragement in bringing the work to completion. My thanks are also due to Elizabeth Kemp, Kay Burton, Liz Critchley and Claire Hook for assistance with various stages in the preparation of the manuscript.

Contents

Part 1
Introduction

Chapter 1 provides a general introduction to the behavioural sciences. It examines their relationship with the social and other sciences and considers man and society as a hierarchical system viewed from different standpoints by the various scientific disciplines. This is followed by a general account of the methodology of the behavioural sciences covering observation, measurement, hypothesis testing, prediction and control. Attention is drawn to various difficulties involved in behavioural science research and its applications, including ethical and moral problems. Finally, four perspectives are described – analytical, developmental, differential and interactional – each of which provides an approach for one of the next four sections of the book.

Chapters 2 and 3 deal respectively with the separate disciplines of psychology and sociology. The plan for each of the two chapters is identical so that the reader may cross refer to the same section in order to make comparisons between the two sciences. The first of these sections is concerned with defining the content and boundaries of each discipline; the rest with their subdivisions and applications, with the four perspectives described in Chapter 1 but now applied to the individual sciences, with the methods of study employed in each and, finally, with some psychological and sociological models.

1

Behavioural sciences

Let us begin by considering a patient. Mr Smith, in bed six in a general medical ward, has had a 'stroke'; there has been an interruption of the blood supply to part of his brain, a 'cerebrovascular accident' or 'CVA', so that he has lost the use of one side of the body. Now an understanding of precisely what has happened from the physical point of view requires a knowledge of human anatomy and physiology. Since it is important for doctors, nurses, physiotherapists and others involved in the treatment of patients to have some such understanding, both subjects are included in the basic sciences studied by students of these various health professions. But is this sufficient? Is Mr Smith just 'the CVA in bed 6' and no different from Mr Jones, 'the CVA in bed 14'? – obviously not. We find perhaps that Mr Smith is very anxious, resentful and demanding – a 'difficult' patient. Mr Jones, on the other hand, maybe a 'good' patient – pleasant, cooperative and compliant with his treatment. Though they are both, as patients, suffering from the same medical condition they are two different individuals each reacting in his own way to the problem of illness, and it is important for those looking after them to take account of this.

But this, it may be said, is obvious and must be well understood. Certainly the importance of considering the whole person and not just the diseased part has always been recognized by the good doctor, while the experienced and sensitive nurse or physiotherapist has likewise been better able to manage the 'uncooperative' patient. If this is the case then is there anything more to understanding patients' behaviour than common sense? It is, unfortunately, a commonly held view that there is not – unfortunate, that is, because it is a view which is usually combined with ignorance of an extensive and well-established body of knowledge about human behaviour and experience which can assist in explaining not only why patients behave as they do, but even on some occasions why they become ill in the first place. To provide some account of this knowledge, to see how it has been obtained and to illustrate its relevance to medicine is a major purpose of this book. At the same time the book will be concerned with the wider psychosocial context in which individual illness occurs and is treated.

The term 'behavioural science', either in the singular or the plural (behavioural sciences), has come to be used in recent years to denote the study of human behaviour both of the individual and of groups of people, small or large. The emphasis tends to be, however, on individual behaviour and on the application of such basic knowledge to medical and paramedical fields, so that we now find behavioural sciences as part of the curriculum for the training of medical, nursing and physiotherapy students. Another term, 'social science' (or again in the plural, social sciences), is used to describe an overlapping area of study but one in which the emphasis is on social rather than individual aspects of behaviour – and as perhaps might be expected, this forms an important part of the training of social workers. There are other health professionals who are also concerned with behavioural and/or social sciences, such as occupational therapists, speech therapists and dieticians. What, then, are the behavioural and social sciences and how do they relate to other sciences?

Behavioural, social and other sciences

Figure 1.1 sets out the relationship between the behavioural and social sciences and other natural (physical and biological) sciences. The earliest of the sciences, the so-called physical sciences of *chemistry* and *physics*, concerned respectively with the study of matter and energy, developed originally out of the much older pursuit of knowledge about the ultimate reality of the universe known as natural philosophy, but distinguished from it by the use of direct observation of phenomena as the starting point or basis for understanding. The distinction between these two sciences, chemistry and physics, has in recent times become blurred with the realization that matter and energy are themselves not entirely distinct, being in fact interconvertible, though in practice it remains easier to preserve the two areas of study as separate sciences.

Biology as a scientific discipline (subdivided into the study of plant life, *botany* and animal life, *zoology*) was a development of the last century, but interest in the form and functioning of the human body goes back much further and became traditional as the basis for medical education in the form of human *anatomy* and *physiology*. *Biochemistry* has been a more recent addition to the basic medical sciences and represents a link between the physical and biological sciences. *Genetics*, the study of the inheritance of characteristics, is one of the

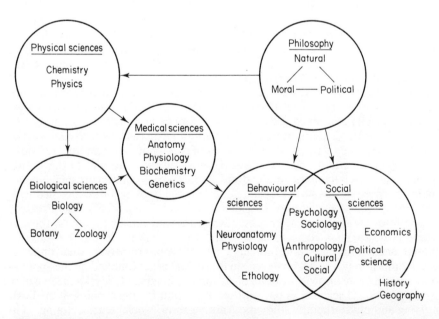

Fig.1.1   Relationships between the sciences

biological sciences which is often included within both the medical and behavioural sciences, since genetic factors may influence both physical and behavioural aspects of the individual. *Ethology* is a branch of zoology involving the observation of animal behaviour in the natural environment, and the techniques used and some of the findings obtained with non-human animals are of relevance to human behaviour.

If we turn now to the behavioural and social sciences, we see that there are two major sciences that each fall into both categories and it is these that will receive the major attention in this book. *Psychology*, which is the study of behaviour and experience (principally in the human individual), forms perhaps the core subject of the behavioural sciences, while *sociology*, which is more difficult to define but may be described shortly as the study of human society, is central to the social sciences. There is, however, much overlap between psychology and sociology, and *social psychology*, the study of social interaction in groups, provides an obvious interdisciplinary link. Historically we may observe that psychology developed out of moral philosophy with its concern about human action and conduct, and sociology from political philosophy which questioned the nature of societies. As with the natural sciences, however, the scientific differed from the philosophical approach in being empirical; that is to say, based on observation and experimentation rather than speculation alone.

Although in this book we shall be dealing with the behavioural rather than the social sciences, a brief reference to the other disciplines within the latter may not be amiss. *Economics* has to do with the distribution of scarce resources within a society, while *political science* is the study of political systems – forms of government and administration within societies. Both are concerned with aspects of society which are likely to have a direct impact on each of its members, and therefore to be of significance in terms of individual behaviour. Two other subjects often included within the social sciences are *history* and *geography*. The study of present day social behaviour can benefit from consideration within a historical and a geographical context, while conversely the nature of such behaviour over space and time has become of increasing interest to the geographer and the historian.

Next we come to *anthropology*, which means the science of man. It includes *physical anthropology*, dealing with the natural history of man (the study of the different human races and their development forming a special subject, *ethnology*, not to be confused with ethology already described), and *cultural* and *social anthropology* (not always clearly distinguishable) concerned with comparing and contrasting social behaviour between, respectively, different societies (particularly those described as 'primitive') and different communities, for example urban and rural, within the same society.

Perhaps finally, the abstract science of *mathematics* and its younger branch of *statistics* should be mentioned since they are fundamental to all the sciences. The problem of measurement in the behavioural sciences is, however, a particularly difficult one, and using such measurements for testing hypotheses requires special types of statistical technique. For this reason, statistics is sometimes included within the subjects considered as belonging to, or at least taught with, the behavioural sciences.

The treatment here, so far, has been to consider all these sciences as distinct entities, but it has already been pointed out that there are areas of overlap between them. Indeed, as far as the behavioural sciences are concerned it may be preferable to look upon them, not as each having a specific and clearly demarcated field of study, but rather as bringing to bear different perspectives, often upon the same subject matter – in this case the social behaviour of man. Such an interdisiplinary approach is also encouraged by the fact that the individual as well as society can both singly and jointly be regarded as a 'system'; a viewpoint which we shall explore in a little more detail.

Man and society as a hierarchical system

The important characteristic of a system is that it is made up from a number of component parts which are interdependent and affect each other. In medicine the term has long been used to describe groups of bodily organs which together serve a particular function; the cardiovascular system, the gastrointestinal system, etc. In order for the system to operate efficiently, functioning of the individual organs has to be integrated. Thus, for example, the output of the heart is regulated to provide the amount of blood required for the circulation at any moment, while the elimination of waste material from the large bowel is stimulated by the intake of more food into the stomach. But the bodily systems are themselves part of a larger system, the whole body, and once again the separate systems are dependent on each other. The individual is, in turn, part of another system – a group of people who are interdependent. Groups then comprise a still larger system, a society, and so on. This principle of the individual parts of one system being themselves systems can thus be seen to operate in a step-like or hierarchical fashion within both the individual and society to form a kind of super system of mankind, and this is illustrated in Fig.1.2. Functioning or behaviour at any level is influenced not only by functioning or behaviour of others at the same level but also by that of the system above, of which it and they form component parts, and by that of its own component parts at the level below. In studying this hierarchical system, interest may be focussed at any level and may then represent the perspective of a particular science.

Let us return to our example of Mr Smith, the patient with the CVA, and see how scientists of different disciplines might view him each from their own

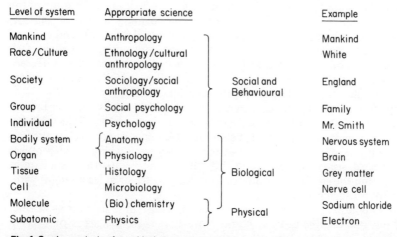

Level of system	Appropriate science		Example
Mankind	Anthropology		Mankind
Race/Culture	Ethnology/cultural anthropology		White
Society	Sociology/social anthropology	Social and Behavioural	England
Group	Social psychology		Family
Individual	Psychology		Mr. Smith
Bodily system	Anatomy		Nervous system
Organ	Physiology		Brain
Tissue	Histology	Biological	Grey matter
Cell	Microbiology		Nerve cell
Molecule	(Bio) chemistry	Physical	Sodium chloride
Subatomic	Physics		Electron

Fig.1.2   An analysis of mankind as a system

perspective but at the same time being aware of the viewpoints of others. Since we are primarily concerned here with individual behaviour we shall start with the psychologist. His interest will be directed to Mr Smith as a person – to his 'personality', in the sense that his present behaviour while ill should be predictable, to some extent at least, from his habitual pattern of behaviour, and in particular, his usual ways of dealing with stressful situations. The psychologist will probably consider Mr Smith's personality to be the result of genetic factors (inherited at birth from his parents) interacting with environmental factors (the life experiences to which he has been exposed, particularly during the formative years of childhood). However, a good psychologist is likely also to be aware of the levels below and above in the system. Below are all those levels of bodily organization which form the subject matter of the biological sciences. Neuroanatomy and neurophysiology are rather directly involved in Mr Smith's case because it is his nervous system which has been damaged by the stroke, but this aspect is really the particular clinical problem and not of primary concern here, though if there has been direct impairment of his mental as well as bodily functioning then this may affect his behaviour. More generally, though, the psychologist is interested in the relationship between brain and behaviour, and this forms an important area of interdisciplinary research.

Continuing down through the levels of the system we can see how each is influenced from above and below. The activity of a nerve cell at any moment, for example, will depend on its position within the nervous system and on the total pattern of neural activity at that time, but it will also be affected by chemical factors within and outside it. The conduction of the nerve impulse along a nerve fibre, on which ultimately depends all the behaviour of the individual, is the result of changes in permeability of the cell membrane to sodium ions. Having entered the cell during the passage of the nerve impulse, the sodium ions have to be expelled again, a process requiring energy. It is the biochemist who studies the complex processes of energy release from organic chemical reactions within the cell. At the lowest level of all we come to the fundamental nature of matter and energy which is the province of the physicist, but on which ultimately depends the very existence of Mr Smith and his behaviour.

Returning to the whole individual, the psychologist should also be aware of the social nature of Mr Smith, that is to say, of Mr Smith as a member of many social groups, some small like his family and some large including his nation. Membership of these groups, as we shall see later, influences his behaviour in various ways, and in small groups this will depend particularly on the relationship between Mr Smith and the other members of the group – parents, wife and children, for example. In turn his behaviour, in this case his way of responding to his illness, will affect others, especially those close to him. Such social interaction is, as we have seen, the interest of the social psychologist.

Sociology proper is also concerned with social behaviour, but more with the regularities and patterns of behaviour within a particular social structure. In our example, Mr Smith would be seen as belonging to a group of people defined as being ill and therefore as playing a particular role, the 'sick role', determined by his membership of the group and in fact prescribed by the society to which he belongs. This role will include, for the moment, not having to work but at the same time being obliged to cooperate with treatment in order to recover as soon as possible. It would seem that our patient is not wholly accepting of this latter aspect of the sick role while Mr Jones, it will be recalled, appears to be doing so.

The sociologist will probably acknowledge that some more individual psychological factors are responsible for this difference between Mr Smith and Mr Jones, but at the same time will also be concerned with the social structure of the institution within which Mr Smith finds himself, namely the hospital as well as the whole health service of which the hospital is a part. Finally, the contrast between Mr Smith and Mr Jones might also be of interest to the social or cultural anthropologist because of recognized differences in the way people from different social or cultural backgrounds perceive and react to illness.

Methodology of the behavioural sciences

Having taken a brief overall look at the behavioural sciences in relation to other sciences, and to man and society as a hierarchical system, we shall now have to narrow our attention to the behavioural sciences themselves and particularly to the subjects of psychology and sociology. It will, however, be a major aim of this book to apply an integrated approach, referring whenever possible to both the psychological and sociological perspectives on any issue. At this point, it may also be appropriate to comment on the question of 'pure' and 'applied' aspects of the subjects and also of their 'relevance' to medicine. Clearly with the already (possibly) overburdened curriculum of most health students, anything which is totally irrelevant to their future needs as professionals should be excluded. However, this does not mean that it would be helpful, as far as behavioural sciences are concerned, only to consider as relevant those areas of knowledge so far derived from the application of psychology and sociology to particular medical problems. This would be of limited value without some appreciation of the disciplines themselves and the concepts and methods they use, particularly in order to be able in the future to assess any new contributions they may make in the medical field. The intention of this book, therefore, is to take a fairly broad view of the theoretical aspects of the behavioural sciences, though with references to clinical applications throughout.

From the outset it is as well to be aware of a number of difficulties facing the behavioural sciences (and social sciences) compared with other sciences. The purpose of science is often summarized as comprising three processes: (1) understanding, or explanation, (2) prediction, and (3) control. Achievement of *understanding* is attempted through the use of the so-called scientific method, which in turn is usually regarded as requiring several steps. The first of these is *observation* – the unbiased, undistorted collection of facts which may then be organized and classified in such a way that generalizations may be induced from them. The process of *induction* or inference of the general from the particular is today, however, not considered to be the cornerstone of the scientific method. This distinction is reserved for what is called the *hypothetico-deductive method*, deduction being opposite in meaning to induction and implying reasoning from the general to the particular. According to this view (Popper, 1959), a suggested general explanation or hypothesis is first put forward, perhaps derived from the original observations; from this is deduced a particular instance which can then be put to a test, either from further observations or in the form of an experiment. If the deduction proves to be incorrect then the hypothesis is refuted and has to be rejected or at least modified to take account of the discrepancy. If, on the other hand, the deduction is found to be correct this only supports and does not establish the hypothesis as 'true', though obviously the more often different deductions are verified, the more likely is it to be so. This means, of course, that a good deal of scientific 'knowledge' generally is (indeed, according to Popper, must be) in the form of unproven hypotheses. Although this strict interpretation of the 'correct' approach to progress in science has been challenged as being out of touch with historical reality, it nevertheless provides a prescription for a healthy, critical scientific attitude towards research (Notturno, 1984).

The problem for the behavioural sciences when compared with others is that it is often difficult to apply the scientific method with the same degree of rigour. Unfortunately, it is also often the case that inductive reasoning alone has been used to construct, from collected observations, explanations which provide apparent understanding but from which it is then difficult, if not impossible, to frame specific hypotheses which can be subjected to any adequate form of testing.

Observations and measurement

There are several reasons for the difficulties facing the scientific study of behaviour. They start with the original observations since the phenomena or 'variables' in which the behavioural sciences are interested are both numerous and difficult to quantify. It is hardly necessary to stress this point if we compare an individual person or a group of people with, say, an element in chemistry or even a simple unicellular organism in biology. There are so many aspects of behaviour that could be studied that some form of selection is necessary, with the consequent difficulty of choosing what to include and what to leave out. Having made the decision there is still the problem of measurement. Again in terms of their quantification the difference between relatively simple physical variables like length and weight and complex psychological and social variables like intelligence and social class is only too obvious. In the first place, such variables have to be defined before they can be measured, and this in itself, as we shall see later, may be a matter of considerable difficulty, often with disagreement as to meaning. Indeed, sometimes the definition is made in terms of the measurement, a so-called 'operational' definition. For example, intelligence may be defined as 'what intelligence tests measure'. The advantage claimed for such a definition is that it is clear-cut and avoids ambiguities as to precisely what it is that is being measured. But this is a somewhat spurious advantage since, to take the example of intelligence again, the tests themselves were originally designed with some kind of theoretical concept or definition of intelligence in mind.

Quite apart from the problem of first defining what is to be measured, the very nature of the phenomena in the behavioural sciences makes them difficult to quantify. In the physical world, measurement is generally made by comparing what is to be measured against some sort of standard measuring instrument. We measure length with a rule which could if necessary then be compared with a standard measure kept at the National Physical Laboratory. It is easy to subdivide into smaller units, yards, feet, inches, metres, centimetres, millimetres, etc. When we record the temperature of a patient we make use of the expansion of mercury with heat to give us a linear measure with a scale in degrees, and we can use fixed temperatures like the freezing and boiling points of water for standardization. Furthermore, we are making use of what is called an *interval scale*, which means that it can be accepted that all units of the same value are in fact equal. Thus the temperature difference of one degree between

42 and 43 degrees is the same as that between 98 and 99 degrees. But it is a different matter when we come to the sort of variables (particular behaviours, emotions, attitudes, motives for example) that are the concern of the behavioural sciences. Using such techniques as questionnaires, ratings of behaviour etc., individuals may be compared with other individuals or groups with groups, thus allowing the allocation of a score (e.g. 5 for extremely aggressive, 0 for no aggression and intermediate scores between) to each individual or group. But such scores are necessarily somewhat arbitrary and this type of scale, which really depends on ranking, is known as an *ordinal scale*. Units at different parts of the scale are not strictly comparable, the value of the difference between 1 and 2 not necessarily being the same as that between 4 and 5, so that a special class of statistics, known as *non-parametric*, has to be used in calculating the statistical significance of any findings. Another difficulty is that there is no 'standard' individual or group against which to compare all others, though, as we shall see for example with intelligence, it is possible to get some kind of standard by finding the average of a large sample of measurements.

Perhaps the most obvious difficulty with measurement in psychology is in the area of subjective experience, since this is available only to the individual person and quantification must depend on accurate reporting by the subject to the investigator. This is clearly a very important matter and we shall return to it in more detail later. However, the risk of distortion is not restricted to the subject of an investigation. The investigator also has to be considered. If we return to the measurement of temperature with a thermometer, we can see that the temperature recorded depends not only on the thermometer but on the person reading it. There is the possibility of *observer error*, and though this is likely to be random it could, in a large sample of subjects, be systematic if the thermometer reader has a tendency to read ievels which fall midway between markings always to the mark above or the mark below. This kind of *observer bias* is a much greater risk with the measurement of behavioural variables – particularly if what is being measured is something which carries some notion of moral value, the observer may unwittingly allow his or her own attitudes to influence the measurement. We shall see later, for example, that this is something which has to be guarded against in the assessment of personality.

There is, however, an even more fundamental difficulty – the possible influence on individual or group behaviour of the process of measurement itself. Apart from the theoretical assertion that observation would alter subatomic processes (described as the Heisenberg Uncertainty Principle after its enunciator), this is generally not a problem facing the physical sciences. Ethologists who, as we have already mentioned, study animal behaviour are aware of the effect of an artificial environment and carry out their observations in as natural a setting as possible. With human subjects the mere knowledge that an investigation is being conducted may produce some behavioural change, while the actual measurements themselves (e.g. administration of questionnaires) may be even more likely to do so.

One example of the effect on people of being studied has come to be known as the *Hawthorne effect*, from the name of the electrical relay works in the USA where an investigation was carried out into the influence on worker output of various environmental changes (Roethlisberger and Dickson, 1939). Each of a series of improvements in the working conditions (increased pay, shorter hours, better lighting and ventilation, etc.) resulted in increased output, but this continued further when the original conditions were restored. It was concluded that a major factor in the increased performance of the workers was the greater interest being shown in them. Precautions therefore have to be taken to minimize, or allow for, such study effects in behavioural research. The usual way of doing this is by the use of controls, and we shall consider this when we deal with the testing of hypotheses.

Before leaving the question of measurement it is necessary to refer briefly to two terms, *reliability* and *validity*, the meanings of which are frequently confused but which should be distinguished. A 'measuring instrument' – examples of which in behavioural science would include interviews, questionnaires, rating scales, etc. – should, like a thermometer, be reliable, meaning that it should give the same result on repeated occasions under the same circumstances or when used by different experimenters. It should also be valid, in the sense that it is in fact measuring what it is supposed to measure. An instrument could be reliable but not valid, i.e. reliably measuring something but not that which it should be. We shall see that an important aspect of behavioural science research is the establishment of the reliability and validity of the measuring instruments used.

Testing of hypotheses

We now come to the most crucial step in the scientific method, the formulation and testing of hypotheses. At its simplest, a hypothesis is derived from the observation that certain phenomena, which may or may not be quantifiable, appear to be related in some way and from this it may be hypothesized that there is a causal relationship between them. Suppose we represent by the letters A and B two quantifiable phenomena or variables which we might measure in a large sample of individuals – e.g. age and blood pressure, body weight at 30 years of age and age at death. If we find that there is a strong tendency for those who have a high measure of A also to have a high measure of B with a similar tendency for low and intermediate measures, we might conclude that there is an association between them. This relationship would be a positive one, but it could be the other way round so that high scorers on A were low scorers on B, in which case it would be a negative association. Could either of these apparent associations just be a matter of coincidence, or is the tendency so great that it is very unlikely to be due to chance?

It is possible to check this by using a statistical measure of association, the *product-moment correlation coefficient*. If the two sets of scores correspond exactly, a correlation of $+1$ will be obtained; if they are exactly opposite to each other (highest to lowest and vice versa, etc.) the figure will be -1; and if there is no relationship at all, it will be 0. Intermediate figures imply lesser degrees of association, but if we know the size of the sample (the number n of individuals involved) we can calculate how likely it is that such an association would arise by chance. This is expressed in terms of the *probability* of such an occurrence. If the probability is very low, for example that it would occur by chance less than one in a hundred times (expressed usually as a decimal, e.g. probability p less than one in a hundred is written as $p < 0.01$, less than one in a thousand as $p < 0.001$, etc.), then we may reasonably conclude that we have a 'non-chance' association. Such a *statistically significant* correlation is, therefore, one which is very unlikely to have occurred by chance. Confidence in the significance of an association may be further strengthened by repeating the measurements on another sample of individuals and demonstrating a similar correlation.

Now it may be noticed that the suggested examples of variables that might be correlated in this way (age, blood pressure, body weight and age at death) could all be measured on an interval scale (time, length and weight), whereas, as we have already seen, most behavioural variables (e.g. anxiety, marital disharmony, group cohesion, etc.) can only be measured on an ordinal scale. This means that for calculating associations between such variables a different type of correlation coefficient should be employed (though in practice it is not uncommon in certain situations to find the product-moment correlation being used). This is a *rank order correlation* which compares the rank order of the two sets of scores (scores ranked from highest to lowest) rather than the actual scores. This avoids the problem, referred to earlier, of the inequality of units from different parts of an ordinal scale. Once the value of such a correlation coefficient has been obtained its statistical significance can again be calculated in terms of the probability of its occurrence by chance.

Some behavioural phenomena are not quantifiable at all in terms of a graded score but are either present or absent – e.g. hospitalized or not, employed or not. Sometimes there are two or more mutually exclusive categories into which individuals may be placed (male, female; single, married, separated, divorced, widowed; etc.). Observation may suggest associations between such *nominal* categories (or attributes) and other behavioural phenomena. Again, certain statistical techniques are required to test whether any associations found are statistically significant.

If a statistically significant association has been demonstrated between two variables or two attributes, what meaning may this have? Perhaps the most usual hypothesis to be suggested is that there is a causal relationship so that one causes the other. Particularly is this likely to be so if one follows the other in time. Thus if delinquency in children is found to be associated with homes in which discipline has been erratic or inconsistent, it may be hypothesized that the former is caused by the latter. As a hypothesis this is quite reasonable, but the danger is that it is regarded as fact rather than conjecture. This possibility of a false interpretation of the significance of events which follow each other is expressed in the Latin tag 'post hoc ergo propter hoc', meaning that if one thing follows another it is caused by it. A visitor from Mars might observe a fairly consistent association between postmen inserting letters into letterboxes of houses and the subsequent departure of the occupants for work, but he would be mistaken in assuming a direct causal relationship between the two events. The correct explanation of the association is, of course, that the occurrence of both is determined by the time of day. In other words, their apparent relationship is explained by their both being related to a third and common factor. Now it would be possible for our Martian to disprove his hypothesis in true scientific fashion by observing that the predicted association between the postman's delivery and the house occupants' departure did not hold for the second postal delivery of the day, while a comparison between days (except Sundays) when houses were visited or not visited by postmen would also show no difference in the likelihood of the occupants setting off for work. These would be examples of testing a hypothesis by making further observation of naturally occurring events which may support or refute it.

An alternative approach might be to alter the conditions artificially so that postmen delivered letters at different times to one group of houses and not another and to observe the effect on the occupants. This would be an example of an *experiment*, and experimentation is the activity which most distinguishes the sciences from other disciplines. Classically, an experiment involves altering one variable, the *independent* variable, and measuring the effect on another, the *dependent* variable. This enables causal relationships to be determined very precisely. To take a well-known example from the physical sciences, the relationships between temperature, volume and pressure of a gas – as stated in the gas laws of Boyle and Charles – can easily be verified by making each in turn the independent variable in an experiment. Note, however, that as there are three variables, each of which affects the other two, it is necessary to hold one of them constant for each experiment. Thus to determine the effect of temperature on volume, the pressure has to be kept constant; for the relationship of temperature to pressure, the volume must remain the same; and so on.

When we turn to the behavioural sciences we find that there are usually a large number of variables which may contribute to the causation of, or have an influence on, any particular behaviour. To test a hypothesis about the causative effect of any individual variable, either by means of further collection of data or by experiment, it is therefore necessary to take account of – or 'control' for – all the variables that could possibly have an influence. Of course it is unlikely to be known at this stage what all these other variables are, and all that can be done is to consider all those which previous experience or theoretical considerations would suggest may be important. Having decided which variables to control, the procedure in an experiment is to hold these constant while varying the one independent variable and measuring the dependent variable. In the case of further observation it may be possible to investigate a number of individuals matched for (i.e. equally affected by) the controlled variables but differing quantitatively in the independent variable, which can then be correlated with the dependent variable. Alternatively, two groups of individuals, again matched for the controlled variables, but differing qualitatively in the presence or absence of the independent variable, may be compared in terms of either the average value of the dependent variable of each if it is a continuous variable measured on an interval scale, or of proportions of different categories if the dependent variable is ordinal. If a difference is found between the two groups a statistical test can be applied to confirm whether it would be unlikely to have arisen by chance, i.e. whether it is statistically significant. Fig. 1.3 illustrates diagrammatically these approaches to hypothesis testing.

Before leaving the question of the scientific method and the behavioural sciences there is a further aspect which distinguishes the latter from other sciences and which produces yet another potential obstacle to the advancement of knowledge in this area. It is the ethical and moral difficulties arising from the fact that the subjects of study are human beings, individual or as a group. Even the variables that are selected for measurement are liable to be subject to attitudes which are often far from objective and emotionally neutral. It is difficult to feel strongly about such physical qualities as length, volume and weight, though certain colours and sounds may evoke an emotional response. It is a very different matter, however, when we come to such behavioural science variables as intelligence and social class. These are likely to elicit quite strong attitudes such as denial, on the one hand, of their very existence or on the other hand, if they do exist, that they should be studied at all. The heated controversy over the question of racial differences in intelligence is a good example of the very strong feelings that can be aroused in politically sensitive areas.

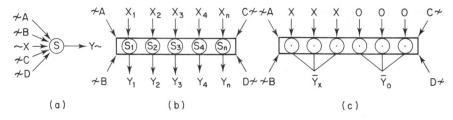

Fig.1.3 Approaches to the testing of hypotheses in the behavioural sciences. (a) An experiment with a single individual or group S in which variables A,B,C and D are held constant (controlled) while the independent variable X is varied and changes in the dependent variable Y are measured. If the latter show a consistent relationship to the former, it may be assumed that X causes Y. (b) Hypothesis testing by observation of a number of individuals or groups (S_1-S_n) matched (identical) for variables A,B,C and D but differing between each other in terms of the independent variable X (X_1-X_n). The correlation provides support for the original hypothesis of a causal relationship between X and Y (X causing Y), since the possibility of the association arising from both being determined by a third variable has been excluded by the control, through matching, of other variables and assuming that the possibility of Y causing X can be dismissed. (c) An alternative approach when the independent variable is qualitative rather than quantitative, i.e. it is either present or absent for each individual or group. Those affected by the attribute X can then be compared with those without (O) in terms of the dependent variable Y, using for each, the means of Y (Y_x compared with Y_o) if it is a continuous variable, or the proportions of different scores if Y is measured on an ordinal scale or of those simply recorded as present or absent

More generally, however, it is not uncommon to find the view expressed that it is somehow dehumanizing to attempt a scientific study of man's behaviour; that it detracts from the essential uniqueness of the individual. Such moral judgments and assertions deserve attention but a pragmatic view would claim that the justification for behavioural research lies in the contributions which it can make to the well-being of mankind. This is not to say that there are not, necessarily, considerable constraints on research when it comes to experimentation with human beings, as indeed there are, though perhaps, to a lesser degree, with other animals. Short-lasting psychological experiments with individuals or groups are often possible, but for the study of longer-term associations it is usually necessary to fall back on the type of observations of naturally occurring situations already described.

Prediction and control

These are the second and third of the three processes that are commonly regarded as the purpose of science. They should follow logically from the first process of understanding, but do not necessarily fully depend upon it. Thus it may be possible, from observations, to make predictions and perhaps even control events without a full understanding of the processes and mechanisms involved. Much of the knowledge of these two areas of behavioural science is of this empirically derived nature, and even then there are difficulties owing to the large number of variables which may influence human behaviour. Yet it is the ability to predict and to control or modify behaviour which is the application most required of the behavioural sciences by the health professions, just as the contribution of other basic medical sciences is to the prediction and control of the bodily changes of disease.

At the same time it is in such capabilities, particularly that of modifying behaviour, that many see potential ethical and moral dangers, already realized in the practice of so-called 'brain-washing'. That something can be used for both good and evil purposes is, nevertheless, a common enough experience, and it must be the responsibility of the health professions to see that, as far as they are concerned, knowledge and techniques derived from behavioural sciences are used by their members solely in the interests of the patient. A particular difficulty may arise when it is not the patient but others who desire a change in his or her, usually socially deviant, behaviour. It may be argued that it is in fact in their own interests as well as that of society that, for example, alcoholics, compulsive gamblers and sexual deviants should have their behaviour changed by health professionals whether they wish it or not. It should be made clear, however, that in this country such behaviour modification would not be attempted without the patient's consent.

Analytical, developmental, differential and interactional perspectives

Behaviour, both of the individual and of society, can be viewed from four major perspectives which will provide the framework for the more detailed consideration of the behavioural sciences, particularly psychology and sociology, in the remainder of this book.

The first of these viewpoints may be described as analytical or reductionist in that it breaks up the whole into component parts. It looks at the psychological structure of the individual or the social structure of the society and at the functions and interactions of the various parts that go to make up the whole.

The second perspective takes account of the changing nature of both the individual and society. Of course the analogy between their respective developments cannot be pushed too far: the time scales are of a different order, and while the human life cycle falls within clearly defined limits and has a biologically determined sequence of stages, this is not the case for the origin, rise and later possible decline and extinction of a society as a social group. Nevertheless, the developmental aspect does provide another link between the two principal behavioural sciences.

The third way of studying both man and society is, in each case, to look not at what all men and all societies or social groups have in common in their structure or development, but at how they differ as wholes.

Finally, the fourth area of psychological and sociological concern is with aspects of behavioural interaction between individuals and social groups.

Further reading

Levitt, E.E. (1961) *Clinical Research Design and Analysis in the Behavioural Sciences.* Springfield: Charles C. Thomas.

Matheson, D.W., Bruce, R.L. and Beauchamp, K.L. (1978) *Experimental Psychology: Research Design and Analysis*, 3rd ed. New York: Rinehart & Winston.

Robson, C. (1983) *Experiment, Design and Statistics in Psychology*, 2nd ed. Harmondsworth: Penguin.

2
Psychology

What is and what is not psychology

In the last chapter we considered psychology to be the study of *behaviour* and *experience*, but now we must begin to examine this definition in more detail to see what it really involves. In the first place, we note that it covers both behaviour, which is something that can be observed not only in man but in other animals, and experience, which is entirely subjective and available only to the human individual through the process of inward observation or introspection. The fact that both aspects of the human condition are considered appropriate for psychological study has not, as we shall see, always been accepted, and even now there are schools of psychological thought which emphasize one or the other aspect. It is also clear that, since man is a 'social animal' and the human individual is normally a member of many social groups, an important part of behaviour is social and involves social relationships between individuals.

Psychology, then, is the science of behaviour and experience and a psychologist is a graduate of the subject.

At this point it is perhaps important to make a distinction between psychology and another discipline with which it is frequently confused, namely *psychiatry*. Whereas psychology is a science and the psychologist is a scientist, psychiatry is a branch of medicine, a specialty comparable with others like neurology, cardiology, dermatology, etc., and the psychiatrist is a medical specialist who has first trained and qualified in medicine and then in psychiatry. As a medical specialty, psychiatry is involved in the study, diagnosis and treatment of psychological disorders – abnormalities or deviations of behaviour and experience – which in our society are regarded as forms of mental ill-health and the proper if not exclusive concern of doctors and psychiatrists. We shall need to refer to psychiatric disorders again on several occasions so we shall not go into further details at this stage. However, there is one other term which is frequently confused with both psychology and psychiatry. *Psychoanalysis* is a subject which we shall also consider in more detail later, but here we can simply say that it refers to a special technique for the investigation in depth and treatment of individuals with particular psychological problems, together with certain theories of personality and psychological development which have been derived from this. It is not synonymous with either psychology or psychiatry, though it has made theoretical contributions to both. A psychoanalyst is a person who has had a special training in the technique of psychoanalysis, which training usually includes undergoing a personal analysis oneself. The analyst may or may not be medically qualified; if he is, he is likely to have also had a psychiatric training so that some psychoanalysts are psychiatrists and some psychiatrists are psychoanalysts. The non-medically qualified psychoanalyst has often, but not necessarily, had a training in social work or psychology before embarking on the analytic training.

Before leaving the question of what is psychology, we should perhaps meet the challenge of those who claim that it is nothing more than common sense. One likely reason for this rather frequent view is that the everyday experience of relating to other people necessitates everyone being his own psychologist – that is to say, one has to have some awareness of the psychological make-up of others in order to be able to predict their behaviour in various circumstances. Some people are particularly gifted in such psychological understanding and many of the best authors, playwrights and poets have been capable of most sensitive and penetrating analyses of character. But this is not to say that all the 'common sense' psychological assumptions and beliefs of the man-in-the-street are correct. It is the purpose of psychology as a science to test such ideas, and while some may be confirmed, others may be found to be quite erroneous. The fact that psychology deals with matters which are within everyone's common experience, in contrast to the traditional physical sciences like chemistry and physics, does not mean that it should be compared unfavourably with them, as of course is implied by the 'common sense' jibe.

Subdivisions and applications of psychology

The science of psychology now covers a wide area of study. Within it, research interests may be directed to particular areas or techniques so that, for example, some psychologists may work exclusively with non-human animals, others may be concerned with the development of language, others with the determinants of perception, and so on. The list is too long to detail here but we shall be referring to many of these subdivisions of psychology throughout the rest of the book.

There are also several branches of applied psychology, including *industrial psychology*, concerned with selection and training of employees and methods and conditions of work in industry (an example of a work study was the Hawthorne investigation referred to in Chapter 1); *educational psychology*, the application of psychological principles to education and educational difficulties in individuals; and *clinical psychology*. It is obviously this last application of psychology to clinical problems which is of most interest to us here.

The clinical psychologist, after qualifying in psychology, undergoes further training in the application of psychology to medicine and psychiatry. His role nowadays is likely to be threefold – research, psychological investigation of patients and psychological treatments of certain kinds. He may be based in a hospital or a clinic (especially child-psychiatric or child-guidance), so that with other health professionals he is a member of the team concerned with helping the individual patient and his family. The position of the clinical psychologist within the UK National Health Service has within recent years moved towards a greater degree of clinical autonomy and responsibility as well as an involvement outside the hospital or clinic; in general practice for example.

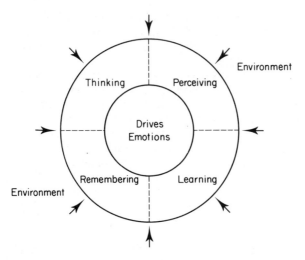

Fig.2.1   Diagrammatic representation of individual psychological structure

Perspectives in psychology

We have seen in the first chapter that there are four major perspectives from which behaviour, both of the individual and of society, can be viewed. Each of these will be dealt with in turn in the next four sections, but in this chapter we are concerned with an overall view of their application to, and how they relate to each other in, the field of psychology.

If we take first the analytic perspective, Fig. 2.1 represents diagrammatically a 'psychological cross-section' of the individual subdivided into various component processes. In the centre are the basic *drives*, *motivation* or *conation*, determining the direction of behaviour towards certain goals, together with the *emotions* or *affects*, experienced and expressed, all of which are probably similar to those present, though at a simpler level, in many other species. Surrounding them are the so-called *higher mental* or *cognitive processes* of *perception, learning, remembering* and *thinking* which are more highly developed in man. The relative positions in the diagram of these two sets of psychological processes is intended to indicate that the expression of the drives and emotions is very much modified during the process of development by the environment, especially social, acting through the cognitive processes. It should be appreciated, however, that the subdivision into these apparently separate processes is somewhat arbitrary and there is, as we shall see, a good deal of interaction between them.

Fig. 2.2 shows the relationships between all four of the perspectives. The psychological processes just described, and shown on the left-hand side, represent a functional analysis of the psychological 'make-up' of the individual. They are, however, biologically based since their existence depends primarily on the structure and functioning of the central nervous system, and their expression in the individual is therefore affected by the stage of physical *maturation* of that system as well as by the original *genetic endowment* from the parents at the time of conception. In addition, however, the developmental changes that are the concern of the second perspective are also, in part, the result

PERSPECTIVES

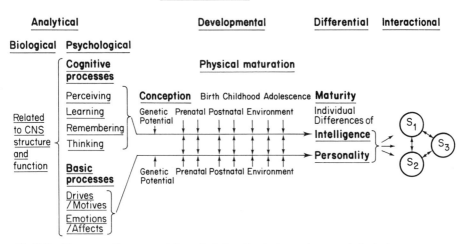

Fig.2.2 Diagrammatic representation of relationships between four psychological perspectives

of *environmental experiences* of the individual, particularly during the formative years of childhood and adolescence. At the other end of the life cycle, but not shown in the diagram, are the psychological changes related to the process of ageing.

The third perspective looks at differences between individuals in terms of *intelligence*, which depends on the development of the cognitive processes and *personality*, which reflects the motivational or conative and the emotional or affective aspects of the person. Such differences of intelligence and personality are usually studied in mature individuals though they may be traced back through earlier stages of development. Most psychologists would, in fact, accept the view that the individual adult's intelligence and personality are the result of a long process of interaction between hereditary endowment and environmental experience but, as we shall see later, there are differing views on the nature of this interaction and of the developmental process generally. Finally, the interactional perspective focusses on the way individuals relate to each other in groups of varying sizes and, as we have seen already, forms the specialized and interdisciplinary area of study of the social psychologist.

Psychological methods of study

In the first chapter we considered something of the scientific method in relation to the behavioural sciences and saw some of the difficulties involved in hypothesis formulation and testing. In later chapters we shall meet particular examples of these two stages in the process of trying to understand individual behaviour and experience, but here we are concerned with the first and basic stage of data collection; with the techniques of observation and measurement used in psychology together with their reliability and validity.

The first decisions that have to be taken are who and what to observe. The human individual is obviously the major focus of attention, though work with other animals may contribute to the understanding of human behaviour. There are, however, two alternative approaches to such study. The first or *ideographic* approach involves the detailed examination of a single individual, often over a prolonged period of time, while with the second or *nomothetic* approach a larger number is studied but in less detail.

The ideographic approach

This may also be described as the *case study* method. It is typical of clinical medicine, and especially of psychiatry which emphasizes the importance of a thorough study of each patient through both history and examination. Probably the most intensive and extensive psychological study of the individual is carried out in the process of *psychoanalysis* to which we have already referred, but which we should now consider a little further.

Psychoanalysis originated with *Sigmund Freud* (1856–1939) who, while practising as a neurologist, found that if a 'neurotic' patient was encouraged repeatedly over a period of time to allow his thoughts to come freely and to be expressed without any kind of conscious censorship (e.g. as being irrelevant, unpleasant or embarrassing), he would gradually be able to recall long-past and apparently forgotten events with their associated emotions, as well as wishes and fantasies, etc., of which he had previously been *unconscious*. This process of *free association* is a fundamental feature of psychoanalysis which involves the subject or *analysand* (not necessarily someone with a psychological disorder) in the gradual recollection of such past events and, with the help of the psychoanalyst, an understanding of how these may be influencing his current attitudes and behaviour – all this usually occupying perhaps an hour a day, four or five days a week, for some years. It is clearly, therefore, a very time-consuming and prolonged form of case study usually undertaken as a form of therapy by a patient or as a training by a would-be analyst.

It is not, however, these aspects which are of concern to us here, but rather its use as a technique of psychological investigation and its contribution to psychological knowledge. These are linked in the sense that it is claimed that the technique of free association reveals information about unconscious mental processes which would otherwise be unavailable and this, together with evidence derived from other sources such as the content of dreams, has led to the construction of theories of psychological functioning and development.

Freud himself put forward the original theories which have subsequently been modified in various ways, and we shall consider these in more detail in later chapters; but here we must comment on psychoanalysis as a technique of observation. There are several points which have to be made. First, all the information which is obtained comes from the analysand and is of a highly subjective nature. It is what he describes as past events in his life, his wishes, his feelings and so on, and there is little chance of verification. Even if others – parents, siblings, etc. – can provide factual accounts of events in his childhood, it is his own perception of these at the time (and liable to further distortion later) which is potentially available for recall to him. It is, of course, these personal perceptions and experiences which may have been of significance in his development, but their subjectivity limits their reliability as scientific data.

The reliability of the analyst himself as an observer is also a crucial question. The completeness of the record made by the analyst of what the analysand says may vary (certainly, sophisticated recording devices were not available to the early analysts), so that the risk of selective distortion is considerable. An even greater difficulty is posed by the relationship between the observer and the subject which, in the course of psychoanalysis, becomes of great significance and a potential source of bias on both sides as far as the reliability of the analytic data is concerned. Support for the acceptance of such data as reliable and valid has largely to depend on its repeated occurrence in the analyses by different analysts of many subjects, both normal and psychologically disordered.

Nevertheless, it has to be recognized that the scientific standing of psychoanalysis as a technique of psychological observation is not very substantial, and there is much debate as to whether it, and the theories derived from it, can be regarded as 'scientific' and dealing with matters of causality or whether psychoanalysis should more correctly be seen as a semantic theory concerned with understanding the meaning and 'language' of the unconscious. According to this latter view, the analyst in relation to an analysand is more analogous to the historian who attempts to understand the present in terms of the past but would not claim that the former could have been accurately predicted from the latter. This is where we shall have to leave further consideration of psychoanalysis for the present; but because of its important influence in the behavioural sciences generally, we shall be returning to various aspects of analytic theory in later chapters.

Before leaving the subject of the ideographic perspective in general – and there are techniques other than the psychoanalytic for the intensive study of the individual – we should note that while it may provide a considerable knowledge and understanding of that individual, it is not necessarily generalizable to others. It may, however, suggest possible lines of investigation to pursue or hypotheses to be tested in larger numbers of subjects, and this brings us to the alternative approach to psychological observation.

The nomothetic approach

This does involve the study, though less intensively, of a *population* of individuals; the term population being used here not to mean all the inhabitants of a geographical area but in the statistical sense of all those individuals having one or more characteristics in common (inhabitation of a particular geographical area could of course be a shared or common characteristic). The nomothetic approach therefore requires some process of selection of those individuals to be studied depending on the purpose of the investigation. A population might be defined, for example, in terms of sex and age, such as 'adolescent girls', or of a medical condition like rheumatoid arthritis.

Whatever the population, however, it is most unlikely that an investigation can examine all possible members – instead, a smaller but representative *sample* has to be used. The simplest way to ensure that a sample is truly representative of the population from which it is drawn is to see that it is *random*. This means that any member of the original population has an equal chance of being selected for the sample. Under these conditions, a large enough sample should contain individuals with all the characteristics (whether these are recognized or not) of the parent population and in the same proportions. When this is the case, observations made on the sample can reasonably be generalized to the total population and other comparable groups within it. This is an important distinction from the ideographic approach, but at the same time it should be remembered that it is not then possible to make precise predictions about any individual within the population from the group data – there is likely to be too much variation between individuals.

Thus the ideographic and nomothetic approaches may be said to complement each other, the former providing detailed observations and an in-depth, though often subjective, understanding of a limited number of individuals, the latter giving a more superficial but objective and quantitative picture of the *parameters* (means and distributions of variables) of a population. It may also be observed that there is a tendency for the ideographic approach to appeal to those (often health professionals) who like to stress the uniqueness of the individual, and the nomothetic to those who prefer the scientific approach which emphasizes the similarities of people.

Variables to be observed

Since psychology is concerned with the behaviour and experience of the individual it is these objective and subjective variables respectively which are likely to be the primary focus of interest, together with their possible determinants or modifiers in the environment and within the individual. It is customary to use a stimulus and response model for these variables, with the individual or organism providing the intervening variable as shown in Fig. 2.3. Various possible associations between variables may then be examined either by observation of natural events or by the use of experiment; for example, the effect of different stimulus situations on response variables; the modification of response variables by organismic factors like sex, age, personality, etc.; the modification in turn of organismic variables by environmental factors such as pharmacological agents, physiological deprivations, past environmental experiences, etc.; and finally, the possible relationships between different response variables, physiological and psychological.

Observational techniques

There is a range of methods of observing and, in particular, of measuring or quantifying psychological variables, detailed examples of which will be found in later chapters. Here we are more concerned with the principles underlying the techniques and with their reliability and validity.

The simplest approach is to observe the *total behaviour* of an individual (human or other animal) and to make a record of the behaviour over a period of time, either by a detailed written account or by some form of audio-visual

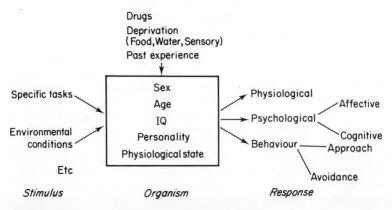

Fig.2.3 Some commonly studied psychological variables

recording which can be examined later. The setting for the observation may be a *natural* one (e.g. pre-school children in a day nursery), in which case the approach is similar to that of the ethologists and may borrow from their expertise and experience; or it may be a *laboratory* situation with experimental manipulation of aspects of the environment.

If these are the techniques concerned with objectively observed behaviour, the equivalent for subjective experience is *introspection* – the detailed description by the subject of the contents of his mind. This was a technique at one time extensively used in psychological research but later rejected as too liable to distortion and inaccuracy in reporting. Nevertheless, psychology is still concerned with subjective experience, and introspection is the only source of direct information about, for example, the hallucinatory experiences induced by certain drugs or conditions of sensory deprivation.

Scientific observation requires, however, a quantitative as well as a qualitative approach. In order to attempt some measurement of behaviour and subjective experience, the observer or subject himself may rate certain aspects on a *rating scale*. This may have defined points for scoring; aggressive behaviour or subjective anxiety might be rated on a five-point scale from 0 for 'absent' to 4 for 'extreme' and/or 'continuous', with intermediate points for 'slight', 'moderate' and 'marked'.

An alternative approach may be to use a *visual analogue scale* which is a straight line, the ends of which are defined (e.g. 'absent' and 'extreme'), and on which the rating is indicated by marking a cross at what is considered the appropriate point. The distance from one end or the middle can then be measured and used as the score. The judgements on which these scores are based are, of course, themselves subjective so that there is a risk of bias, whether by the observer with an observer rating scale or the subject with a self-rating scale. As well as direct observation of the subject's behaviour, the observer may need to enquire into subjective aspects, and here the *interview* is the classical technique. This can be free ranging or *unstructured* or carried out and/or recorded in a *structured* way so that certain topics are covered in a systematic fashion.

A further development in the quantification of psychological variables, especially those concerned with personality – such as emotional responses, attitudes, beliefs, etc. – is the *questionnaire*. This has been refined in various ways as a measuring instrument, but essentially it consists of a series of questions which may be addressed to the subject by the experimenter or completed by the subject himself (i.e. self-administered). Each question may be answered in one of several ways. In some questionnaires the answers may be in the form of 'yes', 'no' or 'don't know'. In others there may be a graded answer indicating varying degrees of agreement with each question, which may then be given a score. All the questions may be designed to measure a single variable, or there may be several variables each represented by a number of questions randomly distributed throughout the questionnaire. After completion of the questionnaire, it is a simple matter to total all the positive answers to each set of questions and obtain a score for each variable. The advantage of the questionnaire over the rating scale and interview is that its scoring is completely objective, but it does not, however, avoid the risk of distortion by the subject in answering the questions. Techniques have been developed to minimize, or allow for, this possibility and these will be described later in relation to particular questionnaires.

Another area of psychological quantification is the measurement of cognitive functions and of intelligence, but these *cognitive tests* will again be examined in some detail in a later chapter.

There is a further set of techniques of psychological observation which give rise to considerable controversy since they derive from psychoanalytic and allied theories and are designed to reveal information about aspects of the individual's unconscious mental processes – a concept which we shall return to later but which is far from universally recognized. These so-called *projective tests* have in common an ambiguous stimulus to which the subject has to respond by describing what it suggests to him (as in the best-known example of these tests – the Rorschach ink-blot test), the idea being that in so doing he 'projects' into his responses certain aspects of himself of which he is unlikely to be fully aware. Having recorded the subject's responses the tester then has to interpret the record (i.e. the significance of the particular responses), and this is where the critics point to the large subjective element and lack of objectivity. It is also essentially an ideographic technique since it is difficult to compare one individual's responses to a projective test with those of another in quantitative terms – though techniques for scoring certain aspects have been devised.

Other techniques with more limited, though none-the-less important, aims include the *semantic differential* which measures the meaning which the individual attaches to particular objects or concepts, and the *repertory grid* which provides a picture of the way a person evaluates or construes his world.

Before leaving the subject of observational techniques, we must consider in general terms the question of reliability and validity of measuring instruments in psychology. A perfect instrument would measure with complete *reliability* – that is to say it would always measure the same thing in the same way and in the hands of different users. Thus if a fully reliable personality questionnaire or intelligence test were to be given to a group of subjects on two separate occasions, the scores for each should be identical, or at least the ranking of scores should be in the same order (the scores of all the subjects might have improved on the intelligence test owing to a practice effect). Similarly if a rating scale were used by two raters simultaneously to rate, say, the degree of anxiety in a group of subjects, then again the perfectly reliable scale would produce complete correspondence between the scores of the two raters. Of course, in either event it would be most unlikely (and highly suspicious) if in practice such perfect agreement were found, and it is therefore necessary to make some assessment of the degree of reliability of a measuring instrument. There are basically three ways of doing this.

Firstly the *test–retest reliability* and the *inter-rater reliability* are obtained by calculating the correlation coefficient between the scores of the same group of subjects assessed, respectively, on two separate occasions but under the same conditions, and on the same occasion by two or more testers or raters. The perfectly reliable test would then have a coefficient of 1.0 and lesser degrees of reliability would be indicated by lower values. The difficulty with the test–retest reliability assessment is that if the two tests are performed too close in time there is a danger of a spuriously high reliability owing to the subjects remembering the responses they gave on the first occasion; while if too long an interval is interposed, an apparently low reliability may actually reflect a genuine change in the subjects between the two tests.

One way of avoiding the problems posed by testing on two separate occasions is to design two forms of the same test and administer both to a group of subjects on the same occasion. Correlation of the two sets of scores then gives the so-called *equivalent-form reliability*. Even here, however, the two forms of the test cannot be completed by the subject at precisely the same time, so that there could be some change of performance between the administration of the two forms.

A way of avoiding this is to measure the *split-half reliability* by correlating the scores obtained by the same group of individuals on two halves of the test – usually split by taking all the even- and all the odd-numbered questions. A high coefficient of correlation indicates a good consistency within the test so that all parts of it are measuring the same thing in the same way.

The *validity* of a measuring instrument is the extent to which it actually measures what it is supposed to. This is not usually a problem with measures of physical quantities like weight and length, but difficulties arise with the quantification of psychological concepts like anxiety or intelligence. There are three approaches to the assessment of validity in such cases. The first is to examine the content of the test, questionnaire, etc., to see whether it appears obviously to be measuring the appropriate variable – obvious, that is, to the observer and to the subject completing it. This so-called *face validity* may be sufficiently convincing for measures of relatively simple concepts but less so for a complex construct like intelligence. A more satisfactory demonstration of validity, if it is feasible, is referred to as *empirical* or *criterion validity* and involves testing the measuring instrument against some other external and independent measure or criterion. The difficulty often is to find a criterion which itself can be accepted as valid. We might, for example, validate a self-administered questionnaire which claims to measure anxiety by comparing the scores of a group of psychiatric patients with ratings of their anxiety made by nursing staff. If there is a high correlation it at least suggests that the question-naire and the nurses are measuring the same variable (validating each other), but it does not confirm that it is anxiety. Nevertheless, if the questionnaire had obvious face validity for anxiety and there was also good inter-rater reliability between the nurses on the ratings of anxiety, the correlation could probably be accepted as good evidence of *concurrent* validity.

It may also be possible to assess the validity of a measure against some future criterion – its *predictive validity* – and this is the case with tests which aim to predict performance on some task. Thus successful predictive validation has been found in the field of industrial psychology for tests designed to select individuals for particular occupations using such criteria as the decline in the number of errors, accidents or amount of unsatisfactory performance of selected employees.

The third type of validity is rather more complicated and is known as *construct validity*. It depends on the variable measured being part of a theoretical framework in which it forms the intervening variable or hypothetical construct between two other variables which can also be measured. Thus within the personality theory of Professor Eysenck (dealt with in greater detail later) the personality dimension of extraversion–introversion is held to be related to the rate at which individuals build up 'cortical inhibition', which in turn will affect their performance under different external conditions. If it is in fact found that, in a group of subjects, behavioural and psychological measures agree with predictions from their scores on the personality dimension, then this may be taken as a measure of construct validity for that personality test.

The experiment

In Chapter 1 we considered the place of experimentation in the behavioural sciences generally, and here we shall refer briefly to its application to psychology. Essentially, this involves the experimental manipulation in the laboratory of stimulus and, when possible, organismic (both independent) variables and the measurement of any resulting changes in response (dependent) variables (as shown in Fig. 2.3). For obvious reasons, much experimental work of this sort is carried out on lower animals but certain aspects of human behaviour and experience can be satisfactorily studied in this way. This particularly applies to cognitive functions (perception, learning, memory, problem solving, etc.), to psychophysiological responses and to the effects of pharmacological agents on behaviour and experience. Social behaviour has also, however, come to be studied experimentally, and at the same time there has been an increased awareness of the social nature of the human psychological laboratory situation and the importance of taking into account the experimenter himself as a possible influence on the results of the experiment. This, of course, only emphasizes the necessity of ensuring that there are adequate controls in any experimental work of this nature.

Psychological models

The term *model* is used here to mean a rather general conceptual framework which is used by scientists as a help to understanding complex phenomena – in this case, human behaviour and experience. Such models are hypothetical; but they are usually more extensive than a single theory in the sense that part of the model may be refuted by later evidence, requiring revision, but not necessarily the destruction of the whole model. Since they are hypothetical, there may be several different models to explain the same phenomena but they may also vary in their comprehensiveness. Some may claim to provide a complete explanation of human behaviour and experience, but others are more limited in their aims, being concerned with certain psychological aspects only. In fact, there is no reason to suppose that any of these models are mutually exclusive and it may be more useful to regard them as representing different perspectives and complementary to each other. It is common for a model to be associated with a particular therapeutic technique for helping individuals with psychological problems.

Before we consider individual models there is one dichotomy of approach in psychology which should be mentioned (though it is largely of historical interest), and there are two basic philosophical issues which have to be faced.

The two contrasting psychological viewpoints – structure and function – are analogous to the two fields of study of physical man, anatomy and physiology.

Structural psychology set out to analyse conscious subjective mental life into component parts called elements, and to determine the connections between them, using the technique of introspection including the quantitative study of sensation or 'psychophysics'. Thus two early structuralists, Wilhelm Wundt (1832–1920) and Edward Titchener (1867–1927), each postulated three basic mental elements – these were, respectively, sensation, feeling and apperception; and sensation, affection and images.

Functional psychology, associated particularly with the philosopher John Dewey (1859–1952), emphasized the functions of mental phenomena using as the basic unit the stimulus–response sequence. Complex acts were seen as being made up of chains of stimulus–response units, each response acting as a stimulus for another response, again studied largely through the process of introspection.

In the early days there was much controversy between these two distinct schools of psychology, but they now remain only as two rather poorly defined perspectives which are generally regarded as complementary to each other, though particular models or theories may emphasize one or the other aspect.

The first of the two philosophical issues has to do with the mind–body problem; that is, the nature of the relationship between man's conscious awareness and his physical body. Without going into the detailed history of the various approaches to this issue, we may consider two main viewpoints.

Dualism, sometimes described as Cartesian after the philosopher René Descartes (1596–1650), sees mind and body as two separate but interacting entities. *Monism* takes the view that they are both aspects of a single entity (essentially the neural processes of the brain), but seen from a different point of view ('double-aspect' theory) or expressed in a different language ('double-language' theory). Current opinion would almost certainly favour the monistic viewpoint or see both mind and body (matter) as abstractions anyway, but a pragmatic dualism tends to persist in everyday practice.

The second philosophical issue concerns the nature of man as viewed from two contrasting standpoints. On the one hand, man may be seen as entirely subject to control by forces within himself and his environment – his behaviour wholly *determined* by his genetic endowment and developmental learning experience. The alternative viewpoint claims for man a degree of *autonomy* and independence from his genes and environment – rejecting determinism and acknowledging the operation of free will and of choice in decision making. The former view tends to be seen as 'scientific' and the latter as 'humanistic'; but even the most ardent determinist admits the impossibility of ever being able to achieve complete predictability of behaviour and experience, while the supporter of the autonomous viewpoint cannot deny the influence of genetic and environmental factors. It will be apparent, however, that one or other of these two viewpoints may predominate in the models that we shall now discuss. Most of these will be considered in greater detail in later chapters, but here we are concerned with a comparison of their basic concepts.

Psychodynamic

This is one of the most comprehensive models, and although strictly speaking there are a number of different psychodynamic theories, they all share certain basic assumptions. The original and most widely known is the psychoanalytic theory of Freud, but from this developed several other psychodynamic 'schools' which departed in various ways from 'classical' psychoanalytic theory. Nevertheless, they have in common a fundamental concept, the *dynamic unconscious* – 'dynamic' because it is held to be the source of the basic biological motivations of the individual which determine much of his behaviour. Another important tenet of psychodynamic theory is that personality development is greatly influenced by early childhood events and experiences. The psychodynamic model is thus a deterministic one subject to criticism not only as being unscientific (because it is largely unamenable to experimental refutation) but also as essentially negative and anti-humanistic.

Behaviourist

This model is often seen as the antithesis of the psychodynamic and indeed there has sometimes been a not always very restrained animosity between proponents of the two views. *Behaviourism* as a school of psychology was founded by J.B. Watson (1879–1958) as a reaction to the introspectionists. He rejected the notion of consciousness as an object for scientific study and claimed that only behaviour and not subjective experience could be so studied. This extreme view has been modified by later behaviourists so that the individual's self report of his subjective mental processes is considered a legitimate piece of behaviour for study. However, the dynamic unconscious as a concept has no place in the behaviourist model, which sees behaviour as being determined by learning experiences which can be studied experimentally both in man and other animals. Differences between individuals may also depend on genetic factors influencing the rate at which they learn or the way they respond physiologically to stimuli. Again this is a model which sees man's behaviour as being determined by factors largely outside his control.

Cognitive

As a contrast to the last two, basically deterministic, models the cognitive view of man sees him as more autonomous and in control of his own destiny. The best-known example of such a model is the *Personal Construct Theory* of George Kelly. According to this view man is regarded as a scientist who is all the time trying to make sense of his world by constructing hypotheses about it which subsequent events either confirm or refute. To take account of his actual experiences, he may – to a greater or lesser extent – alter his hypotheses, but his behaviour is determined by them on an essentially conscious and rational basis with no place for such notions as unconscious motivations.

Phenomenological

This model also views the individual as relatively autonomous but focusses on his *subjective phenomenological experience* of himself and the world as the determinant of his behaviour, in direct contrast to the objectivity of the behaviourist school. It is also a 'holistic' approach since it emphasizes the 'wholeness' as well as the uniqueness of the individual, especially in terms of the concept of *self*, or that part of experience which is identified by the individual as himself. There is a concern with the development and full realization of the self as represented, for example, by Carl Rogers' *self-actualization* and the *ontological security* of R.D. Laing ('ontological' having to do with 'being' and 'existence'). However, the former is essentially a psychological concept and has been the object of research studies, while the latter is derived from existential philosophy and, though contributing to the understanding of human experience, is not open to scientific investigation.

Cybernetic

In the last thirty years, developments in fields outside psychology – concerned with such matters as self-regulation in machines by negative feedback (like the thermostat), the coding of information for transmission purposes, and the construction of electronic computers – have led to the proposal, introduced originally by Norbert Wiener in 1948, that machines may provide analogues for human behaviour and experiences, especially in the area of cognitive functions.

Thus if a machine can be made to simulate a piece of human behaviour then its structure and mode of functioning may throw light on the physical mechanisms underlying that behaviour. Similarly the concepts used in communications engineering and known generally as *information theory* may provide clues to understanding aspects of human communication and of the storage of information in the human memory.

Neurobiological

This is also concerned with the physical basis of human behaviour and experience and links up with the cybernetic model. However, it is based directly on findings from neuro- and psycho-physiological research rather than derived, by analogy, from machines. It represents, of course, the somatic component of the dualistic view of the relationship of mind and body, or the somatic 'aspect' or 'language' of the monistic viewpoint; and it also forms an interdisciplinary research area between psychology and physiology.

Social

The last model is the sociological one which stresses the importance of the individual's membership of social groups in determining his behaviour. It raises, however, such issues as the relationship between the individual and society which we shall be considering in greater detail in the next and later chapters.

Further reading

Coleman, J.C. (ed.) (1977) *Introductory Psychology*. London: Routledge & Kegan Paul.

Taylor, A., Sluckin, W., Davies, D.R., Reason, J.T., Thomson, R. and Colman, A.M. (1982) *Introductory Psychology*, 2nd ed. Harmondsworth: Penguin.

Weinman, J. (1981) *An Outline of Psychology as Applied to Medicine*. Bristol: Wright.

3
Sociology

What is and what is not sociology

It is probably more difficult to arrive at a consensus on a definition of sociology than is the case with psychology. However, it would not be appropriate here to consider the many alternatives which have been suggested and we shall, for present purposes, regard the basic subject matter of sociology as being human social behaviour and relations within and between groups of all sizes. We can see at once that since psychology is also concerned with social as well as other aspects of behaviour, the two sciences have a common interest. The difference between them is really one of perspective; whereas for psychology the major interest is the behaviour of, and its organization within, the individual, for sociology it is how that behaviour is determined by the society and culture to which the individual belongs.

Sociology, then, is essentially the science of social relations and a sociologist is a graduate of the subject.

Just as psychology is often mistakenly thought to be synonymous with psychiatry and psychoanalysis, so the science of sociology is sometimes confused with the political system known as socialism. This is probably in part due to the similarity in the names (as with psychology and psychiatry), but there is also often more than a suspicion in many people's minds that all sociologists are revolutionary socialists. Whether, if this were so, it should be regarded as unwelcome is neither here nor there, but in fact there is no inevitability about such an association between sociology and 'left-wing' politics.

The issue, however, that is raised by such a consideration is the ethical one of the 'objectivity', 'neutrality' or 'non-involvement' of the sociologist as a scientist investigating social systems. Inevitably there are social implications of this type of research, and to a greater or lesser extent the individual sociologist may become involved as a member of his own society – perhaps in striving to bring about social changes which he believes his studies indicate to be necessary. Whether this conflicts with his responsibility as a scientist is a moral question which, together with others arising, as we have already discussed in the first chapter, out of the nature of sociology as a behavioural or social science, cannot be answered in any dogmatic way. (A similar situation exists in relation to the psychologist studying an individual where his own values might lead him to wish to change the behaviour of that individual.) The important point is that the existence of such moral difficulties should be recognized.

Another problem which sociology shares with psychology is that it too is often accused of being nothing more than common sense. Again this is perhaps not surprising if one considers that the 'man in the street' needs to have some understanding of the social system to which he belongs; some awareness of its values, beliefs, controls, etc. His experience, however, is likely to be limited, and while some of his assumptions about the nature of society may be confirmed by sociological study, others may be shown to be false. The difficulty, as with psychology, is that sociology is a science that deals with matters on which the layman is very likely to have an opinion since they come within his everyday experience. As a member of a social system, his views of that system as he sees it may be valuable, but his claim to as much knowledge as the sociologist cannot be justified.

Subdivisions and applications of sociology

Like any other science, sociology as it has progressed from its early beginnings has found more and more areas of specialized study too numerous to detail here. Those, however, which are of particular interest in relation to medicine and the health professions include the sociology of the family, of education and work, of organizations, of crime and social deviance and of medicine itself. As an application of sociology, this last subdivision of *medical sociology* has developed considerably in recent years so that medical sociologists are to be found in hospitals and other medical institutions, particularly in departments of social or community medicine. Their work is largely concerned with research into various social aspects of medical practice and its organization and with the planning of clinical and other services within the hospital and the community. The major difference between the medical sociologist and the clinical psychologist is that the latter, as we saw in the last chapter, has a direct clinical involvement with patients in assessment and treatment and for this purpose has a period of clinical experience and training.

Much closer to clinical psychology as a comparable clinical application of sociology is medical *social work*, and again the term is sometimes confused with sociology itself. The medical social worker has a basic training and qualification in social science followed by field experience in a clinical setting. The majority of social workers are not, however, involved in medical work but are to be found in the community. In fact, following implementation of the Seebohm Report in 1970, most social workers are now employed by local authority social service departments and do not specialize as they once did as mental welfare officers, child care officers, etc. The intention was that they should cover all areas of social work and all types of 'client' – so-called 'generic' social work – but already there is a tendency to return to a limited specialization. Obviously, the medical social worker still works in a medical setting, usually a general hospital, particularly in specialized units like paediatrics, renal dialysis, venereology, etc., while the psychiatric social worker, who has special training in psychiatry, is employed in psychiatric hospitals, clinics and the community. In both cases the social worker is a member of a team of health professionals dealing with the patient and his family. His role includes the investigation of the social circumstances of the patient and help, advice and sometimes 'counselling' of the patient in his social relationships, especially when there are marital or family problems.

Perspectives in sociology

Figure 3.1 represents the same four perspectives described in the last two chapters, from which society and social relationships, as well as individual behaviour, can be viewed. Each will be considered in greater detail in the following sections; but here we are concerned with the overall relationship between the four perspectives together with the introduction of some basic sociological concepts.

If we first take the sociological analysis of a society into its component parts – or in other words look at its *social structure* in terms of social relationships – then the total population is subdivided into groups of individuals according to the pattern of social relationships within and between the groups. Some sociologists also take note of what they regard as the *social functions* of groups in analysing a society. According to this *functionalist* view, each group has a function in maintaining the stability or order of the whole society in a way that is analogous to the parts of a living organism. We shall see later, however, when we consider some sociological models, that this view is not shared by all sociologists. Nevertheless, the interdependence of the various groups within a society is generally recognized by its description as a *social system*.

The term *social group* itself is used to describe a collectivity of individuals who directly or indirectly relate to each other. It may be small like a family or very large like the National Health Service; but, in either case, the individuals are aware of being members of it and of having some kind of relationship with each other. In many instances this pattern of social relationships of a group remains constant over a long period and has a continuing existence independent of the members of the group at any one time, being passed on by teaching from one generation to the next. The term *social institution* is used to describe such a pattern of social relationships (e.g. the family, the church), while a specific type of institution which is set up for a particular purpose and usually has a division of labour and a hierarchical system of authority is known as an *organization* (e.g. the National Health Service).

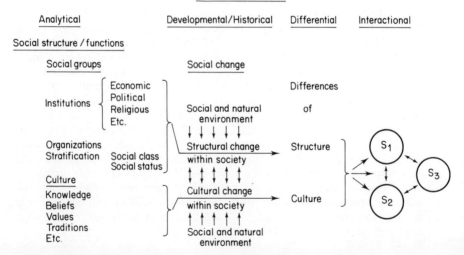

Fig.3.1 Diagrammatic representation of the four perspectives in sociology

Another way of subdividing society into categories is by *social stratification* or the allocation of individuals to different levels or strata of a hierarchical system. This may be, for example, according to economic position – *social class*, or prestige as judged by the community – *social status*.

Whatever form of subdivision or categorization is used in the analysis of society, we have also to consider the regular patterns of behaviour exhibited by the members of different groups. These patterns are determined by what is called the group *culture*, which consists of such things as the shared knowledge, beliefs, values, traditions, etc., of the group and which is transmitted socially from one generation to the next. Not only will the whole society have its particular culture, but there will also be *subcultures* of the various groups within it, often with markedly different sets of beliefs, values, etc. The social behaviour of the individual will thus be considerably determined by his culture, and especially by its *social norms* which establish what is acceptable or unacceptable behaviour. The process by which the society's culture is passed on from generation to generation is known as *socialization*, and the mechanisms by which behaviour is regulated, both formally (the law, etc.) and informally (ridicule, gossip, etc.), are referred to as *social control*. An individual's behaviour is also influenced by his particular *positions* in society, e.g. doctor, father, patient, etc., in each of which he plays an expected *role*.

The second perspective, the developmental/historical, is concerned with the subject of *social change*, both of whole societies and of social groups within them. Such change is probably continuous in all societies, although varying in its extent and rate at different times; but some sociologists tend to stress change while others emphasize the maintenance of order of societies over time. Various factors within and outside the society may operate to bring about both structural and cultural change. External influences include the social and natural environment, but processes within society are the subject of several theories and will be considered in more detail later. An aspect that has received special attention in recent years is the study and planning of social change in the so-called developing countries of the world – a field of applied sociology which has been described as the sociology of development.

The third or differential perspective is perhaps more correctly the concern of cultural and social anthropology, in that the former tends to study whole societies (often 'primitive' and quite distinctive in their social structure and culture) so that they can be compared and contrasted with each other, while the latter examines modern industrial, urban or rural communities in a similar way.

Finally, the fourth perspective looks at the interactions between societies or between social groups within them. Although contact between societies varies, it is generally increasing with improvements in travel and communications, so that most are affected from the sociological point of view by such interaction and interdependence. Of particular current importance are the relations between the 'developed' and the 'developing' nations, yet this area of international relationships is one that has been somewhat neglected by sociologists. On the other hand, relationships between social groups within societies have received much more attention – particularly the question of intergroup conflict and its role in bringing about social change.

Sociological methods of study

In Chapter 2, having concluded that the proper object for study in psychology is the human individual, we went on to examine the various approaches to the observation and measurement of individual experience and behaviour. When we apply the same considerations to sociology we find that the object or unit for study is less specific, since the subject matter of sociology – social relations and social behaviour – can be observed in groups ranging in size from a couple (two individuals) to a whole society. However, just as in psychology there are the two contrasting approaches – the ideographic and the nomothetic – so in sociology it is possible to adopt, on the one hand, the descriptive *case study* approach with its detailed study of a particular group and its emphasis on the unique aspects of the group's social behaviour and relations or, on the other hand, the larger-scale quantitative *social survey* which looks for generalizations about patterns of social behaviour and relations. Again the two are complementary in the sense that case studies can serve as starting points for surveys and may then, in turn, act as tests of specific predictions from generalized sociological hypotheses. Surveys are carried out on samples of people and, as we saw in the last chapter, it is important that they should be representative of the populations from which they are drawn. They are usually cross-sectional in that they deal with a particular moment in time; but sometimes a longitudinal dimension may be added by using the same technique on comparable samples on repeated occasions to measure social changes.

Variables to be observed

If the unit for sociological study consists of a variable number of individuals comprising one or more social groups, then observation may be directed to aspects of the *individuals* themselves or the *groups* to which they belong. These will include quantitative *variables* (i.e. qualities that can be measured on an ordinal or interval scale) as well as qualitative *attributes* which can only be categorized (i.e. 'present' or 'absent' or several mutually exclusive categories).

The choice of variables or attributes to be studied will generally be made with a particular hypothesis in mind, but the difficulty, as with all the behavioural sciences, is to translate complex high-level concepts like alienation, social integration, etc., into something that can be clearly defined and specified for measuring purposes. The usual way to achieve this is to decide on relatively unambiguous *indicators* for various aspects of the concept and to see how these correlate with each other (to form a composite index) and with related variables of known validity.

Observational techniques

A wide range of techniques exists for the collection of sociological data. Use is also made of existing material for so-called *secondary analysis*, in contrast to the making of fresh observations for *primary analysis*. Thus historical documents as well as contemporary statistics gathered for other purposes may be re-examined for sociological purposes, while the products of the mass media or popular literature may be subjected to *content analysis* for the light they throw on sociological issues. There is perhaps an analogy here with the use by Freud and others of works of art and literature for the insights they may provide into the personality of their creator.

As far as fresh data are concerned, the simplest approach, just as with psychology, is the direct *observation* of behaviour in social situations; but a difference is that the observer may become a part of, and even a member of, the group he is studying. This *participant observation* is a common practice in case studies of particular social situations and has been a feature of many classical studies in cultural anthropology (with the anthropologist living and working with the tribe being studied). In the field of medical sociology, participant observation has been applied to the investigation of the hospital, and especially the mental hospital as an institution.

We now turn to the more quantitative approach in sociology. The two techniques used in social surveys of large numbers of people are the *interview* and the *questionnaire*, both of which we have already met as methods of psychological observation. The principles underlying their use are the same in the two disciplines, as are their advantages and disadvantages. There is a tendency for interviews to be conducted 'in the field' (e.g. door to door, on the street corner, etc.) and for questionnaires to be sent through the post, so that the latter is more economical in time and money. The questionnaire is obviously more objective and free from the possibility of observer bias which may be associated with the interview, but at the same time it has necessarily to be relatively simple and superficial. The interview may be *unstructured*, its flexibility allowing a degree of freedom in the expression of opinions, attitudes, beliefs, etc., or *structured*, with restriction to a set of predetermined questions having a limiting effect on the replies but increasing its objectivity and comparability.

A technique called *sociometry* has been developed for the measurement of social relations between individuals within a group so that they can be displayed graphically (in the form of a map of the group members with connecting lines to represent relationships – see Fig. 18.1) or numerically (with figures for each member representing popularity, etc.). The method was initially used by social psychologists to study the social structure and dynamics of small groups and depended upon the observation of the social interaction between the individual members (amount and nature of communication between them, etc.) or, more often, upon each member answering a series of questions about his or her preferences, likes, dislikes, etc., for other members of the group. The technique has since been applied more generally in sociology in order, for example, to discover networks of social relationships within larger groups, starting with one or two key individuals and spreading out through their closest friends or colleagues, and then their's in turn, and so on.

As with psychological techniques, we meet in sociology the problems of *reliability* and *validity*. Much time and effort is spent in improving reliability by revising questionnaires and structured interviews in such a way that the meanings of questions are clear-cut, unambiguous and easily understood by all respondents and interviewees. Distortion in subjects' replies is reduced by careful training of interviewers in technique, while bias of the interviewers themselves may be allowed for in large-scale surveys by employing many interviewers representing a wide range of attitudes and opinions – which should cancel each other out in terms of resulting errors.

Establishing validity, as in all the behavioural sciences, is often difficult. We have seen how a sociological concept has to be transformed into measurable indicators which should have reasonable 'face' validity, but further problems arise with validation against an external criterion. In general there has been less attempt to make assessments of empirical validity in sociology than in psychology, but this may reflect the difficulties inherent in the nature of the concepts used. Thus, even in the area of social stratification there are problems in selecting indices for the two most generally accepted and extensively studied concepts of social class and social status. However, the fact that, as we shall see later, these measures of social differentiation correlate with other behavioural variables and attributes provides some external validation of them as significantly meaningful concepts.

The experiment
Experimentation was a relatively late development in the field of sociology and the reasons are not hard to see. If there are difficulties in carrying out experiments on single individuals, they are multiplied when it comes to social groups. However, it is possible to conduct laboratory experiments in what is perhaps more correctly called social psychology, meaning by 'laboratory' any non-natural environment. The subjects for these experiments have most often been students, and studies have included such areas as the effect of a group on individual behaviour or the development of a 'group culture'.

The experimental investigation of larger numbers usually has to rely on chance natural situations in the 'field' in which, for example, a comparison can be made between two matched groups differing in an independent variable (e.g. the two sections of a single tribe split arbitrarily at some time by an international boundary, or where a group can be studied before and after the introduction of a social innovation (e.g. television).

Sociological models

Just as there are several psychological models which attempt to provide a framework for understanding individual human behaviour, and in particular how and why the mature individual comes to be what he is in terms of his intelligence and personality, so in sociology there are different models concerned with trying to explain the nature of society, and especially how and why social change may occur within it. There are, however, two general issues to be considered before we come to examine the individual models.

The first of these has to do with the concepts of *structure* and *function*. We saw in Chapter 2 how the early psychologists were preoccupied with the distinction between these two aspects but that it was no longer a matter for controversy and that both can be seen to be equally important and complementary to each other. In sociology we find a rather similar state of affairs except that the controversy has perhaps increased rather than decreased. Thus Auguste Comte (1798–1857), who introduced the term sociology (though he first described the new science as 'social physics'), distinguished two forms of sociology, the *static* and the *dynamic*, which he likened to anatomy and physiology respectively. Static sociology was concerned with social existence or *order*, while dynamic sociology studied the 'succession of social states' or *progress*. For Comte, however, this did not represent the conflictual dichotomy that it was subsequently to become with the political implications of social order versus social change highlighted later by Karl Marx (1818–83).

The other issue concerns the relationship between the individual and society, and the extent to which the former is the creator or the product of the latter.

Emile Durkheim (1858-1917) pointed out that although a society is actually made up of a large number of individuals, the whole is more than the sum of the parts, having what he called a *collective consciousness*. Thus there are certain social facts about a society, such as its institutions and its culture, which cannot be wholly explained by qualities of its individual members though it could not exist without them. At the same time, the individual's behaviour is partly determined by his membership of the society, so that there is a complex inter-action in which man is, in part, both the product and the creator of society. The relative importance for human behaviour that is attributed to the individual (and his genes), and to society, and represented by the terms *psychologism* and *sociologism* respectively, is something that has been much debated and has political overtones as *individualism* and *collectivism*.

Having considered these two basic issues, we can now review briefly a few sociological models. We shall meet some of these again in more detail in later chapters but here, as with the psychological models, our concern is with their overall comparison. Most of the models aim to explain either the maintenance of social order or the reasons for social change in a society.

Evolutionary

This model sees society as evolving through a series of stages from a simple to a more complex form, in a way analogous to Darwin's theory of biological evolution. The degree to which the ideas of social and biological evolution are approximated varies between different theories, as does the nature of the evolu-tionary stages. Herbert Spencer (1820-1903), for example, saw society very much in terms of an 'organism' and social evolution as a gradual increase in the complexity and differentiation of society into interdependent parts. He was, however, an individualist, stressing the view that, while in an organism the parts are subservient to the whole, a society exists for the benefit of its individual members. Even Marx regarded civilization as passing through a series of inevit-able stages each of which was destroyed to be succeeded by the next. Such theories with the emphasis on fixed stages have generally not been supported by historical evidence, and the evolutionary model has fallen into disrepute.

Cyclical

Instead of, as in the evolutionary theories, a society progressing in a 'unilinear' fashion from a simple to a complex organization, the cyclical model envisages a number of stages in which increasing complexity may be succeeded by the reverse trend and the whole cycle may be repeated in a society of long enough standing. Thus the sociologist Oswald Spengler and the historian Arnold Toynbee have compared the social cycle to the individual human life cycle from birth to death. Another sociologist, Pitirim Sorokin, describes three cultural phases through which societies pass, each dominated by a particular system of truth: an 'ideational' culture based on faith, a 'sensate' culture based on empirical evidence of the senses, and an 'idealistic' culture dominated by reason. Support for these theories depends largely on an analysis and inter-pretation of historical data and is open to dispute.

Structural–functional

We have already considered, as a general issue, the two concepts of structure and function in sociology and noted their presence from the earliest days of the discipline. The analogy of the living organism as a model for society has long been popular. As we have seen, it was used by Spencer, linked with his view of the evolution of society. It was also used by two well-known anthropologists, Bronislaw Malinowski (1884–1942) and Arthur Radcliffe-Brown (1881–1955).

The model has had a great influence on American sociology, especially through the work of Talcott Parsons whose so-called *equilibrium* theory is based on the concept of homeostasis as used in physiology. The theory is concerned with the way a society maintains a degree of stability in spite of changes in membership and internal and external forces for change. It proposes that this is made possible through the relationships between social structure and functions. Thus: 'Social life persists because societies find means (structures) whereby they fulfil the needs (functions) which are either pre-conditions or consequences of organized social life.' If the equilibrium of society is disturbed it is automatically restored by adjustments, owing to the fact that all parts of the integrated social system are functionally interdependent.

Parsons' equilibrium theory has been criticized for being too 'static' with its emphasis on social stability and neglect of social change, and has been considered to have been used in conservative politics as a support for the status quo.

Conflict
In direct contrast to the equilibrium model, conflict theory is concerned with social change which is seen as resulting from a struggle, rather than a homeostatic equilibrium, between different sections of society. For Marx, the conflict was basically an economic one, at the time between what he regarded as the old system of economic production or 'capitalism' represented by the 'bourgeois' social class, and the future 'socialist' form of production of the 'proletarian' class. The resulting socialist revolution would eventually be succeeded by a 'communist' society with a social structure that would be free from conflict and further revolutions.

Marxian theory has, of course, been associated with radical left-wing politics and formed the basis of the communist regimes, but it is not the only conflict model. Other sociologists, for example Ralf Dahrendorf, consider other causes of inequality and conflict which may not be revolutionary but can still lead to social change.

That conflict and significant changes within societies do at times occur cannot seriously be disputed; but nor can the fact that there may be periods of relative equilibrium and stability, and the two states may alternate with each other. The antithesis between the two models is largely a false one and arises from the different perspectives of their proponents.

Symbolic interaction
Strictly speaking this model is more social psychological than sociological. The model, largely originating with Charles Cooley (1864–1929) and George Mead (1863–1931), emphasizes the cultural rather than the biological nature of human social behaviour, which is seen as occurring in response to symbols (chiefly verbal) which may refer both to objects and to abstract concepts, the meanings of which are acquired during the process of 'socialization'. Such symbols, together with the values defined for them within the 'culture', play an important part in determining the individual's behaviour, as does his definition of himself – his 'self-concept' – including the 'roles' he adopts. Related to this

model is another, associated particularly with Harold Garfinkel and known as *ethnomethodology*, concerned with the regulation of social interaction by shared but tacit and generally unspoken 'rules'.

Sociobiology

This final model (which contrasts particularly with the last viewpoint), though concerned with social behaviour, would be unlikely to be accepted as 'sociological' by most sociologists since it postulates a biological basis for such behaviour. Thus apparently unselfish and altruistic behaviour is considered not to be socially acquired and for the benefit of others but to be genetically determined to ensure the survival of the individual's genes in his or her children. However, it must be emphasized that the theory is at present a relatively recent and controversial development.

Further reading

Cuff, E.C. and Payne, G.C.F. (eds.) (1984) *Perspectives in Sociology*. London: George Allen & Unwin.

Patrick, D.L. and Scambler, G. (1982) *Sociology as Applied to Medicine*. London: Baillière Tindall.

Worsley, P. (ed.) (1977) *Introductory Sociology*, 2nd ed. Harmondsworth: Penguin.

Part 2
The analytical (reductionist) perspective

This section is concerned with the analysis, reduction or breakdown of the whole into its component parts; that is to say, the whole psychology of the individual into some fundamental psychological processes and the whole structure of society into various social groupings.

First, however, Chapter 4 looks at the nature of that overall state of psychological functioning that we call consciousness together with possible variations that may occur in the level of awareness. The next four chapters examine the so-called cognitive processes – perception, learning, remembering and thinking – concerned essentially with enabling the individual to respond appropriately to environmental change. Chapter 9 deals with motivation and Chapter 10 with emotion, both of which are basic to an understanding of individual behaviour. Finally, the concept of social structure is examined in Chapter 11 with particular emphasis on the family as a social institution and the stratification of society into social classes.

Some reference to clinical aspects is made in each chapter.

4
Consciousness and states of awareness

The nature of consciousness

We have seen that psychology is concerned with both objective behaviour and subjective experience. Behaviour can be directly observed and described in all animals, but experience is something which is private to the human individual. We are all aware that we have a mental life in which we perceive the world about us, have all kinds of thoughts, recall events from the past, experience wishes, desires, likes and dislikes and feel various emotions, pleasant and unpleasant. Yet the nature of this state of self-awareness or *consciousness* remains a mystery. We know that it is not present continuously because we lose it each night when we sleep. We observe that other animals also have periods of sleep and wakefulness but we cannot know if they have a comparable state of consciousness. We cannot know because they have no means of telling us; but for the same reason it is unlikely that they do, since to be able to observe one's own mental processes and to have a historical sense of self-continuity necessitates the use of the linguistic symbolic system of verbal communication or language that is unique to man. Only with the ability to name objects, actions and relations, etc. does it really become possible to remember, in the sense of being able to select events out of the past and examine their relevance to the present or future.

Before this stage in evolutionary development an animal's behaviour remains embedded in its experiences – that is to say its behaviour is moulded in a relatively invariant, inflexible and predictable way by its life experiences through the processes of learning which we shall be considering in detail in the next chapter. Only with the acquisition of language is it possible to reflect on previous experiences – to remember them – and then to make a considered prediction as to which would be the best response to make to any current situation. It seems, then, that consciousness – in the sense of self-awareness of mental processes or an inner mental life – has been a necessary evolutionary development in man, associated with an enormously enhanced ability to process information and predict future events.

Another major philosophical problem (to which we have already referred in Chapter 2) concerns the relationship of this subjective, conscious mind to the objective, material body. Even if we adopt in this and other chapters the monistic viewpoint of the single mind–body entity, we shall still find ourselves looking at it from the two aspects represented by psychology and neuroanatomy/physiology. In other words, in relation to any mental process, we could have data from two sources: that which is obtained directly or indirectly (inferred) from the subject's verbal reports or behaviour, and that which is derived from various physiological recordings from the brain and elsewhere.

Thus, to take a simple example, a subject may have electrodes attached temporarily to a number of positions on the scalp and connected to an amplifying machine called an electroencephalograph (EEG) which enables recordings to be made of the minute electrical changes occurring in the brain beneath each electrode. If the subject is told first to relax without any form of mental exertion, and then to perform some difficult mental arithmetic, it is usual to find a difference between these two periods in the pattern of the tracings from the EEG. The subject reports a difference of subjective mental content and the machine demonstrates a difference of electrical activity in the brain. However, such correlations between mental/psychological and physical/physiological processes are relatively crude and are concerned with general levels of activity rather than specific mental events. We shall therefore return to the question of the neurological basis of consciousness when we consider variations in its level involved, for example, in sleep and wakefulness. Before that, we must examine in more detail some psychological aspects of normal waking consciousness.

Limits of consciousness

It is clear that, in the waking state, the conscious content of the mind is derived principally from two sources: the outside world through the cutaneous (touch) and other senses (smell, taste, hearing, sight) by the process of perception, and the inner mental world through the process of remembering. In addition, there is a (usually negligible) contribution of physical sensations from various organs within the body. Fig. 4.1 illustrates this. Consciousness is depicted as being of limited capacity so that there is a restriction on the size of mental content that can be held in conscious awareness at any moment. At the same time there is, potentially, an almost infinite quantity of information which could enter consciousness from the environment and from the collection of memories which is readily available in what was called by Freud the *preconscious* mind. This

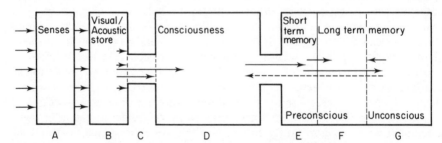

Fig.4.1 A theoretical model of the relationship of consciousness/awareness to the current outside physical world of the environment and the inside mental world of past memories. (A) Stimuli received by the senses give rise to a sensory image which is briefly stored (B), while being processed as meaningful symbols for entry into consciousness (D). Selectivity of attention occurs (C), either through limited capacity or by a filtering mechanism – peripheral or central. Information is briefly stored in short-term memory (E), from which it can be immediately recalled before a proportion is passed into long-term memory (F and G). This is mostly available for recall to consciousness from the preconscious (F), unless it is repressed in the unconscious (G) when it may only appear in disguised form (e.g. in dreams)

means that there has to be an active process of selection of a limited amount of information from the external and internal worlds.

As far as the former is concerned, this is usually referred to as *attention* and, as we shall see, has been an area of considerable psychological study. What is, and what is not, selected for present attention depends on cognitive, affective and motivational factors. This applies equally to what enters consciousness from the past in the form of memories. Indeed, according to psychoanalytic theory this process of control over the content of consciousness amounts to a censorship which results in certain material from the past, together with unacceptable current wishes and feelings, being *repressed* and made entirely unavailable or *unconscious* to the individual though still exerting an influence on that person's present behaviour and experience.

We have already referred to the idea of the unconscious mind in Chapter 2, but our present concern is with its relationship to consciousness. It is a difficult and controversial concept since evidence for the existence of unconscious mental events or processes can, of necessity, only be indirect. Their presence has to be inferred from their supposed effects in certain types of behaviour or experience. These include the frequently bizarre and seemingly inexplicable dreams at night which, as we shall see, were considered by Freud to be the result of unconscious processes, as were the apparently accidental but often embarrassingly revealing 'slips of the tongue' which are a common everyday occurrence.

Whatever may be the truth about the nature of the unconscious, it has by contrast been relatively easy to apply the experimental method to the study of consciousness and to attempt some measurement of its limits. It is not uncommon to speak of the 'stream' of consciousness because of its ever-changing nature, and if we continue the analogy, we may ask how long is the stream as it passes through the mind, how broad is it and how complex; could there, for example, be more than one stream at a time?

Spatio-temporal limits

One way to measure these limits is to see how much information can, so to speak, be pushed into the individual's consciousness – a technique used in some early experiments to measure the so-called 'span of attention'. Thus, Jevons in 1871 examined how much he could take in at a glance by throwing unknown quantities of beans on to a tray and estimating their number. As would be expected, he found that his accuracy fell off as the number increased beyond three or four. This, and later experiments using the *tachistoscope* (an instrument which displays visual stimuli for short durations), suggested quite a low limit to the amount of information that could be recorded. However, what was really being measured was not necessarily what was being registered at the time, but the extent to which this could be recalled after the presentation of the stimulus.

A series of experiments by Sperling since 1960 has shown, in fact, that much more information is initially taken in during the period of exposure, but that this rapidly decays. The initial, very elegant, experiment (Sperling, 1960) involved the tachistoscopic presentation for 50 msec of a display of three rows of letters, after which the subject was required to recall one of the three rows. This row was indicated by the pitch of a tone (high for the top, medium for the middle and low for the bottom row) which was sounded at a variable interval after the end of the visual display. If the tone occurred very soon, the subject was able to recall about three-quarters of the row indicated. Since he had not known which row this would be, the inference was that this amount of information was available at that time for each row, making a total potential quantity of information in excess of that which had previously been thought to be possible within the span of attention. The explanation of this finding was revealed by delaying the tone for one second after the end of the display, when it was found that the number of letters which the subject could recall fell to a level consistent with earlier findings.

It would appear that there must be a *visual store* of considerable capacity but very short duration in which the sensory input is retained as a visual image or *icon*; this then has to be 'coded' or converted into meaningful symbols by recognition as letters, numbers, words, etc., for further processing. Because of the relative slowness of this latter process, only four or five items can be extracted from the visual store before it decays. The advantage of such a visual store may be that it permits very short durations of eye fixation in such processes as reading or viewing a scene, since information can continue to be extracted beyond the brief period of visual attention. In effect this means that the environment is scanned in the form of a succession of very brief 'stills' from which is sequentially built up a total picture of the information it contains.

When we turn to the auditory modality there is experimental evidence for an *acoustic store* or *echoic* memory which, like the visual store, records sensory data but in this case as a sequence of sounds, prior to its symbolic recognition, for example, as speech. It too is of short duration and therefore of limited capacity, but its existence explains the common experience of suddenly becoming aware of what someone has said a second or so after they have spoken. Such an acoustic memory is clearly of value since information conveyed by sound waves is transient and, unlike visual data, cannot be referred to again (unless of course it is recorded and played back on some sound reproducing equipment). Once again the raw data have to be coded or recognized as man-made symbols in consciousness, and this, when reported by the subject, gives a measure of the limit to the amount of auditory material that can be present at any one time; i.e. there is a temporal limit comparable to the spatial limit to visual information.

Complexity and selectivity

The third aspect of attention to have received much study is the question of whether it can be divided so that more than one sequence of stimuli can be attended to or dealt with in consciousness at the same time. Everyday experience such as driving a car while listening to the radio shows that it is possible to do so, provided neither sequence is too complex or unfamiliar. Once, however, it becomes necessary to concentrate on one aspect of the environment, then the rest tends to be ignored. It is this *selectivity* of attention or awareness that has been of particular interest to psychologists. It is sometimes called the 'cocktail-party-problem' because of the difficulty in that situation of trying to listen to one out of several simultaneous, and often equally loud, conversations.

A common experimental technique for the study of selective attention, though criticized as unrepresentative of focussed attention under normal conditions (Underwood, 1976), is known as *dichotic listening*. This involves the use of headphones to provide two auditory inputs to the subject, one to each ear. By this means, stimuli such as sequences of digits or passages of prose, and differing in various respects, can be supplied to the two ears. At the same time, the subject's attention can be directed to one or other of the two sequences (the 'attended') by having to repeat it aloud continuously as it is heard – a process known as *shadowing*. The question then is how much, if any, of the 'unattended' sequence has been registered and can be recalled. In general it is very limited, showing that the subject is able to choose to listen with one ear and to somehow block the other. In order to determine the nature of the selective process involved, many studies have been carried out using the dichotic technique or modifications of it.

Of particular interest has been the question of whether selectivity is based on the physical characteristics, or the semantic or word content, of the auditory input. In other words, is there a *filtering* mechanism as suggested by Broadbent (1958) which acts *peripherally* on the sensory input by blocking certain types of sound, or is there a *central* mechanism which selects on the basis of *symbolic* (e.g. language) content. In favour of the first is the evidence (Cherry, 1953) that changing the unshadowed (unattended) input from English to another language, or from normal to reversed speech, is not noticed by the subject, whereas a change from a male to female speaker is detected.

On the other hand, Moray (1959) found that a few 'significant' words, such as the subject's own name, may reach consciousness from the unattended input, and indeed an instruction preceded by his name may be carried out by the subject, though not if his name is omitted. A galvanic skin response or GSR (a measurement of change of electrical resistance of the skin usually in relation to emotion and arousal – see Chapter 8) can similarly be obtained to an unattended word to which the subject has previously been conditioned (by repeatedly associating the word, presented in prose passages, with an electric shock) even though he may not be aware of it (Moray, 1969). Further support for a central control mechanism came from an experiment (Treisman, 1960) in which inputs were *switched* between ears but subjects continued to shadow the original message for one or two words (i.e. switched attention briefly to the wrong ear) provided the switch occurred at a point where the last word before, and the first word after, the switch had a high probability of being consecutive within the context of the message (e.g. mahogany and table). Where the switch occurred between words with a lower contextual probability the subject would continue to shadow with the correct ear without any interruption.

Finally, in *trichotic* experiments – that is with three different inputs, one to each ear and the third to both ears (Treisman, 1964) – it was found that subjects could shadow the binaural message indicating that half the input to both left and right ears could be blocked. Again this would be difficult to explain on the basis of a peripheral filter.

It seems, then, that divided attention may involve at least two modes of selection: firstly, a peripheral or early selective *filtering*, operating at the level of the sensory storage system (visual or acoustic) and dependent upon the presence of a particular feature of the stimulus (a stimulus 'set' such as we shall meet when we consider perception in the next chapter) but which still allows an attenuated (reduced intensity) rather than completely blocked onward transmission from unattended inputs; and secondly, a central or later process which has been described as *pigeon-holing* (a response set) and dependent upon selective recognition, against representations in memory, of recognized stimulus patterns (Broadbent, 1977; Keele and Neill, 1978). Finally there may be a third, later selective process which determines which of the pattern recognitions are admitted to conscious awareness.

An alternative to the filter model is the 'variable allocation capacity model' of Kahneman (1973) in which a limited capacity for processing information (Moray, 1967) is distributed between tasks. In dichotic listening, most of the capacity is directed to the shadowed input, but in other situations there may be a more equal distribution between two or more familiar tasks – like the previously mentioned driving and listening to the car radio. It is the unpredictability of a task which requires a large component of the capacity and, therefore, a preferential selection of attention.

As well, however, as these cognitive aspects of attention, there are affective and motivational influences on what is selected for entry into consciousness. Thus McGinnies (1949) showed that the *recognition awareness threshold* (i.e. the length of time for which a word must be presented tachistoscopically before its recognition is reported) was raised in some subjects for unpleasant or 'taboo' words, although galvanic skin responses occurred to such words at exposures below the recognition awareness threshold. This suggests that a *recognition* threshold had been reached but not an *awareness* threshold owing to the operation of *perceptual defence* – the concept that we are less likely to see or hear words that are unpleasant to us than neutral words of the same intensity. An analogy is sometimes drawn with the psychoanalytic concept of *repression*, a function of which is to defend the conscious mind or *ego* against unpleasant or unacceptable memories from the past. We shall return to this matter when we consider memory in the next chapter.

Clinical aspects

The limited capacity of consciousness and the selectivity of attention that this necessitates has implications in the clinical field. Thus we may find that an undue preoccupation with memories of recent and/or past events associated, for example, with bereavement (a 'grief reaction'), an anxiety state or a depressive disorder, results in diminished attention to the external world, so that information is not registered and the individual becomes forgetful and unable to pursue a task requiring sustained attention such as reading. Such apparent impairment of cognitive functioning should be distinguished from intellectual deterioration due to organic disease affecting the brain.

A brief reference was made earlier to the usually very small input to conscious awareness from stimulation of internal organs of the body. In various diseases, of course, such stimulation may be considerable and give rise to feelings of discomfort or pain. The question of selectivity of attention and experience of pain is clearly an important one, but we shall leave further consideration of this until the next chapter, when we shall deal with the subject of pain in greater detail. In the healthy individual, however, there is usually little awareness of sensation from the body unless attention is drawn to a particular part. If we do direct our attention in this way, we may all become aware of feelings of pressure arising from our physical position, of our breathing and of the rhythmic beating of the heart or pulsation of certain arteries. In some patients who complain of physical symptoms for which no organic cause can be discovered, it is probable that their complaints are, at least in part, due to an excessive focussing of attention on the site of the symptom and that what they are experiencing is a bodily sensation which does not normally reach the level of awareness.

Just as in some patients input may be selectively enhanced, so in others it may be blocked for psychological reasons. There are patients who, though free from organic disease, present with a loss of skin sensation in part of the body, or of a special sense such as vision or hearing. Such complaints usually do not correspond with those produced by organic disease and they are commonly described as *hysterical*. It has for long been suggested that the mechanism by which they occur is a process of involuntary *dissociation* between a limited part of consciousness (e.g. that concerned with skin sensation from a particular area or with visual or auditory perception) and the rest of consciousness. Thus these parts are dissociated or shut off from the rest of awareness and the individual no longer experiences the appropriate sensations or perceptions. This is only a conceptual model – there is no evidence for such compartmentalization of consciousness – and an alternative model could employ the concept of selective filtering or limited capacity which we have been considering earlier.

Finally, some of the phenomena produced by *hypnosis* may be related to alterations of attention, and indeed the fundamental basis for the process may be a highly selective focussing of attention by the subject on the hypnotist with a corresponding diminution in attention to all other stimuli. Thus in a suitable subject the hypnotist is able to suggest a selective inattention to particular stimuli, resulting in, for example, an area of skin anaesthesia or a loss of a special sense such as vision or hearing. Further suggestion then produces a return to normal functioning.

Levels of consciousness

We have so far considered certain aspects of consciousness as it is experienced in the normal waking state. Everyday experience suggests that natural variations also occur in the overall level of awareness, ranging from sleep and drowsiness at one extreme to a state of excitement and alertness at the other. In addition, alterations of consciousness may be brought about by changes in the general level of external sensory stimulation, by deliberate manipulation of attention by the individual, and by chemical or other organic factors influencing the function of the brain. Closely related to the notion of levels of consciousness is the concept of a continuum of *arousal*, though this, as we shall see in Chapter 6, is concerned more with changes of behaviour and emotion. Before examining some of these aspects in more detail, we must consider what is known of the neurophysiological basis of sleep and wakefulness.

Neurophysiology

It is generally accepted that conscious mental life as we have been considering it depends on electrical activity of the outer layers of the brain or cerebral cortex. However, observation of isolated slabs of cortex shows that such activity does not generally occur spontaneously, but only in response to electrical stimulation, after which it may persist for a few minutes before ceasing. It appears, then, that the cerebral cortex must be continually activated by stimuli from other parts of the nervous system. The structures and mechanisms involved (Fig. 4.2) have been largely identified in the last half century, starting with experiments in the cat by Bremer in 1935. This Belgian physiologist showed that isolating the forebrain by a cut or transection at the top of the brain stem (a preparation known as *cerveau isolé*) resulted in a state of inertness accompanied by a sleep pattern of electrical activity in the EEG (we shall return later to sleep and the EEG). If, however, the transection was made at the base of the brain stem (the *encéphale isolé* or 'whole brain' preparation) then the animal showed alternating wakefulness and sleep associated with the appropriate EEG patterns.

Clearly the brain stem must be essential for wakefulness. Moruzzi and Magoun (1949) showed that electrical stimulation of its central core (called the *reticular formation* because of its network of nerve fibres) in the sleeping encéphale isolé preparation would result in awakening, both behavioural and reflected in the EEG. This suggested that impulses from peripheral sensory stimulation might, in the normal animal, pass to the reticular formation to produce awakening. However, sensory impulses also arrive, via the thalamus, at the cerebral cortex and these might be responsible for awakening.

The solution to this question was provided by Lindsley *et al.* (1950) who used two preparations in the cat. In the first, the upper part of the reticular formation was transected, which resulted in sleep. In the second, the reticular formation was left intact but the ascending sensory pathways to the cortex were cut at the same level, i.e. after collateral (branch) fibres from them had entered the reticular formation. This preparation had normal periods of wakefulness and sleep and could be awakened from the latter by noise, showing that stimulation was activating the animal via the reticular formation. For this reason the term *reticular activating system*, or RAS, is used to describe the anatomical structures involved.

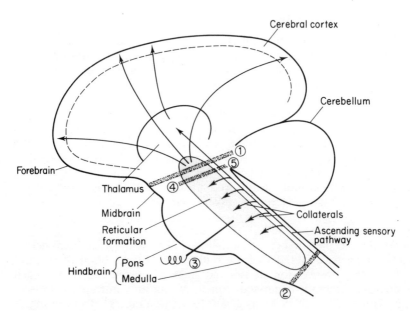

Fig.4.2   The reticular activating system and the classic experiments which demonstrated its function:

(1) Bremer: 'cerveau isolé'→sleep
(2) Bremer: 'encéphale isolé'→alternating wakefulness and sleep
(2) + (3) Moruzzi and Magoun: electrical stimulation of the reticular formation in the sleeping encéphale isolé preparation→awakening
(4) Lindsley: transection of upper reticular formation→sleep
(5) Lindsley: transection of ascending sensory pathways→alternating wakefulness and sleep, waking with noise

The reticular formation, as we have seen, forms the central core of the brain stem and extends from the medulla through the pons and mid-brain to connect at its upper end with the thalamus. There is a diffuse projection of fibres from the reticular formation to the whole of the cerebral cortex, so that when it is stimulated by impulses from the collaterals of the ascending sensory pathways, this leads in turn to stimulation or activation of the cerebral cortex. It is through this system, then, that sensory stimulation arouses and wakens; but why should wakefulness continue in the adult (though not in the infant) after a particular stimulation has ceased? The answer is that the reticular formation is itself subject to influences from the cerebral cortex, activity of which maintains wakefulness and postpones sleep – a process which is learned from experience during development.

The level of consciousness is, then, dependent on activity of the RAS, though there appears to be some difference of function between the lower and upper parts of the reticular formation, the former being concerned with general arousal, wakefulness and sleep and the latter with more transient focussed attention towards a particular stimulus. Evidence of facilitation of perceptual responses by the RAS has been provided by Fuster (1958), who showed that electrical stimulation of the reticular formation in monkeys improved their ability to discriminate between two shapes, and by Lindsley (1957), who found that similar stimulation in man resulted in a shortening of the time interval required for discrimination between two consecutive light flashes. At the same time it has been suggested that the reticular formation is responsible for the filtering of stimuli proposed by Broadbent in selective attention, which we have already discussed. Thus Hernandez-Peon *et al.* (1956) found that the auditory responses to a series of clicks recorded from the cochlear nucleus in the unanaesthetized cat ceased if the animal could see a mouse or smell fish – suggesting a peripheral blocking of the auditory impulses.

To summarize, the RAS is held to be concerned with the general arousal of the cerebral cortex and resultant consciousness, and with selective attention towards stimuli of particular significance. It is the mechanism through which consciousness may be influenced by the various factors to which brief reference has already been made and which we shall shortly be considering further – namely the level of external sensory stimulation, manipulation of attention, and chemical or other organic changes affecting the brain. First, however, we shall consider the unaroused state of sleep, including those periods associated with that form of awareness of mental activity known as dreaming.

Sleep

Sleep may be defined as a recurrent healthy state of inactivity and unresponsiveness to the environment accompanied by loss of conscious awareness. The normal cycle of wakefulness and sleep is of 24 hours' duration and it may be assumed that it is learned by each individual through experience – it has been shown that it is possible to adapt to a different cycle (e.g. 28 hours). However, why sleep should occur at all remains largely a mystery despite being the subject of much study in recent years.

Earlier work was concerned with depth of sleep as inferred from the intensity of a stimulus needed to waken the subject, but later investigations have involved measurement of various physiological changes and particularly of the electrical activity of the brain as recorded by the electroencephalograph or EEG. Studies by Aserinsky and Kleitman (1953) and Dement and Kleitman (1957) have shown that there are two different states of sleep which alternate. One is known as *rapid eye movement*, or *REM*, sleep because it is associated with rapid side-to-side movements of the eyes. During this phase of sleep the EEG shows a fast-frequency low-voltage pattern similar to that seen in the waking state, yet it is more difficult to arouse the subject than at other times in sleep and there is complete muscle relaxation. Because of the confusion over the 'depth' of sleep this phase has also been called *paradoxical* sleep. The most striking feature of REM sleep, however, is that subjects awoken from it will usually report vivid dreams, even those who say that they never dream.

The other type of sleep is termed *non-rapid eye movement*, or *non-REM*, or *orthodox* sleep, and it is not associated with the rapid eye movements of the type just described. If subjects are awoken from it, they may describe having been 'thinking' or if they do report a dream this lacks the vivid imagery of dreams recalled after REM sleep. Four stages of non-REM sleep of increasing depth are described, based on the EEG pattern. The EEG in the normal waking state shows a pattern of low-voltage, fast, desynchronized activity, but in a relaxed, drowsy state a 10 cycles/second *alpha rhythm* predominates. With the onset of the first and lightest stage of non-REM sleep, the EEG shows again a low-voltage mixed-frequency pattern with the addition, in stage 2, of sleep *spindles* – short bursts of 12–14 cycles/second waves so-called because of their characteristic shape (a rising and then falling amplitude). In stages 3 and 4, increasing amounts of increasingly high-voltage slow-wave activity appear (2 or fewer cycles/second or *delta* rhythm). These stages of non-REM sleep are passed through until stage 4 is reached after 30–60 minutes. This corresponds quite well with earlier studies of depth of sleep based on the stimulus required to awaken subjects at different intervals; these showed an increasing depth of sleep to a maximum at about an hour after onset, followed by a gradual lightening through the rest of the night's sleep.

All-night physiological recordings carried out in sleep laboratories (Fig. 4.3) have shown that, after about 60–90 minutes, non-REM sleep is interrupted by a period of REM sleep lasting 8–10 minutes. During this phase, as well as the continuous or *tonic* phenomena of the EEG pattern and muscle relaxation already described, there are other physiological changes of an intermittent or *phasic* nature. These include irregularities of respiration and heart rate, muscular twitches and variable erection of the penis in the male. During the rest of

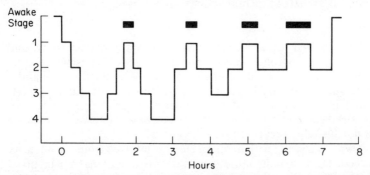

Fig.4.3 Representative graph of EEG stages of sleep as recorded during a typical night. Thick bars indicate periods of rapid eye movements in REM sleep

the night's sleep there are four to six periods of REM sleep occurring in 80–100 minute cycles alternating with non-REM sleep (also termed slow-wave sleep or SWS). The length of the REM periods tends to increase through the night up to about 30 minutes, while the depth of sleep in the non-REM periods gets lighter, with most of the stages 3 and 4 slow-wave sleep occurring in the early part of the night. This means that in the adult about 20–25 per cent of the average $7\frac{1}{2}$ hours sleep is of the REM type.

We considered earlier the neurophysiological basis of consciousness and attributed arousal and wakefulness to activity of the reticular formation. It appears, however, that the onset and maintenance of sleep is not an entirely passive process but depends on inhibition of the activating effect of the mid-brain reticular formation by structures in the lower hind brain part of the system – stimulation of which has been found to produce behavioural sleep accompanied by a non-REM pattern in the EEG. Other studies have shown that destruction of a particular nucleus within the pons (nucleus reticularis pontis caudalis) results in loss of REM sleep without affecting non-REM sleep. Ascending pathways presumably 'activate' the cortex in REM sleep, while a descending inhibitory system produces the accompanying muscular atonia.

Awakening from sleep during the night is brought about by stimulation of the RAS and, as we have seen, the intensity of sensory stimulation required generally depends on the depth of sleep as reflected in the EEG. It is well known, however, that a mother will usually wake to the sound of her baby's cry even if it is not loud, and experimental evidence (Oswald *et al.*, 1960) shows that words that are of particular significance – such as the subject's name, the name of someone close, or a name to be responded to by fist clenching – will lead to arousal. This shows that even in sleep the cerebral cortex maintains some kind of selective vigilance over sensory inputs and stimulates the reticular formation to produce general arousal to particular stimuli.

Before leaving the subject of normal sleep it is important to note the differences that occur during development and between individuals in adult life. The newborn baby has a very short sleep cycle of about 45 minutes spread out through the 24-hour period, with a total sleep time of 15–16 hours. REM sleep forms about 50 per cent of sleep at birth, falling to the adult level of 20–25 per cent by the age of one year. Both total sleep time and the proportion spent in stage 4 sleep gradually decrease during childhood and adult life, so that frequent awakenings during the night are common in the elderly. Differences between healthy adults in their total sleep time are considerable, and the idea that there is a certain amount of sleep which should be taken by all – a view commonly held by doctors and others in the past – is erroneous. Some people are able to live quite normally with as little as three hours of sleep a night, while others seem to need considerably more than the average $7\frac{1}{2}$ hours; EEG studies have shown that the differences are principally in the amount of REM sleep.

This brings us back to the basic question of the function of sleep. One way to seek an answer is to investigate the effect of lack of sleep, and there have been many studies of *sleep deprivation* dating back to the turn of the century. Most have been concerned with detecting changes of behaviour in subjects who had been deprived of sleep for varying lengths of time, and in this the earlier studies unexpectedly failed. Thus measures of hand grip, mental arithmetic and reaction time (speed with which the subject responds to a signal) showed no changes after loss of sleep for two or three days and nights. In recent years, however, studies (e.g. Wilkinson, 1965) have shown that the sleep-deprived subject can perform quite normally on short-lasting tasks requiring active involvement but cannot sustain concentration on those that are longer-lasting, simple, repetitive and monotonous. It would seem that, under such circumstances, it becomes more difficult for the reticular formation to maintain a sufficient level of cortical arousal, and indeed EEG recordings reveal the occurrence of brief periods, lasting a second or two, of sleep (or *microsleep*) which interfere with performance.

As well as these disturbances of psychological function, other behavioural changes may be noted in some subjects and increasingly so the more prolonged is the period of sleep loss – up to 200 hours or more in some experiments. Earlier studies described the development of paranoid ideas such as that they are the object of a plot to harm them in some way and of auditory and visual hallucinations though since another effect is increased suggestibility it is possible that some of the psychological abnormalities might have been induced by expectation. The effects of selective deprivation of SWS and REM sleep will be considered later in relation to dreaming, but from studies of total sleep loss it appears that even if we cannot say precisely what is the function of sleep, at least it has been shown to be essential for normal psychological functioning. Furthermore, after a period of sleep deprivation there is a temporary excess of non-REM and especially stage 4 sleep in the first night's sleep, so that it may be that this is the most important for restorative purposes. Further evidence has been produced in recent years to support this idea, and Oswald (1980) has proposed that orthodox sleep, especially stages 3 and 4, is associated with growth hormone secretion and general bodily protein synthesis, while paradoxical or REM sleep is important for providing periods of complete muscle relaxation.

Dreams

We have already seen that a normal night's sleep includes several periods of REM sleep which appear to be associated with dreaming, revealed by waking subjects during or after such a period. Recall of a dream is, however, found to deteriorate, so that whereas subjects woken at the end of a REM period can usually give a full and vivid description of a dream the subjective length of which appears to correspond quite well with the duration of the REM period before awakening, those woken after a 10-minute interval are unable to relate any dream content. Thus whether an individual recalls a dream on awakening during the night or in the morning depends in part on the length of time that has elapsed since the end of the last REM period. It is also well recognized that there is commonly a rapid forgetting of the content of a dream once the subject is awake, so that unless it is well rehearsed (i.e. repeated by the subject to himself) or written down at the time it may be lost to subsequent recall. All this means, of course, that individuals can only remember a very small fraction of their total dream content, and this is an important fact to bear in mind as we come to consider the possible psychological significance of dreams.

From ancient times, dreams have exercised a fascination for mankind and many cultures have held them to be of religious or political significance. Belief in the prophetic power of the dream is well illustrated by the biblical account, in the Book of Genesis, of Joseph's interpretation of the dream of Pharaoh about seven lean kine devouring seven fat kine as a prediction of a seven year famine. In classical Greece it was through dreams that the gods were believed to speak to mortals, while in 'primitive' societies today events in dreams may be held to have as much significance as, if not more than, reality itself. However, it is, once again, with Sigmund Freud that we meet a systematic attempt to explain the often strange and bizarre content of so many dreams.

For Freud the dream was the 'royal road' to a knowledge of the unconscious, since he believed its purpose was the satisfaction, in fantasy, of forbidden and therefore normally unconscious wishes and desires. At night, during sleep, the censorship exerted by the *super ego* (a psychoanalytic concept roughly equivalent to conscience which we shall consider later in the context of psychological development) was relaxed sufficiently for such repressed wishes to enter and be fulfilled in imagination in consciousness, but nevertheless in a disguised form so that their true nature would not be apparent to, and by arousing anxiety awaken, the dreamer. In other words, the function of the dream was seen by Freud as wish fulfilment but with protection of sleep. He distinguished between what the dreamer actually described, the *manifest* content, and the disguised meaning of the dream, the *latent* content. The difference between the two was due to *dream work* employing various distorting mechanisms, chiefly: *condensation*, one idea standing for several; *displacement*, the transfer of an emotional charge from its true object to another; *dramatization*, the construction of a dramatic sequence of, in the dream, apparently connected though bizarre events; *symbolization*, the use of particular objects to represent other, for Freud exclusively sexual, objects; and *secondary elaboration*, the attempt by the dreamer, on waking, to make some sense of the chaotic dream content. If, through the operation of these processes, there is so much distortion in the manifest content as reported by the dreamer, how was the latent content discovered?

It was this interpretation of the meaning of dreams which Freud considered to be his greatest achievement. To do this he used the technique of free association, which we have already met in Chapter 2 as the basis of psychoanalysis. The dreamer was asked to report any associations that came to mind in relation to each part of the dream, while at the same time certain symbols were interpreted as being of sexual significance (e.g. phallic objects – sticks, umbrellas, posts, trees, etc. – representing the male penis, and hollow objects – pits, cavities, bottles, boxes, etc. – representing the female genitals). Through such processes Freud reached what he believed to be the true meaning of the dream, though other analysts such as C.G. Jung later differed from him in their interpretation of dream symbols. The surrealist school of painting which is concerned with the world of the unconscious mind makes much use of dream symbols so that the paintings often capture the strange and sometimes frightening nature of the dream.

There are, however, difficulties in assessing these psychoanalytic views of the meaning of dreams, not the least of which is the fact, already pointed out, that they are now known to be based on a very small fraction of the total dreams of any individual, and those reported to analysts and then published by them in the literature must, of necessity, be highly selected. In addition the view that so-called sexual symbols are disguises has been challenged by Calvin Hall (1953) who has collected accounts of 'wet dreams', dreams in males in which ejaculation of semen occurs, which show that on some occasions emissions occurred in association with sexual symbols, such as climbing a ladder, but on other occasions, in the same individual, with a frankly sexual content.

As we have already seen, it is difficult in general to submit psychoanalytic theories to any kind of scientific test, but in recent years it has been possible to attempt to modify the content of dreams and such studies seem to confirm some of the mechanisms of distortion described by Freud. Thus Berger (1963) played neutral and significant (boy-friends and girl-friends) names to female and male students during REM sleep and then recorded the dreams on awakening. He was able to show that the content was sometimes (statistically significantly so) influenced by the name in a curious and 'disguised' way. For example, a white girl with an Indian boy friend – a relationship which, owing to racial prejudice, led to some emotional difficulties for her – had, when his name was played, a dream with much sexual symbolism and in which there was an Indian woman who wore glasses, as did the boy-friend. It appears that, through the mechanisms of displacement and symbolization, the boy-friend was represented by an Indian woman with consequent avoidance of the anxiety that might have arisen had the former actually appeared in a sexual dream.

We have devoted some time, though even so rather brief, to examining Freud's ideas about dreaming because they were fundamental to the whole psychoanalytic theory. However, few would now accept them in toto and other, more cognitive, theories have been advanced to explain the purpose of dreams. Hadfield (1954) suggested that they serve a problem-solving function in dealing with unresolved problems of the previous day. Evans and Newman (1964) used a computer analogy and proposed that dreaming is the perception of a process of 'program clearance', i.e. the updating of old programs while the brain, as a computer, is 'off line' as far as processing of new information is concerned. A rather similar theory has been suggested by Torda (1968), with dreaming as an intermittent perception of the continuous process of long-term memory encoding which we shall consider in the next chapter.

Whatever theories may be put forward to explain the content of dreams, another approach to the problem of their function would be to examine, as with sleep, the effects of deprivation. Assuming dreaming to be associated with REM sleep, this may be carried out in a sleep laboratory (Dement, 1960) by waking subjects whenever the latter appears, though it is found that more and more awakenings are required as the night passes because REM sleep appears more frequently. Similarly, an excessive amount of REM sleep is seen in the first night of undisturbed sleep after REM deprivation, though this does not occur after control awakenings from non-REM sleep. These findings were at first claimed to demonstrate a need for dreaming and to provide support for psychoanalytic theories. However, it is now recognized (Vogel, 1975) that dreaming is not exclusive to REM sleep and that it is the physiological REM sleep rather than the psychological dreaming that is required (perhaps, as already mentioned, for muscle resting). Thus addicts to amphetamine, which suppresses REM sleep, are found to adjust to the drug so that after a while they have a normal proportion of REM sleep, i.e. they are not dream deprived. Yet if the drug is withdrawn they are found to have an excess of REM sleep – presumably a physiological rather than psychological effect.

Finally, what of the behavioural effects of REM deprivation? Disappointingly, as far as throwing light on its function is concerned, the answer is that in spite of earlier reports of psychological sequelae, later studies have found remarkably little specifically related to loss of REM sleep (Naitoh, 1975). SWS deprivation, on the other hand, may produce mood changes of depression and irritability.

Should we, then, dismiss the content of dreams as being of little or no psychological significance? This would seem an unjustifiable assumption since, whatever else, the dream, or what is recalled of it, is derived from the individual's recent and past experience and often provides information of considerable personal significance for that person.

Altered states of consciousness

There has been much interest in recent years in the deliberate induction of altered states of waking consciousness for various purposes (social, religious, political and philosophical as well as psychological) and by different means. The major subjective effects of such states are seen in alterations of attention and of perception together with changes in meaning or significance (important in indoctrination or 'brain washing'). Factors bringing about these states are of three types.

The first of these involves sensory under- or over-stimulation. Many studies have been carried out on the effects of *sensory deprivation*, usually by isolating subjects in a sound-proofed room without light and with restriction of bodily movements, or sometimes by immersion in a tank of water at body temperature to reduce even further any proprioceptive sensations from the body. After a variable period of time in these conditions – usually one to four days – subjects begin to experience difficulty in concentration on their thought processes and may become confused as to whether they are awake or asleep. They may even develop visual and auditory hallucinations. In other studies of *perceptual deprivation*, the general level of stimulation may not be reduced but its patterning is removed by the use of translucent goggles and white noise (a 'hissing' sound, played through ear-phones, consisting of all the frequencies in the audible range). Rather surprisingly, such conditions lead to, if anything, greater disturbance of psychological functioning. At any rate, it appears that normal consciousness requires a minimum level of sensory stimulation and/or variation. Fewer studies have been carried out on excessive stimulation or *sensory overload*, but again this is liable to lead to some disruption of normal experience and behaviour.

The second condition which may lead to an altered state of consciousness is a deliberate *alteration of attention*, such that the subject is hyperattentive to a narrow range of stimuli (e.g. the sound of one's own breathing, visual fixation on a particular object, etc.) and hypoattentive to the rest of the environment. As we have already seen, this is met with in hypnosis, but it is also a feature of various forms of meditation.

The last factor to be considered is a *physical change*, usually chemical, affecting the functioning of the brain. This includes the use of certain drugs, particularly the so-called hallucinogens which, as the name implies, may produce vivid hallucinatory experiences.

Clinical aspects

So far, apart from the preceding reference to the effects of certain drugs, we have been considering variations in the level of consciousness in the normal healthy individual. There are, however, disorders of consciousness that occur in association with disease or injury. Head injuries causing temporary loss of consciousness are usually of the 'closed' type with presumed movement of the brain within the skull affecting the brain stem, whereas penetrating injuries through the skull commonly do not cause unconsciousness unless extensive. Diseases affecting the brain stem (i.e. including the reticular formation), such as inflammation (e.g. encephalitis lethargica or sleeping sickness) or pressure from a tumour, can cause drowsiness, sleep or complete loss of consciousness. Conditions affecting the functioning of the brain more generally (e.g. through lack of oxygen or blood supply) may cause a state of *delirium*, with impairment or 'clouding' of consciousness; the patient may become confused or disorientated – not knowing the present time or place – and hallucinated, may have difficulty in concentration and subsequently have little or no memory for events at the time. Finally, episodes of unconsciousness occur in some forms of *epileptic seizure*, a condition associated with an electrical discharge in the brain which, in some individuals, 'epileptics', arises spontaneously from time to time, but can be provoked in anyone by chemical or electrical means (e.g. electroconvulsive therapy or ECT).

Turning to disorders of sleep, the best known and commonest is sleeplessness or *insomnia*. Occasional difficulty in getting off to sleep at times of mental or physical stress (due presumably to the stimulating influence of the cerebral cortex on the reticular formation) is almost universal, but there are some individuals who appear to suffer from primary insomnia, i.e. they are always poor sleepers and complain of the poor quality of their sleep (in contrast to those short sleepers who have no complaint). It should be noted, however, that many people who believe they have slept poorly or not at all have, in fact, had a relatively normal night's sleep, as demonstrated by all-night EEG recordings and failure to respond to a buzzer at intervals. Often, however, genuine and persisting insomnia is secondary to some psychological disturbance, and particularly to a state of *depression*, though the pattern may be one of waking early rather than difficulty at the onset of sleep.

Whatever the cause, insomnia is often treated by the prescription of *hypnotics* or sleep inducing drugs. Unfortunately, this often makes matters worse because many of the drugs have the effect of suppressing REM sleep. When an attempt is then made to stop the drug there is a rebound increase of REM sleep; this leads to difficulties in falling asleep as well as unpleasant dreams, so that the patient continues to take the drug to prevent the withdrawal effects, i.e. has become dependent on it. It may be that some newer drugs do not have this effect, but in general it is probably safer to avoid the use of hypnotics unless there are very good indications for it.

The reverse of insomnia is a tendency to increased sleep or *hypersomnia*. Irresistible attacks of sleep lasting about 15 minutes form part of a syndrome (collection of symptoms that tend to occur together) known as *narcolepsy*. The associated symptoms are *cataplexy* – a sudden and transient loss of muscle tone occurring in clear consciousness and often precipitated by emotion; *sleep paralysis* – a sudden complete muscular paralysis occurring while falling asleep or waking from sleep; and *hypnagogic hallucinations* – vivid hallucinations, again while falling asleep or on waking (this latter experience is quite common among healthy people and is then of no clinical significance). The explanation of these strange phenomena became clear when it was realized that the sleep attacks consist of REM sleep developing directly from wakefulness – a situation which does not normally occur. Intrusion of the REM state into wakefulness but with dissociation between the central and peripheral mechanisms would result in the cataplexy and sleep paralysis from descending motor inhibition, and hypnagogic hallucinations from the ascending and cortical effects. There are other conditions with more prolonged episodes of hypersomnia, but with the sleep being of the non-REM type. Sometimes this is associated with excessive appetite or hyperphagia, so that dysfunction of the hypothalamus has been suggested as an explanatory hypothesis.

In addition to these disturbances of sleep itself, there are other conditions, the *parasomnias*, in which behaviour which is inappropriate occurs during sleep. These include *sleep-walking* or *somnambulism*, which is found to occur in stages 3 and 4 (SWS) of non-REM sleep (so that contrary to popular belief it is not a form of dreaming); *sleep talking* which is also a phenomenon of non-REM sleep but probably in the lightest stage 1 phase; *night terrors* which, although arising from stages 3 and 4 sleep, are actually associated with a waking alpha rhythm of the EEG (in contrast to *nightmares* which develop in REM sleep); and *bedwetting* or *nocturnal enuresis* which occurs during or after a period of non-REM sleep during which, in stages 3 and 4, bladder pressure rises to a higher level than in non-enuretic subjects.

Leaving the topic of sleep disorders, the last clinical aspect to be discussed is that of sensory and perceptual deprivation. We have seen that such deprivation can lead to considerable psychological disturbance and this has to be remembered in relation to several clinical settings. These include patients confined for long periods or indefinitely in respirators or 'iron lungs', those restricted by attachment to various pieces of recording equipment and life-support systems in intensive-care units, and those deprived of sight for a period after eye surgery. Even more generally, we may note that the manifestations of impairment of consciousness in delirious states are commonly worse at night, which may in part be due to the lower level of sensory and perceptual stimulation at this time.

Further reading

Hudson, L. (1985) *Night Life: the Interpretation of Dreams*. London: Weidenfeld & Nicolson.
Oswald, I. (1980) *Sleep*, 4th ed. Harmondsworth: Penguin.

5
Cognitive processes
I – Perception

Cognition

In the last chapter we considered consciousness as a special attribute of man in the sense of a subjective awareness of an inner mental world of the self. Furthermore, there occurs within it, through the use of mental symbols, the process of *thinking* which permits a level of problem solving unattainable by other animal species. Thinking or reasoning, together with the mechanisms of *perception, learning* and *remembering*, which provide the information for decision making, comprise the psychological function of *cognition* and are collectively known as the *cognitive processes*. Although they are generally more highly developed in man, being sometimes called the 'higher mental processes', they are also present, and can in some instances be more easily studied, in other animals. Essentially, they are concerned with enabling the organism to respond continually in an appropriate way to changes in the environment.

Figure 5.1 represents the relationships between the four cognitive processes as parts of a system subserving this adaptive function. Thus information concerning any environmental change is provided through the process of perception and is then related to information derived from past experience through the processes of learning and remembering. Finally, through the organization

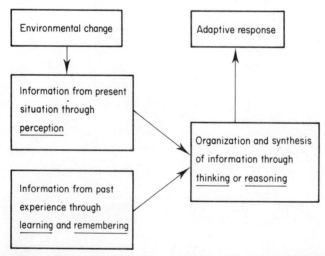

Fig.5.1 Relationships between the cognitive processes as a system concerned with adaptation to change in the environment

and synthesis of all this information in the process of reasoning, an appropriately adaptive behavioural response is initiated. The majority of responses are, of course, made 'automatically' with little conscious awareness of all these processes. This applies, for example, to such everyday activities as car driving when the driver continually responds to traffic signals, road signs, etc., on the basis of previously learned and remembered information, but may be able, if experienced and on a familiar route, to listen at the same time to the radio. Greater conscious effort and awareness is, however, involved in more complex activities, such as a medical consultation when the collection of relevant current information about the patient and his illness, and consideration of this in relation to a body of medical knowledge learned and remembered from teaching, reading and clinical experience, leads to a diagnosis and appropriate treatment.

Although we shall consider each of the cognitive processes separately, it is important to appreciate that they are closely interrelated and their demarcation as distinct functions is somewhat arbitrary. Similarly there is no obvious order in which to deal with them, but we shall begin with the acquisition of information through the process of perception.

Perception

Irritability, or the ability to respond to an external stimulus, is a fundamental characteristic of living matter – even single-celled organisms may, for example, change their direction of movement in response to light. In man, there is a highly developed sensory system through which physical changes in the environment (and within the body) may be detected. Specialized receptor cells in the skin, for example, respond to temperature change or physical contact and initiate nerve impulses which travel to the brain and produce a conscious awareness of such change – a *sensation*. There are also, however, organs of special sense, such as sight and hearing, which – while responding in a similar way to the physical stimuli of light and sound, giving rise to the appropriate sensations – are at the same time able to provide a meaningful interpretation of the external world.

It is this process of obtaining information from the environment that is known as *perception*, and it depends primarily on 'distance receptors' such as the eye or ear, which are capable of responding not only to the energy characteristics of a stimulus (i.e. light and sound waves) but also to the informational content (i.e. the patterning of light and sound which represents the external world). Whether there is such a fundamental distinction between sensation and perception as was at one time supposed is now considered doubtful, and the two processes are generally held to represent the first and second stages respectively in the response of the organism to a stimulus.

What is certain, however, is that perception is not just a passive, mechanical response to external stimulation like that of a camera or a sound recording device, but involves an active process of organization of the sensory input influenced by various factors, both innate and learned. This can be seen quite clearly if we examine the working of the visual system. (Similar principles apply to the auditory system, but space does not allow further consideration here.) There is the three-dimensional external world as it really is – called the *geographical environment* or *distal stimulus* by Koffka (1935). This is then represented by a two-dimensional image at the back of the eye and the pattern of sensory stimulation to which this gives rise in the retina and visual cortex of the brain – the so-called *proximal stimulus*. But what is actually 'seen' by the individual, the *behavioural environment*, may differ in some respects from the pattern of stimulation and the most familiar examples are the phenomena of three-dimensional or depth perception, perceptual constancy and perceptual illusions.

Depth perception
   The ability to locate objects in the three-dimensional space of the real world is clearly important for adaptive behaviour, and yet the visual image on the retina is in two dimensions. The perception of the third dimension of distance or depth depends on the use of a number of cues. Over a rather limited range of distances, there may be feedback information from the muscles involved in *accommodation* (focussing of the lens of the eye) and *convergence* (directing the axes of the eyes so that the image of an object falls in corresponding positions on the two retinae).
   More important are the so-called *parallax* effects – binocular and monocular. The former depends mainly on the fact that the two eyes, being several centimetres apart, differ slightly in their respective views and therefore in their retinal images, which are then, by some central mechanism, combined to give a three-dimensional percept, just as the two slighly differing photographs produced by a stereoscopic camera give an impression of depth when viewed, one by each eye, in a stereoscopic viewer. Monocular parallax provides depth cues, even with vision restricted to one eye, and depends on the relative apparent or actual movements of objects at different distances. If, for example, the head is moved from side to side, nearer objects appear to move faster and further than those more distant, and the same applies to objects actually in motion at equal velocities.
   Finally there are a number of cues derived from features of the two-dimensional retinal image which assist in depth perception. They are, in fact, those that are consciously employed by artists for the same purpose in two-dimensional painting and include perspective, shadows on or cast by objects, the relative apparent sizes of similar objects at different distances, etc.

Perceptual constancy
   This refers to the fact that objects are actually seen as having their characteristic appearance in terms of shape, size, colour, brightness, etc., despite the fact that, depending on their lighting, position and distance from the observer, their retinal images may vary considerably. Thus a man will look normal in size whether close or far away, a coin will appear round even when viewed from an angle so that the proximal stimulus is in reality elliptical, and coal is black and snow white, under a wide range of light intensities. Cues for these perceptual constancies include familiarity with the object, awareness of its distance and position in relation to the observer, and comparison of it with its surroundings.

Perceptual illusions
   In this third example of discrepancy between 'geographical' and 'behavioural' environment, the perception is inaccurate – a misinterpretation – and is therefore described as an *illusion*. There are several well-known visual illusions, named after their originators, and three of these are illustrated in Fig. 5.2.

There is no single, generally accepted, explanation of all these illusions, but it seems likely that many depend on interaction between the constituent parts and the whole figure. Thus in the Muller–Leyer illusion, the apparent lengths of the horizontal lines reflect the overall size of the whole figure of which they form a part, whereas in the Ponzo illusion the two cross lines, being separated from the two obliques, are not integrated within the whole and the line further from the apex appears the shorter owing to the larger gaps between its ends and the obliques. Illusions of movement are found in the so-called phi-phenomenon – the apparent to and fro motion of two adjacent lights that are switched on and off in succession within a range of time intervals, or in the appearance of movement of the moon behind the passing clouds.

Perceptual organization

What the three phenomena of depth perception, perceptual constancy and perceptual illusions clearly demonstrate is that perception involves a process of organization of the sensory input. This was the subject of much study by a school of psychology founded by three Germans, Max Wertheimer (1880–1943), Kurt Koffka (1886–1941) (to whom we have already referred) and Wolfgang Kohler (1887–1967), in 1912 at about the same time as behaviourism in America. Named *Gestalt* psychology from the German word for 'form' or 'pattern', it was concerned with the study of conscious experience through the use of intro-spection, but taking account of 'holistic' impressions rather than attempting an analysis into component elements like Wundt and Titchener before them

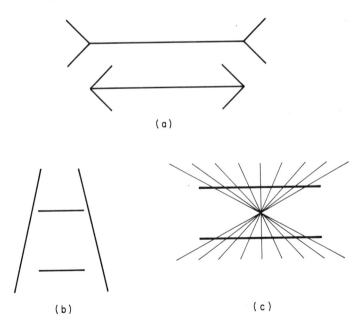

Fig.5.2 Visual illusions. (a) The Muller–Lyer illusion – horizontal line in the upper figure appears longer than that in the lower. (b) The Ponzo illusion – the upper of the two horizontal lines appears longer. (c) The Hering illusion – the horizontal lines, though straight and parallel, appear bent by the radiating lines

(see Chapter 2) – the underlying assumption being that 'the whole is more than the sum of its parts' (similar to Durkheim's view of society – see Chapter 3).

A number of principles of perceptual organization were described by the Gestalt psychologists and some of these are illustrated in Fig. 5.3. The basic process in perception was held to be the identification of shape or 'form' by its contour or outline. Individual objects in the environment are seen as differentiated from their surroundings – as standing out from the background – and this phenomenon is described as the *figure–ground* experience. Attention is directed to the 'figure' separated from the 'ground' by its contour. Sometimes figure and ground may alternate so that each is equally meaningful, such as in the well-known 'vase or profile' (Fig. 5.3(a)).

Another important aspect of perceptual organization in Gestalt theory is the *Law of Prägnanz* (good form), meaning that patterns of stimulation tend to be

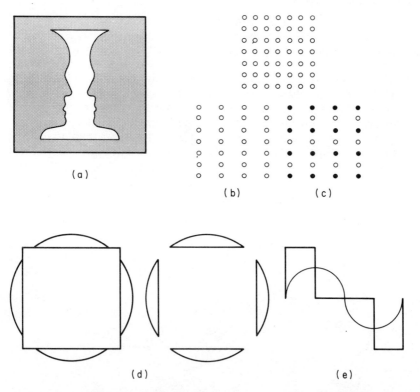

Fig.5.3 Gestalt principles of perceptual organization. (a) The principle of *figure and ground*. In this well-known example of the vase or profile, we see alternately a white vase figure against a black ground or two black profile figures against a white ground. (b) The principle of *proximity*. Compared with the pattern of equally spaced dots above, proximity results in these dots appearing to be grouped in vertical columns. (c) The principle of *similarity*. Though the spatial relationships of these dots is identical to those in (b), similarity causes them to appear as horizontal rows. (d) The principle of *closure*. In the left-hand figure, the circle appears whole despite the missing portions obscured by the square. In the right-hand figure both the circle and square can be perceived as wholes though the four complete segments are more conspicuous. (e) The principle of *continuity*. The continuity of the curved and straight lines results in their perception as a whole rather than constituting parts of each of the four enclosed areas

seen as stable wholes, the pattern being, if necessary, modified for the purpose. Various principles of organization are involved, including those of *proximity* – stimuli close together are grouped together (Fig. 5.3(b)); *similarity* – stimuli that are similar are grouped together (Fig. 5.3(c)); *closure* – figures tend to be organized into complete wholes even if the stimulus pattern is incomplete or interrupted (Fig. 5.3(d)); and *continuity* – continuity of line or border takes precedence over other principles (Fig. 5.3(e)).

Perceptual determinants

The organization of perception described by the Gestalt psychologists was held by them to be determined by innate mechanisms and to be independent of experience (i.e. learning), but since then the relative importance of these two factors has been the subject of much debate and numerous studies. Some neurophysiological support for an innate mechanism for the perception of contours came from experiments by Hubel and Wiesel (1962), which showed that single cells of the cat's visual cortex responded to lines falling on the retina in a particular orientation only (e.g. horizontal, vertical, diagonal). Later experiments, however, by Blakemore and Cooper (1970) on kittens that had been brought up in the dark except for brief daily exposure to black and white vertical or horizontal stripes, showed that all cells of the visual cortex tended to respond either to vertical or horizontal lines only – depending on the earlier experience.

That learning, or at least re-learning, may be a significant factor is also suggested by the capacity of the visual system to adapt to deliberate distortion of input. As long ago as 1897 Stratton found that he was able, after about a week, to cope quite well with everyday life in spite of wearing spectacles which inverted the visual field of one eye – the other being covered. Many similar experiments have been performed since then, but it remains uncertain to what extent the visual perception actually changes (i.e. the world appears the right way up again) or the individual learns to cope with the inverted input.

Other studies directed at solving the innate versus learning controversy have used subjects who have had no learning opportunities – such as newborn or adults deprived of vision during development. An example of a study involving the former was that of Walk and Gibson (1961) into depth perception in the young of several animal species using a piece of apparatus known as the 'visual cliff'. This consisted of a raised central platform with a sheet of glass on each side. Under each sheet was a black and white chequered surface; but on one side it was immediately beneath the glass, while on the other it was some distance below, giving the appearance, through the glass, of a steep drop. There was thus a 'shallow' side and a 'deep' side, and it was possible to observe which of the two would be chosen for movement by a young animal placed in the centre. The fact that a clear preference was generally shown for the 'shallow' side by all species, including human babies who avoided crossing the 'deep' side to crawl to their mothers (while doing so on the shallow side), indicates an early ability to perceive depth from the visual clues available. The possibility that this was, even in such young animals, dependent on learning from experience prior to the development of locomotion (the stage at which testing was performed) was excluded by demonstration of the same findings in animals that had been reared in the dark since birth.

Depth perception was thus shown to be an innate process. Further studies showed that it was the use of the parallax cues for this purpose which was independent of learning, while use of the visual clue to depth provided by the difference in apparent sizes of the chequered pattern on the 'shallow' and 'deep' sides proved to be dependent on learning. It appears from these and other studies that the organization of perception is, like most psychological processes, in part innate and in part learned from previous experience.

Other influences on perception

So far, we have considered the nature and determinants of perceptual organization in general terms, but now we must examine some other factors which affect what the individual perceives of the environment. These will include his cognitive, affective and motivational state as well as his personality and even the culture to which he belongs.

Perceptual set

This term refers to the tendency to perceive certain stimuli in the environment rather than others. It may be of short duration and induced by the current situation, or may be a persistent feature of the individual and derived from past experience. Laboratory experiments have shown, for example, that subjects presented with brief-duration (tachistoscopic) exposures of 'nonsense' words will tend to misinterpret them as real words but differing according to the category that they have previously been told to expect (e.g. names of animals).

In everyday life, such perceptual sets may have both advantages and disadvantages. Thus the pathologist, by developing sets for the perception of certain histological or cellular features, becomes skilled at the rapid and accurate recognition of pathological changes, as does the radiologist in the interpretation of the X-ray. On the other hand, there is some danger from the expectations associated with a particular set. Biology and medical students, for example, were shown by Johnson (1953) to misperceive biological specimens and X-rays because they tended to see what they were expecting on the basis of their teaching and textbooks. If the concept of perception is taken to extend to the total assessment of a patient, another example of the risks of perceptual set was provided by Rosenhan (1973). A number of healthy individuals presented themselves (in the USA) to psychiatrists claiming (falsely) that they were hearing a voice when no-one was present. Following admission to hospital with a diagnosis of mental illness, they continued to be perceived by the staff as showing abnormal behaviour consistent with the diagnosis, despite the fact that they no longer spoke of their 'hallucination', in fact behaved quite normally, and were recognized by the 'genuine' patients to be normal.

Affect and motivation in perception

The role of these factors in perception has received a great deal of attention. Examples of evidence in support of their influence include: the differential perception and recognition of ambiguous objects and words as being related to their particular needs by hungry and thirsty subjects; the effect of reward and punishment on judgements of length or weight, and of success and failure in performance of a difficult task on subsequent perception of ambiguous pictures or tachistoscopically presented sentences; and finally, the many experiments involving the differential recognition of anxiety-arousing 'taboo', and emotionally neutral words, such as that of McGinnies which we considered in the last chapter as suggesting the operation of perceptual defence.

Some difficulty arises, however, in the interpretation of much of this type of evidence, since the usual indication of perception in human studies is, of course, the verbal report of the subject and it could be a motivated 'response' rather than 'perception' which is being elicited (i.e. a subject might be unwilling to report a taboo word even though it is perceived). If such motivated perception – or rather 'non-perception' – does occur, it raises another difficulty since it implies that a stimulus must, in the first place, be 'recognized' as anxiety-provoking in order to be 'defended against' and subsequently not identified. This may be explained by proposing an autonomic, affective response which may precede and sometimes inhibit the process of verbal identification, but it may also exemplify the distinction between conscious and unconscious mental processes which we considered in the last chapter.

Personality, culture and perception

Only brief reference will be made here to attempts to relate aspects of perception and personality since we shall be considering the whole subject of personality in a later chapter. The tendency has been to look for 'perceptual types', although within the field of personality study the concept of the 'type' has become somewhat outmoded. Individuals have been classified into such dichotomies as 'synthetic' and 'analytic' perceivers according to whether the perceptual field is perceived respectively as an integrated whole, or broken up into its component parts; 'levellers' and 'sharpeners', the former tending to be less influenced than the latter by the effects of previous perceptions; and the 'field dependent' and 'field independent', distinguished by whether they rely on perception of the external environment or on bodily sensations for spatial orientation. An application of the concepts of both motivated perception and individual differences of perception is found in the field of 'projective' testing, to which reference has already been made in Chapter 2 and to which we shall return again in relation to the study of personality. In this technique of psychological assessment the individual's perception of deliberately ambiguous material (e.g. ink blots) is used to draw inferences about largely unconscious psychological processes.

Perceptual differences between individuals of different cultures have attracted much interest, in part because they might throw additional light on the question of innate or experiential determination of perception. As early as 1901 the anthropologist, W.H.R. Rivers, found that Murray Islanders were less prone to the Muller–Lyer illusion than were Europeans. Subsequent studies have tended to confirm the greater susceptibility of Europeans to visual illusions, especially those involving perspective – and attempts have been made to relate these and other cross-cultural differences to ecological factors. Thus the environment of the European, in contrast to that of many non-Europeans, has been described (Campbell, 1964) as 'carpentered', with straight lines generally set at right-angles so that acute or obtuse angles in the retinal image tend to be interpreted by the European as representing a right-angle in space. A contrast is also drawn between the rather 'horizontal' world of a plains dweller and the 'vertical' world of the inhabitants of a rain forest as influencing their respective perceptions of height and width.

General clinical aspects

We have seen that what is perceived by an individual is a subjective internal representation of the external world which is determined not only by the reality of the environment, but also by innate organizational processes, by influences from past experience, and by the individual's current emotional and motivational state.

This active modification of the sensory input is reflected in certain clinical situations. It affects the nature of the perceptual experience of patients with sensory defects. The Gestalt principle of closure, for example, enables the patient with a neurological lesion causing loss of vision in one half of the visual field – a hemianopia – to nevertheless 'see' a complete circle even though one half of it lies within the blind half of the field. In general, patients with sensory defects are thus able to compensate to a certain extent for their disability.

Another and more extreme example of discrepancy between external world and internal awareness are those perceptual experiences known as *illusions* and *hallucinations*. We have already discussed the visual illusions which are the subject of study by psychologists, but these are a universal phenomenon – i.e. they are misperceived to a greater or lesser extent by everyone. An illusion in the pathological sense is also a false perception which is due to distortion of an external stimulus but is not shared with others. In clinical practice it is usually associated with some organic process or disease which affects the function of the brain, resulting in 'clouding' of consciousness or delirium. One of the commonest examples is the child with a fever who wakes in the night and talks of frightening objects which he 'sees' on the wall or the curtains – a misinterpretation or misperception of the pattern that is actually there. The fact that this is more likely to occur at night in the dimly lit bedroom suggests that it is encouraged by the vagueness and ambiguity of the visual stimulus.

An hallucination, in contrast, is a false perception in the absence of an external stimulus, so that its content must be entirely derived from within. It may occur in any of the sensory modalities – auditory, visual, olfactory, tactile, etc. – and can arise in a variety of circumstances. We have already referred in the last chapter to the hypnagogic hallucinations which a proportion of normal healthy individuals experience in the state between wakefulness and sleep and which is probably a form of REM sleep. Another situation in which a quite normal person may experience an hallucination (or, strictly, a 'pseudo-hallucination' if its unreal nature is realized by the individual) is bereavement, when it is not uncommon for grief to be associated with hearing the voice of, or even 'seeing', the deceased. Sometimes this may be due to misinterpretation of an auditory or visual stimulus, i.e. an illusion, but this is not always so. In either event, the content of the subjective experience in this situation is clearly determined by the state of mind of the bereaved person.

Apart from these examples of hallucinations in healthy individuals (and a few others such as those in sensory deprivation experiments which we discussed in the last chapter), the phenomenon is generally taken to indicate the presence of some pathological condition. We have already considered (in the previous chapter) drug-induced alterations of consciousness, but delirium due to chemical intoxication, drug withdrawal or acute organic disease affecting the brain is often dominated by hallucinations – commonly visual. Finally, however, it is the so-called 'functional psychoses' (the severer forms of psychiatric illness not due to recognizable organic disease) that are most frequently associated with hallucinations – the commonest being auditory in the form of a voice or voices. The explanation of these experiences has yet to be unravelled, but the content is, once more, usually related to the mental state of the individual (e.g. a voice talking about his past misdeeds and how he will suffer for them in a patient with a severe depressive illness).

Clinical aspects of pain

We have been considering clinical aspects of the perception of the external world, but we are also aware of course of a sensory input from different parts of the body and it will be convenient here to consider some psychosocial aspects of one of the commonest physical symptoms complained of by patients.

Surveys have shown a high incidence of pain in general practice (64 per cent), in medical clinics (90 per cent) and even in psychiatric clinics (60–70 per cent), while its relief or management has long been a traditional function of the doctor. Pain is a subjective experience which is generally taken to indicate the presence of physical injury or disease: 'an unpleasant experience which we primarily associate with tissue damage' (Merskey and Spear, 1967). However, there is clinical and experimental evidence to show that the severity of that experience is not necessarily related to the extent of the damage – lack of correspondence being due to a variety of intervening psychological factors. In fact, rather than simply considering pain as a sensation produced by stimulation of a particular physiological system (pain receptors and neuronal pathways), it may more usefully be viewed as a *multidimensional* (physiological, subjective and behavioural) experience (Fordyce, 1978) involving nociception (activity of the physiological system) perceived as a subjective sensation and as an associated unpleasant, distressing, affective (emotional) response which then leads to various forms of pain behaviour (communication of the distress to others and actions to reduce the pain).

A neurophysiological model to account for such influences on the perception of pain is provided by the *gate control theory* of Melzack and Wall (1965). This proposes a neural 'gate' in the spinal cord through which the input from peripheral pain receptors has to pass on its way to the brain. The opening or closing of the 'gate' is controlled by other afferent inputs; this may provide an explanation for the effectiveness of acupuncture in pain relief which appears to be greater than can be explained in terms of a placebo response (Richardson and Vincent, 1986). In addition there is considered to be an influence from descending pathways from the brain, the latter enabling 'higher' (psychological) processes to modulate or influence the ascending passage of 'pain' impulses to the brain (and thus the subjective pain experienced). Another possible means by which psychological variables may effect pain perception is via the release of the natural opiate substances known as endorphins, known to block pain behaviour in experimental animals.

The subjective nature of pain poses obvious problems for its measurement. Experimental approaches have employed such stimuli as heat, electrical stimulation, ischaemia, etc., and determination of the level of stimulation at which the subject just feels pain, the *pain threshold*, and the highest intensity which can be borne – the *pain tolerance* level. Clinical studies have attempted to measure the physiological (e.g. the electrical activity in muscles in tension headaches), subjective (rating scales and questionnaires) and behavioural (e.g. observation of analgesic consumption) components of pain.

It appears, then, that pain is not simply a function of the amount of tissue damage but is a highly personal experience depending on cultural learning, the meaning of the situation and other factors unique to the individual. We shall now examine some of these influences.

Cultural influences

A frequently quoted example of cultural differences is the experience of pain in childbirth. Anthropologists have described cultures which practice 'couvade', where the woman shows little or no distress during labour, returning soon afterwards to work, leaving the baby with the husband who, by contrast, has retired to bed in pain. In Western culture childbirth is generally seen as somewhat dangerous – a culturally determined fear which may enhance the experience of pain for the woman. Even so it is not infrequent for Western husbands to notice aches and pains around the time of their wife's labour (Trethowan and Conlon, 1965). Another example of a cultural influence is the Indian ritual of hook hanging in which a subject is suspended by hooks piercing the flesh of the back – apparently in a state of trance with freedom from pain and minimal injury and subsequent rapid healing.

Experimental studies (e.g. Sternbach and Tursky, 1965) have claimed to demonstrate different pain thresholds and tolerance levels in different ethnic groups, but not all studies have shown such clear-cut differences (Merskey and Spear, 1967). Zborowski (1952) described cultural differences of attitudes towards pain and of pain behaviour between 'Old Americans' and those of Jewish and Italian descent, with the latter two groups showing more complaining behaviour than the former but with the Italian group ceasing to complain once the disorder had been treated and the Jewish group continuing to express concern – a difference interpreted as indicating an Italian present-orientated concern about the pain itself and a Jewish future-orientated anxiety as to its meaning. In terms of subjective experience rather than behaviour, however, Flannery *et al.* (1981) found no differences in pain ratings at episiotomy (incision of the perineum during childbirth to ease the delivery and prevent tearing) between five ethnic groups.

Social influences

Experimental studies reviewed by Craig (1978) measuring pain perception in subjects in the presence of models apparently receiving the same level of stimulation but actually simulating little or much pain, have shown that they can be induced to tolerate high levels of stimulation or report pain at low levels respectively. It is suggested that the effect of the model is to alter the affective quality of the pain experienced by the subject, and this could have significance for clinical situations where patients come into contact with others who are in pain.

Social experience within families (e.g. children influenced by their parents) may in a similar way affect the liability to experience pain. Thus Apley (1975) found that parents of children with recurrent abdominal pain were more likely than parents of control children to complain of pain themselves (i.e. to comprise 'painful families'). It may well be that parental attitudes towards pain and their behaviour towards their children when suffering from minor injuries can result in similar and persistent attitudes in the next generation.

Evidence for the effect of past experience on pain perception in dogs was found by Melzack and Scott (1957); scottish terriers who had been raised in isolation cages from infancy, and thus deprived of contact with other dogs and of other normal environmental stimuli including minor injuries, failed to respond normally to a variety of noxious stimuli, in contrast to their litter mates reared in a normal environment.

Meaning of the situation

The French writer and philosopher Montaigne in 1580 referred to the lack of pain from wounds received in the heat of battle. Similarly, during the Second World War Beecher (1956) found that recently wounded soldiers frequently denied any pain or felt so little that they did not want any analgesics for it. After the war he observed that civilians with surgical wounds were far more likely to complain of severe pain and to ask for analgesics. Beecher's interpretation of these findings was that for the soldiers the injury meant relief and thankfulness at escaping alive from the battlefield, whereas for the civilians major surgery was an unwelcome event.

At a more mundane level, the role of personal evaluation of the situation in determining the response may be seen in a child's reaction to a slap on the behind; laughter if received in the course of play, tears if seen as a punishment. This effect was even seen in conditioning experiments carried out by Pavlov; if dogs were repeatedly given food after an electric shock to a paw, the conditioned response became one of salivation and signs of pleasure, rather than the previous violent pain response. The new response was, however, limited to the paw that had been stimulated – shocks applied to other paws still produced pain behaviour.

Attention

We have seen that because of the limited extent of conscious awareness there has to be a selectivity of attention. In situations that attract intense prolonged attention other stimuli may therefore be unattended, and this can include painful stimulation. Common examples are the injuries in battle just described, and those in sports such as boxing and football.

We have also seen that hypnosis may be explicable in terms of manipulation of attention, so that intense focussing on the hypnotist may result in the successful suggestion of analgesia; a similar effect may occur in deep meditation. We have already referred to the opposite situation when attention is drawn to a particular part of the body and a bodily sensation which does not normally reach consciousness may be experienced and may even be perceived as painful, as when a bereaved person experiences symptoms resembling those of the deceased. An 'attention redirection' technique of pain management has been devised which may affect the sensory component of the pain experience.

Anxiety

Although largely indirect, there is evidence that anxiety increases the experience of pain. In experimental studies (Hill *et al.*, 1952) the intensity of pain has been demonstrated to be reduced if the subject's anxiety is lowered by his being led to believe that he has control over the noxious stimulus. Clinically it has been shown that preoperative encouragement and instruction of patients results in a reduction of postoperative pain as judged by fewer requirements for analgesics (Egbert *et al.*, 1964). Since the instruction included how to relax as well as what to expect in the postoperative period, it seems likely that lessening of anxiety was the means by which the pain was reduced. In fact relaxation as a technique for the management of pain appears to be effective in reducing the affective component (in contrast to the 'attention redirection' technique described above).

Suggestion
We have already noted the role of suggestion in the inducement of analgesia during hypnosis, but the most common example of its effectiveness in reducing pain perception is the so-called placebo response. The word placebo is usually applied to a pharmacologically inert preparation made up to look like an active drug and administered with the suggestion that it will have a therapeutic effect, though the term may also be used for a procedure designed for the same purpose. In relation to pain relief, Beecher (1959) in a review of clinical studies found a placebo to be effective in approximately 35 per cent of patients. It is probable that a number of variables are involved in the placebo response, but it seems likely that a major factor is the reduction of anxiety dependent on the patient's expectation of relief from the placebo.

Psychogenic pain
In view of the importance of psychological factors in the experience of pain, it is perhaps not surprising that it may occur in some patients in the absence of any organic disease. Sometimes this may arise from muscle tension, and therefore peripheral nerve stimulation; but this is not always present and the pain then appears to exist as a purely 'psychological' phenomenon.

A possible explanation for such 'psychogenic' pain may be sought in the association of pain with bodily damage, resulting in its being considered generally as a consequence of the perception of a threat. Such pain may then take on other characteristics of a communicative or symbolic nature – representing, for example, punishment for the expression of hostility. That this may not be entirely fanciful is supported by the fact that the word 'pain' is derived from poena (Latin) and poine (Greek), which suggest punishment, though in modern English it has lost this meaning except in such expressions as 'on pain of death'. At the same time pain has a second meaning as the opposite of pleasure – something a person feels when hurt both in body and mind – so that it is perhaps not surprising that pain may occur in association with states of mental depression.

Another approach to the problem of non-organic pain focusses on the behavioural component. Responses to pain that are rewarded (e.g. by increased attention from others or avoidance of unpleasant activities by the individual – associated as discussed elsewhere with the concept of the 'sick role') may become learned patterns of behaviour which are repeated in stressful circumstances, even in the absence of pain-producing organic disease. Such 'learned pain behaviour' (Tyrer, 1986) is an example of abnormal illness behaviour which will be considered in greater detail in Chapter 20.

Further reading

Barber, P. and Legge, D. (1975) *Perception and Information Processing* (Essential Psychology Series). London: Methuen.

Lindsay, P.H. and Norman, D.A. (1977) *Human Information Processing*, 2nd ed. London: Academic Press.

Melzack, P. and Wall, P.D. (1983) *The Challenge of Pain*. London: Basic Books.

Pearce, S. (1983) Pain. In: *Psychology Survey No. 4*, ed. B.M. Foss. Leicester: BPS Publications.

6
Cognitive processes
II – Learning

Having considered the way in which information is obtained from the environment through the process of perception, we must now examine how such experiences can have consequences extending beyond immediate awareness. The process responsible – learning – may be defined as the means by which a lasting modification of behaviour occurs as a result of experience. It is of vital importance in enabling the organism to adapt to its changing environment on the basis of previously successful and unsuccessful behaviour. It has, however, to be distinguished from behavioural changes that are due, not to any effect of experience, but to the process of maturation or physical development largely of the central nervous system, which permits the appearance of new behaviour. It should perhaps be noted here that this definition may not appear, at first sight, to correspond with the concept of learning probably held by most students; namely the acquisition of a body of knowledge. Nevertheless, the application of such knowledge clearly enables the performance of new and often highly complex pieces of behaviour (e.g. practising a profession). There are, in fact, a variety of different types of learning from the simplest to the most complex and there have been a range of theories to explain them.

Classical conditioning

This is the simplest form of learning and is sometimes also known as Pavlovian conditioning after the Russian physiologist Ivan Petrovich Pavlov (1849–1936) who first studied it systematically. Pavlov had noticed that his experimental dogs salivated not only to the sight of food but sometimes also to the sight of the experimenter or the sound of his footsteps. To study this phenomenon, he examined the effect of associating the presentation of food to the dog (which elicits the reflex response of salivation) with another stimulus such as the sound of a bell. He showed that after a number of such associations the sound of the bell alone would produce salivation, though at a rather lesser rate and without some of the other responses (e.g. stomach contractions) that occurred with the food.

Certain terms are customarily applied to these stimuli and responses, so that Pavlov's classical experiment may be rephrased as follows. Food, the *unconditioned stimulus* (UCS), elicits salivation, the *unconditoned response* (UCR). As a result of repeatedly sounding a bell, the *conditioned stimulus* (CS), at the same time as, or just prior to, the presentation of the food, the process of conditioning takes place, so that eventually the bell (i.e. CS) alone produces salivation (though slower and of lesser quantity than in the UCR) – the *conditioned response* (CR).

Many other examples of classical conditioning have been described in man as well as other animals, including the eye-blink (to a puff of air as the UCS), the knee jerk and the galvanic skin response or GSR (usually to electric shock as the UCS). The essence of this type of learning in all cases is that an already existing, innate, involuntary reflex response to a specific UCS (sometimes called *respondent* behaviour) comes to be elicited by a different stimulus.

There are, however, some further aspects of the classical conditioning process which require consideration. First, the timing of the CS and UCS is of great importance, the strongest conditioning being produced by a CS which immediately precedes, and terminates with the onset of, the UCS, while very little conditioning occurs to a CS which follows the presentation of the UCS.

A second feature of the conditioning process is the necessity for *reinforcement* of the CR by the UCS. If the CS (e.g. sound of bell) is presented repeatedly without reinforcement by the UCS (e.g. food), the CR gradually diminishes in amplitude and eventually ceases – a process known as *extinction*. After an interval, however (i.e. with no reinforcement), *spontaneous recovery* may occur, although the CR is weaker than previously.

Finally, the characteristics of the CS are significant in that the CR is elicited not only by the original CS but also by other similar stimuli (e.g. a bell of a different tone in Pavlov's experiments). This is known as *stimulus generalization*. It is found that the more closely the stimulus corresponds to the original CS, the greater is the CR. The relationship between the similarity of the stimulus to the original, and the intensity of response, can be represented graphically as a *gradient* of stimulus generalization. At first, after a conditioned response is established, stimuli fairly different from the original may elicit some response. If, however, the original conditioned stimulus continues to be reinforced by the unconditioned stimulus while no reinforcement is given after presentation of the other stimuli, then what is called *stimulus discrimination* occurs; only the original or very similar stimuli produce the CR, i.e. there is a steep gradient of stimulus generalization.

How important is this type of learning in human behaviour and experience? We shall consider later the question of clinical application, but in general it seems that many emotional responses, both pleasant and unpleasant, may be classically conditioned, and this may be significant in the process of psychological development. Thus the small child who gets burnt by touching a hot stove will acquire a fear of it and of other stoves which, provided it is not excessive, is adaptive in helping to avoid further injury. Similarly it may be that a mother, in the early days of a child's birth, becomes for the child a CS to the emotional feeling of pleasure and contentment which follows her satisfaction of its bodily needs, especially for food, and this may play some part in the 'bonding' between child and mother.

Operant or instrumental conditioning

This type of learning is of more obvious significance to everyday behaviour since it corresponds essentially to the traditional ways of training both children and non-human animals by the use of reward and punishment. It differs from classical conditioning in that it is concerned primarily with voluntary and *operant* behaviour emitted by, and not elicited from, the organism. Certain pieces of behaviour are encouraged or discouraged by their consequences, resulting in the gradual shaping of overall behaviour in particular ways.

Just as classical conditioning may be called Pavlovian, so operant conditioning is sometimes described as Skinnerian after the American psychologist, B.F. Skinner, who has, over many years, made an extensive study of the subject. His approach is fundamentally behaviourist and he has argued for the application of such ideas to create a Utopian society (Skinner, 1948).

Skinner designed a piece of apparatus which has come to be known as the 'Skinner box'. It consists of a cage in which is placed a small animal such as a rat or bird and in which there is also a mechanism by which a small quantity of food is delivered if the animal presses a lever or pecks at a disc. Initially, such 'reward' occurs only when the animal happens to operate the mechanism (which can be recorded automatically) purely by chance; but after a time the repeated rewarding or *positive reinforcement* of this particular piece of behaviour leads to its more frequent occurrence (a higher response rate), i.e. the animal has 'learned' to produce it in order to receive the positive reinforcing stimulus or *positive reinforcer* which follows.

Thus operant conditioning involves the reinforcement of a specific item of operant behaviour selected from the total behaviour of the organism. A new behavioural response is learned, in contrast to classical conditioning where an already existing response comes to be elicited by a new stimulus. However, as with classical conditioning, extinction of the response may occur after repeated lack of reinforcement, though with spontaneous recovery after a period away from the conditioning situation.

The ease with which extinction occurs or, conversely, the strength of a conditioned response (as measured by the response rate) is also affected by certain aspects of the conditioning process. First, as might be expected, the strength is greater the sooner reinforcement occurs after the response. (An exception is the aversion towards a poisonous food which may be acquired by some animals through a single experience of becoming ill some time after eating the food.) Rather less predictable (and in contrast to classical conditioning) is the fact that a conditioned response has a greater resistance to extinction if it has been acquired by a process of *partial* or *intermittent* reinforcement, i.e. during the conditioning procedure not all responses are reinforced. Various types of partial reinforcement or 'schedules of reinforcement' have been extensively studied by Skinner, who found the most effective to be the *variable ratio* schedule in which reinforcement of responses occurs in an unpredictable fashion except that the average – say one in every five responses – remains the same over a long period.

So far we have considered only positive reinforcement or the presentation of a positive reinforcer (reward) in operant conditioning. There are two other outcomes of a response which can affect its rate of occurrence. *Punishment* involves the presentation of an unpleasant stimulus (*negative reinforcer*) or removal of a positive reinforcer, and this leads to a reduction and possibly complete suppression of the punished behaviour. Evidence suggests, however, that such suppression is generally only temporary and the behaviour returns once punishment is removed. *Negative reinforcement* (a term which is sometimes confused with, but is not the same as, punishment) occurs when a particular behavioural response leads to the removal of a negative reinforcer. Thus a Skinner box may be provided with a grid/floor which can be electrified but in such a way that pressing the lever in the box switches off the current.

An animal placed in the box can learn to escape from the shock by pressing the lever - an *escape* response. Furthermore, if the electrification of the grid is signalled by a light being switched on a few seconds beforehand, the animal can learn, by the same response, to avoid the shock altogether - an *avoidance* response.

We have been considering operant conditioning chiefly as demonstrated in the Skinner box, but there are many other experimental situations used for this purpose. Thus animals may learn to find their way through a maze - turning right or left at T-junctions - for a reward at the end. This is a form of *discrimination* learning, i.e. to make a choice between alternative stimuli.

We have seen that operant conditioning is concerned with the modification of behaviour that is under voluntary control and it was generally considered to exclude responses under the involuntary control of the autonomic system. However, studies by N.E. Miller (1969) suggested that some visceral (internal autonomic) responses - such as heart rate, blood pressure, gastrointestinal activities and even renal function - could be modified by rewarding changes in the required direction (e.g. heart rate increased or decreased, blood pressure raised or lowered). Although it has subsequently proved impossible to replicate these findings, they were followed by similar research in human subjects which led to clinical applications in the form of 'biofeedback', which we shall shortly be considering.

Most of the study of operant conditioning has, in fact, been carried out under laboratory conditions on non-human animals, but similar data have been obtained from human subjects. Indeed, this form of learning is of vital importance to the acquisition, by the developing individual, of appropriate behaviour, especially social, through the process of socialization. Thus the practice of child rearing usually consists of a combination of positive reinforcement or negative reinforcement of socially approved behaviour and punishment of socially disapproved behaviour. Positive reinforcement takes the form of obvious rewards (sweets, toys, treats, etc.) at an early age, followed later by social rewards such as approval and praise, and generally this is very effective in producing persisting behavioural change. Negative reinforcement is used in the form of *aversive control* when behaviour is performed in order to avoid a threatened punishment, i.e. a form of blackmail. This can also be very effective, even in the long term, but it does depend on the continuing existence of a threat, which is liable to cause resentment in the child. It can also be a two-edged weapon since the child may retaliate by using the same technique against the parent, resulting ultimately in a battle of wills. Lastly, punishment in the form of a noxious stimulus (e.g. a slap) or withdrawal of a positive reinforcement (e.g. television) is generally effective, but usually only in the short term unless positive reinforcement is given for some alternative behaviour. We shall return to this subject when we consider child development and rearing in a later chapter.

We have so far emphasized the *differences* between classical and operant conditioning, but they have in common the fact that the response to be learned has actually to occur and to be reinforced in some way on a number of occasions before conditioning is established. There are, however, some examples of experience bringing about a modification of behaviour, or at least of behavioural potentiality, which do not have these requirements; these are sometimes described as *non-associative*.

Non-associative forms of learning

The first of these is known as *latent learning* or learning that is not immediately reflected in performance. An early experiment by Tolman and Honzik (1930), for example, showed that rats that were allowed to 'explore' a maze for a few days without any reward for traversing it correctly, exhibited little or no improvement in performance compared with others receiving a regular reward, but very quickly did so – even overtaking the latter – once rewards were given to both groups; the latent learning that had occurred thus only becoming manifested in performance with the introduction of reinforcement.

A second type of non-associative learning is based entirely on sensory stimulation with no behavioural participation on the part of the subject. Known as *imitation* or *observational* learning, the subject simply observes the behaviour of another, the model, and later may perform the same behaviour in spite of having had no previous practice or reinforcement. An important role has been claimed (Bandura, 1962) for imitation in social learning in children, and we shall discuss this further in relation to development in Chapter 12.

Next we come to a process which is not always classified as a type of learning and has been studied principally by ethologists (see Chapter 1). It is concerned with the formation of an *attachment* between an organism and another object and is known as *imprinting*. Thus Konrad Lorenz (1937) found that newly hatched birds of certain species would form a permanent attachment to, and follow, any moving object (which would normally be the mother bird) that was presented at the right time – the so-called *critical period*. This is an example of a *species specific* behaviour, the stimulus for which is imprinted through sensory exposure.

The role of imprinting in mammals is less well established, but H.F. Harlow (1959) showed that young rhesus monkeys deprived of their mother would develop an attachment to a cloth-covered wire frame to which they would exhibit a clinging response. When frightened, they would rush to the 'cloth mother', apparently lose their fear and begin exploratory activity again. It was further found that the cloth mother was preferred to a similar wire structure which was not covered in cloth, despite the fact that milk could be obtained from the latter and not the former. 'Contact comfort' seemed to be more important than food in this context. Whether imprinting is of importance in the development of the human infant is uncertain, but again we shall return to this question in the appropriate chapter.

The last process to be considered here is known as *learning how to learn* or the formation of a *learning set*. Harlow (1949) found that monkeys showed improvement in solving discrimination problems (choosing which of two objects had a reward underneath it – a different set of objects being used for each problem) the more they solved. In other words, they had developed a strategy for learning or a learning set for this type of problem. Harlow explained this by postulating *error factors* which interfere with correct responses (e.g. always chosing the left-hand object) and which were gradually eliminated in the process of developing a learning set. This phenomenon may also explain what is known as *transfer of learning* – the positive facilitatory effect that one learning task may have on a succeeding one. More generally, it suggests the need for a revision of the distinction which used to be made between learning that was called *trial and error* (trying out different responses to a problem until the correct solution is hit upon and then learned) and *insightful* (rapid learning based on insight into the nature of the problem). It seems, rather, that these are different phases in a continuous learning process, with the former preceding the latter.

Learning of skills

Skills, leading to the efficient performance of particular activities, are important in human behaviour. As well as those involved in specialized sensorimotor tasks such as operating a lathe, playing tennis, driving a car, etc., we may also include various social skills required in different types of interpersonal relationship. However, it is the process of learning a sensorimotor skill that has received most study, especially during the Second World War, because of its obvious application to improving training methods.

The progress of performance (measured by speed, accuracy, etc.) with length of learning may be represented graphically as a *learning* curve. This generally has a characteristic shape (Fig. 6.1) indicating an initial rapid learning (steep slope) which gradually falls off to a plateau (level section) followed by further phases of learning with intervening plateaux. These spurts of learning probably correspond to phases of insightful learning such as we have just mentioned, but what are the basic processes underlying them in this situation? It seems, from the evidence, that to a large extent this is a matter of perceptual organization; of appreciating the redundancy in the total available sensory information and selecting from it only the important sensory cues for attention, together with learning the likely sequences of incoming signals, i.e. which are likely to follow which. The necessity for this perceptual organization stems from what is sometimes called the *single channel hypothesis* – a cybernetic concept derived from communications engineering, meaning that human perception may be viewed, as we saw in the last chapter, as a single-channel communication system of limited capacity. Perceptual selection is therefore important in order that the maximum amount of information is received through the limited channel.

Unconscious behavioural learning

Clinical evidence from amnesic patients has suggested that, despite their inability to recall events, they may nevertheless still be able to learn from them

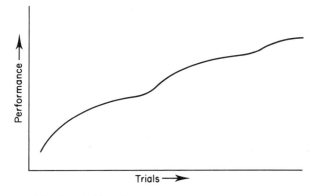

Fig.6.1   A typical learning curve

in the sense of a change in behaviour. This has been termed *procedural* learning. Studies have shown that such learning can include motor and perceptual skills – learning to type, play a new tune on the piano, reading inverted writing, etc. – despite the patient being unable to recollect the circumstances in which the learning occurred (Baddeley, 1982). It has been suggested, therefore, that there is a separate system for this 'unconscious' behavioural learning which can remain intact despite impairment of recollection of the learning experience.

Neurophysiological aspects

Since much learning – at least at the level of classical and operant conditioning – depends on the establishment of an association between a stimulus and a response, neurophysiological theory has tended to focus on the neural pathways between the former and the latter. The Canadian psychologist, D.O. Hebb (1959), postulated the build-up of what he called *cell assemblies* and *phase sequences* during the process of learning. Cell assemblies are composed of all the cells and their connecting fibres that are active in a particular situation – when we perceive an object in the environment for example. Phase sequences consist of progressive activity in a series of individual cells or cell assemblies, so that the firing of one part leads to activation of the whole sequence. Learning then occurs through the development of cell assemblies and phase sequences through repetition of situations activating these particular cells.

The concept of establishing specific neuronal circuits or links between stimulus and response is, by analogy with a telephone system, sometimes referred to as the 'switchboard' approach; it contrasts with the Gestalt viewpoint which postulated 'patterns' of neural activity in the cerebral cortex. Such patterns would be the result of multiple sensory inputs modified by the traces of past experience and thus subject to a process of organization before a response is produced.

Physiological theories of these kinds are difficult to subject to experimental verification, but some evidence is derived from studies of the effects on learning of destruction of various parts of the brain. As far as the cerebral cortex is concerned, Lashley (1929) showed, in rats, that when learning depended on multiple sensory cues – visual, auditory, olfactory, etc. – impairment was not related to destruction of any particular area but rather to the total *amount* of cortical damage and the complexity of the learning task. He concluded, therefore, that one part of the cortex could replace another in learning and spoke of this ability as *equipotentiality*. Later work, however, in which stimulation was restricted to one sensory modality showed that destruction of those parts of the cortex associated with that modality (e.g. visual cortex with vision) would result in loss of learning ability.

Since, as we have seen, much learning depends upon the mechanism of reinforcement, interest has also been directed to the effects on learning of stimulation or destruction of those parts of the brain thought to be concerned with emotion and motivation. We shall, however, defer further consideration of such studies to Chapters 9 and 10, which are devoted to these two psychological processes.

Clinical aspects

Since learning is fundamental to the development and modification of behaviour, knowledge concerning the process may be usefully applied to many clinical situations involving human behaviour - not only of patients but also of staff.

Disorders of behaviour and experience

In the first place perhaps the most obvious application is in the field of psychiatry which, as we saw in Chapter 2, is the medical specialty concerned with abnormalities of behaviour and experience. To what extent could some, at least, of the phenomena of psychiatric disorders be explained on the basis of learning?

Pavlov demonstrated what was claimed to be an *experimental neurosis* in dogs that had been trained by classical conditioning to discriminate shapes (e.g. a circle and an elipse), the difference between which was then gradually reduced until discrimination was extremely difficult. The dogs, which could be presumed to be in a state of conflict over whether or not to respond, began to show signs of a behavioural disturbance with trembling, whining, barking and refusal to eat. It is doubtful whether this is strictly comparable with human 'neurotic' behaviour, but problems over discrimination may nevertheless be disturbing. Thus a child may have difficulty in discriminating between rewarded and unrewarded (or punished and unpunished) behaviours that differ in ways that he cannot appreciate (e.g. expressing a differing but reasonable opinion and 'answering back').

Another early experimental demonstration of the possible importance of learning in the causation of some psychiatric conditions was performed by J.B. Watson, the founder of the behaviourist school of psychology. Watson and Rayner (1920) succeeded in inducing a fear of furry animals and similar inanimate objects (the CR) in a small boy, famous in the history of psychology as 'Little Albert', by associating the presentation of a white rat (the CS) with a loud noise (the UCS). The fact that he became afraid of other furry objects as well as white rats was, of course, due to stimulus generalization. The behaviourist view is, then, that *phobias* - i.e. excessive and irrational fears of objects and situations - are actually learned emotional responses (and not due to unconscious conflict, etc., as suggested by psychoanalytic theory), with the implication that 'treatment' should be directed to 'unlearning' the fear.

Methods of treatment derived from theories of learning and known as *behavioural psychotherapy* or *behaviour therapy* are employed, in suitable cases, generally by psychiatrists, clinical psychologists and 'nurse therapists' (nurses who have received special training in the techniques). Two principal techniques have been employed in the treatment of specific phobias (Marks, 1969). The first of these was developed by a South African psychiatrist, J. Wolpe (1958), and is known as *systematic desensitization*. It is a gradual process and involves the deconditioning of the fear (CR) to the phobic object or situation (CS) by association of the latter with a feeling of relaxation which inhibits the fear - *reciprocal inhibition*. The first step consists of drawing up, with the patient, a list of objects or situations which increasingly resemble the phobic stimulus itself, so that, passing from the bottom to the top of the hierarchy, they would evoke increasing intensities of fear. The patient, having been trained in attaining a state of physical and mental relaxation, is then presented in reality, or in imagination, with a stimulus from the bottom of the list. This is stopped as soon as any anxiety is experienced, but after repeated presentations the anxiety ceases and the next stimulus in the hierarchy is dealt with in the same way. Eventually the phobic object or situation itself is reached and the fear extinguished. A typical example might be the removal of a cat phobia by using a hierarchy stretching from a piece of fur-like material, through photographs of cats to a real kitten which then gradually matures into an adult cat.

The other behavioural technique for treatment of phobias contrasts considerably with systematic desensitization since it involves exposing the patient (with full consent and cooperation) to the full effect of the phobic stimulus and preventing any escape from it. Known as *flooding* or *implosion* therapy, it depends for its efficacy on the fact that the state of fear induced cannot be maintained indefinitely at a high level, so that the phobic stimulus fairly rapidly comes to be associated with lessening and eventually complete absence of fear. An example of this form of treatment might be a patient with an excessive fear of heights who would be taken by the therapist to the top of a high building and encouraged to remain looking towards the ground in spite of the great fear induced at first.

The variety of phobic stimuli met with in practice is considerable and includes many clinical objects and situations which can prove obstacles to the treatment of disease (e.g. fear of hospitals, doctors, injections, operations, etc.). It is easy to see how many of these fears may have been conditioned by unpleasant and frightening experiences, especially in childhood, and much can probably be done to minimize such occurrences – by, for example, careful preparation of a child before admission to hospital and of women before childbirth.

The principles of operant conditioning have also been applied to various clinical problems. One example concerns the attempt to improve the social behaviour of long-stay patients in psychiatric hospitals. Many patients who were admitted to such hospitals in years gone by, especially those suffering from the condition known as schizophrenia, unfortunately remained as inpatients instead of, as is usually the case today with modern treatments, being discharged within a few weeks. After long periods in an institution, even if the original condition which necessitated admission has largely disappeared, the patient may become 'institutionalized' with little apparent inclination to do anything and with very poor socialization. Using operant conditioning, however, it is possible to encourage more active and appropriate social behaviour by applying rewards, which may take the form of plastic discs or 'tokens' that can then be exchanged for material goods in the hospital shop or for special privileges. This particular technique, known as *token economy* has been used with success in such circumstances; but the principles can be applied more generally to the management of patients in general and psychiatric hospitals.

Other conditions of clinical interest where operant conditioning principles may be important – both in causation and treatment – are those disorders of behaviour which are maladaptive in the sense of being harmful to the individual, yet have become habitual. Excessive gambling may be so extreme and compulsive as to be termed pathological; but if we consider the nature of the gambling situation and the likelihood of winning, we can see that it corresponds very closely with the variable ratio schedule of reinforcement which we saw earlier was the most effective form of conditioning. Application of operant conditioning techniques to the extinction of this particular form of behaviour has been shown to be successful in some cases.

Other examples of maladaptive behaviour familiar to general medicine as well as to psychiatry include excessive food and alcohol intake, drug abuse and cigarette smoking. In spite of warnings of the health hazards involved, patients frequently find it extremely difficult if not impossible to modify these habits. With alcohol, drugs and cigarettes there is, of course, an additional pharmacological factor, but learning principles are also of importance. The main difficulty lies in the time relationships of the 'rewards' and 'punishments' in such cases, with the former occurring early and the latter later. The satisfaction of a cigarette is immediate, the damage to the respiratory and cardiovascular system long delayed; the intoxicant effect of alcohol is rapid, the harmful effects of excessive intake come much later – even the 'hangover' is not until next morning! In terms of reinforcement, the immediate 'rewards' are more powerful than the delayed 'punishment'. Similarly when it comes to treatment, the rewards of reduced intake or complete abstinence in terms of improved health are also somewhat delayed, so that intermediate targets may have to be set (e.g. a reduction of so many cigarettes or so much weight), the passing of which can be rewarded.

Finally, we have seen that some animal studies had suggested that operant conditioning could also be applied to certain autonomic responses. Experiments in man involved the use of signals to indicate to the subject whether or not a particular physiological change had occurred (and for this reason became known as *biofeedback*). It has been claimed that changes may be produced in the level of skin resistance (as measured by the GSR), in heart rate, in blood pressure and in the amount of alpha rhythm in the EEG. Attempts have been made to apply the technique to treatment not only of anxiety (by inducing relaxation as indicated by the GSR and EEG) but also of disordered rhythm of the heart and of high blood pressure. In general, however, the initially high hopes for biofeedback have not been fully realized, and it appears often to add little to what can be achieved by relaxation alone (Lynch, 1973).

Training in clinical skills

We have considered some applications of learning theory to clinical problems of patients, but techniques of learning could clearly also be of importance to the acquisition of clinical skills by health professionals – particularly skills required in interpersonal relationships such as those between patient and doctor, nurse, physiotherapist, etc., or between different members of staff. This is not just a question of a good 'bedside manner', nor is it something that is innate to the individual who either possesses it or does not. Although personality differences may contribute to variation in this respect, clinical skills have to be developed through the process of learning. Of course a good deal of this has always been, and still is, based on imitation by the student of the behaviour of more experienced health professionals, but more specific training programmes may have a place in the acquisition of particular skills such as those involved in history-taking, dealing with 'difficult' patients, bereaved relatives and various other distressing situations. All this is really concerned with the learning of a professional 'role', a sociological concept which we have already met in Chapter 3 and to which we shall return in Chapter 11.

Training for this purpose may involve the student in 'role playing', i.e.

playing the part of a doctor, nurse, etc., with perhaps another student taking the part of a patient or relative. The whole session may be videotaped so that the student has the opportunity of observing his performance, which can also be commented on by other students and teachers. Such training in clinical skills is beginning, in a limited way, to be applied and evaluated (e.g. Maguire and Rutter, 1976), but the future may see its more widespread use. We shall return to this matter in Chapter 18 when we consider aspects of doctor–patient communication.

Impairment of learning and its assessment

So far we have dealt only with applications of learning theory to various clinical situations, but there are also certain disorders in which the individual's ability to acquire new information is impaired. This may occur in states of clouded consciousness (see Chapter 4) where attention and concentration and, therefore, registration is limited; but more often it is due to chronic organic disease directly affecting the brain – so-called *dementia*. Disturbance of memory is also found in dementia, but this is not solely due to the learning deficit and will be dealt within the next chapter.

Clinical psychologists have developed tests to detect and measure the extent of impairment of learning. These are generally based on the speed with which new material can be learned by the patient. This may consist of a set of words not included in his vocabulary and whose meanings he has to learn (e.g. the Walton Black Modified Word Learning Test), or a number of pairs of unrelated words (e.g. chair–apple) which he has learn to associate so that he can give the second when supplied with the first of each pair (e.g. the Inglis Paired Associate Learning Test).

Further reading

Bandura, A. (1969) *Principles of Behaviour Modification*. New York: Holt, Rinehart & Winston.

Bower, G.H. and Hilgard, E.J. (1981) *Theories of Learning*, 5th ed. New Jersey: Prentice-Hall.

Rimm, D.C. and Masters, J.C. (1979) *Behaviour Therapy: Techniques and Empirical Findings*. New York: Academic Press.

Walker, S. (1975) *Learning and Reinforcement* (Essential Psychology Series). London: Methuen.

7
Cognitive processes
III – Remembering

We have seen how the environment is selectively perceived and how experience of events occurring in that environment can result in modification of behaviour through the process of learning. An obvious and important additional fact of human mental life, however, is that such perceptions may subsequently be remembered and recalled into conscious awareness. It is important because it is the ability to remember past information that enables the individual to benefit from previous experience (his own, and that of others passed on through teaching) in responding and adapting to current circumstances. It is not surprising, therefore, that the study of remembering and its converse, forgetting, has a long history within psychology. In recent years developments in other fields such as computer technology have led to new approaches, but many questions still remain to be answered.

The whole process of remembering can be regarded as consisting of a sequence of stages beginning with the initial *registration* of information which has then to be *retained* until such time as it is *recalled* to consciousness or at least *recognized* (e.g. on being presented with the same or a similar current situation). The input or registration of information involves, of course, the processes of perception and learning which we have already considered, and it is with the later stages of retention, recall and recognition that we shall be concerned here.

Forgetting

Just as, when we considered consciousness in the last chapter, we noted its limitations and the selectivity of perceptual attention which this necessitated, so we must now consider the limitations of human memory. Clearly we are not able to recall every item that has ever been present in our conscious awareness. Remarkable though it may be, the human brain, like its electronic counterpart the computer, must have a finite capacity to store information, so that unless it is to be 'filled up' prematurely there has to be some restriction to the amount of acquired information that is to be preserved for further use.

One approach to the study of memory is, in fact, to investigate the way in which learned material is forgotten over a period of time. This technique was used in a classical series of experiments carried out by the German psychologist, Hermann Ebbinghaus (1850–1909). As in most of the research on remembering, Ebbinghaus used verbal material but of a non-meaningful kind; for this purpose he invented what was called *nonsense syllables* – words made up from two consonants and an intervening vowel – baf, gic, lod, for example. The advantage of these was that from a learning point of view each was of equal value since, having no meaning, they were all 'unknown' to the subject. To study the process of forgetting, Ebbinghaus himself learned lists of nonsense syllables and then, at different intervals after successful learning, relearned them. By seeing how long it took to relearn a list compared with the time originally required (giving a so-called 'savings score'), he was able to estimate how much of the original learned (i.e. registered) material had been forgotten and, conversely, retained.

Figure 7.1 shows a representative curve, which corresponds with the general finding that forgetting is initially rapid and then gradually tails off until a stage is reached when there is no further loss – at least for the duration of the experiment. This, of course, corresponds well with everyday experience that we can remember in some detail events that have just occurred but that, with the passage of time, the amount that can be recalled becomes very much less. It also raises questions which have as yet not been fully resolved; is there, for example, one memory system or are there at least two – one concerned with short-term and another with long-term remembering? and what actually brings about forgetting – do the memories just decay with time or are they interfered with by other material that is being learned? These two questions are in some ways related, but we shall look first at whether or not there is more than one kind of memory.

Short- and long-term memories

The fact that the shape of the curve of forgetting takes the form that it does rather than a straight line – together with the experience of everyday life that we find ourselves in some situations where we need to remember some information for a short period only (e.g. an unfamiliar telephone number just long enough to dial it) while on other occasions we depend on information that has been learned and retained for a long period – suggests that there may in fact be two different types of memory, short-term (STM) and long-term (LTM). The alternative concept is of a single memory system, and controversy between the unitary and dichotomous viewpoints has depended on the demonstration of similarities and differences respectively between STM and LTM, especially in

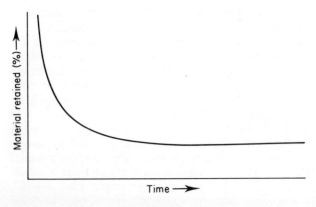

Fig.7.1   A typical curve of forgetting

terms of the nature of the process of forgetting in each case. Though not unequivocal, the evidence, as we shall consider in more detail later, has on the whole tended to support the distinction, the most influential modal model being that of Atkinson and Shiffrin (1971). We shall therefore consider the two forms of memory separately.

First we should recall that there is a third form of ultra-short memory of limited capacity which we considered in the last chapter – the visual (iconic) and acoustic (echoic) memory concerned with an initial storage of sensory information before it is *processed* or *encoded* and passed on to the categorical memory systems with which we are concerned here (see Fig. 4.1).

Short-term memory

Having been registered, information passes into a short-term memory store from which it may or may not also enter into the long-term memory store. If it does not, it is lost to later recall and its duration in short-term memory is limited by a process of rapid forgetting. To demonstrate this it is necessary to prevent the subject from maintaining the information by rehearsal, i.e. repeating it in consciousness. This may be done, for example (Peterson and Peterson, 1959), by getting him to count backwards after the presentation of the material to be remembered and during the interval before testing. Under these conditions very little can be remembered after about eighteen seconds. It seems then, that we are dealing with a storage system of limited capacity from which information is lost after a short period unless it is passed into long-term memory.

We shall return to consider the nature of the forgetting process itself, but here we should note the importance of having such a short-term storage system for the understanding of information contained in a temporal sequence of stimuli such as speech or music. Full analysis of the meaning of such information cannot be instantaneous but must depend on the ability to store a sequence (e.g. of words or musical notes) for processing as a whole; similar considerations also apply to the analysis of spatial patterns.

Long-term memory

It is clear from the foregoing that, while short-term memory provides a limited storage of all the information that has been perceived and registered by the individual, only a selected proportion of this enters into long-term memory. The latter, however, has by comparison an almost unlimited capacity and information in it may be stored indefinitely. Which information enters into the storage system will depend on a number of factors, including its intensity and length of presentation, whether it has been rehearsed in STM and whether there is a 'set' for its selection. This, however, as we have already considered, is only the first stage of the process of remembering; information, once it has been registered and put into the memory store has not only to be retained but has also to be retrieved from it when required. This necessitates some kind of organization of memory and we shall return to this shortly. First we must consider further the problem of forgetting and why it occurs.

Theories of forgetting

This is the other major area of controversy in relation to memory, and it is also connected with the question, just discussed, of whether there is more than one memory system since support for the dichotomous viewpoint might come from differences in the processes of forgetting in STM and LTM.

Two principal explanations of forgetting have been advanced by experimental psychologists though it is now generally recognized that they are not mutually exclusive. The first of these is known as the *trace decay* hypothesis which proposes that information is lost simply through fading or weakening of some form of memory trace with disuse and the passage of time. The alternative theory involves the concept of *interference* whereby stored material is affected by previous or subsequent events – known respectively as *proactive* and *retroactive* interference.

Much research has been carried out into these two theories of forgetting which were initially related to the unitary/dichotomous memory controversy by the proposal that trace decay is responsible for forgetting in STM and interference for that in LTM. However, the situation does not appear to be as simple as this. If we return to the experiment on STM to which we have already referred, it will be recalled that the subject was prevented from rehearsing the items to be remembered by some intervening activity such as counting backwards. Now it could be that the forgetting resulted from simple decay with time or it might be that the intervening activity itself had a retroactive interference effect.

Waugh and Norman (1965) separated these two factors by independently varying the time interval and the amount of intervening material. Their so-called 'serial probe' technique involved first presenting a sequence of 16 digits and then asking the subject to name the next digit after a particular one selected from any position in the sequence. This enabled the time interval since the required digits to be varied, but in addition two rates of presentation of the digits were used (1 or 4 per second) which allowed a choice of number of digits presented in that time interval. The results showed that elapsed time was of less importance in forgetting than the number of items presented during that period – supporting the notion of interference or the displacement of old by new items in a memory store of limited capacity. At the same time, however, there was evidence of less marked forgetting for the more rapidly presented digits, and this would be consistent with trace-decay theory. So that it appears that both processes may be involved in forgetting in STM.

Assuming that information has remained sufficiently long in STM to have been able to pass into long-term storage, what determines its persistence there? It is, of course, only possible to discover whether it has been retained by seeing whether it can be recognized or recalled, but does the absence of such retrieval necessarily indicate that the information has been lost? We shall return to this question, but the experimental evidence on forgetting in LTM has stressed the importance of interference, though the theory has been modified in recent years and has moved away from a primary concern with the learning and remembering of associations between a stimulus and a response.

In the first place though, the theory proposed that forgetting was due to interference between an original association and a new one, especially when the same stimulus was associated with a different response, and experiments usually involved subjects learning lists of pairs of items (e.g. nonsense syllables). In the first list to be learned – called the A-B list – the stimulus item A was followed by the response item B, but in a subsequent list, A-C, the response which followed A was a different one, C. Learning the A-C list resulted in less recall of the A-B list than in a control situation when only the latter was learned – due to retroactive interference. At the same time, recall of the A-C list was also affected by the prior learning of the A-B list through proactive interference.

It was argued from this and other experiments that forgetting is due, not to decay of a response, but to its *competition* with another response when recall is required. Later evidence, however, where the effect of competition was minimized by allowing unlimited time for recall of both responses to the same stimulus, necessitated a revision of this theory since it appeared that retroactive interference does lead to some 'unlearning' of the original response. It seems, then, that as far as learning associations are concerned, particularly when there are two different responses to the same stimulus, faulty recall may be due to interference both from competition or confusion between two responses, and from some actual unlearning of the early association during the process of learning the later response – a 'time-factor' explanation of forgetting. Although such situations do arise in everyday life (e.g. the English visitor to Italy who has to learn that the tap marked C should produce hot and not cold water, *caldo* meaning hot, they are not particularly common and interference of this kind is unlikely to be the explanation for all forgetting. In fact the concept itself of learning as the establishment of stimulus–response associations has considerable limitations, as does a model of memory based solely on it.

Another approach was that of the *Gestalt* psychologists who maintained that the processes involved in memory are subject to the same sort of influences as are those of perception. Stored information would thus be liable to modification in various ways so that it would not necessarily represent an undistorted record of the original event as perceived at the time. Evidence for this was based on repeated testing of learned material, visual or verbal, which showed that distortion may occur in terms of greater organization and meaning of the material, often in the context of the individual's previous experience. This again is something we shall return to when we consider the organization of memory.

Finally, there is another theory of forgetting which is also concerned with memory distortion brought about by individual experience but which lays greater emphasis on affective and motivational than on purely cognitive factors. This is the Freudian concept of *repression*, which postulates an active process of forgetting those ideas and events which would prove threatening to conscious awareness. According to this view the memories are not actually 'lost' but become inaccessible in their original forms. They may, nevertheless, appear in distorted forms under certain conditions (e.g. dreams) and be correctly recalled in special circumstances (e.g. during psychoanalysis or under hypnosis). It must be conceded, however, that support for such a notion comes largely from clinical experience, though there is some laboratory evidence for motivated forgetting in terms of better recall of pleasant than of unpleasant events.

Alternatives to, and recent developments of, the dichotomous concept of memory

We have noted some evidence supporting the idea of a dichotomy between a temporary short-term memory store and a more durable long-term memory system – information being fed from sensory buffer stores into the former where it is held for a limited time and then, depending in part on the length of that period, being transferred to long-term storage. Not all the available evidence has confirmed the model, and this has led to alternatives to and refinements of the concept (Baddeley, 1984).

Further supportive evidence for the dichotomy has come from two sources. First, experimental work on the role of encoding in memory has suggested differences in the process. In STM, such as the immediate recall of a list of unselected letters or words, there is a major reliance on the sound of the material (i.e. acoustic coding), with items that are phonologically similar being much less accurately recalled than those that are dissimilar (e.g. BVTCPD versus KWYQRL or MAN CAD MAT MAP CAN versus PIT DAY PEN COW FAR). Similarly, for remembering meaningful material such as a piece of prose the exact wording can only be recalled if tested immediately, whereas the meaning of the passage is more long-lasting (i.e. semantic coding). Secondly, clinical evidence shows that patients with Korsakoff's psychosis have a normal short-term memory despite gross impairment of their long-term learning ability, while the converse may be found in patients with a specific left hemisphere lesion.

Against these supportive findings, however, has been other evidence demonstrating acoustic coding in long-term memory (which in any case should be expected if one is to be able to learn to speak a new language) and for semantic coding in short-term memory. Similarly, investigation of patients with impaired short-term memory has shown that long-term memory performance may be normal – suggesting that information does not necessarily have to pass through a short-term store for long-term learning to occur.

In the face of this conflicting evidence an alternative to the dichotomous model of memory was proposed by Craik and Lockhart (1972). This related the durability of memory to the level of encoding or processing of the material rather than to separate memory stores. Thus the more deeply the material is encoded – ranging from sensory characteristics (brightness, loudness, etc.) to categorization at different levels (from recognition of words to abstraction of meanings) – the more will it be retained. Experimentally this was supported by measurement of subjects' ability to learn material that they were required to process at different levels – for example, deciding whether each of a list of unrelated words was written in upper or lower case, rhymed with a particular word, or fitted into a particular category of meaning. However, although this *levels of processing* model has proved a useful concept – particularly the notion of depth of processing in LTM as a continuum rather than as a series of separate stages – it has proved less successful in other areas (e.g. in amnesia).

Further developments of the dichotomous approach have included attempts to move away from the concept of a single short-term and single long-term memory system. It has been proposed by Baddeley and Hitch (1974) that the old idea of a unitary STM of limited capacity for the storage of verbal information for a few seconds should be expanded. It had already been recognized to function as a *working memory*, in the sense that it was involved in a range of information processing activities that required temporary information storage, such as problem solving and speech comprehension. The new approach conceived of the working memory as composed of modules or subsystems comprising a limited-capacity central processor or *central executive*, together with two subsidiary 'slave' systems – an *articulatory rehearsal loop* and a *visio-spatial sketch pad*. Briefly, the central executive maintains received information at a flexible level of processing by rehearsing it and keeping it in conscious awareness – the quantity of information depending on the depth of processing involved. Using such techniques as giving a subject the task of temporarily remembering a number of irrelevant digits while at the same time engaging in some other activity such as verbal reasoning, understanding a prose passage or learning a list of words, it was shown that the amount of interference with these activities was less than would be expected with a unitary working memory system. The 'slave' subsystems are therefore seen as providing back-up temporary storage – the speech-based articulatory loop being associated with subvocal rehearsal and the visio-spatial sketch pad with visual imagery. They are also assumed to have a general role in other tasks – the former with a system for comprehending and producing speech, and the latter with a system for maintaining orientation in space.

Attempts have also been made to replace the concept of a unitary LTM system with two or more subsystems. Tulving (1972) proposed a distinction between *semantic* memory comprising a store of organized knowledge about words, their meanings and use, which in effect means a general knowledge of the world (a marigold is a flower, Madrid is the capital of Spain, water boils at 100°C, etc.) and *episodic* memory covering memories of specific personal events (the weather on one's wedding day, where the last holiday was spent, etc.). However, while the distinction between these two types of memory has proved useful, the evidence does not provide strong support for two separate underlying systems.

Organization of memory and retrieval of information

We have already referred to the limitations of a stimulus–response, associationist view of memory, and indeed it has largely been replaced by concepts derived from computer technology and more specifically from computer programming. An important function of the computer is the storage of information and its retrieval as and when required. This requires some form of organization of storage and retrieval, so that individual items of information can be rapidly located, and it is assumed that an analogous system may exist in the human brain for the large-capacity LTM system.

We have also seen that, at an earlier date, Gestalt psychology was concerned with the organization of material in memory. The Cambridge psychologist, Sir Frederick Bartlett (1932), in a series of experiments using realistic everyday material (pictures, stories, etc.) in contrast to the nonsense syllables of Ebbinghaus, showed that subjects tended to organize the information (by omissions, inventions and alterations), sometimes in a highly individual way, in order to increase its meaningfulness to them.

If we turn for a moment from laboratory experiments to a consideration of the popular systems for improving memory known as *mnemonics*, we shall see that they all depend on some form of meaningful organization of the material to be remembered. Probably the earliest known example of such a system was that of the Greek poet, Simonides, who based it on his experience of having been able to identify, by recalling the places in which they had been sitting, the unrecognizable bodies of fellow guests at a banquet, all of whom had been killed by a collapse of the roof after he himself had left. His system, which was employed by Cicero and other Roman orators in order to memorize long speeches, depended upon visualizing a room with the various items to be remembered placed in different localities. Examples of popular present-day simple aids to memory include the rhyming couplet 'i before e, except after c', and numerous mnemonics (mostly unprintable!) used by medical and perhaps other health students in learning lists of anatomical structures such as the cranial nerves.

Is there, however, more experimental evidence of organization of information within long-term memory? Two examples only will be described here, but they both demonstrate the importance of categorization of material for storage purposes – at least in semantic memory.

Mandler (1967) presented two groups of subjects with 52 cards on each of which was a single word. One group was instructed to organize the cards by sorting them into 2–7 categories of their own choice, while the other group had to distribute the cards, each one in turn, to seven piles. Thus the first group categorized the cards within some meaningful system while the second group simply arranged them according to their (random) position in the pack. Prior to the sorting of the cards, half the subjects in each group were told to learn the words, with no such instruction to the rest, but after five trials all were tested for recall. This showed that only those subjects given no instruction, either to organize or to learn, recalled fewer words than the rest. Thus the process of organizing the material alone resulted in its retention, which suggests that learning, which was equally but no more effective, may itself be based on a similar process of organization.

The other study we shall consider is that of Bower *et al.* (1969) in which subjects were given 112 words to learn under two different conditions. In the experimental group the words were organized in a hierarchical fashion into categories and subcategories; for example, minerals, subdivided into metals and stones, each further subdivided – the former into rare, common and alloys and the latter into precious and masonry – with the words in the last subcategory being limestone, granite, marble and slate. For the control group the words were presented in an entirely random order, and after a single trial the mean recall score for these subjects was only 21 compared with 73 for the hierarchical group.

These and other studies suggest that information stored in LTM is organized in such a way as to aid its location and retrieval, and it is to this last stage of memory that we shall now turn our attention. We all have some subjective awareness of the process when we find that we have difficulty in recalling, say, a name and yet are certain that we know it – we say that it is 'on the tip of the tongue'. Introspection shows us that we usually try several approaches as we search for the name – we think of the size and sound of the word, its beginning or ending, its associations with other names, etc. This suggests an analogy with a filing system with cross-references so that an individual document may be recorded under several different titles. The efficiency of such a system depends, of course, on correct filing in the first place; if an item is misfiled it may never be found unless every file is searched.

The tip-of-the-tongue phenomenon is concerned with recall of information and this has to be distinguished from recognition – a process which by comparison is generally easier. If, for example, when we are unable to recall a particular name we are presented with a choice of several names including that which is required, we can usually recognize it at once.

In everyday life retrieval of information by recognition or recall is generally not difficult and proceeds smoothly and accurately; but assuming that stored information is organized in the ways we have already discussed, how are the memory stores actually searched? In a recognition situation, for example, are all the items in a store 'scanned' in turn to find a match for the stimulus presented, or does the scanning stop as soon as the required item is found? Common sense would suggest the latter as being obviously more efficient, but Sternberg (1966) claimed on the basis on some very ingenious experiments that this is not so. Although his conclusions have not gone unchallenged, his experimental technique is of great interest as, in contrast to previous work on memory, it does not depend on mistakes on the part of the subject but on speed of error-free memory.

The first experiment concerned STM (though similar results have been obtained for recognition in LTM). Subjects were presented with a sequence of between one and six digits and two seconds after the last of these were shown another 'probe' digit. The subject then had to pull a lever marked 'yes' or 'no' according to whether the probe digit had been present or not in the original sequence, and the time taken to do this was noted. When the reaction times were plotted against the number of digits presented, a straight line was obtained, indicating that each additional digit produced the same increase in reaction time (actually 38 msec per item). Furthermore, the slope of the line was the same for 'yes' or 'no' responses. Now, if we take the 'yes' responses first, the linear relationship between the number of items in the memory store and the time taken to search it for a positive recognition supports Sternberg's contention that the store is scanned serially, i.e. each item is compared in turn with the probe rather than several at the same time.

Evidence for the second assertion – that the search is also exhaustive rather than self-terminating – comes from the similarity betweeen the 'yes' and 'no' responses. Clearly a complete search of the memory store is required before the probe can be excluded as having been in the sequence (a 'no' response), whereas a positive recognition (a 'yes' response) could occur at any point in the search, and on average only half the store would need to be scanned. The slope of the number of items/reaction time graph should in this case be half that of the negative responses which, as we have seen, it was not.

Neurological basis of memory

In our discussion so far we have examined only psychological models of memory, but we shall now consider how far these may be related to known brain structure and function (see Fig. 7.2).

Evidence pointing to the anatomical structures concerned comes largely from ablation studies in animals, with some support from clinical observations in man. Attention has focussed on the so-called *limbic system*, consisting principally of the *limbic lobe*, a ring of structures on the inner side of each cerebral hemisphere surrounding the junction with the *diencephalon* or middle part of the forebrain. These limbic lobe structures form part of the *rhinencephalon*, which developed relatively early in the process of evolution and was concerned largely with the sense of smell, though this is of minor importance in man. They include the *septal area*, the *cingulate gyrus*, the *hippocampus* and *amygdala* – which together with certain other structures, the *anterior thalamus* and the

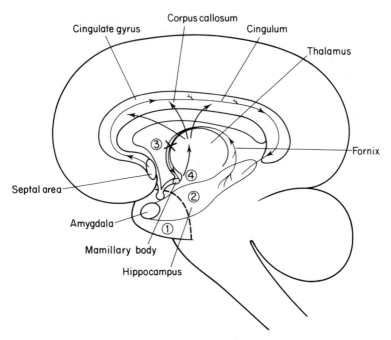

Fig.7.2   The limbic system and its role in remembering. Memory for recent events is impaired with damage to: (1) temporal lobes (Klüver–Bucy syndrome); (2) hippocampi; (3) fornix; (4) mamillary bodies

hypothalamus, comprise the 'limbic system'. In 1937, Papez proposed that anatomical connections between most of these structures formed a circuit (which has come to be named after him) concerned with the experience of emotion, and we shall consider this aspect in the next chapter. About this time, however, a series of experiments involving the removal, in monkeys, of the temporal lobes (containing the amygdala and anterior hippocampus) were performed by Klüver and Bucy (1939) which pointed to these structures being also concerned with memory. Later animal experiments identified damage to the hippocampus as being responsible for the disturbance of recent memory, and this is supported by clinical evidence in cases of bilateral hippocampal damage or surgical removal in man. The hippocampus is connected to the *mamillary bodies* (part of the hypothalamus) by the *fornix* and section of these fibres also results in a failure of memory for recent events. This does not mean that information is actually stored in these structures but that they are probably concerned with the laying down of such memories in other parts of the brain, and possibly also with their retrieval.

Where then, are these memories stored? Just as Lashley proposed equipotentiality of the cortex for learning (see Chapter 6), so there is no evidence to show that any particular memories are lost as a result of localized cerebral lesions; which suggests the likelihood of fairly widespread distribution in the cerebral cortex. There is, however, some interesting experimental work in animals using the so-called split-brain preparation (Sperry, 1964, 1974) in which the connecting fibres (chiefly the corpus callosum) between the two cerebral hemispheres are cut, which shows that each side of the brain can act very largely independently of the other in terms of both learning and remembering. Indeed, contradictory information can be acquired by the two hemispheres (with experimental training procedures taking advantage of the fact that sensory information to each hemishere comes from the opposite side of the body), so that the same stimulus may produce a positive or negative response depending on which hemisphere is perceiving it. There is also some evidence from studies of patients with neurological damage for the existence of separate STMs for verbal and visual information in the left and right hemispheres respectively – a correspondence perhaps with the working memory subsystems referred to earlier.

Perhaps the most intriguing question, and certainly one which has attracted much attention, is the form in which information is stored. All activity within the central nervous system depends upon the conduction of electrical nerve impulses along nerve fibres and chemical transmission from one nerve cell to another at points of close contact known as *synapses*. If a mental event such as the conscious awareness of some external happening is represented at the physiological level by nerve impulses passing along certain neuronal pathways or circuits, then later recall of that event may depend upon activation of the same or similar circuits.

Applying such a concept Hebb (1949) proposed a two-stage physiological theory of memory which corresponds closely with the dichotomous psycho-logical model of short- and long-term memory that we have already considered. STM of a stimulus was held to be due to a continuance of the resultant neuronal activity in a circulatory self-stimulating fashion – *reverberatory activity* (the *activity trace*) – which if it persisted long enough would result in permanent facilitation (a lowered threshold of excitation) of the synapses involved through *structural changes (structural trace)*, so that the same activity could be easily evoked on later occasions as recall of an LTM. The activity trace would theo-retically be relatively unstable and liable to interference compared with the structural trace, and there is some supporting experimental evidence for this. Thus various procedures which may be assumed to interfere with electrical activity within the brain, such as the passage of an electric current, anoxia or hypothermia, all produce impairment of recent learning while previously learned behaviour is retained. The supposed structural changes producing alteration in synaptic transmission in LTM are likely to be biochemical and probably involve continuing protein synthesis in the postsynaptic membranes.

Clinical aspects

Various disorders of memory are found in clinical practice, some of which have already been touched on because of their theoretical significance. Inability to recall events that have occurred within an individual's waking experience is referred to as *amnesia*. A distinction is made between *retrograde* amnesia and *anterograde* amnesia, which refer respectively to loss of memory for events before and after a particular incident such as a head injury. During recovery from such an injury, involving loss of consciousness or 'concussion', there may be for a time, even if the patient appears to be conscious and aware of his surroundings, an inability to register, or at least retain, current events so that there is subsequently an amnesia for that period – an anterograde amnesia.

Depending on the severity of the head injury, there may also be a loss of memory, of greater or lesser extent, for events preceding the trauma – a retrograde amnesia. During the process of recovery there is usually a progressive return of memories, starting with the oldest and working forwards to the more recent past. It appears that recall of these more recently past events is more vulnerable to disruption that that of more distant times. Even after complete recovery there may be a persistent retrograde amnesia for events during a short period just before the injury, and this is assumed to be due to interference at the time with the passage of these memories into long-term storage.

Similar, though less severe and fortunately reversible, effects may be seen in psychiatric patients given the treatment (usually for depression) known as *electroconvulsive therapy* or *ECT*. In this, an electric current is passed between two electrodes applied to the head of the anaesthetized subject in order to induce an electrical discharge of the brain of the same type that occurs spontaneously in an epileptic fit (though with ECT the associated convulsive movements are usually prevented or at least modified by the use of a muscle relaxant drug). The purpose of the treatment is not, as is sometimes supposed, to produce an impairment of memory – which is in fact an unwanted side-effect. Indeed it has been found in recent years that it can be largely prevented by a modification of the technique in which the electric current is passed through only one side of the head and, therefore, one cerebral hemisphere – provided this is on the non-dominant side (i.e. the right hemisphere in right-handed subjects). However, it is of some interest from the theoretical point of view because it confirms the experimental work using electric shock in other animals.

Probably the commonest memory defect met with in clinical practice is that associated with chronic, usually irreversible, organic brain disease or *dementia*. It is combined with other cognitive defects of learning and reasoning and with deterioration of personality, and is most frequently due to the degenerative changes of the brain that occur in a proportion of the elderly – senile dementia. Again it is striking that it is the memories for recent happenings that are the first to be lost while those for events in childhood continue to be recalled with great vividness.

A rarer form of memory impairment, to which we have already referred, found usually in alcoholics and due to deficiency of thiamine or vitamin B₁ was described in 1887 by a Russian physician, S.S. Korsakoff, and is named after him. The dominant feature of *Korsakoff's psychosis* is defective ability to acquire new information, so that the patient has no memory for anything that has occurred since the onset of the condition – a complete anterograde amnesia – but may have excellent recall of everything he had learned prior to this. Pathological changes are found in the medial thalamus and mamillary bodies.

Finally, we come to loss of memory which is not due to any organic disease – so-called *hysterical* amnesia. The patient may claim that he has no recollection of his past life nor even perhaps any knowledge of his identity – yet, paradoxically, he is able to perform various tasks and skills based on previous learning. Such a state of affairs would not occur with organic disease and, in fact, like all hysterical symptoms, it represents the patient's ideas of what amnesia is like. This is not to say that he is deliberately feigning illness – which would be malingering – rather is it an involuntary avoidance of all remembering which may afford an escape from some unpleasant or frightening situation; a pathological exaggeration of the kind of motivated forgetting which we all experience when we forget something we do not really want to do (e.g. to attend a lecture – or to give one!).

Further reading

Baddeley, A.D. (1976) *The Psychology of Memory*. London: Harper & Row.
Gregg, V. (1975) *Human Memory* (Essential Psychology Series). London: Methuen.
Lindsay, P.H. and Norman, D.A. (1977) *Human Information Processing*, 2nd ed. London: Academic Press.
Loftus, G.R. and Loftus, E.F. (1976) *Human Memory: the Processing of Information*. London: Wiley.

8
Cognitive processes
IV – Thinking

Thinking, the last of the cognitive processes to be considered, is certainly the most difficult to define and to study. For centuries before the advent of psychology as a scientific discipline it was a major concern of philosophers. Aristotle regarded it as the defining characteristic of man and it is clearly of central importance to an understanding of man and his nature. Indeed the French philosopher, René Descartes, starting from a position of universal doubt, held thinking to be the one activity which was of such self-evidence as to be beyond question and which provided confirmation of his existence – 'Cogito, ergo sum' (I think, therefore I am).

What, though, do we understand by 'thinking'? Consider some of the everyday uses of the term: I was trying to think of the name . . . I thought it was wrong of him . . . I think it is a matter of fate . . . I'm thinking whether I should go . . . I think it is going to rain . . . I'm thinking how to solve number four across . . . I must think of a title for this book. Although there are obvious differences of meaning – concerned with remembrance, judgement, belief, decision, expectation, solution to a problem, creativity, etc. – what seems to be common to all is the notion of some kind of ongoing mental activity with internal representation of the outside world of which the subject is aware but which is unobservable by another person. It may or may not have been induced by an external stimulus and it may or may not result in some overt action on the part of the thinker. Since the process itself is entirely subjective much of its study has depended upon introspection and verbal report by the subject. This was the traditional approach of the philosophers and, later, of the early psychologists, but we shall see that it has also been possible using experimental techniques to draw inferences about thinking from behavioural observations.

We have so far spoken as if thinking is a cognitive process restricted, as Aristotle suggested, to the human species, but is this assumption justified? Do other animals think? Here we come again to a question of definition, but if we consider thinking to involve internal representation of outside events, we may infer its presence wherever a correct behavioural response is made in the absence at the time of relevant cues in the environment. Thus an animal may be able to carry out a *delayed response* when it has been prevented from responding immediately – implying some internal representation of the earlier, but no longer present, stimulus during the interval. Even more strikingly, some animals may be taught a *delayed alternation* task involving a sequence of right and left turns at the same T junction in a maze (e.g. RLRL or RR LL RR LL), which again implies that they are capable of an internal representation of the sequence.

We may say, then, that thinking involves the manipulation of internal or covert representations of external and overt events or behaviour, but that in man this ability is greatly enhanced because of the existence of language. Language developed as a means of communication, but like any other external behaviour it may be represented internally, and much human thinking involves a kind of internal speech. Indeed a great deal of attention has been directed to the relationship between language and thought, but there are also many examples of non-linguistic thought as when a composer 'hears' in his mind music that he is creating or an artist 'sees' a painting he will put on to canvas. These are, of course, only instances of the more general phenomenon of *mental imagery* – the ability, which varies between individuals, to experience 'internally' something resembling but not identical with a percept; visual, auditory, olfactory, etc. These mental images may be memories of previous events, scenes, etc., or apparently original as, for example, in the case of some creative artists. The ability to experience vivid and detailed images which are then projected into the environment and perceived as if external is known as *eidetic imagery* and is relatively common in children but rare in adults. It may also be noted that images may occur spontaneously in some situations, while on other occasions they may result from a conscious effort on the part of the individual. These may be referred to as *autonomous* and *controlled* imagery respectively. This difference may be extended to all thinking so that a distinction is made between what may be described as purposive and fantasy thinking – the difference depending essentially on the degree of control exercised by the thinker.

Purposive and fantasy thinking

In purposive thinking a close control is exercised over the thought process, so that it is directed along a particular path towards a goal such as the solution to a problem. Fantasy thinking, on the other hand, occurs in situations when such conscious control or direction is relaxed and thoughts are allowed to come apparently spontaneously as in *day-dreaming*. We may also note that there is a difference between these two modes of thinking in terms of their relation to reality, and McKellar (1957) has described an approximately equivalent dichotomy between what he calls *reality adjusted* or *R-thinking* and *autistic* or *A-thinking* respectively. R-thinking is logical, rational, takes account of external reality and, clearly, is involved in reasoning and problem-solving. A-thinking, in contrast, is 'primitive', non-logical in its association of ideas and is not subject to correction by reference to reality. It depends primarily on the use of images rather than language, and while some autistic thinking may occur in day-dreaming, it is found most typically in dreams at night (see Chapter 4) and, possibly, in the thinking of some psychotic patients.

McKellar has also suggested, however, that A-thinking may usefully interact with R-thinking in some situations. Thus both scientific advance as well as artistic creation may result from spontaneous A-thinking, providing an original idea which is then subjected to critical evaluation and development through the process of R-thinking. One of the best examples of such a sequence of events was the discovery by the chemist Kekulé of the molecular structure of benzene. Having been unable to solve the problem and while in a half-awake state, Kekulé had an image of a snake swallowing its own tail, thus forming a circle, which enabled him to see that the carbon atoms could be linked in such a ring structure. The rest of the night was spent in working out the consequences of the idea, i.e. in purposive or R-thinking. There is much anecdotal evidence of similar contributions to the solution of problems from unconscious imagery occurring in dreams or hypnagogic (half-awake) states, but whether A and R forms of thinking should be regarded as distinct and separate or rather as representing differences of degree of conscious control and reality testing is as yet uncertain.

Convergent and divergent thinking

Another dichotomy between two forms of purposive thinking was suggested by Guilford (1956) and later developed by Hudson (1966). *Convergent* thinking applies to problem-solving which involves a focussing on to the one and only correct answer – the sort of problem that has commonly been used in conventional tests of intelligence (e.g. 'fat is to thin as tall is to . . .?'). *Divergent* thinking requires the production of as many answers as possible (e.g. 'how many uses can you think of for a flower pot?') and has been considered to be important in relation to creativity. It has also been suggested that ability in convergent and divergent thinking is a personality characteristic distinguishing between the 'scientist' and the 'artist' respectively, and we shall return to this later when we consider individual differences of intelligence and personality.

Problem-solving

Of the various processes to which the term thinking may be applied, the one that has probably been most studied by psychologists is problem-solving – in both humans and other animals. Solving a problem implies that the organism is faced with a task the solution to which is not immediately apparent, but which it is able to solve after an interval during which the problem-solving activity including thinking or reasoning has occurred. In other words, problem-solving involves the acquisition of an appropriate response to a novel situation.

Gestalt and behaviourist views

To avoid the difficulties of the introspective method of studying the reasoning process, experimental psychologists have made direct observations of what the organism actually does when faced with a problem. Early work with animals reflected, just as we have seen in other areas, the different approaches of the learning theorist (behaviourist) and the Gestalt schools of psychology.

The American psychologist, Edward L. Thorndike (1874–1949), working largely with cats, used an experimental apparatus called a *puzzle box* from which the animal could escape by making a certain response (e.g. pulling a chain which released the door). Thorndike observed that a successful response would initially occur only by chance, but that the animal then gradually improved in the time it took to escape over a number of trials. He concluded that problem-solving occurred through a process of *trial and error* which we have already met as instrumental or operant conditioning. (Strictly speaking Thorndike measured time to solution of a problem described as 'instrumental' conditioning, while Skinner was concerned with rate of responding which he termed 'operant' conditioning; but the two processes are usually regarded as identical.)

The Gestalt view of problem-solving, as one would expect, is a more holistic one. Instead of a solution proceeding gradually by small steps as proposed by Thorndike, the Gestalt school considered that it is either reached or it is not. Furthermore, when it does come, it is sudden through the organism having seen the problem as a whole as well as elements within it, resulting in *insight* into its nature. Support for this viewpoint came from a famous series of experiments by Köhler (1925) working primarily with apes. Probably the best known of these involved a chimpanzee in a cage, with a banana outside which could only be reached with the aid of a long stick, which in turn was outside the cage at the other end. Inside was a smaller stick with which the larger could be pulled into the cage. After a certain amount of what could be regarded as trial and error behaviour, there might be a pause in activity, after which the correct solution to the problem appeared to be discovered quite suddenly. In man the abrupt development of insight into a problem is sometimes spoken of, for obvious reasons, as an 'aha' experience. The important point, of course, is that such insight, once present, cuts out any further trial and error behaviour.

It is doubtful, however, whether such a clear-cut distinction can be drawn between the two forms of problem-solving, and it may be that to a large extent the supporting evidence for each reflects differences between the animal species used (i.e. non-primate versus primate) and the experimental situation in which they were placed (i.e. possible solution visible or not visible to the animal).

When we turn to problem-solving in man we find, as would be expected, that studies have employed much more complicated tasks. Nevertheless, the same dichotomy can be distinguished between the behaviourist and the Gestalt approaches, the former placing emphasis on previous training and the latter on perceptual reorganization leading to insight. Again, however, the distinction may be more apparent than real, resulting from different interpretations of essentially the same process according to the particular orientation of the experimenter. Alternatively, the appropriateness of the two explanations may depend on differences in the nature of the problems themselves.

A proponent of the Gestalt view, Duncker (1945) speaks of problem-solving as involving a change in the 'psychological structure of the situation as a whole or of certain significant parts'. In one of his most crucial experiments which happens also to be a clinical interest, he gave the following problem to subjects. 'If a human being has a stomach tumour and surgical operation proves impracticable, how can the tumour be destroyed by ray treatment: the difficulty is that the rays destroy healthy tissue as well as diseased tissue and the tumour is completely surrounded by healthy tissue.' This is, in fact, a genuine problem which has been solved in practice by rotating the source of a beam of X-rays round the patient with the tumour at the centre where it receives the maximum intensity with the intervening tissues exposed to the radiation only intermittently – once in each rotation. However, the interest of Duncker's experiment lay in the way subjects attempted to reach a solution to the problem. Several unacceptable solutions were usually suggested before the correct one (which at the time was considered to be the use of a number of weak rays from different directions to converge at the site of the tumour). These incorrect solutions were not, however, inappropriate; they were only impracticable for one reason or another (e.g. sending the rays down the oesophagus, or making the healthy tissues insensitive to the rays by an injection). The first of these examples is only one of several proposed *functional solutions* within the *general range* concerned with avoiding contact between the rays and healthy tissue – another would be the removal of healthy tissue in the path of the rays. Similarly, an alternative functional solution within the general range aimed at desensitizing healthy tissue, might be to immunize it by repeated exposure to weak rays. The 'correct' solution falls within the third general range aimed at lowering the intensity of the rays on their way through the healthy tissue. From this and other experiments on problem-solving, Duncker concluded that most solutions are achieved through the application of previous experience to the current situation but by means of 'cognitive–perceptual responses'. The subject responds to his total perception of the problem and, after several reformulations, reaches a solution through a particular reorganization of the 'psychological field'.

A behaviourist interpretation of the same data by Maltzman (1955) proposes that any stimulus, in this case the problem, evokes a range of possible responses with different strengths – a *habit-family hierarchy*. A complex problem may include several hierarchies and solution involves the gradual elimination, by lack of reinforcement, of the more dominant but incorrect responses of a hierarchy until either a correct response is produced or, following extinction of the whole hierarchy, a new one becomes dominant.

However, if reinforcement plays a significant part, it is perhaps surprising that a solution once seen is usually immediately remembered for subsequent application, and indeed this seems more consistent with the Gestalt concept of insight through a restructuring of the problem. Yet with some problems – such as the familiar metal puzzles where two or more parts have to be separated – full insight often requires several successful solutions, so that it appears that both the behaviourist and the Gestalt explanations may be applicable in different situations.

Set, einstellung or functional fixedness

So far we have spoken of problem-solving in terms of a final correct solution, but a common observation is that people sometimes persist in making a particular response though it is incorrect and may even be inappropriate. This phenomenon, which Duncker called *functional fixedness*, was well illustrated by one of his experiments in which subjects were asked to fix three small candles to a door. As well as the candles, they were provided with several other objects including some drawing pins and three boxes of roughly the size of a match box. The solution was to use the boxes as platforms for the candles after fixing them to the door with the drawing pins; but subjects who had been given the boxes filled with matches, drawing pins and candles had difficulty visualizing them as having any other use than as containers, in contrast to subjects for whom the boxes had been empty.

Another well-known experiment performed by Luchins (1942) demonstrated a similar inappropriateness of behaviour due to the induction of what he called a *set* or *einstellung*. Subjects were set a problem in which a given volume of water was to be obtained using three jars of known volume. For example, given jars of 127, 21 and 3 pints capacity, obtain 100 pints. The solution is to first fill the 127-pint jar and from this to fill the 21-pint jar once and the 3-pint jar twice, i.e. $127 - 21 - (2 \times 3)$. The subjects were then given further examples of the same problem with different values but where the same principle of using all three jars was required, e.g. 24 pints from jars of 126, 76 and 26 pints; $126 - 76 - 26$. Finally some problems were introduced which could be solved more simply by using only two of the jars, e.g. 18 pints from jars of 39, 15 and 3 pints; $39 - 15$

– (2 × 3) but more simply 15 + 3. Subjects were less likely to realize the simpler solution than a control group who had been exposed to problems the solution to some of which required three and to others two jars. In other words, the experimental group had acquired a 'set' for solving the problem using three rather than two jars. The tendency to 'see' how to solve the problem in one way only is, of course, comparable with the concept of perceptual and learning sets discussed earlier.

Concept formation

We have considered thinking as involving the internal representation of external events, but it is evident that we generally neither respond behaviourally to, nor manipulate within our minds, each and every event as if it were unique, but usually as belonging to one or more classes of events. This classification or categorization of events is of great importance in enabling the individual to adjust to the environment, associated as it is with the formation of *concepts* which are learned responses to classes of events. Thus we are aware of a class of animals which we call 'dogs', together with a concept which includes the name itself (i.e. a learned *symbol* which represents the class) and various approach or avoidance responses towards any member of the class. Our concept will depend on our past experience – what we have been told about dogs and our direct experience of them. Such a concept is relatively simple, but others may be more complex, often abstract and built up by a combination of several, more basic, concepts. We have already met with many instances of higher-order concepts in the behavioural sciences (e.g. consciousness, conditioning, perception).

It is clear that thinking, and especially problem-solving, depends very considerably on the use of concepts, and so the process of concept formation has received much attention with studies tending to fall into two main areas. The first of these is concerned with the way in which children acquire some of the basic concepts essential for thinking, and we shall return to this aspect later in relation to intellectual development.

The second area of study is the process by which an adult attains a new concept. Probably the best-known work of this type is that of Bruner, Goodnow and Austin (1956). These psychologists first defined a concept as a 'category', and they further made a distinction between two kinds of category: *identity* classes when a variety of different objects or events are recognized as being the 'same' (e.g. a boy and an adult man being the same person), and *equivalence* classes where different items are regarded as 'equivalent' for some purpose (e.g. hammers, chisels and screwdrivers are all 'tools'). Bruner and his colleagues then suggested that the process of allotting items to a particular class depended upon identifying their *attributes* and then basing the classification on their presence or absence. Attributes may be sensory features such as colour, shape, smell, etc., possessed by an object; but they may also be determined more arbitrarily, such as a blood pressure higher than a certain level. Classificatory concepts may also vary in the way that attributes are combined in their definition; *conjunctive* concepts are those requiring the joint possession by members of more than one attribute, e.g. a + b + c; *disjunctive* concepts require only one of a number of attributes, e.g. a or b or c; and *relational* concepts specify a particular relation between attributes, e.g. a larger than b.

Having, with these definitions, clarified the area of study, Bruner *et al.* set about examining how an individual attains a new concept. The experimental technique involved presenting the subject with an array of objects differing in certain attributes, from which he had to discover the required concept (chosen by the experimenter). An individual example was pointed out which possessed the correct attributes, after which the subject chose others and was told each time whether or not they fell into the right category.

In one experiment, 81 cards were presented representing all the possible combinations of four 'attributes', each of which had three 'values', i.e. shape (cross, square, circle), colour (green, red, black), number of figures (one, two, three) and number of borders (one, two, three). Each card then had one value for each attribute, e.g. two green crosses with one border or three black squares with two borders. Conjunctive concepts consisted of any set of particular values for up to three attributes, e.g. 'circles' (27 positive examples), red squares (9 positive examples), 3 crosses with 2 borders (3 positive examples).

From these and other experiments it was possible to discover the different *strategies* or *cognitive styles* used by the subjects and which reflected the reasoning processes involved. A number of 'ideal' strategies were described, of which two may be contrasted in terms of their effectiveness in discovering conjunctive concepts. A wasteful strategy called *successive scanning* consisted of formulating a hypothesis about the concept based on part of the attributes of the initial instance given by the experimenter, and then trying to confirm this by looking for more positive examples. Thus, if the instance given were 'two black squares with one border', the subject might start with the hypothesis that the concept is 'two squares' of which there would be nine instances. If the correct concept were 'black squares', a negative instance would be met with in a short while, e.g. 'two red squares' and the subject would have to start again with a new hypothesis. The important point is that confirmation of the hypothesis depends on positive instances and the number of tests required is unpredictable, with many redundant and inconsistent guesses. The much more economical strategy of *conservative focussing* starts with the hypothesis that the initial instance is the whole concept and then depends on finding negative instances by varying the values of each attribute in turn. With the 81-card experiment just described, for example, the correct concept can always be identified in four trials. Let us see how this can be done using the above example, i.e. given a card with two black squares with one border. Four cards are chosen in turn, for example:

(1) *3* black squares with 1 border – positive, therefore 'number' of figures irrelevant.
(2) 2 *red* squares with 1 border – negative, therefore 'black' is part of the concept.
(3) 2 black *circles* with 1 border – negative, therefore 'square' is part of the concept.
(4) 2 black squares with 2 borders – positive, therefore 'number' of borders is irrelevant. 'Black squares' must, therefore, be the required concept.

There are obvious similarities here with the importance of refutation of scientific hypotheses by negative evidence to which we referred in Chapter 1.

Thinking as information processing

Just as, in relation to other cognitive functions such as remembering, we have seen that modern developments in communications engineering and computer technology have led to new ideas about the processes involved, so attempts have been made to view thinking as a form of information processing and to simulate it by the use of computers. This has involved writing programmes for both concept formation (e.g. Hunt, 1962) and problem-solving (e.g. Newell and Simon, 1963). The performance of the computer may then be compared with that of the human individual in terms of the sequence of operations carried out. Such comparisons have generally shown quite encouraging similarities between the simulated and the 'genuine' thinking, and despite the obvious danger of equating the two processes it seems likely that the technique will prove fruitful in this area of research.

Neurological basis of thinking

In view of its complexity and dependence on other cognitive functions, it is perhaps not surprising that little is known about the neurophysiological aspects of thinking, and evidence has come mainly from clinical studies of patients with brain lesions. Loss of linguistic ability or *aphasia* is known to be associated with damage to relatively specific areas of the cerebral cortex, but this has largely been of concern to neurologists – indeed Freud in his earlier career as a neurologist published an important monograph on the subject. Since, in man, thinking and language are so intimately related it is obviously a matter of some interest whether the former is affected by impairment of the latter. The difficulty, of course, is that the aphasic patient is seldom able to communicate adequately for this purpose, though there is anecdotal evidence from patients who have recovered from a period of aphasia that they were able to think clearly during the episode.

The Russian psychologist, A.R. Luria, who, on the basis of studies of children, has regarded the internalization of speech as the major factor in the development of thinking, has also shown (1973) that patients with lesions of the frontal lobes may suffer from loss of speech control as well as more general disorganization of behaviour, and presumably of the thinking process underlying it. Milner (1963) has also found that frontal lobe patients show impairment on a card-sorting task in which cards can be categorized in terms of colour, form or number, the correct sorting principle being learned by the subject from the tester's confirmation or otherwise of each choice. If the principle is changed (e.g. from form to colour), the patients tend to persist in sorting according to the original principle – a so-called *perseveration* of behaviour.

There are, however, other disturbances associated with frontal lobe damage, including a motivational deficit, so that the suggested association of this part of the brain with the process of thinking can only be regarded as tentative.

Clinical aspects

Thinking in medicine

Before we consider some abnormalities of thinking which are met with in clinical practice, it may be worth taking a brief look at the nature and place of thinking in medicine. Indeed, Sir Frederic Bartlett chose this as the title of a paper which he delivered in 1953 to the British Postgraduate Medical Federation. Starting from his rather striking definition of thinking as 'the expansion of evidence in accord with the evidence, to fill up the inevitable gaps in evidence', Bartlett considered its application to the processes of diagnosis, experimentation and prognostication (forecasting the course and outcome of an illness). He concluded that it is unlikely that there is anything peculiar to medical thinking (i.e. that renders it unique), but he emphasized the importance when making clinical observations of the identification of similarities together with a refusal to neglect differences. He also advocated, as had others before him, the cultivation of a wide and varied range of interests by the individual in order to promote original ideas. At the same time, Bartlett drew attention to the lack of experimental work on the processes of medical diagnosis and prognosis.

In recent years, however, the development of computer technology has again led to renewed interest in clinical decision-making and its logic (e.g. Card and Good, 1971). The process of diagnosis, prognosis and treatment may be represented in the form of a 'decision tree' – with the ends of the branches as diagnoses reached by taking decisions at the various forks based on elements of evidence or 'indicants', such as answers by the patient to a question, the presence of a physical sign on examination or the result of a laboratory test. It then becomes possible in some situations to programme a computer to carry out a diagnostic process and to compare its performance with that of clinicians (e.g. Taylor *et al.*, 1971). This is, of course, a similar procedure to that used in the experimental study of thinking by computer simulation, but it has been shown that clinicians themselves differ widely in their diagnostic behaviour. A further application has been the construction of computer programmes actually to aid diagnosis in specific clinical areas such as congenital heart disease and thyroid disease.

Disorders of thinking

It is customary in clinical medicine to make a distinction between the content and the form of a patient's thinking – between what is being thought about and the way in which the thinking is being pursued.

We have seen that the content of conscious awareness at any moment is derived from our perception of the outside world and our recollection of past experience – it is based on reality, and if we consciously fantasize an imaginary world, we are aware of its unreal nature. We have a similar appreciation of the sometimes bizarre and unreal content of our dreams at night which probably depend on what McKellar called A-type thinking and Freud described as 'primary-process' thinking (contrasted with R-type or 'secondary-process' thinking respectively). Such thinking is minimal in waking thought, but patients with certain psychiatric disorders may develop ideas or beliefs which are out of touch with everyday reality. These false beliefs or *delusions* may be held with firm conviction despite all the evidence against them (e.g. that the BBC is controlling the patient's thoughts and actions with radio waves or that all the suffering in the world is the direct consequence of his own, often grossly exaggerated, misdeeds).

While it may be that ideas of this sort are based on the same kind of thinking as occurs in early childhood and in dreams, there is really very little experimental evidence on the subject. There is, perhaps, an analogy with the scientist who, having formulated a hypothesis, may be unwilling to change it in the light of negative evidence. Wason and Johnson-Laird (1972), in a series of experiments on formal reasoning, found that in a task involving the discovery of a 'rule' for a sequence of numbers, normal subjects would often be reluctant to change their hypothesized rule in spite of conflicting evidence. It seems, in fact, that there is a general tendency towards the seeking of verification rather than falsification, and one possible explanation may lie in the likely under-valuation of denials in early learning – for the young child it is more important to know what something is than what it is not. So in the deluded patient, one may suppose that there is a selective attention to apparently confirmatory evidence and avoidance of contradictory evidence. The same phenomenon may certainly be seen in relation to strongly held prejudices, which perhaps only differ in degree from delusions.

If we turn to disorders of 'form' of thought, there are two psychiatric disorders in which the sequence of thoughts may be so disturbed as to make speech difficult, if not impossible, to understand (in the absence of any organic disease affecting speech itself). In the condition known as *mania* – which is essentially a prolonged disturbance of mood in the direction of elation – thinking may be greatly speeded up; and this, together with impaired concentration and increased distractibility, results in a rapid, ever-changing stream of thoughts described as *flight of ideas*. The connection between one idea and the next may be rather loose and based on casual association (e.g. similarity of sounds of words in rhyming, punning, etc.), but it is generally possible for the listener to make out the overall trend of ideas and to understand the associations between them.

In *schizophrenia*, however, a type of thought disorder may occur in which the connection between one thought and the next is inexplicable to the observer. For this reason the disorder is sometimes described as a *knight's move*, from the unusual nature of the moves of this piece in the game of chess. Again, this has been attributed to the intrusion of A-type or primary process thinking into waking consciousness, but experimental studies have claimed that it is due to an attention or memory deficit. A distinction has been made between thinking as expressed in language (as just described) and a disorder of thinking in terms of reasoning or problem-solving. A hypothesis advanced by Bannister (1963), and derived from the Personal Construct Theory of George Kelly to which we have already referred in Chapter 2, attributes the disorder to the fact that the schizophrenic is operating with a *loose construct system*, which in turn is due to what he calls *serial invalidation*. Briefly it is argued that if an individual's constructs (i.e. the way he evaluates objects and events) are repeatedly invalidated so that he has to keep changing them – for example, he sees his mother alternately as loving and hating, depending on her behaviour – then gradually the relationship between this and other constructs becomes weaker and the environment largely unpredictable, with consequent confusion of the thinking process. A test of this loosening of constructs based on the repertory grid technique (see Chapter 16) was derived by Bannister and Fransella (1967) as a diagnostic test for schizophrenic thought disorder, and this is used quite commonly in clinical practice. However, neither it nor Bannister's hypothesis have received much support from later experimental observations.

Further reading

Elstein, A.S., Shulman, L.S. and Sprafka, S.A. (1978) *Medical Problem Solving – an Analysis of Clinical Reasoning*. Cambridge: Harvard University Press.
Greene, J. (1975) *Thinking and Language* (Essential Psychology Series). London: Methuen.
Hudson, L. (1966) *Contrary Imaginations*. London: Methuen.

9
Motivation

Motivation and emotion

In the last chapter we considered how the organism – and man in particular – through the cognitive processes acquires information from the environment, thereby constructing an internal representation of the outside world and gaining an understanding of it which facilitates adaptation to environmental change. We have also seen that these processes – perception, learning, remembering and thinking – can often be studied experimentally in both man and other animals, and that useful analogies may sometimes be drawn with similar processes performed by electronic computers. It is commonly said that all this has to do with the 'how' of behaviour and experience, whereas in this chapter and the next we shall be concerned more with the 'why'; why do people behave and experience in the way that they do?

The distinction is, once again, a somewhat arbitrary one, but we may consider some other differences between the two areas of study. Whereas the cognitive processes are sometimes referred to as the 'higher mental' processes because of their greater development in man, it is generally assumed that our more basic drives and emotions are probably little different from those of other animal species. Their overt expression is, however, modified by the process of socialization and, perhaps as a consequence, emotional and motivational disturbances are common features in psychiatric disorders. Because of this there has been much clinical interest in these psychological processes, with the formulation of theories of their normal development and functioning based on observation of abnormal behaviour and experience. There is, of course, a well-established precedent for this in the contribution to the understanding of normal physiology from the study of pathological changes in organic disease; but it must be conceded that psychological theories originating in this way tend to be highly subjective and largely unsusceptible to experimental verification or refutation. At the same time, however, there are more objective aspects of motivation and emotion which are open to scientific study by, for example, experimental psychologists and neuro- and psycho-physiologists.

Finally, before we proceed to a consideration of the two processes separately, we should bear in mind that there are many important relationships between them so that neither can be fully examined in isolation from the other.

Motivation

The term *motivation* is applied to the process or processes which determine activity directed towards a goal. It implies that the organism is not simply a passive responder to external stimuli, but that behaviour may have at any one time a particular direction, and an intensity which is liable to vary between different occasions.

Everyday experience certainly confirms that human behaviour is guided and controlled by the individual with particular objectives in mind, but there is less certainty as to the extent to which the motivation for such 'goal directed' activity is fully conscious or at least partially influenced by unconscious factors, and how much of it is innate and how much learned from experience. What is clear, however, is that the occurrence of a particular behaviour may depend both on the internal state of the organism and on stimulation from the environment. Motivation is, in fact, determined by a variable combination of biological, psychological and social conditions. It is therefore an area of interest to a wide range of disciplines within the behavioural sciences, but here we shall be chiefly concerned with the psychological aspects.

There have been many approaches to this subject, reflecting the particular orientations of their proponents and the organisms they studied. In general, however, attention has been directed to three aspects: the nature of what has come to be called the underlying *drive* towards a particular behaviour, its purpose or *goal*, and the factors that *reinforce* its occurrence.

Instinct

Following *Charles Darwin's* (1809–82) recognition, and inclusion within his theory of evolution, of the importance of the behaviour of animal species for their survival, it became fashionable to look to man's ancestry for an explanation of his behaviour and to assume that he is born with a number of unlearned biological *instincts* to perceive and act in particular ways towards certain objects.

How many instincts there were and what happened to them during development was the subject of controversy. The American psychologist and later philosopher, *William James* (1842–1910), listed in 1890 a large number of transitory instincts such as sucking, biting, chewing and licking. Although present at birth, these were supposed to remain active for a short period only, by which time necessary learned habits had been formed. *William McDougall* (1871–1938), an English physician who later became a psychologist, in 1908 produced a list of seven human instincts each paired with its corresponding primary emotion (an example of the close association between motivation and emotion to which we have already referred). These were: flight–fear, repulsion–disgust, curiosity–wonder, pugnacity–anger, self-abasement–subjection, self-assertion–elation, and parental care–tenderness. McDougall added other instincts not associated with specific emotions: reproduction, gregariousness, acquisition and construction. There were many more of these early lists of instincts; but while they may be useful from a descriptive viewpoint, an obvious weakness of them as theories of behaviour is that they were largely tautological, since an instinct was defined by a piece of behaviour which in turn was attributed to the instinct.

In contrast to these multiple instinct theories, *Freud*, on the basis of his analysis of neurotic patients, attempted to derive all motivation from two basic 'instincts' arising from the *id*. Freud actually used for this purpose the word 'trieb', which was translated as 'instinct', and this has persisted though what he was describing is perhaps more comparable with the idea of 'drive' which we shall be considering shortly. Freud's concept included the notion of a supply of energy associated with the instinct which was 'discharged' with performance of the behaviour specific to it – the *aim*, and in relation to a particular *object*. Failure to find this object and to achieve the instinctual aim led to frustration, tension and 'pain' (in the sense of psychological distress rather than a physical sensation). Behaviour was thus, in accordance with the so-called *pleasure-principle*, directed to keeping instinctual tension at an optimum or minimal level.

In terms of behaviour reinforcement this is similar to the ancient doctrine of *hedonism*, which claims that human action is aimed at increasing pleasure and decreasing pain. At a primitive level this may be immediate and purely *sensory* (sexual stimulation, sweet taste, heat, cold, etc.), but *rational* hedonism assumes that the thinking individual will be prepared to defer immediate small pleasures for the sake of ultimately greater satisfaction; according to Freudian theory the pleasure-principle gives way to the *reality-principle*. When we consider the nature of the two instincts themselves, we find that Freud revised the theory several times. His final view was that they comprised a *life* instinct or *Eros* and a *death* instinct or *Thanatos* – the former concerned in part with self-preservation as well as with perpetuation of the species through sexual reproduction (the instinctual energy being known as *libido*), and the latter with a drive towards self-destruction and a return to the original inorganic state with its freedom from psychological tension. It is not surprising that such an inherently unbiological concept as a self-destructive instinct should have evoked much opposition, and whereas Freud himself saw outwardly directed aggression as being a means, brought about by the self-preservative instincts, of avoiding the danger of self-destruction from it, most analysts would contend rather that the drive is basically one of aggression which may at times become inwardly directed, as in suicidal behaviour. It is still, however, a concept of a primary drive towards aggression, in contrast to the alternative view which sees aggressive behaviour always as a response to frustration (we shall return to this question later). It tends also to be equated with destructiveness rather than with the more positive meaning of self-assertiveness and striving.

Although Freud's concept of motivation in terms of instinctual energies which behave as if obeying physical laws now seems old-fashioned, reflecting contemporary neurophysiological ideas, the hostility aroused at the time by his description of the importance of sex and aggression in human behaviour seems equally out of tune with our present-day tolerant attitudes towards sex and violence as, for example, displayed in the media.

In more recent years, the notion of instinct has been given a new impetus under the influence of *ethologists* such as Konrad Lorenz and Nikolaas Tinbergen, who study animal behaviour outside the laboratory and in a natural environment. Strictly speaking, ethology is concerned with instinctive or unlearned, relatively stereotyped, behaviour which tends to be specific to a particular animal species but without any preconception about such behaviour being due to instincts as such. In particular, ethologists have set out to discover what environmental cues are responsible for evoking instinctual behaviour. An *innate response* is said to be elicited by a *specific sign stimulus* through an *innate releasing mechanism*. Thus, to take an example from Tinbergen (1951), the (innate) fighting response of one stickleback towards another is actually elicited by the (specific sign) stimulus of the latter's red belly, and any small red object will produce the response. Similarly the more complicated sequence of male and female behavioural responses involved in stickleback mating is innately determined, with each movement of one of the pair acting as a stimulus for the response of the other, which in its turn provides a stimulus to the first, and so on.

Many examples of these, often quite complex, specific innate behaviours or *fixed motor patterns* have been studied in several animal species. It has been found that if such an activity is not carried out for some time the threshold for its releasing stimulus falls, so that it is more easily elicited and may even occur spontaneously. Furthermore, the animal begins to search actively for the stimulus – a form of activity described as *appetitive behaviour*. It seems that each individual instinctive behaviour pattern has its own 'drive' in addition to the more basic physiological drives such as those concerned with feeding, reproduction, etc.

We shall return to a further consideration of ethological concepts when we consider the process of development, but an obvious question is how much these instinctive behaviours of 'lower' animal species are relevant to human activity. Clearly, if present at all they are likely to be rapidly modified through the process of learning, and supporting evidence has therefore to be sought in the earliest stages of development. The best example is the response of the human baby to the sight of a face. In a series of experiments, Fantz (1961) showed that infants in the first few weeks of life paid more attention (fixated with their eyes) stimulus patterns resembling a human face. Such crude representation will also elicit a *smiling response*, and it may be that this has an instinctual unlearned basis. It has even been found (Bower, 1977) that newborn babies are, presumably innately, able to imitate the facial gestures of other people. However, Carpenter (1974) has shown that a 3-week-old infant can discriminate its mother's face from others, suggesting that learning must occur even at this early stage of development.

Physiological drives and their neurological basis

With the decline in interest in the idea of instincts, psychologists began in the 1920s to turn to the concept of homeostasis as formulated by the American physiologist, Walter B. Cannon (1932) and the notion of *drives* which impel the organism to satisfy an internal *need*. According to Cannon, regulating mechanisms exist to maintain the relative constancy of what Claude Bernard had called the 'internal environment' of the body – the level of temperature, blood gases, osmotic pressure of the body fluids, etc. Any significant departure from the normal limits was considered to stimulate specific local sense organs, which led to behaviour aimed at eliminating the unpleasant sensation. Thus contractions of an empty stomach associated with hunger would lead to eating, a dry throat with thirst to drinking, etc.

Later observations have shown the concept of local irritation to be an insufficient explanation for these so-called *biological* drives which, on the basis of electrical stimulation and ablation studies, are now believed to be controlled by inhibitory and excitatory regions within the *hypothalamus* (either as 'centres' or, more probably, particular nerve tracts). These in turn are subject to influences of various kinds, including the bodily sensations described by Cannon but also particularly to internal chemical and hormonal changes reflecting a disturbance of the internal environment. Thus a change in the chemical composition of the blood in a food-deprived animal will result in stimulation of an *excitatory* part of the hypothalamus controlling appetite, resulting in the 'food consummatory response' (eating!). Satisfaction of this particular need then causes activity of an *inhibitory* or *satiation* 'centre' in the hypothalamus, so reducing the level of drive and cessation of the response. It is possible that the *amygdala* (see Fig. 10.1) also plays a part in halting food consumption after a certain amount of activity and before the chemical changes from the digestion and absorption of the food have occurred (perhaps as a conditioned reaction to gastrointestinal sensations), since bilateral ablation of the amygdala in monkeys results in overeating or hyperphagia as part of the so-called Klüver-Bucy syndrome. A similar homeostatic mechanism is concerned with the state of hydration of the body tissues by controlling fluid output via the kidneys and intake through the thirst drive and drinking.

As well as these *self-preservative* drives designed to satisfy the basic physiological requirements of the individual, the 'need' to perpetuate the species is met by the *sexual* drive which is also controlled by the hypothalamus under the influence of sex hormones produced by the *gonads*. In some species the latter in turn are stimulated to cyclical activity by *pituitary* hormones, also controlled by the hypothalamus and triggered off by external seasonal influences such as a rise in temperature or increase in the length of day. In man such a cyclical effect is negligible and there is less dependence on sex hormones since removal of the testes or ovaries does not necessarily abolish sexual drive and behaviour. In any event, the occurrence of sexual activity itself is also dependent on the presence of the appropriate sexual stimuli – tactile, auditory, visual, olfactory, etc. (though in man this may be in imagination), and human sexual behaviour is, in addition, subject to considerable modification by learning during the process of development. Cessation of sexual activity after each performance may, like that, of eating, be brought about by action of the amygdala, since hypersexuality is also a feature of the Klüver–Bucy syndrome.

It is clear, then, that a proportion of behaviour is directly determined by these basic, innate, physiological drives – which are also sometimes called *primary* to distinguish them from learned or *secondary* drives which we shall be considering shortly. However, their more general significance for psychology lay in the realization that satisfaction of such drives could lead to the establishment of stimulus–response connections involved in learning, thus providing the answer to the 'why?' of this process. In the last chapter we considered the role of reward or positive reinforcement such as food in operant conditioning, and we can now see that this actually involves the satisfaction of a primary drive. In fact the American neobehaviourist, Clark L. Hull (1943), developed a complex theory of learning ultimately based on the principle that whenever a response to a stimulus (e.g. pressing a bar in a cage when a light is switched on) results in a reduction of a biological drive (e.g. reduction of hunger by food), the strength of that stimulus–response association is increased. Of course, as a behaviourist Hull was not concerned with the subjective experience, like hunger, associated with a drive, and indeed his conception of drive was solely as a *theoretical construct* – an *intervening variable* which would relate antecedent, independent variables (e.g. length of food deprivation) to dependent response variables (e.g. speed of feeding response).

The notion of reward and reinforcement again raises the concept of 'pleasure' – whether there is some kind of pleasant subjective experience which underlies the satisfaction of any drive – and here there is interesting neurophysiological evidence for the existence of so-called *pleasure centres*, originating from a chance discovery of two Canadian neuropsychologists. James Olds and Peter Milner (1954) found that rats would repeatedly operate a lever which resulted in their being electrically stimulated in certain parts of the brain – particularly the hypothalamus and neural pathways entering and leaving it. In fact subsequent work on a variety of animal species, including observations during neurosurgery in man, has shown that within the limbic system (see Fig. 10.1) there are some areas which are reinforcing and others which are 'aversive' – motivating the animal to terminate the electrical stimulation. It appears that here we may have a neurophysiological basis for the principle of hedonism which we considered earlier – behaviour being directed towards whatever will result in activity of the 'pleasure centres' (Campbell, 1973). However, this does not in itself explain why particular behaviours are 'pleasureable', so that we have still to identify the individual drives themselves.

Other primary or innate drives

As well as the biological drives of hunger, thirst and sex – which we have seen are largely determined by the internal physiological state of the organism – there are others which are also innate but which are primarily dependent on environmental circumstances.

One of these, the drive for *bodily contact*, is in some species of great importance in the development of the dependent relationship between the newborn animal and its mother on which its survival may depend. Thus Harlow (1959), as we saw in Chapter 6, showed that infant monkeys would display a 'clinging response' to a cloth-covered wire 'surrogate mother' if deprived of their real mothers.

Another set of drives is concerned with the active application of cognitive functions, and the members are for this reason sometimes described as *cognitive drives*. In this sense, we may also regard them as providing an essential distinction between the active living organism and the passive computer as information processing machines. Thus there is a *stimulus seeking* drive which seeks to maintain the level of general sensory stimulation within a certain range, as we discussed in Chapter 4 where we saw that not only over- but also under-stimulation is harmful to normal function.

In addition to this concern with keeping the whole cognitive apparatus functioning at an optimal level, there is evidence for the existence of an *exploratory* or *curiosity* drive, more directly related to the processing of information (Berlyne, 1966). Observation shows that animals of many species, including man, will tend to cease present activity and pay attention to any novel occurrence. Exploratory behaviour itself usually consists of a series of alternating approach and withdrawal responses towards any new object until it has become familiar (non-frightening). The assumption that the behaviour can be regarded as a manifestation of 'curiosity' depends, of course, on inference unless the subject is human and can describe his subjective state at the time. There is, however, experimental evidence that expression of the drive is rewarding in that the opportunity to explore can be used as a positive reinforcer in instrumental conditioning.

An allied *manipulative* drive has been described by Harlow and his co-workers (1956). Monkeys repeatedly solved a mechanical puzzle without any other apparent motive or reward (it is hardly necessary to point to similar problem-solving behaviour in man – crossword puzzles, mathematical problems, etc.). The manipulative behaviour does, however, increase in frequency and efficiency with age, so that it may provide its own reinforcement. Clearly, these cognitive drives assist the organism in acquiring information from the environment, which we have seen is essential for adaptive behaviour; but in man we may speculate that they play a part in stimulating creative activity in the sciences and the arts.

Fear and anger

Although *fear* is clearly an emotion it is characteristically associated with certain behaviours, notably withdrawal and avoidance. Since it can in some respects be regarded as a drive it is appropriate to give some consideration to it here. There is ethological evidence for the existence of innate fears in particular species, elicited by specific stimuli, and we have seen in the last chapter with the 'visual cliff' that the young of many species show fear, or at least avoidance, of heights. Intense stimulation of any sort also evokes a probably innate fear but, in general, learning plays an important part in the adult organism's fear responses.

This can occur in two ways. Firstly, the animal may learn what is safe in the environment, fear then being a response to the unfamiliar. A similar process occurs in animal species which early on become imprinted to safe stimuli such as the mother, but remain fearful thereafter of all other stimuli. Secondly, the animal may learn, through classical conditioning, a fear response to stimuli associated with an original painful situation. Thus the American psychologist, O.H. Mowrer (1950), who developed and expanded Hull's theory of learning, took the view that fear is generally a secondary learned drive which in turn can lead to the acquisition, through instrumental conditioning, of various avoidance behaviours which have proved effective in reducing the drive.

Just as fear is related to avoidance behaviour, so *aggressive* behaviour is, in man, usually associated with the emotion of *anger*. There has, however, been much controversy over the question of whether such behaviour is the result of a primary aggressive drive which exerts a relatively continual effect – a view which, as we have seen, was taken by Freud – or whether it is always due to frustration as proposed by Dollard and his co-workers (1939). Ethologists have described in many species (as we have already seen in the stickleback) aggression which is released by particular stimuli and which is concerned with predatory (food seeking) activity or territorial defence. In relation to the latter, however, the aggressive behaviour between members of the same species tends to be ritualized in such a way (with appeasement signals, submissive postures, etc.) that serious injury is generally avoided, while retaining the evolutionary advantage that it is the fittest who are able to breed. Lorenz (1966) has suggested that such intra-species innate competitive aggression also exists in man, and that an example of the ritualized form is to be found in sport; but in most other respects, and particularly because of the invention of destructive weapons, it is vastly more dangerous (Storr, 1968).

Against the idea of aggression as a spontaneous innate drive, Dollard and his co-workers produced evidence that such behaviour always occurred as a response to frustration and that its magnitude was related to the strength of the frustrated drive. Although aggression is normally directed towards the frustrating agent, it may be *displaced* on to some other object or person, including the self. This suggests that the act of aggression itself wherever directed may be consummatory or drive-reducing, and this is supported by the reduced tendency to aggression immediately afterwards. Whether or not the frustration–aggression hypothesis is a sufficient explanation for all aggressive behaviour seems, however, doubtful, and certainly frustration itself can result in reactions other than aggression – including *regression* to earlier patterns of behaviour.

What is certain, however, is that learning plays a significant part in determining the amount of aggressive behaviour displayed by an animal, and especially by man, and we shall return to this later when we consider development of personality in Chapter 13. All we need note here is, on the one hand, the obvious positive reinforcement which aggressive behaviour may receive from success in competing with other young children, and on the other hand, the punishment which it may also attract from parents and others who wish to reduce it.

The neurophysiological basis for these behaviours is clearly concerned also with the related emotions, fear and anger, and will be considered in Chapter 10.

Cognitive determinants of motivation

In recent years there has been a greater emphasis on the importance, in human motivation, of cognitive determinants even of the basic drives which we have so far been considering. Instead of the rather simple mechanistic stimulus–response approach of the behaviourist, a stimulus is seen rather as a source of information which the individual processes and then responds to in terms of its *meaning* to him. Thus even with food or water deprivation, the amount of hunger or thirst experienced by the subject depends in part on his appraisal of his need, and this may be artificially manipulated in an experimental setting. For example, subjects given no incentive to undergo a period of voluntary deprivation felt less hunger or thirst than control subjects given adequate compensation (Brehm, 1962). This is consistent with the *cognitive dissonance* theory of Festinger, which we shall be considering shortly since it reduces the amount of dissonance between the realization of having agreed to undertake an unpleasant task and the absence of reward for it.

Similar cognitive determinants have been demonstrated for fearful and aggressive behaviour. Lazarus (1966), using 'threatening' films viewed by subjects, has shown that the individual's reaction is dependent on his appraisal of the potential danger, and this can be reduced by introducing various psychological defence or coping mechanisms such as the suggestion that the people in the incident shown are actually actors. Mallick and McCandless (1966) showed that aggressive behaviour induced in subjects by having a 'stooge' frustrate their completion of a task was less if they were told that the frustrator was tired and upset than if no explanation was given.

Social drives

So far we have considered drives which are concerned with self-preservation, perpetuating the species and facilitating adaptation to the environment, and which, although modified by learning, are likely to be largely innately determined. Man, however, is also a 'social animal' who displays a number of social needs and attendant drives, many of which are acquired by learning during the process of development. There is less agreement, however, on a comprehensive list of such drives. The American psychologist, Henry A. Murray, described a large number of 'needs' or motives derived from studies of overt behaviour and fantasy, the latter revealed in his Thematic Apperception Test or TAT (1943) which we shall consider later in relation to individual differences or personality. Murray's list included such needs as autonomy, aggression, abasement, achievement, dominance, deference, affiliation, nurturance, succorance, play and many others too numerous to consider here.

More recently the British social psychologist, Michael Argyle (1972), has listed the following seven 'motivational sources of interpersonal behaviour'.

Non-social drives which can produce social interaction

These include the largely innate biological drives which we have already considered but the satisfaction of which may lead to cooperative or competitive behaviour. An obvious example is the acquired motivation for work which, through the money earned, indirectly enables the basic needs to be satisfied. Another important acquired drive is the need for achievement which manifests itself in many social situations.

Dependency

Beginning in infancy and childhood with the child's close and submissive relationship with its parents, and probably deriving in part from the innate need for bodily contact which we have already described, adults show varying dependency needs and these may be associated with the opposite need for dominance – sometimes on different occasions in the same individual with the so-called 'authoritarian personality'.

Affiliation

This is manifested by a need for intimacy, closeness and acceptance by others. Individuals with a high affiliative drive are strongly motivated to interact with other people, especially those similar to themselves.

Dominance

This is a need for power over, and recognition and admiration from, others. Ethological studies of monkeys have shown that dominance is established by displays of aggression, and most of the time a stable hierarchy is maintained in the group. A similar process occurs in children and, as we have seen, the rewards of such aggression and domination of the peer group are likely to be reinforcing.

Sex

In man sexual motivation may be seen in a social context as a social approach drive towards close social interaction, usually with attractive members of the opposite sex, but with great internal and external restraints on the overt expression of sexual activity itself.

Aggression

Although, in origin, an innate self-preservative drive, the display of aggression has great social significance and is much modified by learning. There are considerable variations in aggressiveness between individuals and between cultures, as we shall see later when we consider personality in more detail.

Self-esteem and ego-identity

This is associated with the need for approval from others and for a clear and consistent self-image. Obviously this will be related to the kind of evaluation of the individual made by parents and others during childhood, and will determine the way he sees himself. Again there are cultural differences in the importance attached to self-esteem and 'loss of face'.

Unconscious motivation

We have seen that motivation or the operation of a drive is present when behaviour is observed to be directed towards a goal. In man, of course, there is frequently conscious subjective awareness of the presence of such motivation, but this is not always so and some behaviour appears to be determined by motives of which the individual is quite unaware or *unconscious*. Their existence can, by definition, only be inferred from the behaviour itself such as some 'slips of the tongue', 'accidents', lapses of memory, etc.; but additional quite striking examples of unconsciously determined behaviour may be provided by the phenomenon of post-hypnotic suggestion. A suitable subject may be given a suggestion, while hypnotized, that he will later perform a particular piece of behaviour such as taking off his shoes at a given signal by the hypnotist, but he will have no recollection of being given this instruction. Subsequently, the action will be carried out but the subject will invent an explanation for it; in the example just given he might say that his feet were unbearably hot.

Motivation and performance

So far we have paid little attention to the question of the *strength* of a drive and its relationship to behaviour. It has for long been recognized that, just as too little motivation may be responsible for poor performance at a task, so too can extreme activation of a drive be disruptive. This leads to the notion of an optimum level of drive with its associated physiological *arousal*, which was first demonstrated experimentally in a number of animal species as early as 1908 by R.M. Yerkes and J.D. Dodson. The relationship between motivation/arousal and performance has come to be known as the Yerkes–Dodson law; it states that increasing activation or arousal has an energizing effect which at first increases performance but later leads to deterioration – the relationship being represented graphically in the form of an inverted U as in Fig. 9.1.

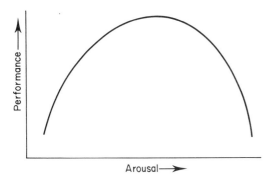

Fig.9.1 Graphical representation of the Yerkes–Dodson law

Conflict

The concept of conflict between opposing motives is one which is common to both of the otherwise contrasting psychodynamic and behaviourist schools. In Freudian theory the conflict is unconscious, occurs between the instinctual sexual and aggressive impulses of the id and the repressive control of the super ego, and is inferred from such material as the content of dreams or the associations to projective tests. The behaviourist approach views the conflict, at the simplest level, as being between pairs of drives which fall into one, or both, of two categories described as *approach* and *avoidance* and which in experimental animals can be manipulated in order to study the resultant behaviour. In fact such animal studies, especially those of the American psychologist Neal Miller, have provided a model which can be applied quite successfully to the human 'intra-psychic' conflicts of Freudian theory (intra-psychic meaning that the conflict arises not from external obstacles to a drive but 'within' from internal restraints acquired chiefly from punishment in the past).

Miller (1944) considered three possible kinds of conflict in an approach–avoidance context. Firstly there could be *approach–approach* conflict when there has to be a choice between two equally desirable but mutually exclusive goals. After some indecision, the animal would move towards one of the two goals, thereby providing greater motivation to approach it with increasing proximity, while motivation to approach the other goal would fall off with increasing distance. The second type of conflict was an *avoidance–avoidance* conflict typified by the expression 'between the devil and the deep blue sea'. Here the individual withdraws and avoids both goals if possible, but if this is impossible tends to vacillate back and forth between them.

The third type of situation, the *approach–avoidance* conflict, is the one most extensively studied experimentally by Miller. For example, rats were fed at a point indicated by a light at the end of a straight passage. The strength of the approach drive to the food at different distances from it could be measured by the amount of pull exerted on a harness worn by the rat. The relationship between drive and proximity to the goal, the *gradient of approach*, proved to be linear as shown in Fig. 9.2. A second experiment was performed with another group of rats given an electric shock on two occasions at the end of the same passage. This resulted in their running away when placed there again, despite not receiving a shock. The strength of the avoidance drive was measured by the

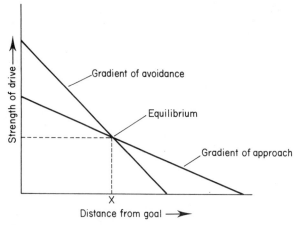

Fig.9.2   Approach–avoidance conflict. The experimental animal stops at the point X where the approach and avoidance drives are in equilibrium

same technique and found also to relate linearly to the distance from the point of shock. However, the *gradient of avoidance* was steeper than that for approach. Further experiments showed that the strength of the drives was also related to the intensity of the needs as increased by food deprivation and a higher-voltage electric shock. Finally, another group of rats was given both food and an electric shock at the end of the passage. If then placed at the entrance, they would approach a certain distance and then stop at a point predictable from the intersection of the approach and avoidance gradients, i.e. when the two drives were in equilibrium. Hesitant behaviour of the animal could also be observed and in general the conflict between the two responses was found to increase with the strength of the needs, thus confirming the Freudian theory that evidence of strong fear and avoidance of an object may also indicate a strong desire for it.

In human behaviour, however, motivation is often more complex than this. Any activity may involve a combination of several different drives with a choice of goals, the positive and negative values of which have to be weighed up against each other in reaching a decision – frequently a demanding cognitive task. Various strategies may be employed to deal with these difficult situations, including tossing a coin to decide between two courses, or denying the existence of some aspects of the problem in order to simplify the choice. Festinger (1957), to whom we have already referred, put forward a theory of *cognitive dissonance* to explain how the individual may resolve a conflict or dissonance between two cognitions or attitudes towards a particular behaviour or goal by minimizing one of them. Thus the cigarette smoker deals with the conflict between the wish to smoke and the knowledge of its harmful effects by belittling or denying the latter.

Clinical aspects

There are basically two ways in which knowledge of motivation may be of value from a clinical point of view. First, it can be of help in understanding the wide range of behaviours of patients in relation to their illness and treatment.

We shall return to this subject in the last chapter when we consider the psychological response of patients to their illness – but, to take one example, it is clear that the effect of a disabling disease is likely to differ according to the degree of dependency or dominance needs of the patient.

The other clinical aspect is concerned with problems which arise directly from abnormalities of drives or their goals. Thus the aggressive drive appears to be expressed to a pathological degree in some individuals, who may thereby be a danger to others – the so-called aggressive psychopath. Sexual deviations occur in which the aim and object of the sex drive depart to varying degrees from the statistically usual goal of heterosexual intercourse, sometimes with an admixture of aggression as in sado-masochism. Such 'abnormalities' are generally not clearly demarcated but represent, as so often in psychological disorders, an extreme position on a continuum from 'normal' behaviour – the decision as to normality or abnormality at intermediate points being somewhat arbitrary. Hypotheses as to the possible causes of these sexual deviations vary; but one explanation may be derived from the approach–avoidance model where, possibly owing to earlier experience, the 'normal' sexual object is both attractive and frightening, so that either an intermediate position between approach and avoidance is chosen, (e.g. voyeurism or indecent exposure) or a less aversive object (e.g. small girls instead of adult women).

In the rather more clearly defined condition of schizophrenia, a common feature – particularly in the later stages of a chronic illness – is a loss of motivation so that the patient becomes apathetic and generally inactive.

Other disorders of motivation are found in such conditions as alcohol and drug dependence and over-eating leading to obesity. In the latter instance, it is not uncommon to find that the excessive intake is due less to actual feelings of hunger than to eating becoming associated with needs other than the food itself – to reduce feelings of anxiety or unhappiness, for example. In general terms, motivation for apparently self-injurious behaviour has to be understood in terms of the needs that it satisfies or the rewards that it brings – though often in the short term. The child who repeatedly gets into trouble through 'misbehaviour' knowing full well that he will be punished may be motivated (though without being aware of it) by the fact that only by so doing will he receive more attention from others.

The degree of control exerted over the overt expression of basic drives such as sex and aggression may be weakened by organic disease affecting the functioning of the brain. The first signs of such disease may sometimes be the appearance of behaviour quite out of character for the individual. Such a change of personality may therefore be an important indication for clinical assessment for neurological disease.

Finally, the measurement of motivation is generally part of the assessment of personality since this is considerably influenced by the individual's pattern of drives – particularly social drives. We shall therefore return to this later in relation to personality.

Further reading

Cofer, C.N. and Appley, M.H. (1964) *Motivation: Theory and Research*. London: Wiley.
Hinde, R.A. (1974) *Biological Bases of Human Social Behaviour*. New York: McGraw Hill.
Evans, P. (1975) *Motivation* (Essential Psychology Series). London: Methuen.

10
Emotion

Emotions or *affects* provide a good example of the importance in psychology of considering both behaviour and experience. An emotion involves, on the one hand, a subjective awareness of a particular state of mind which has various qualities such as pleasantness or unpleasantness, and can be recognized and verbally labelled by the individual as fear, anger, unhappiness, etc.; and on the other hand, objective physiological changes (of heart rate, blood pressure, etc.) and expressive motor behaviour (running away, aggressiveness, etc.) which are observable and may be directly measureable. A full understanding of emotion, therefore, requires an appreciation of all three aspects – psychological, physiological and behavioural – and their relationship to each other.

The James–Lange theory of emotion

The first clear, coherent theory of emotion was put forward by William James, to whom we have already referred in connection with his list of innate instincts. It began with an article by James in 1884 entitled 'What is emotion?', but the following year a Danish anatomist and physician Carl Lange published, quite independently, some physiological data supporting a similar though not identical view, and thereafter it became known as the James–Lange theory.

The theory was conceived within a dualistic mind–body framework and was concerned with the relationship between the subjective awareness of an emotion and the accompanying physiological changes. Against the common sense view that the perception by the individual of some outside event leads to a subjective mental state of emotion, which then gives rise to the bodily changes, the theory reverses these last two processes so that it is the physical changes which follow the perception and it is the subjective awareness of these changes that constitutes the emotion; we feel sad because we cry, afraid because we run, etc.

Although, as we shall see, the theory has ultimately been discarded, it has proved to be heuristically of great value in terms of the amount of research it has generated. James himself based the theory on the results of introspection which, he claimed, showed that for any emotion nothing would be left if all bodily sensations were to be abstracted. Not everyone agreed with this on the basis of their own introspections, and later studies by Mandler and his co-workers (1958) have in any case shown marked differences between individuals in their ability to observe changes in their own physiological state.

However, it has been on more objective grounds that the theory has been challenged over the years, particularly by physiologists, promoting in the process much useful study of the physiological aspects of emotion. Starting with the English physiologist, Sir Charles Sherrington (1857–1952), and his studies of dogs (1906), and followed later by Cannon (1927) with similar findings in cats, it was demonstrated that animals could still display expressive emotional behaviour despite extensive severence of the sensory feedback from the viscera (body organs) and skeletal muscles by which they would have been aware of bodily changes. Of course, we cannot know whether such animals actually 'felt' any emotions, but evidence from clinical observations on human patients with spinal cord injuries and, therefore, a similar loss of sensory feedback has shown no apparent loss of emotional experience. Perhaps even more striking findings were obtained by Wynne and Solomon (1955), who showed that dogs deprived of their entire autonomic nervous system could still learn, though more slowly than normal, to avoid an electric shock and would retain previous avoidance learning – fear being, of course, the drive for this learning of avoidance behaviour.

We have seen, then, that one prediction of the James–Lange theory – namely that absence of awareness of the normal physiological changes accompanying emotion would abolish the emotion itself – is not supported by the evidence. A second prediction, the obverse of the above and again pointed out by Cannon, is that the artificial induction of physiological changes should result in the experience of emotion. This has been tested by the injection of adrenaline and noradrenaline (Wenger *et al.*, 1960); but despite the production of marked autonomic changes, subjects reported no feelings of emotion with either drug – once again failing to confirm the theory though, as we shall see later, such artificial autonomic arousal can enhance the emotional response to a particular situation.

A third consequence of the James–Lange theory to which Cannon drew attention, and which he believed was not supported by the evidence, is that different emotions should show different patterns of autonomic activity. This is an important question to which much attention has been directed, and we shall deal with it next as a separate issue; but here we can note that there is, in fact, some support for physiological differences between the two most studied emotions – fear and anger.

It appears that most of the evidence fails to support the James–Lange theory of emotion in its original form, but this is not to deny the importance of bodily changes as part of the total experience of emotion.

Patterns of autonomic response in emotion

It will be necessary at this point to refer briefly to the organization of the *autonomic* nervous system or ANS – so-called because it is not directly under voluntary control. Many internal or visceral organs (heart, stomach, colon, etc.) and glands (sweat, salivary, etc.) throughout the body are under the control of the ANS. The majority are innervated by each of the two divisions, the *sympathetic* and the *parasympathetic*, which tend to exert opposite effects. The ANS is in turn organized by the *hypothalamus* – the posterior part, near the mamillary bodies, being concerned with the sympathetic system and the anterior region with the parasympathetic. Much of our knowledge about the ANS came from the classical experiments of the Swiss physiologist, W.R. Hess (1954), who showed by electrical stimulation that the posterior hypothalamus–sympathetic system is concerned with an energizing state of alertness and arousal in support of defensive reactions such as fight or flight, and described as *ergotrophic* (autonomic changes including acceleration of the heart rate, rise of blood pressure, etc.); while the anterior hypothalamic–parasympathetic system, in contrast, is involved with vegetative events when the organism is at rest, such as digestion, and described as *trophotrophic* (with decrease of heart rate, fall in blood pressure and stimulation of activity of the alimentary tract).

Another difference between the two divisions is that sympathetic activity tends to be more general while the parasympathetic can have relatively localized effects. This is partly structural in origin; but it is also because sympathetic activation leads to secretion by the adrenal medulla, into the blood stream, of the hormones adrenaline and noradrenaline which have widespread though differing effects.

At any moment, however, there is a state of balance between the two systems, with one showing apparent dominance over the other as revealed by various autonomic measures such as heart rate, blood pressure, sweating (as measured by the galvanic skin response or GSR). Since several of these autonomic measures may be taken simultaneously they provide a 'pattern' of responses, and our concern here is with how these may relate to emotion. Before doing this, however, we shall consider more generally the question of patterns of autonomic activity in relation to a stimulus situation.

Response to novelty

Exposure of the organism to an unexpected or intense stimulus will lead to neurophysiological and behavioural changes described as 'arousal'. We referred to this in passing in Chapter 4 since, in man, they are associated with alteration of conscious awareness. However, Cannon (1932) drew attention to the autonomic changes, primarily sympathetic, which also occur in such circumstances and which he considered to be a preparation for, and to result in greater efficiency of, any required emergency action, i.e. fight or flight. According to Cannon, the response pattern was the same for either reaction – i.e. associated with both anger or fear – but we shall return to this question shortly. The full development of Cannon's *emergency reaction* generally depends upon an appraisal by the organism of the danger of the situation, but it may be preceded by faster responses to a novel stimulus. Thus the *startle reaction* is rapid in onset and lasts only a few seconds. The Russian, E.N. Sokolov (1960), has divided it into two types: the *orienting reaction* which results from a stimulus change (e.g. onset or offset) and diminishes rapidly with repetition of the stimulus (*habituation*); and the *defence reaction* which is a response to a stimulus of abnormal intensity and which increases with stimulus repetition.

Stimulus–response specificity and individual response stereotypy

There have been attempts to demonstrate particular patterns of autonomic activity associated with different stimulus situations – a relationship described as *stimulus–response specificity*. Thus R.C. Davis (1957), using a whole battery of autonomic indices – including psychogalvanic reflex, pulse rate and pulse pressure – as well as other physiological measures such as electromyogram (muscle activity) and respiratory rate, presented subjects with three stimuli: simple visual, cutaneous (pressure, warmth) and complex visual (e.g. pictures of a nude woman for male subjects). Definite differences were found between the responses evoked by the three stimuli.

Other studies (Lacey, 1950; Schnore, 1959) have established the principle of *individual response stereotypy* by demonstrating that individual subjects showed a consistent autonomic response pattern in different situations (e.g. a mental or physical task at different levels of motivation), while the patterns differed considerably between subjects. In fact it has been shown in studies of patients with high blood pressure (Engel and Bickford, 1961) that both forms of response specificity – stimulus and individual – can exist in the same person.

Response patterns in fear and anger

Attempts to differentiate autonomic response patterns associated with different emotions have generally chosen fear and anger for study. We can first refer to a classical series of observations by S.G. Wolf and H.G. Wolff (1943) on an experimental subject whose name 'Tom' has become part of the history of physiological psychology. Tom, an Irish American, had a fistula (or opening) into his stomach via the abdominal wall, through which he had had to feed himself since an accident as a child had damaged his oesophagus. Over a prolonged period during which Tom was employed in their research laboratory, Wolf and Wolff were able to make observation, through the fistula, of both the activity of the stomach and the appearance of its lining in relation to various situations in Tom's life, both natural and artificial. They were thus able to note that fear was regularly associated with a reduction in gastric activity and blood flow, while with anger stomach contractions and a red engorged stomach lining were seen.

Further evidence for such autonomic differentiation of fear and anger was provided by an ingenious study of Ax (1953), in which a state of fear was induced in subjects by Ax pretending that there was a danger of electric shock from a short-circuit in the physiological recording apparatus, and of anger by an assistant behaving in a provocative fashion accusing them of being uncooperative. Anger was found to have a greater effect than fear in raising the diastolic blood pressure, while the reverse was the case for increase of systolic blood pressure, pulse rate and skin conductance.

This pattern suggested that anger might be associated with greater secretion of noradrenaline and fear with adrenaline; but this has not been supported by studies of urinary excretions of those hormones in subjects watching fear or aggression-arousing films (e.g. Levi, 1965). Other evidence (e.g. Elmadjian *et al.*, 1957) has pointed to an association between noradrenaline and active coping with an emotionally arousing situation (e.g. a game of hockey), while adrenaline is higher in the passive spectator.

Cognitive determinants of emotion

Although it appears that there may be some differences in the patterns of autonomic response in different emotions, we have also seen that there is little evidence to support the James–Lange theory that it is awareness of these physiological changes that is actually responsible for the subjective experience of an emotion. In recent years an alternative *cognitive* approach has been proposed, rather in line with that which we discussed in relation to motivation. Thus according to one theory – which has been called *cognitive labelling* – the individual identifies and 'labels' his stirred-up state of physiological and psychological arousal in terms of the immediate situation which has precipitated it, and it is this which determines whether he is, for example, 'angry', 'fearful' or 'happy'.

Evidence for this *attribution* theory of emotion was provided by an experiment of Schachter and Singer (1962), in which subjects were first given an injection of adrenaline, supposedly to test the effect of a 'new drug', though without being aware of its true nature. Some were told correctly what effects to expect, others were deliberately misinformed and others were given no information at all. A fourth group were given a placebo instead. Subjects were then placed in a waiting room with another person who was actually a 'stooge' who attempted to induce an emotional reaction by acting either as angry and provocative or euphoric and friendly. On the basis of observed behaviour and self-ratings, greater appropriate emotion was felt and expressed by those subjects who had been artificially aroused with the adrenaline but misinformed or not informed of its effects, than those who were given placebo or, if given adrenaline, were informed correctly of its arousing effect. The results can be interpreted, therefore, as supporting the view that emotional experience is determined by both arousal and cognitive awareness of the cause of that arousal – though it must be said that not all attempts to replicate Schachter and Singer's findings have been successful.

The emotional effect of the subject's perception of his autonomic reactions has also been studied using false feedback (Valins, 1970), so that, for example, he is given the impression in a given situation that he is more or less aroused by providing false information about his heart rate. Results suggested that these beliefs by the subject, although untrue, were significant in determining the emotional response. Again replication has proved unsuccessful, and it has been suggested (Hastrup and Katkin, 1976) that self-perception of arousal is only important for some emotional experiences – termed primary – while others (secondary) are learned from previous experience of a primary emotion and are not so dependent.

Perhaps the most cognitive theory of emotion is that of Lazarus (1966) who, as we saw in Chapter 9, stressed the individual's cognitive appraisal of any situation (influenced by past experience and current availability of strategies for coping with threat) as the determinant of the emotional response, including its accompanying physiological changes.

Overall, then, we may conclude that the evidence suggests that cognitive appraisal of the external situation plays a primary role in the experience of emotion, with a variable contribution from perception of the internal physiological state.

Neurological basis of emotion

We have seen that the autonomic manifestations of emotion are under the control of the hypothalamus, though electrical stimulation in human patients has shown that it is not itself the seat of emotional experience. The hypothalamus in turn is linked with other forebrain structures comprising the limbic system, to which we have already referred in the last chapter in relation to memory. Fig. 10.1 shows the chief anatomical connections between these structures which, together with clinical experience and animal studies, led the neurologist, J.W. Papez (1937), to propose that they form a circuit, activity (possibility self-reverberatory) of which might underlie the experience of emotion. Shortly after this Klüver and Bucy (1939) performed their famous series of experiments to which we have also referred more than once, since their temporal lobectomized monkeys showed abnormalities of behaviour in several areas – the so-called Klüver-Bucy syndrome. The animals showed a remarkable change in eating habits, putting any movable object in their mouths; they displayed increased sexual activity – including copulation with sexually inappropriate objects; they seemed unable to recognize familiar objects; and they lost their fear of normally dangerous objects. These behavioural changes can be attributed to perceptual defects from loss of the temporal neocortex, recent memory impairment from damage to the hippocampus (as discussed in Chapter 7), and loss of the fear response from removal of the amygdala.

Studies of the amygdala itself show that both fear and rage-like reactions can be produced by ablation and stimulation of particular areas within it, and similar effects are found in relation to the anterior end of the cingulate gyrus. Damage to the septal area consistently produces an increase in aggressive behaviour, as does a lesion in the anterior hypothalamus; but the effects of both can be abolished by damage to the amygdala. It seems that there is, therefore, some kind of push–pull control over aggressive behaviour exerted by these three structures – the septal area, amygdala and anterior hypothalamus.

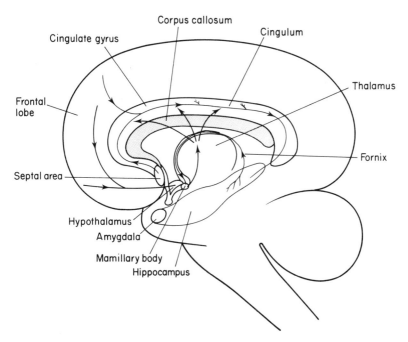

Fig.10.1 The limbic system and its role in emotion. Pathways shown include: (a) the Papez circuit which passes from the hippocampus, via the fornix to the mamillary body (part of the hypothalamus), thence via the mamillothalamic tract to the anterior thalamus, from which it returns via the thalamic radiation and the cingulum to the hippocampus; (b) the frontolimbic pathways from the frontal lobe to the hypothalamus and thus the limbic system as a whole. Pathways not shown exist between the amygdala and the hypothalamus and hippocampus. There are also connections between the limbic system and the reticular fromation (see Fig.4.2)

Electrical stimulation of some of these limbic structures in man has confirmed their involvement in emotion; stimulation of the cingulum region results in emotional responses while anxiety, aggression and autonomic effects are found with stimulation of the hypothalamus or amygdala.

The limbic system is itself under a higher control mechanism located in the frontal lobe, and exterpation of the under-surface of the frontal lobe in primates leads to docility and lack of fear.

The concept of arousal

We have used the term 'arousal' on more than one occasion with a meaning roughly equivalent to 'activation'. We should note here that it is now generally held (Routtenberg, 1968) that such arousal may arise through two neurophysiological systems: the reticular activating system which we considered in Chapter 4 as being responsible for *cortical arousal* brought about by sensory stimulation, and the limbic system which, as we have seen, is concerned with emotional and *autonomic arousal*. The two systems are, however, to a large extent interdependent through anatomical connections between the reticular formation and the hypothalamus. Thus, cortical arousal can result from both sensory stimulation and emotion, though the latter will also be associated with autonomic arousal.

Individual emotions

Just as with motives, there have been various classifications of the emotions. Watson, from observation of infant behaviour, concluded that there were three basic, innate emotions – fear, rage and love – from which all others were derived through the process of conditioning. We have already seen (in Chapter 9) that McDougall listed seven *primary* emotions, each paired with a corresponding 'instinct', which he distinguished from *complex* emotions (e.g. admiration, envy) and *sentiments* (e.g. love, hate, respect). Others have made a similar distinction, regarding the sentiments as habitual responses to an object involving a persistent disposition to respond in a particular way – either for or against. Freud, however, emphasized what had already been recognized before, that sentiments can be *ambivalent* – that we can have both positive and negative feelings towards the same person though we are not always fully aware of this.

There is, perhaps, less concern now with distinction between emotions and other feelings and all are often referred to as emotions. We shall not be able to consider many individual emotions in detail, but there are three which deserve special attention.

Fears and anxiety

We have already discussed the motivational aspect of these, the most commonly studied of the emotions. In general we may say that fears are normally aroused by situations of danger which threaten the individual, while anxiety arises from anticipation of future threat not actually present. Many fears, as we have already seen, are learned from experience, but there is evidence that they are ultimately derived from certain innate fears. Watson (1924) held that there are three innate stimuli for fear – loud noise, sudden loss of support and pain – from which all subsequent fear-producing stimuli are learned through association by classical conditioning.

This has proved, however, to be an over-simplification, and a more recent view (Gray, 1971) supposes that all fear stimuli can be subsumed under one of four principles: intensity, novelty, 'special evolutionary dangers', and stimuli arising from social interaction. *Intensity* of stimulation is fairly obvious and covers two of Watson's suggestions – pain and loud noise. *Novelty* has also been referred to already as a cortically and emotionally arousing stimulus, but it may also produce a fear response and Watson's 'loss of support' may include both intensity and novelty of stimulation. *Special evolutionary danger* refers to certain species-specific fears of stimuli which are characteristic of particular dangers to the species. Such fears as that of snakes displayed by both man and chimpanzee and the fear of the dark in man are likely to have been of evolutionary survival value. The last class of stimuli – those arising from *social interaction with con-specifics* (i.e. members of the same species) – are examples of the sign stimuli described by the ethologists, which we have already illustrated in relation to the stickleback behaviour with the male's red belly acting as a threatening stimulus to another male.

Another important observation by ethologists, well illustrated by Robert Hinde of Cambridge in a series of experiments on the so-called 'mobbing reaction' of the chaffinch to an owl, is that innate fear responses may not become evident until a particular age – dependent on the process of maturation and not learning. Evidence from humans suggests that the, probably innate, fear of snakes does not become manifest until a child is about four years old. Jersild and Holmes (1935), in a study of the relative frequencies of various fears in children of different ages, showed that while some declined, others increased with age; some may well have been due to maturation while others were probably learned. Fears present at birth but thereafter gradually decreasing included noise and agents of noise; strange objects, situations and persons; pain; falling and loss of support, high places, etc. Those that were minimal or absent at birth but gradually increased included animals; ridicule, robbers, dreams, death; dark, alone, imaginary creatures in the dark; threat or danger of harm, traffic, drowning, fire, gaol, etc; and signs of fears in others.

It is, of course, clear that in man many fears are learned through the process of classical conditioning, as we saw demonstrated in Chapter 6 when 'Little Albert' was conditioned to fear a rat and other furry objects. Even this, however, is evidently not quite as simple as it at first appears. The English psychologist, C.W. Valentine (1930), repeated a modified version of Watson's experiment on his own year-old daughter but was unable to induce in her a fear of a pair of opera glasses by sounding a loud whistle. He was successful, however, with a 'woolly caterpillar', which Valentine attributed to the presence of an already existing innate 'lurking fear in the background'.

Anger

Again, we have considered the important aggressive drive associated with this emotion which has otherwise received relatively less attention as a subjective state than has fear and anxiety. In keeping with the frustration–aggression hypothesis, McKellar (1949, 1950) found from his own introspective observations, and those of others, that one group of anger-provoking situations which he called 'need situations' involved a thwarting of the individual in his pursuit of various goals. The other source of anger lay in 'personality situations' in which he felt himself to be the subject of attack, injury or humiliation – an attack, in fact, on his personality or that which he valued and which thereby provoked him to a position of defence. McKellar further distinguished between the anger resulting from these two situations as respectively, warm-blooded anger of short duration directed to removing an obstacle, and cold-blooded hostility of longer duration with a tendency to malice and revenge. He also found that as far as the expression of anger was concerned, most of the subjects (who were adults in the London area) said and did nothing, though fantasy and imagery might occur; verbal expression of anger was rare and physical aggression was very rare indeed.

Mood variation

An important aspect of the emotional state of an individual is his position on a continuum of 'mood' from unhappiness to happiness, which is likely to vary within limits according to how he perceives his current situation. There has, however, in general been relatively little contribution from psychologists to the study of mood variation as a normal phenomenon, and this may in part be due to the difficulty of producing a recognizable equivalent in lower animals in contrast to fear and anger which can be evoked with comparative ease.

The relationship of depressed mood to depressive thinking has received much attention. Obviously a person who is feeling depressed is likely to have unhappy thoughts, but there could theoretically be a causal relationship in either direction – the mood causing the thoughts or vice versa. Generally speaking, most psychiatrists have considered the disturbance of mood to be of primary importance, but Beck (1967, 1974) proposed primacy of depressive thinking. In fact, there have been two influential theories suggesting that certain attitudes may actually predispose a person to becoming depressed. Beck himself claims that depressed people have a *negative cognitive set* in which they take an over-critical view of themselves, the world and the future – a so-called 'negative cognitive triad' – and that this arises from early traumatic experiences.

The other cognitive approach is the *learned helplessness hypothesis* of Seligman (1975), which considers (Miller *et al.*, 1975) that depression results from an underlying belief of the individual that he is unable to exert any control over the outcome of events – in technical terms he perceives a lack of contingency between his responses and the outcome and is likely to attribute this to personal failure. This in turn is believed to be a consequence of repeated failures and defeats in childhood – instead of the more positive sense of mastery following earlier successes.

Both of these theories have generated much research, leading to the development of 'cognitive' therapies (see also Chapter 16) aimed at changing the depressive individual's negative self-cognitions to give a greater degree of self-esteem and self-confidence associated with improved mood (Beck *et al.*, 1979). Comparison with drug treatment for depression has given encouraging results (Blackburn *et al.*, 1981) but not all experimental and clinical evidence has been positive.

Psychiatrists, on the other hand, are very much concerned with disturbances of mood to abnormal degrees – both to extreme elation or extreme depression – and there has been much research into their basis. Freud (1917) drew attention to the similarities between the condition of pathological depression, or *melancholia* as it was then called, and the state of *mourning* or *grief* which normally follows bereavement. In both, the depressed mood was held to follow loss of an *object* – in the latter case external (the deceased person), and in the former a hypothesized *internal object* (an internal representation or image of a significant person such as the mother, about whom the depressed person has had ambivalent feelings and which he imagines he has destroyed but cannot survive without). Again this is a hypothetical psychodynamic model, and attention nowadays has shifted to the possible biochemical basis of pathological depression which is often considered to arise *endogenously* or 'from within' (sometimes contrasted with those cases in which it is said to be *reactive* to external circumstances). In general, though, we may assume that normal depression of mood occurs in response to a loss – real or imaginary, objective or abstract (such as self-respect) – and that this may also play a part in many pathological depressions.

Clinical aspects

While it is clear that a wide range of emotions are experienced in normal everyday life, they may at times become extreme in intensity or inappropriate to the current situation, and they may then present as a psychiatric problem. Thus there may be fears or *phobias* of particular objects or situations (some relatively common, like a fear of enclosed spaces, others uncommon such as a fear of cats). We have already seen how such fears may be learned through the process of conditioning and how they may be treated by forms of behaviour therapy (see Chapter 6). These, of course, are based on the behaviourist view of irrational fears or anxiety as a learned phenomenon.

In psychoanalytic theory, anxiety is generally seen as arising in one of two ways. The commonest is known as *signal* anxiety and is regarded as an alerting mechanism which warns the conscious *ego* of an impending threat from the repressed instinctual forces of the *id* – a threat, that is, to gain expression or at least entry into consciousness against the control of the *super ego* – a conflict to which we have already referred. It is a signal to the ego to employ some form of defence against the threat, and we shall be considering the various so-called *defence-mechanisms* in Chapter 14. Anxiety may, therefore, also be said to arise from a failure of such defences. Less common is *primary* anxiety – which is evoked by separation from a necessary object (also, therefore, called *separation* anxiety) or by dissolution of the ego (by instinctual forces of the id) as occurs temporarily in a nightmare. Once again we must recognize that however much it may be claimed that these ideas are supported by psychoanalytic experience they are still essentially hypothetical and unsubstantiated by rigorous scientific evidence, though some experimental verification has been attempted and we have already referred to the approach–avoidance studies of Miller in relation to intra-psychic conflict. However, it may also be that in our present 'permissive' society, as compared with the restricted Viennese society of Freud's day, anxiety is likely to result less from 'internal', 'intra-psychic' threats of the type we have been considering than from external stresses from interpersonal conflict, difficulties in coping with a competitive society, and so forth.

It is possible to combine the behavioural and psychodynamic views in the sense that the latter may provide an explanation for the initial state of anxiety which tends to be lacking in behavioural accounts of the development of a phobia – apart, that is, from those with an obvious traumatic onset (such as a car travel phobia following a crash). Whether a phobia then responds to desensitization treatment may depend on how much it is by now just a learned 'habit' or how much there are still external or internal psychodynamic causes for continuing anxiety.

Another aspect of anxiety which is of great importance from the clinical point of view is related to the James–Lange theory. Even if the autonomic changes are not the 'cause' of the emotional state, awareness of them certainly acts like a positive feedback mechanism in many patients. Anxiety may be increased, for example, by a fear that the rapid pulse which they may feel as 'palpitation' indicates heart disease. Preventing some of these autonomic effects by the use of a beta-blocking drug (a drug which blocks some of the effects of activity of the sympathetic nervous system) can be very effective in reducing the anxiety of those patients in whom bodily symptoms are pronounced, but less so when anxiety is experienced as psychological (Tyrer, 1976).

Another clinical condition of neurophysiological interest in relation to emotion is epilepsy originating in the temporal lobes. The electrical discharge in that part of the brain (which we have seen includes the amygdala) may give rise to a transient state of intense fear.

Still related to the neurological basis of emotion, we may refer briefly to the various surgical procedures which have been attempted to alleviate the suffering of psychiatric patients – particularly those with chronic anxiety or prolonged depression which has not responded to other treatments. Such operations are used much less frequently now than in the past, and they have been considerably modified in order to minimize unwanted effects which with the original procedures could be quite pronounced. Most of the techniques involve selective division of some of the connecting pathways between the frontal lobes and the limbic system, but bilateral lesions in the amygdala have also been claimed to reduce abnormally aggressive behaviour in some patients.

A curious disorder of the emotions may be found in schizophrenia. It is described as *incongruity of affect*, indicating lack of correspondence or congruity between thought content (usually revealed in conversation) and emotional expression; a patient may giggle or laugh while describing a sad or distressing event. After the schizophrenic illness has been present for some time, a *flattening of affect* may be observed – a lack of emotional responsiveness to outside situations and events.

Finally, the emotions, and particularly the physiological changes accompanying them, are considered by many to be of great importance in relation to psychosomatic medicine – the idea that psychosocial factors may contribute to the causation of, or affect the course and prognosis of, organic disease (see Chapter 20).

Psychopharmacological aspects

Psychopharmacology (which is concerned with the so-called *psychoactive* or *psychotropic* drugs) is a relatively new discipline, since it really began with the introduction of the antipsychotic drug chlorpromazine in the early 1970s. The idea that drugs could exert a major influence on an individual's behaviour and subjective experience was, of course, of considerable significance in relation to the issue of the mind–body relationship. It is an area of interest not only to clinical medicine, and particularly to psychiatry, but also to the behavioural sciences – and especially psychology since it has thrown much light on the neurophysiological mechanisms underlying behaviour. Evidence in this field has been both descriptive – clinical and anthropological (e.g. accounts of the use of preparations from certain plants, etc.), and experimental – controlled studies, both animal and human, under laboratory conditions.

We are not primarily concerned here with many of the factors that may influence the effects of a drug on behaviour, such as dosage (the behavioural response to a drug often showing an inverted U shaped rather than a linear relationship to dosage, the maximum effect occurring over an optimum range); route of administration (behavioural effects being influenced by the rate of entry of the drug into the body, and especially into the brain, via different routes); the site of action (some drugs and not others being able to cross the so-called blood–brain barrier); and the presence of multiple effects (all drugs have more than one effect, the predominance of which will depend on other factors such as dosage, situation, etc.).

Of greater importance in the present context are two non-pharmacological variables. First there are psychological influences arising from the subject's perception of the situation in which the drug is administered (which include the so-called *placebo* effect to which reference was made in relation to pain in Chapter 5). Thus the effect of a drug may be deliberately distorted – by suggesting to a subject, for example, that a stimulant drug is actually a sedative when the effect produced may be one of slowness and drowsiness rather than excitement. The second influence is related to the personality of the subject and affects the response to stimulant and depressant drugs. From the Yerkes–Dodson inverted U shaped relationship between arousal and performance (see Fig. 9.1), it would be expected that the effect of a stimulant or depressant drug would be influenced by the existing state of arousal of the individual (i.e. whether it is optimal in terms of performance on a task, or too high or too low). This resting level of arousal in turn has been found to be related to two personality characteristics, neuroticism–stability and introversion–extraversion (which will be discussed in Chapter 16), such that the neurotic introvert has a high arousal and a neurotic extravert a low arousal. The former therefore needs a larger dose of a depressant drug to produce sedation (a high sedation threshold) than the latter (a low sedation threshold).

If psychoactive drugs are able to affect behaviour and experience, they must do so by altering neuronal activity in the brain in some way. Clinical and experimental evidence suggests that this in turn is brought about by modulating the transmission of nerve impulses at synapses via excitatory and inhibitory neurotransmitters. The three parts of the CNS which are likely to be involved in drug-induced behavioural changes are the neocortex for cognitive functions, the reticular activating system for level of arousal, and the limbic system for emotional states, and such a relationship between site of action and effect has received support from experimental work with particular drugs.

It is not the intention here to detail the various drugs with their clinical indications, dosages, therapeutic effects and side-effects. However, we may note briefly that they can be divided into four major categories – depressants, stimulants, antidepressants and psychotomimetics–hallucinogens.

The first group, as their name implies, exert a *depressant* effect on neural activity within the central nervous system. The *sedatives*, of which the major representatives are the barbiturates, have a widespread depressant action throughout the CNS, including the neocortex, so that in high doses intellectual functioning can be impaired – a condition that may occur in elderly patients who become confused if given a barbiturate as a sleeping tablet. As would be predicted by their calming effect, and in higher dosage induction of sleep, the barbiturates exert a direct action on the RAS, confirmed by the finding of a raised threshold to electrical stimulation by implanted electrodes and the fact that, in a sedated animal, blocking occurs of both the behavioural arousal and the arousal pattern in the EEG which are normally seen when the animal is stimulated.

In contrast to the barbiturate sedatives the class of drugs known as *tranquillizers* have a more restricted and selective action both behaviourally and within the CNS. They are themselves subdivided into so-called minor and major tranquillizers. The *minor* tranquillizers (of which the main examples are the *benzodiazepines*), as their alternative name *anti-anxiety* drugs would suggest, are used to reduce anxiety when this is excessive or inappropriate to circumstances. They do not induce sleep in high dosage, though they may be used to improve sleep where this is impaired by the anxiety. This is consistent with the fact that their main CNS effect is to depress the limbic structures with little action on the RAS or neocortex. Experimental animal studies have also demonstrated that these drugs diminish a passive avoidance response which has been induced by operant conditioning – analogous perhaps to helping a patient to overcome irrational fears which cause avoidance of certain situations. There is no doubt that used carefully and usually for limited periods, these drugs are of value in this way; but it has become evident that some patients can develop a dependence on them which can itself be difficult to manage.

The *major* tranquillizers or *neuroleptics* (of which the largest group comprises the phenothiazines) are used for patients with the severer forms of mental illness such as schizophrenia, though at lower dosages they may be used in the same way as the minor tranquillizers. As far as their ability to reduce agitated, disturbed or overactive behaviour is concerned, this can be related to their ability to reduce the excitability of both the limbic system and the RAS – in the latter by blocking afferent impulses arriving by collaterals from the ascending sensory pathways. The fact that they also appear to have a more specific antipsychotic effect in reducing and often abolishing the symptoms of schizophrenia appears to depend upon their effect on neurotransmission via the neurotransmitter dopamine. We shall not consider this further since it is of less relevance from the behavioural sciences point of view.

The *stimulant* drugs such as amphetamine have a brief stimulant effect on behaviour, probably due to direct action on the RAS. Because of the risk of dependency they are little used in clinical practice.

The *antidepressants*, or perhaps more correctly the *antidepressives* since their action is not to counteract a 'depressant', are used for the treatment of patients suffering from a pathological state of depression and have little or no direct stimulating action. Their therapeutic effects are often delayed and assumed to relate to certain changes that are brought about in brain neurotransmitter metabolism – particularly that of the monoamines, noradrenaline and 5-hydroxytryptamine. Again this will not be pursued further here since it has less direct relevance to the behavioural sciences, except in so far as it further demonstrates the interrelationship of what we describe as mind and body.

Finally, the *psychotomimetic* or *hallucinogenic* drugs are so called because of their ability to cause changes of behaviour and experience, including hallucinations, which in some ways resemble those seen in the psychoses. Many are derived from particular plants and have been used for religious rituals in various cultures. The best known are lysergic acid diethylamide (or LSD) and mescaline, and most research has been carried out with the former. It appears to have an effect on perceptual mechanisms – broadening attention while at the same time increasing arousal – in contrast to the normal inverse relationship where greater arousal leads to narrowed attention. This suggests that LSD alters arousal indirectly, rather than having a direct action on the RAS, by making the individual more sensitive to incoming information.

Further reading

Gray, J. (1971) *The Psychology of Fear and Stress*. London: World University Press.
Mandler, G. (1982) *Mind and Emotion*. Melbourne: Krieger.
Rachman, S. (1974) *The Meanings of Fear*. Harmondsworth: Penguin.

11
Social structure and the individual

The concept of social structure

Having, in the last three chapters, considered how individual behaviour and experience can be conceptualized as composed of a number of separate but interrelated psychological processes, we now move further up the hierarchical systems scheme discussed in Chapter 1. We shall consider whole societies and the ways in which they can be analysed in terms of their so-called *social structure* – a concept of central importance to sociology yet subject to differing inter-pretations.

We have earlier (in Chapter 3 where many of the concepts to be examined in this chapter were introduced briefly) considered sociology to be concerned with social behaviour, and especially with social relations between persons. Clearly, the larger the number of individuals the more complex the network of relation-ships which may exist between them, and to understand these it is necessary to look for regularities which point to the existence of various groupings – some small like a family, others large, such as the church, a profession, a trade union, etc. What all these *social groups* have in common is that definite relations exist between their individual members who are conscious of the group and its organization of rules and regulations.

Sometimes a distinction, though a rather indefinite and fluid one, is made between social groups proper and 'quasi groups' such as a particular sex or age group, which do not posess an organization and whose members have less awareness of the group itself. Many social groups, on the other hand, may be deliberately set up as *organizations* to pursue particular goals, and for this purpose have a division of labour, a formal power structure and decision-making machinery.

Of course groups and organizations may come and go, but it is recognized that within a society there are certain patterns of social relationships which persist over long periods of time despite changes of membership, and these are known as *social institutions*; chiefly family and kinship, political, economic, religious and educational. At the same time, recognition of the interdependence of the various groupings within a society has resulted in their frequently being referred to as *social systems*.

We shall be considering some of these concepts in more detail. However, in general terms we can say that it is the complex of the major groups and insti-tutions of a society which provides a relatively stable and enduring framework within which individual social relationships take place; they constitute, in fact, the social structure of the society.

It is important to note that such a view of social structure is concerned with relatively permanent general patterns of relationships and ignores transient variations from them. In this respect it resembles the notion of personality, which is likewise based on the relatively stable and enduring aspects of the individual's behaviour and experience (see Chapter 16). Both concepts are open to the criticism that they support a conservative acceptance of the status quo and minimize the possibility of change within the individual or society. Such a charge has been levelled particularly at the *structural-functional* school of sociology, and especially at the *equilibrium* theory of Talcott Parsons which, as we saw in Chapter 3, asserts that the 'functions' of the 'structures' which we have been considering is to fulfil the needs of, and thereby maintain the stability of, the whole society. Such a view presupposes that a society, like a person, has a purpose which is served by its constituent groups, whereas opponents deny this anthropomorphic analogy and claim, rather, that the social structure bene-fits some groups at the expense of others – the so-called *structural conflict* theory.

These are still matters of controversy, but as we suggested earlier (in Chapter 3) the antithesis between the two contrasting view points (though they are of great political significance) may be largely a false one. At any rate, it seems reasonable to suppose that the major social systems or institutions of a society, at least during a period of comparative social stability, fulfil particular func-tional requirements of the society. These will include the need to ensure a flow of new members who must be *socialized* so that they are familiar with the culture of the society – both functions being provided by the family and kinship system; a system of communication; an economic system concerned with the production and disbursement of goods; a system of authority and distribution of power; and finally, perhaps, a system of ritual which helps to maintain social cohesion and awareness of the values of the community. Clearly we shall be unable to deal here with all the major groups and institutions but will have to restrict further consideration to those with special relevance to medicine.

So a society may be analysed in terms of its social structure composed of groups and institutions. There is in addition another subdivision of the popula-tion into categories which cuts across these elements in what may be regarded as a 'horizontal' fashion, since it allots individuals to a hierarchy of social posi-tions. This *social stratification* may be by economic level (*social class*) or by prestige (*social status*), and we shall be considering its relevance to illness and health care.

So far we have considered the structure and stratification of a *society* without examining what we mean by the term itself. It is, of course, the largest social unit into which the total world population is subdivided, though there are other ways of categorizing by race, religion, etc. But by what criteria are the limits of a society determined? Unless a population is physically isolated by its geograph-ical situation, which is a relative rarity nowadays, it is impossible to define precisely the boundaries of a society. The most commonly used criterion is that of *political independence* – the notion of a 'political community' that manages its affairs independently of external control. Of course, political independence is relative since communities may at times have to submit to a greater or lesser degree of domination from another and more powerful society.

In general, however, we may recognize a population as a society if it is essentially politically independent and has a distinct social structure. From this, it also follows that if there is a major change in most or all of its institutions we should regard the society, after such a change, as a new society, distinct from the old. Having delineated individual societies, it is then possible to make comparisons between them and to attempt a classification into various 'types', and we shall return to this question when we consider the differential perspective in sociology.

The individual and society

In our examination of the basic psychological processes based upon neural activity within certain structures of the central nervous system, we have so far been largely concerned with the innate, biological determination of individual behaviour (and experience), and its modification by learning from the environment. The importance of the social environment in that process has been stressed, and we must now look at the relationship that exists between the individual and the society of which he is a member. This raises a fundamental and controversial (and, indeed, political) question as to the nature of this relationship – to what extent is man the creator of society or under the control of it?

In a sense this could be dismissed as a meaningless question since 'society' is a concept, an abstraction, and we are in danger, once again, of treating it as an object which has a purpose. Nevertheless, as the French sociologist Emile Durkheim (1858–1917) pointed out, a society is more than just a collection of persons – in other words is something more than the sum of its parts – while it certainly has a discernable reality for the individual member.

There is, then, a long history within sociology of two contrasting views on the nature of the relationship between man and society. According to the predominant doctrine, of which Durkheim was a proponent, the individual's actions are derived from the social system of which he is a member; that he is, in fact, a product of the external society which exerts a coercive influence over his behaviour through its given norms and expectations. Others, however, have taken the view that social structure itself is ultimately deducible from the characteristics of the human mind – a notable contemporary exponent of this approach (bearing the name of *structuralism*) being the French social anthropologist, Claude Levi-Strauss. At an individual level, the idea that a person is able himself to construct his own 'social world' has received more support in recent times. It would seem, however, more reasonable to suppose that the two views are complementary and that individual and society interact and are interdependent. In a sense, this problem also reflects the contrasting perspectives of psychology and sociology, while the field of study of the bridging discipline, social psychology, may be said to be the interplay between individual character and social structure – with an approach which tends to be derived either from biology or from sociology.

H.H. Gerth and C. Wright Mills (1954) have proposed that a key concept in understanding the relationship between the individual and the social structure is that of social *role*. This in turn is based on the popular sociological notion of the individual as an *actor* whose part is determined by his *status* or *position* within the social structure. Thus a man may be a member of several groups and organizations, in each of which he has a position associated with a role which he acts out in appropriate situations; his *multiple roles* may include that of husband/father within a nuclear family, church warden of the local church, or consultant surgeon within the National Health Service. He may also, at times, himself be an ill patient – a position associated with what Parsons (1951) has called the *sick role* – a concept to which we shall return in later chapters. For each of these roles he is provided with a 'script' which complies with the norms and expectations ascribed by society to that role, but he himself may then play the part according to his own characteristics. Here we can see how the concept of role links the psychological approach which will emphasize the individual's interpretation of the role and the social structural perspective which will trace the way that shared norms and expectations create networks of social privileges and obligations associated with a particular status.

An obvious distinction can be made between *ascribed* roles over which the individual has no choice (such as those associated with sex and age) and *achieved* roles which are acquired (marital, occupational, etc.) and whose range and number can obviously to some extent be a matter of individual choice. Sometimes, *role conflict* may occur when two roles demand conflicting behaviours – a common example being the spouse who is faced with competing duties to a husband/wife and an occupation/career. We can see that such a conflict quite closely corresponds to the approach–approach conflict situation which we considered in the last chapter.

We have spoken of the norms and expectations associated with particular roles and ascribed by society, but we should now examine, in a little more detail, this important aspect of society. The shared norms, values and beliefs of a society are referred to as its *culture* – the term being used in a technical sense and not in its common usage. Culture differences exist, of course, between different societies, and we shall examine some of these when we consider the differential perspective. Within a particular society there are also likely to be many *subcultures* associated with individual groups. Social *norms* are concerned with the acceptability or otherwise of various forms of conduct – that which departs from the norm being regarded as *deviant*.

The process by which the culture of a society is transmitted from one generation to the next is described as *socialization*, and the main agencies for this are the family and kinship group, and then school, religious institutions and the mass media. Through such means, the individual learns the values and norms of his culture which will regulate his behaviour – a process referred to as *social control*. This regulation will be largely 'internal', i.e. by the individual himself, and we shall return to the question of internalization of controls when we consider childhood development in Chapter 13. It may be contrasted with the external regulation of behaviour by force (e.g. the law), but the two are not always clearly demarcated.

Having dealt in general terms with the structure of society and how this relates to the individual, we can now examine in more detail some aspects which are of particular concern to medicine and the health care professions. Thus, although we may refer to other social institutions in later chapters, we shall here restrict our consideration to the family and kinship system, since not only is it of the greatest and most immediate significance for the individual, but it also provides the context within which much clinical practice occurs. We shall also take a look at the question of social stratification, since this is a concept of relevance to the later examination of patterns of disease and use of health services.

The family and kinship

Of all the social institutions, the family is central to the relationship of the individual to society, providing as it does the earliest and most intimate interface between the two. At the same time, cross-cultural studies (Murdock, 1949) have shown the family to be virtually universal, though with wide variations of pattern between societies which we shall consider later in relation to the differential perspective (Chapter 15). Even within Western society there have been, over the years, changes in the structure of the family, and the association between these and developments of the larger society have been of interest to sociologists and social historians, as we shall also see later when we consider the developmental perspective (Chapter 12). Here we shall concentrate on the family in contemporary Britain though, even in this context, a variety of patterns of family life may be associated with different segments of society.

The nature and extent of the family

Like many other concepts in the behavioural sciences, the family is so familiar (note the linguistic similarity) to everyone that its meaning seems self-evident until its strict definition is attempted. Obviously, in the first place, it may be considered to consist of a group of individuals who are related to each other in ways that are socially approved – by kinship (i.e. genetic), by marriage or by adoption – but this still leaves the actual extent of the family ill-defined. Another feature that is often regarded as characteristic is that the members of the family live together. Even this criterion of common residence can, however, be open to different interpretations depending on the type of living arrangement (e.g. house, flat, farm, camp, etc.). It appears that it is impossible to be precise in defining the family since it will vary from place to place and from time to time. This serves to emphasize the social nature of the concept, despite its obvious biological foundation in mating and reproduction. In many species where the young require a period of protection and nurturance, a relationship may be observed between the mother and her progeny, sometimes also involving the father and thus providing a rudimentary form of family structure. Although more complex patterns have been described in primates they are still relatively stereotyped, and it is only in man that we find such a variety of family arrangements reflecting different cultural and subcultural norms and values.

A distinction is commonly made between two types of family in terms of the number of kin included within it. The *nuclear* or *conjugal* family is the most basic family unit and consists of father, mother and their children (Fig. 11.1(a)). It is also, at the present time, the typical form of British family, in contrast to the previously more usual *extended* family – extended 'vertically' to include more than two generations (e.g. grandparents, parents and children as in Fig. 11.1(b)) or 'horizontally', with more than one nuclear family (e.g. brothers and/or sisters and their families) sharing a common residence (Fig. 11.1(c)). Extended families are today more likely to be found in rural areas or among immigrants in the cities, where living together provides a sense of security and serves to preserve the customs of their particular culture.

Whatever the type of family, its existence, as we have said, obviously depends upon the biological foundation of mating between man and woman. However, the majority of societies have customs or laws regarding the setting up of the relatively stable and permanent heterosexual relationship which *legitimates* any offspring of the union and is known as *marriage*. The commonest form of

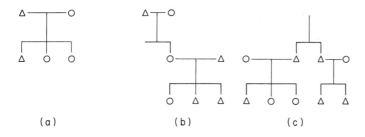

Fig.11.1 (a) Nuclear family; (b) 'vertically' extended family; (c) 'horizontally' extended family

marriage in all societies is *monogamous*, even in those societies where *polygamy*, including the marriage of one man to two or more women (*polygyny*) or of one woman to two or more men (*polyandry*), is permitted, or indeed regarded as ideal. We shall return to this when we compare different societies and cultures (Chapter 15); but in Western society, owing to the influence of Christianity and the sacred view of marriage, monogamy has in any case been the rule.

Regulations also exist in most societies as to which couples may marry or indeed have a sexual relationship. Thus *incest taboos* prohibit sexual intercourse between particular individuals – usually those closely related by descent – so that mating has to occur outside the nuclear family (*exogamy*) with an exchange of males and females between existing families. From a biological standpoint this has the advantage of ensuring a greater genetic heterogeneity (by intermingling of genes from different hereditary stock); but from the social point of view it carries with it consequences in terms of residence and descent. As far as the former is concerned there is, of course, no problem if the new family has its own new and separate accommodation (*neolocal* residence); but with vertically extended families the question arises as to whether the newly-weds continue to live with or near the husband's family (*patrilocal* residence) or the wife's family (*matrilocal* residence).

Related to these varieties of residence is the whole concept of kinship, which includes the tracing of lines of descent or *lineage* from one generation to another. Social anthropologists have described several types of descent in different societies which here we can only summarize (Fig. 11.2) as *matrilineal* when it is traced through the female line (i.e. with husbands being outsiders to the family), *patrilineal* when the line is perpetuated by the males who import

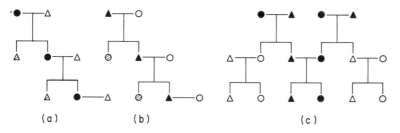

Fig.11.2 (a) Matrilinear lineage; (b) patrilinear lineage; (c) cognatic lineage. ● or ▲ = the line of descent; ⊘ or △ = members who may or may not be within the kinship; ○ or △ = outside the lineage

their wives from outside, and *non-unilineal* or *cognatic* which implies that a man or woman can belong to both the father's and the mother's lineage. There is, however, an alternative approach to the designation of a family kinship; instead of, as in the lineage method, starting with an ancester and tracing the descendents downwards, it is possible to work backwards from an individual and consider as *kindred* all those related to him. In Britain kinship is largely of this type, though the inheritance of surnames and succession to some titles is patrilineal. The cognatic lineage occurs in the Scottish clan and in some family businesses and can also be observed at such events as marriages and funerals. Young and Willmott (1957), in a study of working-class families in Bethnal Green in the East End of London, found that daughters tended to retain a close emotional tie with, and to remain in fairly close geographical proximity to, their mothers – a situation somewhat resembling the matrilineal family structure. In general, however, kinship tends to be of minor influence upon the social structure of modern industrial societies, though it may be of greater significance within immigrant subcultures.

The functions of the family

Having looked at the structure – or rather the variety of structures – of the family, the question arises as to its functions. Despite the reservations concerning the use of the structural – functional approach, it seems quite evident that the family plays an important part in the continuing existence of the individual and of society, and in this sense we can speak of its functions for both. It can be argued, however, that several of the traditional functions of the family in relation to the individual have been largely taken over by society during the process of industrialization; while at the same time it is claimed that the decline of the extended family and emergence of the nuclear family has been of advantage to, and facilitated, industrial development since it permitted greater geographical mobility and a larger variety and flexibility of roles – a question to which we shall return in the next chapter when we consider social change. Here we shall examine in turn some of the functions of the family and how they have changed in Britain.

Sexual

This need, of course, forms the biological basis for the social institution of marriage, which may then be said to provide for its satisfaction within the sanction of society, and, when appropriate, the church. It is clear, though, that sexual behaviour has never been restricted to marriage and although the lack of reliable data from earlier times makes it difficult to draw firm conclusions, there is evidence (Kinsey *et al.*, 1948) to suggest that, while the use of prostitutes has declined in recent years, pre-marital and extra-marital sexual intercourse has increased. Nevertheless, Michael Schofield (1965) found that promiscuity among teenagers was less widespread than was commonly supposed at the time, and when sexual intercourse had occurred it was usually with a steady partner and the relationship progressed to marriage. The practice of couples living together before marriage has, however, increased considerably in the last few years: of women aged 16–34 who married for the first time in 1970–74, 8 per cent had lived with their future husband, while the comparable figure for 1979–82 was 24 per cent. Cohabitation among widowed, divorced or separated women is actually higher than among single women; the figures for 1982/83 being 17 and 10 per cent respectively. However, the majority of couples who get divorced marry again (of women who separated between 1970 and 1974 before the age of 35, 23 per cent had remarried within three years and 52 per cent within six years) – presumably in most cases to those with whom they have had an extra-marital relationship (Fletcher, 1966).

Reproduction

If the sexual function of the family is important for the individual, its reproductive function is vital to society. This should perhaps be qualified by the fact that procreation can, of course, occur outside marriage and a family, though most societies condemn such births by designating them as 'illegitimate'. In Britain, however, not only has the percentage of illegitimate conceptions shown a tendency to increase (from about 12 to 22 per cent since the last war), especially in the under-20s, but also the proportion that are legitimated by marriage of the parents before the birth of the child has fallen (from roughly 60 to 30 per cent), again largely brought about by mothers aged under 20, so that there would seem to be an increasing proportion of young unmarried mothers. The practice of such a mother keeping her child and rearing it within an incomplete nuclear or 'one parent' family has also become much commoner than in the past, associated with a sharp decline in the last ten years of non-parental, and to a lesser extent parental, adoptions of illegitimate children. On the other hand, the fact that there has been, over the same period of time, an increase in the proportion of illegitimate births registered jointly by both parents (from 46 to nearly 60 per cent) suggests an increased likelihood, at least up to the time of birth of the child, of the single woman maintaining a stable relationship outside marriage with the father.

Another important aspect for society of the family's reproductive function concerns the actual numbers of children being born, as this has obvious implications for social and economic planning. The birth rate is clearly related to the average number of children born to each married woman during her reproductive life, and the statistics for Britain show that over the last one hundred years there has been a decline from a figure of about six to the present two children per family. This cannot be due to any reduction in reproductive capacity of women and must be the result of a deliberate decision by parents to restrict their families by using the various methods of contraception that became increasingly available during the period. Since family planning is now actively encouraged, it might seem that the reproductive function of the family is being deliberately limited, while at the same time society has taken over some aspects of this function by providing such support as maternity benefit, child allowance, etc.

Economic

This is another feature of the family that has been greatly affected by the process of industrialization. Whereas in earlier times the family was generally the centre of production – with all or most of its members involved in similar work such as farming or a 'cottage' industry – the development of the factory as the unit of production meant that more and more people were employed outside the home, while the family itself became the consumer of the goods produced. Thus the economic function of the family generally changed from one of production to one of consumption.

Socialization

We have already referred to this important function by which the culture of a society is passed on to the next generation and to the role of the family as a major agent in the process. Certainly it is within the family that the child first learns the customs and traditions of the culture and subcultures to which its parents belong, as we shall see later when we consider childhood development; but once again an increasing proportion of this function has been taken over by the educational system, while the media (especially television) also exert a considerable influence.

Roles and relationships within the modern family

Although our concern in this chapter is not with the question of changes, we have noted that the present-day Western family is, in many ways, different from its predecessors owing to such social influences as the industrial revolution and the taking over of family functions by the state. A concomitant change of great significance for marriage and the family has been the gradual emancipation of women and the breakdown of the patriarchal system in which authority was vested in the male head of the family. All this has resulted in something of a shift of emphasis from the concept of marriage as a legal contract involving mutual rights and duties, towards a view of it as a relationship concerned with the satisfaction of personal needs.

An earlier change was the development in Europe in the middle ages of the idea of romantic love, which then, only much later, became associated with marriage. Prior to this, love and marriage – which we nowadays assume should, in the words of the song, 'go together like a horse and carriage' – tended to be dissociated. Marriages took place for a variety of reasons other than love – an experience which was then frequently sought in relationships outside wedlock. Even today, marriage in the majority of societies is 'arranged' – often between young men and women who may never have previously met. In Western societies, however, marriage is usually by consent between the partners, and there has been much study of the psychological and social factors which may influence the choice of a spouse. In general, it is found that such choosing is by no means random but that there is, as we might have supposed, a tendency for couples to resemble each other in certain physical, psychological and social characteristics – a phenomenon known as *assortative mating*.

Theoretically, of course, there is a potential for meeting and mating between any two opposite-sexed people, from anywhere in the world, but in practice there are, in addition to the incest taboo, limitations of geography, race, culture, religion, social class, etc. Although there is evidence that greater geographical and social mobility has led to increased intermarriage between members from different groupings, or *marriage isolates*, there is still a high incidence of assortative mating between those from the same geographical area – *circumscribed marriage*; from the same social class – *class endogamy* (where differences do occur it is more common for women to marry into a higher social class, a channel for upward mobility more open to them than the occupational routes used by men); from the same religious faith – *intrafaith marriage*; and, most strictly of all, from the same *ethnic* or *racial* background.

Although we are, here, chiefly concerned with the social influences on the selection of spouses, we may also note the importance of physical and psychological determinants since couples have been found to resemble each other in height and in eye and hair colour, as well as in temperament, intelligence and attitudes and interests. The latter, of course, are in any case more likely to be similar in those from the same social and educational background. In fact, education appears to be more important than social origin in choice of a spouse, especially for those with a professional or university education.

We can see that psychosocial factors play an important part in determining how husbands and wives choose each other, but even more striking are the cultural influences on their subsequent behaviour in the marriage. Each spouse may be regarded as playing a role which is defined by society and is related to the even more basic concept of *gender*. While men and women are biologically differentiated as male and female, their gender, or the way they behave in their masculine and feminine roles, is largely determined by the expectations of the particular society and acquired through the process of socialization. We shall return to this subject when we reconsider, in Chapter 15, the very marked differences in gender roles which may be found between different cultures; but here we are concerned with the way that the behaviour of husbands and wives is determined by the socially defined gender roles within British society. Thus it has been, and still largely is, expected for the man to be the main provider for the family and the woman to be the 'housewife' concerned with running the household and bringing up the children.

These, then, were the traditional rights and duties of the marriage contract, but as we have seen the pattern of marriage has become much less rigid and generally more democratic, though considerable variations may be met with between different subcultures. Most attention has been paid to social class differences, particularly in relation to the effect of kinship ties and the greater tendency for working-class husbands and wives to lead relatively separate lives, with the former spending much of their leisure time outside the home and the latter remaining closely attached to their mothers (Young and Willmott, 1957). Even this pattern has been found to change, however, with rehousing of families in new estates, when the couples become more integrated and the marriages home-centred instead of 'mum' centred. Studies of middle-class families (e.g. Young and Willmott, 1960) show fathers to be more involved with their families and to maintain important links, through financial support, with their married children.

While changes in the role of the husband/father have been noted, it is the position of the wife/mother that has attracted most attention since it has been greatly influenced by the increasing political and social emancipation of women. With the greater educational and occupational opportunities open to her, the traditional notion that 'the woman's place is in the home' has been called into question. Encouraged by such concomitant factors as the smaller size of families and the development of labour-saving devices and 'convenience foods', more and more women are 'working wives', both before and after they have fulfilled their still usual role of child-rearing. Surveys (e.g. Jephcott *et al.*, 1962) have shown that, for the majority of working married women, the advantages of this arrangement appear to far outweigh the disadvantages in terms of interest, satisfaction and companionship, as well as the additional income.

Related to this is the frequent dissatisfaction of the young mother who has had to give up work and may become socially isolated and sometimes virtually 'house-bound' while her children are maximally dependent on her – a situation described in a small survey of working-class and middle-class wives by Hannah

Gavron (1968). Some women, especially those with professional occupations, return to work even sooner by employing nannies or au pair girls to look after the children, while women in less well paid jobs may make similar arrangements with a relative or friend. There has been much discussion of the possible effects on children of these changes within the modern family, and especially of mothers going out to work. This is a matter to which we shall return in Chapter 13 when we consider child development, but in general there appear to be no harmful effects on children over the age of three provided the substitute care is stable.

What is clear from all these changes is that the roles of husband and wife have become much less clearly defined and that this has affected the nature of the marital relationship. The husband is no longer the dominant patriarch to a subservient wife, and both are now likely to share some at least of the domestic tasks in the family within a relationship of equality – described by Young and Willmott (1973) as a *symmetrical* family. We shall, however, leave further consideration of the more psychological aspects of the marital relationship until we deal with the interpersonal perspective in Chapters 18 and 19. We may note here though, that the breakdown of the traditional power structure of the family includes the children, who are more likely to be treated as individuals in their own right to be consulted about family matters and not arbitrarily subject to the authority of the parents.

Family breakdown

Since a family generally owes its origin and continued existence to the marriage of the parents, its dissolution may be brought about by the termination of that marriage not only by death but more commonly by separation or divorce. The causes and consequences of marital breakdown are clearly of great importance and interest to several institutions and disciplines – for example the law and the church, as well as psychology and sociology (Dominian, 1968). The dramatic increase in the number of divorces in recent years has given rise to much concern and to speculation that the family as an institution is in decline.

The statistics need, however, to be interpreted with caution, since there have been a number of legal and social changes which have made divorce easier to obtain and less socially stigmatized. Thus it was only after the Matrimonial Causes Act of 1857 that divorce became a civil and not an ecclesiastical matter, and even then it was both extremely expensive and very restricted as to the grounds for divorce. Later legislation, however, has been increasingly liberal, culminating in the Divorce Reform Act of 1969 which came into effect in 1971, since when the sole ground for divorce has been the irretrievable breakdown of the marriage – doing away with the previous necessity for evidence of a matrimonial offence like adultery. At the same time legal aid has been more available for, and social attitudes more tolerant towards, divorce. In fact the divorce rate per thousand of the married population, though generally rising throughout this century, has shown fluctuations which relate quite strikingly with changes in the law and financial assistance to litigants, though there was an additional rise (associated with the Second World War) which reached a peak in 1947.

Bearing in mind these social influences we should obviously not assume that the rise in the divorce rate necessarily reflects directly a true increase in marital instability and breakdown since, though evidence is lacking, it is likely that in the past very many couples remained legally married for religious, social or financial reasons despite complete breakdown of their relationship. Nevertheless, the statistics for divorce do allow us to examine certain aspects of marital breakdown. First, the incidence of divorce shows a strong association with social class; in 1979 the rate for husbands in unskilled manual occupations was more than four times that for husbands in professional occupations – the difference being even greater for younger men. The rates for the unemployed were higher still for all age groups – in each case about double that of the national average. It seems likely that these differences in divorce rates are in part a reflection of other divorce-associated factors, such as the presence of a premaritally conceived child or a wife in her 'teens.

Age at marriage is related to divorce rates, with a much higher risk for teenage marriages. In 1982, 13 per cent of divorces involved husbands aged less than 20 at marriage, and in 37 per cent the wife had been under 20. The likelihood is that almost three in five teenage husbands and one in two teenage brides will eventually divorce, compared with one in three for all marriages. For all age groups it is the early years of marriage which seem to be most vulnerable – nearly 50 per cent of all divorces in 1983 occurred within the first ten years of marriage – the peak being after six to seven years and separation even earlier, most commonly in the first year.

It seems likely that both of these vulnerability factors – early age and early years of marriage – are associated with difficulties in establishing the marital relationship, both physically and emotionally. Once this phase has been passed marriages seem to remain relatively stable, though with a later increase in breakdown after twenty years or so when the children have become largely, if not entirely, independent. Breakdown at this time may be due to the possibility of ending a long-since unsatisfactory marriage held together for the sake of the children, or to the inability of the couple, particularly within the nuclear family, to adjust to their altered circumstances and especially to the increased involvement with each other now that the children are 'off their hands'.

An obvious concern from the point of view of society is the question of what happens to the children when marriages break up. The size of this problem is somewhat reduced by the fact that there is an inverse relationship between the likelihood of divorce and the number of children in a family, with about a third of divorces involving childless couples. We shall, however, defer further consideration of the effects of divorce on the children until we deal with child development in Chapter 13 – except to note here that in relation to their own marital happiness, there is evidence of an association between success or failure of marriages between generations, i.e. parents with satisfactory marriages tend to produce children with similar marriages, and vice versa.

Alternatives to the family

We have seen that the family is a virtually universal phenomenon. Furthermore, despite the increasing rate of overt marital breakdown in Western society, the majority of divorced couples remarry so that there appears to be no decline in the popularity of marriage as an institution. The traditional (at present) nuclear family has, however, come in for a good deal of criticism in recent years as being insular, restrictive, repressive, etc., and there are several alternatives available including single-parent families, 'common-law' marriages in which couples live together in a long and stable relationship but without being legally married, and various types of group living in a 'commune' – a structure which in some ways resembles the extended family but without the members being related to each other. Many communes are short-lived, but the best known and longest existing example at present is the Israeli kibbutz in which child rearing and socialization is communal – a situation to which we shall refer again when we consider child development in Chapter 13.

Clinical aspects of the family

The fact that a frequently used alternative name for the NHS General Practitioner is the 'family doctor', indicates the importance of the family in relation to the practice of medicine in the community. It is usual for a whole family to be registered with a single GP or group practice, so that the doctor is likely to become well-acquainted with all the family members. In hospital, too, there are obviously many occasions when meetings occur between medical, nursing and other staff caring for a patient, and the relatives who come to visit, and this opportunity for communication can be valuable on both sides.

Hospital medical social workers are often very much concerned with helping patients' relatives with psychological and social problems. Outside hospital, the importance of the family as the focus of attention for community social workers was recognized within the reorganization of the social services by the concept of the generic social worker, who would be concerned with any member of a particular family in need of help, rather than having specialist social workers to deal with special problems of different individuals within the same family. (In practice, however, this has not been a complete success and the need for some degree of specialization has now been realized.)

The significance of the family in relation to health and illness lies, of course, in the fact that almost every patient, or potential patient, has been, and/or is, a member of a family and that interaction within it is a two-way process. Thus the family may be considered from two points of view: on the one hand as a possible causative or modifying agent in a patient's illness and, on the other hand, as the more immediate social environment within which the illness occurs – including the reaction of other family members to it. Since both of these aspects will receive more detailed examination in later chapters, they will not be considered further here.

Family pathology, or 'sickness' of the family itself, whether or not it culminates in actual breakdown in the form of separation or divorce of the parents, may also be a frequent matter of concern to doctors as well as other professional workers. While the Marriage Guidance Council specifically provides a counselling service for couples with marital problems, others such as priests, probation officers, social workers and doctors (especially psychiatrists) may also be involved in this way. Sometimes, however, the difficulties extend to all the members of a family, and then help may be offered to the whole family in the form of 'family therapy'. This is a common practice in many departments of child psychiatry since psychological disturbances in the child often reflect more widespread disorder in the family. Again we shall return to the question of marital and family disharmony when we consider the interpersonal perspective in Chapters 18 and 19; but here we may note that as well as difficulties stemming from individual characteristics of personality in spouses, there may frequently be divisions brought about by 'role segregation' when the husband and wife lead largely separate and non-communicating lives owing to the exclusive involvement in their respective roles as worker and housewife.

Cultural factors may also be important in immigrant families when conflict arises between the first and second generation owing to exposure of the latter to the influence of the host culture while they are growing up – an example being the daughters of Asian immigrants who rebel against the practice of arranged marriages. Similar difficulties may arise when upward social mobility of children leads to an intergenerational conflict of class values.

Social stratification

Just as the family is apparently a universal institution, so there has been, and still is, in all societies some form of social differentiation in terms of wealth, power or prestige. Sometimes this has a religious basis, as in Moslem countries where women may be regarded as being of inferior status to men, or in the Hindu caste system of India where life-long membership of a particular *caste* is believed to be determined by good or bad conduct in a previous life so that advancement through the caste system may be achieved by correct behaviour in a series of incarnations – a form of social control over behaviour rather similar to the Christian belief in the importance of the quality of life on earth in relation to existence in an 'after-life'.

In Europe the social differentiation found in the feudal system was based on the possession of land – granted originally in return for military service to the king. Gradually, however, as trade and commerce developed this *estate* system changed into the *class* system as we know it today. Industrialization was important in this process, and in the last century, Karl Marx, who stressed the economic basis of class differentiation, distinguished between the capitalists or *bourgeoisie* – the owners of the means of production, and the working class or *proletariat* who provided the labour force. We shall return to Marx's views when we consider the possible functions of social class, and again in Chapter 12 when we deal with the question of social change; but here we must now examine in more detail, and in relation to present-day society, precisely what we mean by some of the terms used in this area.

In the first place the differentiation of social structure into a hierarchy of prestige and power may be made in several ways: sometimes the scaling may be along a continuum without any clear-cut subdivision; more often it is viewed as a series of supposedly clearly demarcated layers like geological strata – giving rise to the term *social stratification*.

The German sociologist, Max Weber (1864–1920) drew a distinction between two concepts which exemplify this difference: *social status* – a hierarchical continuum depending upon the social *prestige* or *honour* attaching to particular positions in society (such as those with titles, members of particular professions or holding certain offices, etc.); and *social class* – a division into strata based on position within the economic system (or what Weber called the 'market situation') but with each stratum having a particular culture shared by its members.

Since these earlier theories it has, in recent years, been possible for sociologists to make empirical studies of social differentiation by examining both the distribution within society of certain measurable indices such as occupation, income, education, power and ethnic group, and the amount of prestige attached to these by various groups of people. In general the results have shown a measure of agreement both within and between different industrial countries as to the social ranking of different occupations, and at the same time there is a fairly high degree of *status consistency*, i.e. congruity between an individual's ranking on different criteria – occupation, education, income, etc.

Another aspect to be considered in relation to social status is that it may be *ascribed* or conferred on a person by virtue of some quality which he possesses, often from birth, such as skin colour, or *achieved*, for example by obtaining qualifications or being promoted. The relative significance of these two types of status in Britain today is uncertain, but the more that society approaches a so-called *meritocracy* (Michael Young, 1965) the more important does achievement become in determining social position.

It is, of course, clear that there must be a large subjective element to social ranking, and that it is indeed a cultural phenomenon since it depends on shared values within the society. Some sociologists speak of social *perception* and social *imagery* (see also Chapter 18) to describe the way individuals 'see' and think about their society, including some idea of its stratification. In fact, as we shall see, there may be differences of social perspective between members of different social classes which are reflected in contrasting social perceptions – just as we saw in Chapter 5 that perception of the physical environment by the individual involves an active process in which its meaning is influenced by various factors, and especially by learning from past experience.

Even more subjective and open to value judgements, yet nevertheless often considered to be important in social stratification, are such indices as speech (including both accent and vocabulary), 'manners', and 'tastes' (artistic, dress, etc.). All this means, of course, is that, once again, what may appear at first sight to be a fairly obvious and straightforward feature of social structure turns out on closer examination to be much less precise and more difficult to investigate and measure objectively. However, we must now consider in more detail what is known of the social class structure of Britain in order to be able later to relate this to various aspects of health and illness.

Social class differences in Britain

We have seen that the concept of social class involves the subdivision of society, essentially on an economic basis, into a number of strata, each with its own common attitudes, values and norms. Definition of social class is, however, as we have also recognized, difficult and there may not always be agreement as to which social class an individual occupies – there may, for example, be a difference of opinion between himself and others as to which it is. The only solution to the problem in practice is to consider the various attributes that are customarily associated with the different social classes and then to assess any individual in relation to these.

It is generally assumed that there are, in Britain today, three main social classes – the 'working', the 'middle' and the 'upper' classes – though, as we shall see, their relative proportions have changed since the industrial revolution and are probably still doing so. Awareness of belonging to a particular class, or *class consciousness*, arose with the greater concentration of people in towns brought about by industrialization. This was especially true of the *manual* or *working* class, who at that time were poor, ill-fed, shabbily dressed and living in overcrowded accommodation. Conditions gradually improved, however, and in recent years social legislation and so-called affluence have brought considerable social changes affecting the working class – a matter to which we shall return when we consider social mobility. The origin of the *middle* class as a major social group also lies in the industrial revolution, which brought an increase in the need for a variety of forms of *non-manual* work in commerce and public service as well as for the professions – medicine, law and the church. Again we shall see that there have been subsequent social changes affecting the middle class. Finally the *upper* class has always been numerically much smaller, consisting of the *aristocracy* or 'landed gentry' and the *plutocracy* or *nouveaux riches* who have made large fortunes in one way or another – recruitment to the aristocracy has continued into the present century with the creation of new peerages, some of which have been hereditary, while additions to the ranks of the millionaires have come to include such newcomers as film and pop stars.

For fairly obvious reasons, there has been relatively little sociological study of the upper class, though there has been much interest in its possible role as a 'dominant' or even 'ruling' class – at least in the past. Most attention has been directed to examination of differences between the working and middle classes. Much of the recent work in this area has been carried out at Oxford by John Goldthorpe and his colleagues (Goldthorpe *et al.*, 1969) who have described differences of attitudes or *social perspective* reflected in differences of *life style* between the two classes.

The working-class or manual-worker perspective, which may be characterized as *collectivism*, sees the social order as dichotomous – divided into 'them' and 'us', separated by an unbridgeable gap so that life has to be 'put up with'. Related to this is the view of working-class solidarity and a belief in the effectiveness of collective action – especially trade unionism; also a degree of fatalism which encourages present enjoyment as against planning for future achievements, and which restricts aspirations for children to levels of education and jobs that will not remove them from the family, either geographically or socially.

The middle-class, non-manual-worker perspective may, by contrast, be described as *individualism*, which views the social order as hierarchical – a stratification in terms of life style and prestige which is relatively open to advancement by the individual according to ability and determination, and the achievement of which is his own responsibility. To this end (i.e. 'getting on') it is worth making short-term sacrifices, and this may also involve parents in giving their children 'a good start' in education and a job that will lead to a still higher level in the social order.

Of course it is not suggested that these attitudes would be found in every individual within each of the two classes, and a blurring of the distinctions between the two subcultures is likely to occur, especially in those with occupations on the borderline between manual and non-manual work. The same reservations also apply, of course, to behavioural differences such as those in styles of communication and of life in general. Studies by Basil Bernstein (1971, 1972 and 1975) have, however, shown class differences in the use of language in terms of both grammar and words. Thus working-class people use what Bernstein calls a *restricted* code – a limited use of adjectives and adverbs within relatively short and grammatically simple sentences – which communicates *particularistic* meanings specific to particular contexts (i.e. the meaning of what is said is derived only in part from the speech itself and depends also on clues provided by the context or by non-verbal expressive movements). Middle-class speech, by contrast, is described as *elaborated*, using an *extended* code which conveys *universalistic* meanings. Since this is the dominant form of speech in society – especially in the media and in education – working-class children are at a relative disadvantage compared with those from the middle class, who are able to use both restricted and extended codes on different occasions.

Social class differences in life style in terms of leisure activities and sociability have probably become well known to most people through the media, and especially the so-called 'situation comedy' series on television. These differences have, however, been examined by sociological studies such as those by Young and Willmott (1973), who found more reading of books by non-manual than manual workers and more and different activities outside the house for non-manual workers (e.g. dinners, theatres, evening classes, art galleries, museums, etc., for the middle-class workers and darts for manual workers), and by Goldthorpe and his co-workers (1969) who found less entertaining at home and a geographically more limited circle of spare-time companions (usually relatives and neighbours) among manual than non-manual workers and their wives. It is interesting that this evidence of a relatively restricted life style was found among affluent manual car workers in Luton as well as in the more traditionally working-class environment of the East End of London, where it would more easily be explained by overcrowded living conditions.

The measurement and distribution of social class in Britain

Having briefly examined the nature of these three traditional social classes in Britain, we must now consider how in practice people are allotted to different social ranks for statistical and other purposes. Although we have seen that several factors – occupation, income, education, etc. – are concerned with social ranking, it is occupation that is most easily identified and most often used for determining social class.

The idea of dividing the population up into occupational groups which later came to be regarded as social classes began in 1911 when the British Government started to include such data in the ten-yearly census. For this purpose, occupations were allotted to five classes according to what is usually referred to as the Registrar General's social scale: Class 1 – professional and managerial, occupations such as civil service administrative officers, company secretaries, ministers of religion, lawyers, doctors and professional engineers; Class 2 – intermediate occupations such as farmers, retailers, local authority officers and teachers; Class 3 – skilled occupations in industry such as coal-miners and many factory workers, together with shop assistants and clerical workers; Class 4 – partly skilled occupations such as bus conductors, plumbers mates and window cleaners; Class 5 – unskilled occupations such as labourers, street sellers and watchmen. Over the years some modifications have been made, with particular occupations being reallocated to different classes; but otherwise the scale has remained essentially unchanged. Criticisms of it include the fact that it is rather vague and that it is limited in range.

In 1950, John Hall and D. Caradog Jones obtained ratings of various occupations by a group of people and from these evolved the 'Hall–Jones scale' which has been used in much sociological research. It is a seven-point scale thus: 1 – professional and high administrative, 2 – managerial and executive, 3 – inspectional, supervisory and other non-manual (high grade), 4 – inspectional, supervisory and other non-manual (low-grade), 5 – skilled manual and routine grades of non-manual, 6 – semi-skilled manual, 7 – unskilled manual. Again the scale may be criticized as having rather broad groupings and for being based on the attitudes of a rather biased sample of the population, since the members were largely non-manual workers. Indeed a study by Young and Willmott (1956) showed that a sample of manual workers tended to produce a somewhat different ranking of the same list of occupations as well as showing less agreement between themselves on the ranking.

More recently, John Goldthorpe and Keith Hope (1972) have devised another classification of occupations into seven classes according to ratings of desirability. Classes 1 and 2 include managers of firms, senior civil servants, doctors, landowners, etc., and are described as the 'service' rather than the conventional 'middle' class. The intermediate classes 3 to 5 include rank-and-file white collar workers, small shopkeepers and supervisors of manual workers, while the industrial manual workers are placed in classes 6 and 7.

Social mobility between classes

The term *social mobility* is used to describe the extent to which a society shows movement between its different social strata or classes; but since, as we have seen, it is occupation that is the major determinant of social class, most studies of social mobility have actually been concerned with occupational mobility. Two kinds of such mobility may be distinguished: intragenerational mobility involving occupational change within an individual's career, and intergenerational mobility shown by occupational differences between generations – usually fathers and sons.

Studies of *intragenerational* mobility carried out for the government (Thomas, 1949; Harris and Clausen, 1966) have shown that, although a certain amount of movement occurs within the occupational structure (about a fifth of workers having moved between categories over a ten-year period), the actual range of movement is limited. Most moves are to adjacent occupational groups and there is little crossing of the boundaries between manual and non-manual categories.

There have been two important studies of *intergenerational* mobility in Britain separated by about a quarter of a century. The first, carried out in 1948 by David Glass (1954) and his colleagues at the London School of Economics, examined the occupational status of a national sample of men and of their fathers, using the Hall–Jones scale to which we have already referred. By comparing the two generations, the amount of occupational change could be determined for each group. The results showed that a considerable amount of movement had in fact occurred, with only a third of the total sample of sons being of the same occupational status as their fathers. The range of movement was again, however, limited – usually to adjacent ranks – though there was less of a division between manual and non-manual occupations so that there was a movement across the boundary in both directions of about a third of each group. The degree of *internal recruitment* (i.e. where sons have occupations in the same category as their fathers) was higher in some groups (especially 1 and 5) than others, but this could in part be a spurious finding depending on similarities between the unequal distributions of occupational ranks of the two generations. A statistical technique was devised to overcome this which gave an *index of association* between statuses of father and sons, indicating the chances in each category of a son having the same status as his father compared with his chances if there were random mobility (i.e. equal probabilities of movement for all persons). The highest indices were for categories 1 and 2 where the chances of recruitment to father's occupational status were about 13 and 6 times greater, respectively, than would be the case with random mobility, while indices for the remaining categories were mostly between 1 and 2. We may conclude that in 1948 intergenerational social mobility in Britain was generally quite widespread but of short distance, with entry to the top two occupational categories being particularly difficult. The total occupational structure remained, however, quite stable, since upward and downward mobility balanced each other.

The other major study of intergenerational mobility was more recent and was carried out in 1972 by the same group at Oxford to whom we have already referred. Goldthorpe and his colleagues (Goldthorpe and Llewellyn, 1977), using the Goldthorpe–Hope classification of occupations, found a much greater mobility with more upward mobility of the sons of both manual workers and men in the intermediate classes – not balanced this time by an equal downward mobility. Self-recruitment to class 1 was also only three times greater than chance – much less than it had been 25 years previously. All this would, of course, suggest a change in the distribution of occupations, and indeed the findings showed that there had been a shrinkage of the working class and an expansion of the middle class. Goldthorpe's team examined the class distribution of their 1972 sample of workers according to their year of birth. Of those born in the decade 1908–17, only about 22 per cent were members of the 'service' classes 1 and 2 (i.e. roughly equivalent to middle class), whereas the figure for those born between 1938 and 1947 was nearly 30 per cent, despite the fact that they were still relatively young and might rise further in their careers. The increase was, of course, balanced by a decrease in the proportions of the intermedite classes 3 – 5 (32 to 27 per cent) and of the industrial workers, classes 6 and 7 (45½ to 43½ per cent). Goldthorpe suggests that this trend towards upward mobility was due to an expansion in the 1950s and 1960s of highly skilled and well-paid jobs, especially in the service industries and the public sector, which together with better educational opportunities enabled much larger upward movements to occur so that 15 – 20 per cent of those with working-class backgrounds were entering classes 1 and 2 (the service classes). It seems likely, however, that this net upward mobility has now ceased and the occupational structure has stabilized again.

A question that obviously arises from these changes of class structure is whether there has been a corresponding change in class culture. A view which gained popularity as the *embourgoisement* theory was that the affluent workers were identifying themselves with the middle-class style of life – were becoming 'bourgeois'. However, Goldthorpe and his colleagues (1969), in their study of the Luton car workers to which we have already referred, showed that this was not in fact the case. Although these workers were better off, they tended to retain their traditional working-class attitudes and were not assimilated by their already middle-class neighbours. This means that the nature of this new, expanded, middle-class itself has changed in such a way that Goldthorpe describes it as having 'low classness' in the sense that it has less of a sense of class consciousness. At the same time the working class is becoming more homogeneous since it has lost its more successful members and has received fewer of those who have slipped down the social ladder.

In summary, it would appear that greater general affluence has led to greater intergenerational upward mobility but little change in intragenerational mobility – the inference being that social advancement occurs through education and job opportunity in the first 20 years or so of a person's life, but that if he has not gained the requisite qualifications by this age there is relatively little opportunity for subsequent progress of more than a limited extent.

Individual aspects of social mobility

So far we have been considering the extent of social mobility between classes and how this may be influenced by such social factors as greater affluence or improved educational opportunities. Since, however, only a proportion of individuals born into a particular social class achieve upward mobility, there must be other determining factors in this process. While these are likely to be considered more psychological than sociological in nature, it is perhaps appropriate to examine them briefly here.

Clearly the most obvious characteristic of the individual which might be supposed to be related to 'improvement' of social class position would be his ability – consistent, of course, with the notion of a meritocracy, a concept to which we shall return shortly. Ability, in turn, may be assumed to reflect innate intelligence, but as we shall see in Chapter 17 this is by no means a simple matter. The extent to which such innate intellectual capacity is realized in achievement may depend on other factors, some social, which will thereby influence the likelihood of social mobility. Thus equal educational opportunity may be more apparent than real, even within the state system, owing to the relatively poor stimulating influence of the home environment, together with cultural values, including lower aspirations of many working-class families, and this is particularly true in respect of higher education.

As well as intelligence and ability, another individual factor that has received attention is the *need for achievement* which can be considered an aspect of personality – a matter to which we shall return in Chapter 16. The achievement motive (which we have also mentioned in Chapter 9 as a social drive) is also, however, likely to be influenced by social factors such as child-rearing practices, including early training in independence.

Associated with upward mobility is another phenomenon known as *anticipatory socialization*, in which individuals assume the attitudes, values and behaviour of a *reference group* which is a higher social class, prior to actually changing their social position. As a consequence they are non-conformist within their own social group – an aspect of personality which results in alienation from their class of origin and facilitation of upward mobility.

Theories of social class and its function

Since social stratification appears to be a universal phenomenon, its nature and possible functions have been the subject of much debate. We saw that Karl Marx regarded social class as economically based and due to the division of labour brought about by the process of industrialization. Thus, in contrast to the earlier feudal economy where each family was more or less self-sufficient, the new society was one in which some members began to accumulate surplus wealth and gained ownership and control of the means of production – the bourgeoisie – while the bulk of the remainder formed the proletariat who sold their labour for wages. A relatively small middle-class or 'intermediate' stratum of craftsmen, artisans, self-employed professional men, etc., also existed, but Marx believed this would disappear and society would be split into 'two great hostile camps'. In fact he saw the social stratification of the nineteenth century as simply a stage in the development of society – a consequence of the capitalist system – which would later be replaced by a socialist, classless society following the victory of the workers in the conflict between the classes. Subsequent events have, of course, only partially fulfilled these predictions.

Communist countries have arisen following worker revolution, but gradually the post-revolutionary equality and classlessness has been followed by demands for increased efficiency and economic growth and the re-emergence of inequalities associated with the need for a higher degree of division of labour (see below). At the same time in Western societies, Marx's intermediate stratum, far from disappearing, has expanded as a new type of middle class, while the working class has not exhibited great militancy. This is not to say that conflict does not exist, and Dahrendorf (1959) has argued that the class struggle is now a question of power rather than ownership of property – the power to control material resources and conditions of work – and that this would arise even in a fully socialist society. Such 'conflict' viewpoints, then, see the class struggle as a permanent feature of all organized societies.

An alternative, 'functionalist' theory of class was put forward in 1945 by Kingsley Davis and Wilbert E. Moore, who argued that the universality of social stratification is due to its function of motivating individuals to fill the various functions required by the division of labour and to carry the responsibilities of these positions. Social inequality with unequal distribution of rewards is necessary for this purpose in order to obtain the most qualified persons for the most important positions. Thus, it is claimed, every society must differentiate people in terms of prestige and esteem and must, therefore, possess a degree of institutionalized inequality. A system of this sort may be termed a *meritocracy* since it assumes that an individual's social status depends upon his ability and achievements; but this is an idealistic view that has been criticized as somewhat naive, since it ignores the extent to which obstacles may be placed in the way of individual achievement by the class system itself, as well as the strategies which may be used to increase income differentials – such as restrictive practices with limited entry to particular occupations by trade unions and professions in order to strengthen their bargaining positions.

Once again, it seems unnecessary to consider these two approaches – the conflict and the functionalist theories – as mutually exclusive. In any society, it seems likely that there are opposing forces working towards egalitarianism on the one hand and inequality of social structure on the other. While policies of greater equality of opportunity and some redistribution of income are likely to be pursued in most democratic societies, there would seem to be a need for some measure of inequality for economic efficiency.

Clinical aspects of social stratification
Before we refer briefly to the question of social class and health and illness, it is worth summarizing again the main differences between the social classes, particularly the manual and non-manual workers – since therein lies the importance of social class for medicine and the health professions. We have seen that the major contrasts are in material conditions, including type of occupation, level of income, etc., in attitudes and life styles, and in the nature of communication and of relationships with other people.

The material conditions and life styles of individuals within a social class may influence not only their susceptibility to particular diseases, but also even their life expectancy, and we shall examine these relationships in Chapters 19 and 20.

Similarly, differences of social perspective are probably in part responsible for the differential utilization of health services by working-class and middle-class patients.

Finally, the different styles of communication to which we have referred may lead to difficulties in the relationship, and particularly of understanding, between patients who come from one social class and health professionals from a different social class.

Further reading

Anderson, M. (ed.) (1980) *Sociology of the Family*. Harmondsworth: Penguin.
Bottomore, T. B. (1965) *Classes in Modern Society*. London: Allen & Unwin.
Fletcher, R. (1973) *The Family and Marriage in Britain*, 3rd ed. Harmondsworth: Penguin.

Part 3
The developmental/historical perspective

The theme of this section is change, both of the individual and of society. Chapter 12 is concerned with the latter and considers first some general theories of social change advanced by sociologists past and present, followed by more specific aspects relating to three areas: the family, industrialization and urbanization, and migration.

Chapter 13 deals with the psychological development of the individual from birth to maturity, describing the theories of Jean Piaget, Sigmund Freud and Erik Erikson in relation to cognitive, personality and psychosocial development respectively. After an examination of the relationship of psychological to neural development, consideration is given to environmental influences, including the role of social learning, especially in moral development, and finally the importance of child rearing practice to psychological development.

Chapter 14 looks first at the concept of psychological maturity and the role of mental mechanisms in maintaining psychological stability. This is followed by a description of the effects of ageing on cognitive functions and personality. Finally, consideration is given to the ending of the life cycle – to the process of dying and its effects on others as mourning or grief.

Reference to relevant clinical aspects is made whenever appropriate.

12
Social change

We have already met with the concept of social change in Chapter 3, where we saw that most of the major theoretical schools of sociology have been concerned with explaining the maintenance of social order or the reasons for change in societies. Again, in the last chapter we considered briefly some aspects of change in relation to the institution of marriage and the family and to social class structure – at least in recent years.

These two introductions may serve to represent two approaches within sociology to the study of social change – the first concerned with general, all-embracing theories and associated particularly with the earlier founders of the subject, and the second, and later, emphasizing empirical studies of more specific and limited aspects of change.

Awareness of the fact that societies do change, and sometimes quite dramatically, has been of crucial importance to sociology, and indeed the discipline originated in Europe largely in response to the social upheavals of the French revolution. At the same time the obvious political significance of social change may pose a problem for the individual sociologist, with a choice between neutral, unbiased observation aimed only at understanding, and an involved, active participation in trying to encourage social stability or, perhaps more often, radical social change.

General theories of social change

So far we have spoken only of social *change*, and this has now come to be adopted as the usual descriptive term in preference to earlier concepts such as *progress, evolution* and *development*, each of which has implications as to the nature of social change that may be unwarranted. Social change, then, refers simply to historical variations in human societies as well as more specific changes within them. We shall first consider briefly the theories of social change advanced by four of the 'founding fathers' of sociology – Comte, Spencer, Hobhouse and Marx – and then take a look at some later and current views.

For Auguste Comte (1798–1857), the French mathematician/philosopher to whom the discipline owes its name, social change resulted from man's intellectual development and involved an inevitable progress through successive stages of increasing superiority – a concept taken over from earlier thinkers and known as the 'law of three stages'. Thus the first, or *fictive* stage, was characterized by a supernatural, theological mode of thought in which events in the world were explained in terms of external powers. The second, or *metaphysical*, stage involved thinking and reasoning aimed at discovering inherent truths, but not based on the systematic observation and experimentation which was to come later with the third and final stage of *positivism* in thinking. This intellectual progress was accompanied by a corresponding moral development and changes in social institutions. Indeed it was Comte's ambition to develop sociology as the highest of the 'abstract' sciences (those that deal with general laws) which would provide the basis of a new and better way of life. Such notions were, however, highly speculative, and it was chiefly as the originator of positivism in philosophical thought that Comte made his most enduring contribution.

The sometime railway engineer and later subeditor of the *Economist*, Herbert Spencer (1820–1903), outlined a model of social change which was, as we saw in Chapter 3, derived by analogy from the Darwinian theory of biological evolution. Thus, comparing society to a living organism, social evolution was concerned with increasing complexity and differentiation of function within expanding societies. As in biological evolution, social change was dependent on conflicts and adaptations operating through the process of natural selection and the survival of the fittest. Such an analogy is superficially plausible, but there are important distinctions to be made between historical change and biological evolution. Thus while mutational biological changes are accidental and transmitted by the genes, changes in human cultures are deliberate and brought about and passed on through the process of learning.

Our third theorist of social change was another Englishman, Leonard Trelawny Hobhouse (1864–1929), who turned from academic philosophy at Oxford to journalism with the *Manchester Guardian* before becoming, in 1907, the first professor of sociology in the London School of Economics, in addition to being a psychologist of considerable distinction. Hobhouse spoke of social 'development' for which he proposed four criteria – increases in scale, efficiency, mutuality and freedom – which he suggested was correlated with the growth of mind and increasing rationality of thought as evidenced in advances in scientific knowledge, in the ethico-religious sphere and in art. The correlation would not, however, necessarily be complete, so that there could be discrepancies between developments; and indeed this has since become apparent in the unevenness of development in different parts of the world and the failure of ethical and social changes to keep pace with scientific and technological developments (a phenomenon described later in 1922 by the American sociologist William Ogburn as 'cultural lag').

We have referred on more than one occasion to Karl Marx (1818–83) whose name has, of course, become very familiar through the political application of his revolutionary views in communist countries and elsewhere. Whether Marx should, strictly speaking, be regarded as a sociologist is open to debate. In his own lifetime, the last 35 years of which were spent in England as an exile from his native Germany, his chief contribution was considered to be in the field of economics, while in the first half of this century he was thought of largely as a philosopher. Be that as it may, many sociologists have been much influenced by marxist views, and this is especially true in relation to social change which is seen as resulting from the class struggle and to have an economic basis. Another feature of Marx's 'conflict' theory of social change is its emphasis on the inevitability of the progression through capitalism and the proletarian revolution to a socialist society – all largely without the awareness of the participants in the process since they have a 'false consciousness' of the real nature of society and their position within it. We have already seen, however, that these predictions have largely failed to be confirmed by subsequent events.

Leaving these earliest general theories of social change, we turn to the more limited views of the 'classical' theorists – so-called because they are considered to be the founders of modern sociology. A feature common to most of these theories is the notion of a movement from an 'old' to a 'new' or emerging social order. Thus Emile Durkheim (1858–1917), who grew up in a turbulent period of French history and held successively the Chairs of Social Science at Bordeaux and Sociology at the Sorbonne (of which Comte had been the first holder), was particularly concerned with the social bonds which united individuals in societies and saw social change as reflected in a change in these bonds brought about by increasing division of labour (Durkheim, 1964). He described this change as being from *mechanical* to *organic solidarity* – the former being characteristic of simple, homogeneous societies where social ties are total, very strong and based on similarities between people, while the latter occurred in more advanced, heterogeneous societies in which relations between individuals outside the family are frequently partial and specific to certain situations (e.g. a business deal or professional consultation) – the social solidarity being based on inter-dependence of different groups of people. Such a social change was seen by Durkheim as leading to greater individual freedom and liberty, but at the cost of an increased threat of personal insecurity from the state of deprivation of social ties. He called this *anomie* and we shall consider it again later in relation to his studies of suicide.

A similar view of social change was put forward at about the same time by the German sociologist Ferdinand Tönnies (1855–1936), who distinguished two types of social life which he called *Gemeinschaft* and *Gesellschaft* – usually translated as 'community' and 'association' respectively. Tönnies saw social change as a progression from the former form of social order based on intimate, direct relationships between people towards the latter, characterized by indirect, superficial, impersonal, contractual relations. Actually the two ways of life were not regarded as mutually exclusive categories, but the degree of Gesellschaft was considered to be increasing at the expense of Gemeinschaft, a change which Tönnies himself regretted as reflecting a dehumanization of modern man. Later sociologists who made the same type of distinction between old and new social orders, though in relation to more limited aspects of social change, include C.H. Cooley, who in *Social Organisation* (1909) contrasted *primary groups*, characterized by 'intimate face to face association and cooperation', with other groups which later authors came to refer to as *secondary groups*; and R.M. MacIver who, in *Society* (1937), distinguished again between a *community* with individuals sharing 'the basic institutions of a common life' and an *association* organized specifically for some purpose.

Another classical contributer to the theory of social change was the German sociologist Max Weber (1864–1920) who, on the basis of his comparative historical studies of different cultures and religions, emphasized the role of ideas rather than economic factors in historical change. Thus he claimed a causal association between the origins of capitalism and certain aspects of the new Protestant religion – notably what he called 'inner-worldly asceticism'; a concern with the affairs of this world rather than an exclusive preoccupation with an after-life. The followers of Calvin, especially, came to look upon worldly success as proof of their ultimate salvation, and the economic activity required for this, including self-denial and hard work – the so-called *protestant ethic* – was, according to Weber (1952), fundamental to the development of modern capitalism.

Another concept of central importance to Weber's ideas on social change was that of *authority* – the relatively durable and legitimate exercise of control over people's conduct (Weber, 1964). Three major types of authority were distinguished – *traditional, charismatic* and *rational–legal* – in terms of the basis for their legitimacy. Thus traditional authority is accepted simply because 'it has always been so', whereas rational–legal authority is derived from a system of clearly defined principles or laws. Charismatic authority, in contrast, is by its very nature revolutionary and concerned with social change, since it is based upon the claims of a charismatic individual or group to be able to speak with certainty and authority against the previously existing authority and social structure. Charismatic leaders, religious or political, are of course not always successful, but when they are, may bring about radical social change. Such charisma does not usually last beyond the generation of the leader himself, and if the new social order is to persist it has to be *routinized* by becoming either *traditionalized* by establishment of a dynasty among the descendents of the leader or, more commonly, *rationalized* through the setting up of a bureaucratic administration. It was Weber's contention then, that charisma and rationalization have been the major forces for social change in history, though he did not deny the role of economic and other factors.

Another sociologist who also held that social change was related to ideas was the Russian, Pitirim Sorokin (1889–1968), who distinguished three successive stages in the views of man about the nature of truth – each of which determines the nature of the society itself and its culture. An *ideational* culture is one in which religious views of the world predominate; this would be followed by a *sensate* culture in which truth and reality depend upon the experience of the senses, and finally the *idealistic* culture which involves a realistic or rational view of the world. An additional feature of Sorokin's theory, in contrast to the previous *linear* theories, is that these stages of social change may be *cyclical*, and indeed he thought that modern society was becoming increasingly sensate and thus retrogressing.

The American sociologist, Talcott Parsons, who (as we saw in Chapter 3) was one of the founders of 'structural–functionalism', saw social change as occurring *within* society, and then only within the framework set by established values, so allowing the continued survival of the system without changing to another kind of society. A basic, and essentially evolutionary, concept involved in social change from pre-industrial to industrial society is that of *progressive social differentiation* – the separation of different functions of society, each performed by an institution specialized for that purpose. No new functions have been created, however – the same functions are still being fulfilled by society but in a different way. In terms of changes in social relations associated with modernization, Parsons has described shifts in what he calls *pattern variables* pertaining to categorization of people and attitudes towards them. Thus there is a shift in relation to the former from *particularism* (in which the status of an individual is ascribed by his membership of a particular group), to *universalism* (where status is determined by achievement within equality of opportunity), and in relation to the latter from *affectivity* (when social relations are based upon strong emotional ties) to *affective neutrality* (when certain social ties are maintained in the absence of such emotionality). There are obvious similarities of course between these transitions and those described by Durkheim and Tönnies.

Although Parsons considered these aspects of change within societies, the emphasis in structural–functionalism has been on the stability of social systems and cultures, with social change tending to be seen as an exceptional occurrence. Such a view has been attacked by more radical sociologists such as C. Wright Mills who, in his book *The Sociological Imagination* (1959), criticized most sociology at the time for avoiding research into controversial areas such as the power structure within a society (which Mills himself studied in the USA). There has since been a resurgence of interest in conflict theories of social change – some more explicitly Marxist than others. However, much conflict may exist other than between social classes within society, though this has received the major attention.

Conflict between societies themselves has obviously played a crucial role historically in bringing about social and cultural changes, but in modern times too, international conflict has been and is equally important. Intergenerational conflict is another rather neglected area which may nevertheless be significant for social change, since otherwise the process of socialization would, theoretically, ensure the continuance of social traditions and ways of life quite unchanged from one generation to the next. By criticizing and rejecting some of these cultural values, the younger generation can introduce social changes, and this phenomenon has been observed in both industrialized and developing societies.

Reviewing the various theories of social change, we can see that most have tended to emphasize a particular factor as being of causative significance. Nevertheless, they generally recognized the complexity of the problem, and indeed it is likely that, just as in the development of the individual (as we shall see in the next chapter) and in changes of personal behaviour, so in historical changes of, and within, societies, the determining influences are multifactorial.

There are, however, two central issues which deserve special consideration. The first concerns the extent to which social change is brought about by individuals or by *social forces*. The latter term refers to values and tendencies which, while they depend on social interaction between a number of individuals who each contribute to them, yet are seen by any single person as being external to him and largely outside his influence. Social change may then be perceived only when a sufficient number of individuals start behaving in a different way. At the opposite extreme from this relatively humble contribution of the individual to social change is that of the outstanding person or charismatic leader in Weber's sense. Even then, however, it may be argued that such people owe their influence to the fact that they represent social forces that are already dominant in their time, rather than that they are the sole determinants of social change. It is likely, in fact, that social environment and personal qualities combine to allow such an individual to put forward, in a persuasive way, ideas that prove to be acceptable to a large number of people.

The second issue which arises out of these theories of social change is the role of *ideas* versus *material* factors. This is epitomized by the dispute between the views of Marx and Weber concerning the origins of modern capitalism, which Marx attributed to economic factors and Weber to the influence of ideas – specifically those associated with the so-called protestant ethic. Again it is more reasonable to suppose that both ideas and material circumstances can determine social change, and in any case the two factors are likely to be interrelated since the growth of knowledge affects economic development.

Having looked at the question of social change largely from a historical standpoint, we may now ask what is the position at the present time in relation to our own and other societies? In this context it is difficult to avoid some concept such as development, since obviously some countries are more advanced or developed than others - at least in terms of industrialism and technology. However, this is a matter to which we shall return in Chapter 15, when we consider the differential perspective; though here we may note that the distinction which we have just examined - between material aspects and ideas in social change - provides a means of categorizing contemporary societies according to their level of technological development (developed and under-developed) and social ideology (capitalist or communist) respectively.

Specific aspects of social change

Turning from social change as a general phenomenon, we shall now consider three examples of more specific changes occurring within societies - those related to the family, industrialization and urbanization and, finally, migration.

The family

Social changes within the family and kinship system - particularly in terms of its pattern of relationships and of its functions - were referred to briefly in the last chapter. Here we shall examine in more detail the possible relationship between these changes and the process of industrialization. The questions that arise in this context are, first, is there in fact an association between the 'isolated' nuclear family and industrial society; secondly, is it causal; and thirdly, if there is such a relationship, what is its direction - is the family pattern a necessary precondition for, or a consequence of, industrialization?

The argument starts from the proposition that with the industrial revolution there was a change from a previous pattern of an extended family to that of a nuclear, conjugal family which was relatively isolated from other kin. Such an association has been seen as demonstrating a congruity or fit between this type of family and the needs of an industrial economy. These included the requirement that workers could be recruited according to their skills and achievements rather than their kinship; that they should be geographically mobile and therefore able to break away from family ties; and that they should be able to devote themselves whole-heartedly to their work without being distracted by family concerns. All this was further facilitated by the protestant ethic which put devotion to God and the brotherhood of all men before the special ties of kinship. At the same time the smaller family size was more appropriate to its new role as a unit of consumption rather than production.

All this would suggest that such a family pattern might have provided the preconditions necessary for industrialization; but the alternative view would be that the family changes were actually a consequence of that process. Thus it might be supposed that kinship ties had already been weakened by agricultural developments which preceded the industrial revolution, and in which small family farms were combined into larger estates using hired labour and more efficient farming methods. Industry then took some of the excess labour force, women also began to be employed outside the home, families moved to where the work was, and finally the State started to take over some of the traditional roles of the family – hence the lessened need for the extended family.

Historical and comparative evidence to support one or other of these viewpoints is, however, not at all clear-cut. In the first place the family pattern in present-day industrial societies has been shown still to include an external network of kin beyond the nuclear family – a 'modified extended family'. It is uncertain how important these kinship ties may be, but they are likely to be more so for women who stay at home than for men who go out to work; 'isolation' of the nuclear family may therefore be more relevant for men than for women, though even then, kinship ties may still be important for entry into some occupations, both working-class and professional.

Another feature of modern industrialization and urbanization is the use of migrant labour from rural areas or from other, more rural, countries – a situation which must inevitably lead to some breaking of kinship ties. Nevertheless, such workers do maintain important ties with their families left behind – often including financial support for them. At the same time they may provide many kinds of assistance to related newcomers, so that quite an extensive network of relationships exists.

As well as this contemporary complexity in the relationship between family structure and industrial society there is also historical evidence to show that there has not, in fact, been as much change in the composition of the family since pre-industrial times in England as was at first supposed. Even then the norm was the nuclear family, though it may be that the present-day family is more 'autonomous' with less emphasis on 'duty' in relationships outside it.

It seems that it is impossible at present to say, with any certainty, whether there is a definite cause and effect relationship between the nuclear family and the process of industrialization. All we can say is that there does appear to be a reasonable degree of congruence or fit between the two systems – family and economic.

Industrialization and urbanization

We have referred to *industrialization* as a major factor in bringing about social change, and a feature of this change which has received particular attention has been the growth of towns and cities – a process described as *urbanization*. Although cities were already in existence some thousands of years ago they have, until recent times, been relatively small and surrounded by rural areas. Only in the last 150 years have societies become urbanized to the extent that most of the population lives in towns and cities. Britain was the first to attain this state, so that now four-fifths of the people are urban dwellers – living in towns and cities of more than 50,000 inhabitants. The same pattern exists in most other industrialized nations where urbanization has been closely related to economic development. However, a similar process is also occurring in less industrialized countries, especially those in the so-called Third World, largely owing to the rapid rise in the total population – a situation which, in the absence of rapid industrial growth, can lead to great social distress with lack of employment and conditions of poverty.

Social problems have, however, long been considered to be associated with the change from a rural to an urban society, with social changes characterized, as we have seen, by Tönnies as progressing from Gemeinschaft to Gesellschaft – a decline in the traditional community with its sense of belonging, towards a more superficial, impersonal way of life for a large, heterogeneous population concentrated into a small area, and leading to conflicts and such signs of social pathology as high rates of crime and delinquency, mental illness, etc.

In the present century, much attention has been directed to the field of urban sociology, especially in the USA, starting with a series of studies in the 1920s and 1930s by Louis Wirth and the so-called Chicago school of sociologists, who were early users of the technique of participant observation. Wirth formulated the concept of *urbanism* defined by three factors of large size, high density and marked heterogeneity of population, and summarized in his 1938 essay 'Urbanism as a way of life' in which he contrasted 'urban-industrial' with 'rural-folk' societies – the former characterized by secondary, functional rather than primary, close contacts, a decline in the social importance of the family and disappearance of the 'neighbourhood'. In an attempt to overcome some of these features of social isolation, city dwellers tended to join formal organizations of various sorts to facilitate social contacts.

Later studies, of which there have been several in Britain, have shown that some of Wirth's ideas need qualification. Thus neighbourhoods within the city may remain important for many inhabitants, and while voluntary organizations are certainly common in urban communities, their membership tends to be restricted and chiefly drawn from the middle-aged and middle class. Nevertheless, the association of urbanism with social 'normlessness', or the *anomie* of Durkheim, especially among the unskilled, low-income and often immigrant population of the decayed central areas of cities, has been confirmed by recent studies (e.g. Banfield, 1970).

Part of the reason for this unsatisfactory aspect of urban life must lie in the unplanned nature of the rapid growth of urbanism in the nineteenth century. Lack of control over the expansion of cities and towns often led to large areas of slums and further and further spread into the surrounding rural areas – a process known as *urban diffusion*. Those who were able to, tended to move to the outskirts, leaving the central areas to neglect and decay. This *laissez-faire* approach to the development of towns and cities contrasts with that of the ancient Greeks who were concerned to prevent disorganized growth by limiting the size of urban communities.

This idea was taken up in Britain in the early years of this century by Sir Ebenezer Howard, who introduced the idea of 'garden-cities' – relatively small cities of about 30,000 population which would include industry, commerce, local government, education and various social activities as well as residential areas.

The end of the Second World War saw a need for an extensive housing programme, and much of this followed a similar pattern with the development of 'new towns', planned in such a way as to meet all the requirements of their inhabitants. At the same time, however, private and municipal housing estates were built on the outskirts of existing towns, and these have, in fact, accommodated a larger proportion of people than have the new towns. There are also some differences in the process of selection of new inhabitants for the two types of community – those in new towns tending to have moved there because of employment in local industry, compared with those in fringe council estates who were selected in order of priority from the housing waiting list of those requiring rehousing from poor and overcrowded conditions – differences which may have implications for the health of the two communities.

Migration

We have spoken of the process of geographical *migration* both within and between countries, occurring especially as part of the social changes associated with urbanization. The scale of migration from one country to another has, however, varied considerably at different times and in different places, as have its causes.

As far as Great Britain is concerned the composition of the population has been altered over the centuries by successive influxes of newcomers from overseas, initially by invaders and later by immigrants who came for various reasons – religious, political or economic. For much of the time the size of the total population has not been significantly affected by the process, since the numbers of *immigrants* who have entered the country has been balanced by the numbers of *emigrants* who have left. During the fifty years or so straddling the turn of the century, however, the size of the emigration to the colonies – chiefly Canada, Australia and New Zealand – was massive with the loss of over two million people, mostly young men, which accentuated the already existing excess of females in the population.

For the last hundred years there has been a series of waves of immigration, following on from the Irish who came to escape the conditions of poverty at home, through the refugees from European countries changing from monarchies to republics and later fleeing from the Nazi persecution, up to the more recent arrivals from Commonwealth countries such as the West Indies, India, Pakistan and East Africa. In the late 1950s and early 1960s the rate of this latter immigration exceeded that of emigration, until legislation was introduced in 1962 to restrict the numbers coming into the country from the Commonwealth.

Each group of immigrants has, of course, brought with it its own customs and culture, and these have, over the years and to varying extents, contributed to changes within British society itself. In the first place, however, immigrants have to be gradually *assimilated* by the host society since they start off as 'outsiders' – a *minority group* – and for this reason are frequently subject to discrimination of various sorts. For a period after their arrival immigrants tend to form small communities within large towns and cities, usually in the more run-down central areas; some districts such as the East End of London have seen a succession of immigrant populations.

The ease and speed with which the immigrant minority is then assimilated by the host society depends very largely on the degreee of similarity between the two communities in terms of language, culture, religion, appearance, etc. In the case of the earlier refugees from Europe the only requirement was to learn the English language, and within a generation they were unrecognizable as a distinct group – their major legacy today being their surnames. Where religious and cultural differences exist, however, assimilation is more difficult, and immigrants who wish to protect and perpetuate their customs and beliefs tend to form communities of their own. This applies, for example, to many Jews who are more orthodox compared with others who feel less 'Jewish' and tend to identify themselves as more 'British'.

However, it has only been in relatively recent times on any significant scale in this country that the colour of an immigrant's skin has been such an obvious distinguishing feature from the rest of the population and one which, apart from interracial breeding, will persist through to succeeding generations. Once again, the coloured immigrants from the West Indies, India and Pakistan have settled in the large industrial cities, where in some areas they outnumber the local white population – a fact which is apparent to the casual observer in a way that would not, of course, have been the case with earlier white immigrants.

It is, perhaps, this obvious difference in appearance that has been responsible for the greater degree of discrimination practised against the coloured than other immigrant minorities. There have been, and still are, some fairly deep-rooted attitudes and beliefs associated with the idea of skin colour independent of other characteristics. We shall, however, defer further consideration of this aspect until we deal with social attitudes and prejudice in Chapter 18.

It is clear that the process of immigration is associated with social change within a society, but the extent to which all minority groups are assimilated and integrated into the whole is likely to be variable. Indeed it is questionable whether this should necessarily be an ultimate goal provided there is protection of such minorities against discrimination, and tolerance and respect exists on both sides for religious, cultural and other differences.

The individual and social change

In the last chapter we were concerned with the relationship between the individual and society in terms of his position within its structure – a relatively static situation; but here we must take a more dynamic view of this interaction since we have seen that some measure of social change over time is present in most societies. This means that man has to be able to adjust and adapt to changes in his social, no less than in his physical, environment – an aspect of psychology to which we devoted considerable attention in earlier chapters. There are, however, as we have also seen, variations in the rates of social change at different times and in different places. In Western society, the changes over the last two generations have been enormous and the difficulties experienced by the older members in assimilating these changes result in the so-called 'generation gap' – a phenomenon which has probably always existed but which is widened at times of rapid social change.

Clinical aspects

From the clinical standpoint it is clear that problems for the individual may arise from difficulties in adjustment to social change, and we shall consider three examples.

Suicide

Durkheim was the first to attempt to relate the act of suicide, an apparently most personal piece of behaviour, to social factors. Based on a systematic study of statistics collected in France in the latter part of the nineteenth century which enabled suicide rates to be related to such characteristics as age, sex, marital status, etc., Durkheim in his book *Du Suicide*, published in 1897, concluded that there was an inverse relationship between suicide risk and the degree of integration of individuals into social groups – the higher the level of integration the less the likelihood of suicide. He went on to describe three types of suicide, but the only one with which we are concerned here was the *anomic* – occurring in periods of rapid social change. Under these circumstances – for example, both in times of economic collapse or economic boom – lives of individuals are disrupted and the social environment becomes less secure, associated with a decline in the established norms and values that usually control behaviour; a collapse of what Durkheim called the *collective conscience*. Thus, he claimed, while it seems obvious that financial loss which results in an individual being unable to live according to his previous standards may lead him to feel frustrated, depressed and consequently to contemplate suicide, so too, the sudden acquisition of wealth may lead people to feel free from societies' controls, to develop unrealistic expectations beyond possible fulfilment, and therefore also to become frustrated and suicidal.

Some of Durkheim's findings and views on suicide have been challenged by later workers – the assumption, for example, that official statistics of death by suicide as recorded by coroners' verdicts accurately reflect the true suicide rate has been shown to be unwarranted in some countries, especially those whose religious attitudes to suicide are strong; but in general the importance of alienation of an individual from his group in increasing the likelihood of suicide has been confirmed. Clearly, though, we are faced once again with an example of an interaction between individual and environment in determining suicidal, as any other, behaviour, and it is necessary to keep both in mind – though the health professional is most likely to be concerned with the more personal factors in dealing with an individual case.

New communities

We have already referred to the massive programme of rehousing in Great Britain following the Second World War – chiefly of people from inner city areas to peripheral housing estates or new towns. It was clearly of great interest to see what effect this might have on the health of these populations, though this raises all the methodological difficulties of such surveys when trying to measure the true prevalence of illness rather than its rate as seen by medical agencies – necessitating, in fact, interviewing of a sample of the population. As far as physical health is concerned it seems to be generally held to have improved, especially among the children, but there is less agreement on the question of mental health.

Just before the war Taylor (1938) had described what he called *suburban neurosis* occurring, particularly among women, in the housing estates which had developed around the larger cities as part of the process of urban diffusion, and which he attributed largely to social isolation in the new environment. An early study of a post-war housing estate by Martin, Brotherston and Chave (1957) showed that an apparently similar situation still existed, with higher than average mental hospital admission rates, general practitioner consultations for neuroses and proportion of individuals with nervous symptoms interviewed in a sample of the population. Again this was put down to the social isolation of the inhabitants compared with their previous life.

Later studies, however, have cast some doubt on the supposed adverse effects of life in these new communities. Hare and Shaw (1965) compared a new peripheral housing estate with an older central town area from which many of the inhabitants had moved, and found no difference in the amount of neurosis. There was, however, in both populations, a vulnerable group of people who were more prone to develop both physical and mental illness and also to complain of their surroundings – the nature of the complaints differing in the two areas. Similar findings were obtained by Taylor and Chave (1964), who examined measures of mental health in three communities – a new town, a peripheral estate and an inner city area. Again, a constitutionally vulnerable group suffering from 'subclinical neurosis syndrome', and expressing dissatisfaction with their environment and feelings of loneliness, was identified in all three areas and was a similar size in each. In fact, Taylor dismissed his earlier concept of suburban neurosis in view of these findings.

It seems that the social changes involved in rehousing are most pathogenic for individuals already of vulnerable personality – once again an interactional phenomenon. Whether placement of such persons in an 'ideal' social environment would abolish neurosis has yet to be demonstrated.

Migration

The health implications of migration, both internal and between different countries, have attracted much attention. Probably the most obvious of these is the importation of disease into one country from another, though as far as serious infectious disease is concerned this is related less to immigration as such, than to rapidity of travel by air. The presence of imported diseases which are seldom seen in the indignious population sometimes makes for difficulties in diagnosis for doctors of the host country unless they maintain a high level of vigilance.

In relation to psychiatric illness, studies have shown higher hospital admission rates for foreign than for native born – though the difference decreases with succeeding generations. One explanation could be that those liable to develop certain mental illnesses are more likely to emigrate, and support for this came from an early study by Ødegaard (1932) who found a higher admission rate for Norwegians living in Minnesota, USA than for Americans or native Norwegians (i.e. migration was thought to be related to the early stages of the disease or the pre-existing personality). Astrup and Ødegaard (1960) later found a reversed selective process for internal migration in Norway with lower admission rates for those who had moved.

For milder illnesses the actual stress of immigration may be more important – a *culture shock* – adjustment to which has been likened to that following bereavement. Sometimes this may be sufficient to produce a florid *immigrant psychosis* which may be 'cured' simply by returning to the country of origin.

Nevertheless, results of studies in recent years have challenged the belief that immigrants invariably suffer a higher rate of mental disorder. Murphy (1977) has argued against such a unitary concept and has, instead, proposed that the mental health of an immigrant group is determined by three sets of factors related respectively to the society/culture of origin, the circumstances of the immigration and the society of resettlement.

Further reading

Bernard, J. (1982) *Future of Marriage*. London: Yale University Press.
Frankenberg, R. (1966) *Communities in Britain*. Harmondsworth: Penguin.
Young, M. and Willmott, P. (1973) *The Symmetrical Family*. London: Routledge & Kegan Paul.

13
Psychological development from birth to maturity

In the last chapter we considered social change as seen in different societies over different periods of time, together with some theories advanced to explain such historical variation. When we turn to the individual, however, it is at once apparent that there is a recognizable pattern of psychological changes associated with the life cycle from birth to death – an invariant sequence of age-related changes generally described as *psychological development* up to maturity and *ageing* thereafter. (The latter will be dealt with in the next chapter).

It is, of course, also clear that these behavioural changes accompany a similar succession of stages of physical development – the order of which is also always the same despite differences in rate of growth between individuals. This pattern of structural changes of, and within, the body is largely under genetic control and is referred to as *maturation.*

Behavioural development is, then, contributed to by two processes: on the one hand, physical maturation – especially of the central nervous and endocrine systems, and on the other hand, *learning* from the environment. We should recognize, though, that even the latter is, within a society, likely to vary systematically according to the age of the individual (e.g. at first the cot and the mother, through increasing contact with others in the family and later outside, then school etc.). In other words, the extent of psychological development of a person as reflected in his behaviour and subjective experience at a particular age will be determined both by the stage of physical maturation and by his past and current life experience.

Because these two factors of maturation and learning are so intricately related it is difficult to separate out their relative contributions to psychological development. Evidence for the role of maturation has, however, come from several sources. The first of these, the most obvious, and one to which we shall return in greater detail later in this chapter, concerns the correlation of stages of behavioural development with the progress of structural maturation; certain types of behaviour only making their appearance when sufficient physical maturation has occurred.

Other evidence comes from experiments which attempt to exclude the effect of learning – for example, by anaesthetizing animals for a period of time during which controls of the same age are developing a particular piece of behaviour, and demonstrating that on recovery from the anaesthetic the animals that have thus been deprived of any learning experience are just as proficient in the particular behaviour.

Such work has not, of course, been performed with humans but the different effects of applying the same learning experiences at different stages of human development does suggest the importance of maturation. In a classical experiment by Gesell and Thompson (1929), one member of a pair of identical twins was given special practice in stair climbing while the other was kept from the stairs. When the second twin was later allowed to climb the stairs she reached a degree of skill similar to that of her sister within a shorter space of time.

The role of genetic factors in controlling behavioural maturation has also been investigated in man through the use of twins. The same pair of investigators, Gesell and Thompson (1941), found very similar patterns of development in both members of a single pair of identical twins whom they followed up from early infancy to adolescence. More recently Freedman and Keller (1963) showed a greater similarity in the developmental patterns of identical than of non-identical twins in the first year of life.

We have already used the term *stages* in relation to psychological development, and a familiar example of such a notion is provided by Shakespeare's 'Seven ages of man'. We shall see shortly that most of the major developmental theorists have made use of the concept of qualitatively different periods of development which, despite differences between individuals in their ages of onset, always follow each other in the same sequence. This is not to suggest that there is not a continuous, quantitative development of particular behaviours, but that at certain times there is a relatively sudden change in behavioural organization resulting in the appearance of new types of behaviour and loss of others. Thus to take an example, the emergence of walking can be quite rapid over a short space of time but may, nevertheless, be seen to be the result of a reorganization of several individual elements of behaviour that have been developing steadily over a longer period.

So far we have spoken of psychological development as a unitary or holistic process, but it is customary to make a distinction between cognitive and personality (emotional and motivational) aspects as we saw earlier when we considered the analytic perspective. Clearly there must be a very close interrelationship between the two, and though we shall consider them separately, we shall later attempt to relate them both to physical maturation.

Various methods of study have been employed in this field, including direct observation and detailed description of infants and children in their natural setting from which schedules of normal development may be derived; investigation of responses of children of different ages to experimental manipulation of the environment – both natural and laboratory; psychological testing of groups of children of different ages or the same children at different ages; retrospective studies to relate later behaviour to early experience; prospective longitudinal descriptive studies of large numbers of children from birth; and, finally, psychoanalysis, often clinical, of both adults and children.

Knowledge of development thus comes from a wide range of studies of varying degrees of objectivity and subjectivity, covering both normal and abnormal behaviour and experience. Going beyond such observations, however, a number of explanatory developmental theories have been put forward, and we shall now consider three of the more important of these. Each is associated with a particular individual, though other workers have often been involved in their testing, extension and modification. The process of language development will then be examined separately.

Jean Piaget and cognitive development

We shall defer until Chapter 17, consideration of the way that intelligence, as measured by intelligence tests, changes in its manifestation during childhood development. Here we are concerned with a brief examination of the most systematic and coherent view of intellectual development to date – constructed over a lifetime of work by a Swiss, Jean Piaget. Many of his ideas are complex and not easy to comprehend, but they have been extremely influential in developmental psychology. Piaget, though a psychologist, started his career as a zoologist and had in addition always been deeply interested in mathematics and philosophy. Indeed, his studies of cognitive development form part of a more general concern with that major area of philosophy known as *epistemology*, the theory of knowledge. Where Piaget differs from most philosophers in his approach to the nature of knowledge is in his claim that, since knowledge is only acquired by an individual through the operation of psychological processes, then a proper theory of knowledge must rest upon an understanding of such processes. In other words, knowledge is itself a suitable subject for scientific study rather than philosophical speculation. The capacity for rational thought and the creation of knowledge is regarded as having been a necessary evolutionary development in man, but since it is now virtually impossible to trace this process historically, Piaget adopts a technique from biology and replaces phylogenesis (evolutionary development) by ontogenesis (individual development).

Thus, for Piaget, the study of the way that a child's thinking develops is the key to an understanding of the way that the structure of knowledge itself has developed in mankind's remote past – a theory of knowledge which Piaget describes as *genetic epistemology*. Though it would be tempting to pursue further this aspect of Piaget's work and to compare it with other epistemological theories – empiricist, rational, phenomenological, etc. – this is not our purpose and we must leave it as an introductory background to our present concern, which is the description of cognitive development in childhood.

A concept of central importance is the notion that a child's knowledge of the world is acquired not by a purely passive learning process but by an interaction between his internal mental structure and the constantly changing environment. The idea of mental structure in terms of *schemata* is another of Piaget's basic concepts. An action schema refers to the organization of an action which has a particular pattern and a tendency to be repeated, ranging from a simple response to a stimulus to a complex piece of behaviour; it is thus a mental structure whose function is to produce a particular action. Schemata are, however, conceived as mobile and flexible, so that they are constantly modified by interaction with the environment until a state of temporary *equilibrium* is obtained – temporary, that is, until environmental change leads to further modification. This process of *adaptation* to the realities of the environment has two components (Fig. 13.1). The first is called *assimilation* and involves the integration of something new into an activity, as when a baby grasps a rattle for the first time – the 'grasping schema' assimilating the rattle as an 'object to be grasped', or when the 'sucking schema' comes to include visible objects at a distance as well as those that actually touch the mouth. The process of assimilating a new object is likely, however, to result in a *disequilibrium* between the new aspect of the environment and the existing schema, which then has to

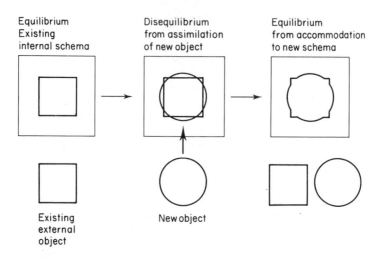

Equilibrium
Existing
internal schema

Disequilibrium
from assimilation
of new object

Equilibrium
from accommodation
to new schema

Existing
external
object

New object

Fig. 13.1   Diagrammatic representation of Piaget's concept of the adaptation of internal schemata to external reality

take account of the characteristics – size, shape, weight, etc. – of the object; a process of modification called *accommodation*. The grasping schema, for example, has to accommodate so that the child is able to shape the hand and fingers to fit the rattle he is about to grasp.

As the child develops, so the surrounding environment is progressively assimilated with consequent accommodation of the existing schemata – according to Piaget, 'an ever more precise adaptation to reality'. In a sense the two processes are in conflict, and development consists of a succession of states of disequilibrium between the two, followed by temporary resolutions. Sometimes one process predominates and sometimes the other; accommodation exceeding assimilation results in imitation, as when a child adopts the actions and manners of an older person, or uses adult phrases, but inappropriately; assimilation predominating over accommodation may be seen in play when everyday external objects are imagined to fit a phantasy schema – a wooden box becomes an aeroplane, a boat, a car.

In summary, Piaget's concept of mental development implies that the child is not a passive recipient of environmental stimulation but actively organizes his inner mental world in terms of his experiences of, and activities in, the external world.

Four stages of development are described by Piaget, the sequence being always the same despite individual variation in ages of onset of the different stages.

1 Sensori-motor stage

This, the first stage of cognitive development, extends from birth to about 18 months. It is characterized by behaviour which occurs in the absence of symbolic thought, and depends upon simultaneous activity of the perceptual and motor apparatuses; activity mostly of a simple reflex kind but governed by genetically determined schemata present at birth – sucking, grasping, etc. All appropriate objects are at first assimilated by these schemata which accommodate to them, but gradually there appears an ability to differentiate between objects. At the same time there is an organization and coordination of simple into more complex schemata, such as thumb-sucking, and looking at and grasping objects.

Another important achievement during this stage of development is the creation of a *schema of object permanence*. In the first few months of life an object which is hidden under a cloth within full view of the infant has apparently ceased to exist as far as he is concerned – if he has been about to grasp it the activity immediately ceases. Only by about nine months will he search for it in the place where it disappeared, indicating that the object is now perceived as having a stable, persistent existence separate from the child. It is assumed that, prior to this, there is no definite differentiation between the self and the world outside – between 'me' and 'not me' – a so-called *radical egocentricity* in which the universe is seen entirely in relation to the child's own actions. The new advance from this position also allows the development of some notion of causality since the child can observe how some events are dependent and some independent of his actions. He observes that he can, for example, drop things out of his pram in order that someone will pick them up!

By the end of this stage the child has a practical but limited understanding of objects and events in the world in so far as he has been directly involved with them. At the same time he is beginning to form sensori-motor representations in his mind and to be able, in a given situation, to perform simple internal or mental actions which he can then apply to actual activity (e.g. to solve a simple problem without using 'trial and error') – a kind of interalized action which can be considered as *sensori-motor thinking* and from which symbolic thought will emerge in the next stage of development.

2 Pre-operational stage
This starts at the end of the sensori-motor stage in the second half of the second year, and continues to the age of about seven years when, as we shall see, the child becomes capable of true 'operational' thinking. It is, however, divided into two substages.

2a Symbolic thought
This emerges out of the sensori-motor internal representation and thinking which preceded and continues in parallel with it. The action schemata which the child has developed can be seen as *symbols* of the environment which he is now able to apply to new situations. The ability to recreate past activity as a mental image is called by Piaget *deferred imitation*, and it is this which allows the progression to symbolic thought. This differs from sensori-motor thinking in that, whereas the latter only occurs as a result of external activity, the former actually gives rise to such activity. Thus whereas the younger child may find ways of playing in an experimental way with familiar objects in the environment, the two-year old will now be able to use them to represent other objects that have also been internalized as symbols (a stone as a sweet, for example, in a pretend game of eating, with awareness of its symbolic nature being shown by the fact that the child does not actually eat it!).

A feature of the child's view of the world at this stage is still his *egocentrism*, in the sense that reality is interpreted in a very self-centred way. He will believe that inanimate objects have feelings like his own, that his thoughts can actually change events, and he has no idea of viewpoints other than his own. His thinking is also dominated by what he perceives of the environment – a so-called *percept-centred* view of the world.

At about the same time as symbolic thought is beginning to develop there is also a rapid increase in the use of language by the child. Words are, of course, also symbols in that they represent objects, events, etc., but the relationship betweeen a word and that which it symbolizes is usually quite arbitrary and has to be learnt by the child. Nevertheless it is Piaget's view that the increasing use of language at this stage is based upon the emergence of symbolic thought, and that there is subsequently a gradual integration between, on the one hand, the private symbolism of the child based on his unique past experience of objects and events and his actions in relation to them, and on the other hand, the public symbolism of language which depends upon socially agreed meanings of words and grammatical rules. Language is thus first assimilated into the private symbolism which then accommodates to it.

2b Intuitive thought

This stage begins at the age of about four years but is not clearly demarcated from the previous one. By this time the child is able to communicate with, and think in, language; but again his use of it is immature and very personal or egocentric, so that words may still have private meanings not shared with others. Gradually, however, with increasing social involvement and interaction he comes to acquire a shared or communal form of communication and thought. The latter, however, is still 'pre-operational' – in the sense that mental 'operations' or transformations of mental images cannot be performed.

This *static representation* together with another feature of thought at this stage known as *centration*, is well illustrated in a famous experiment of Piaget's with eggs and egg-cups (Fig. 13.2). The five-year-old child is shown a row of eggs and egg-cups (a), and agrees that there is the same number of each. The eggs are now removed from the egg-cups and placed close together, with the egg-cups still spread out (b). The child now says that there are more egg-cups than eggs. If the eggs are then spread out over a greater distance than the egg-cups (c), the child says there are more eggs than egg-cups. Piaget's explanation is that the child is only able to attend to a part of the complex whole and fixates or *centres* on one aspect of the changing relationship between the eggs and egg-cups. If either is more spread out then its number appears to have increased. At the same time that the child is thus unable to *decentre* his thought, he is also unable to relate the different arrangements to each other and to see them simply as transformations – he has in fact only a static representation of the objects.

Similar limitations are revealed by another well-known experiment with

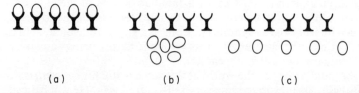

(a)   (b)   (c)

Fig.13.2 Piaget's experiment with eggs and egg-cups, illustrating the failure of the 'pre-operational' child to appreciate the conservation of number with rearrangement

beakers of different sizes (Fig. 13.3). if water is poured into two beakers of the same dimensions so that the levels are the same (a), a 'pre-operational' child will agree that there is an equal quantity of water in each. If now the water from one beaker is poured into another that is taller and narrower (b), the child says that there is more water in it, despite having witnessed the procedure. Similarly, if the water is now poured into a shorter and wider beaker (c), it is held to have decreased in quantity. The explanation is again in terms of the child's 'centring' on a particular feature of the problem – namely the tallness of the beakers and of the level of the water within. Once more the child has failed to appreciate what Piaget calls the concept of *conservation* despite changing conditions – in this case, the conservation of 'quantity' with change of shape and, in the case of the eggs and egg-cups, the conservation of 'number' with change of spatial distribution.

Such limitations are considered to be further examples of the egocentrism of thinking at this stage which, although fully representational, can only comprehend one set of relationships at a time among objects and therefore leads to denial of others.

3 Concrete operational stage

Starting at the age of about seven years and lasting until about ten or eleven, this stage sees the development of operational thinking and a loss of some of the limitations of the preceding stage. A mental *operation*, according to Piaget, is an internal action, or set of related actions forming an integrated whole, performed by the mind but which has evolved from the internalization of actions that had originally been performed on the external environment. In such an operation, mental representations are combined in various ways to form new representations, but another important feature is that the process is reversible. There is, however, a limitation at this stage in that operations can be performed only on data derived from actual experience, past or present, and for this reason it is described as *concrete* (in contrast to abstract). Nevertheless, this allows the child to perform such tasks as classifying objects in different ways. For example, if he is shown a set of wooden beads of which the majority are brown but a few are white, he will agree that there are more brown than white beads and that all are made of wood. However, if asked whether there are more brown beads or more wooden beads, a pre-operational child will reply that there are more brown beads and will persist in that view despite agreeing that all the beads are wooden. He explains his answer by saying that there are more brown beads than white beads. He is unable to compare part of the whole (brown beads) against the whole (wooden beads) but only against another part (white beads). The older, operational child is able to give the correct answer by saying that

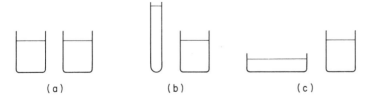

Fig.13.3 Piaget's experiment with beakers of water, illustrating the failure of the 'pre-operational' child to appreciate the conservation of volume with change of shape

there are more wooden beads than brown beads because the white beads are also made of wood – he is able to create both classes of brown and white beads as well as the inclusive class of wooden beads, and to reverse the process.

Similarly, the concept of conservation becomes attainable because the child can keep in mind, at the same time, different measurements – such as, in the beakers experiment, the height and width of the liquid in the beakers, with mental reversals of the processes which had been performed on it during the experiment. Simple tasks of logic are also possible so that the child is able to appreciate at once that, given relationships between objects of different sizes, if A > B and B > C, then A > C. A younger child would have to discover this by making actual comparisons between the objects themselves.

4 Formal operational stage

This, the last stage of cognitive development, brings us to the threshold of the adult form of thinking that we have considered in Chapter 5. The child at the age of ten or eleven becomes capable of reasoning free from dependence on actual environmental experience. He can formulate hypotheses to solve problems and make logical deductions from them. The level of abstract reasoning ultimately achieved will, of course, vary from one individual to another – a question, in fact, of individual differences of intelligence to which we shall return in Chapter 17.

To summarize, Piaget's view of cognitive development involves a progressive adaptation of internal mental structure to external reality, necessitating an increasing departure from the percept-centred and egocentric view of the world that dominates early childhood. Thinking progresses from an initial stage of internalized action, to the use of symbols and especially language, thence to the ability to carry out mental operations based on 'concrete' objects, until finally abstract and fully logical thought is attained.

Criticism of Piaget's work has included the fact that his observations, at least in the earlier years of his studies, were often made on small (and perhaps unrepresentative) samples of children. Results of studies of perception in infants – such as the fact that (as we saw in Chapter 9) the newborn can imitate the facial expression of others (Bower, 1977) – have cast doubt on Piaget's emphasis for cognitive development on physical interaction with the environment through 'action schemata' rather than direct perception. Other criticisms include a failure to recognize the importance for cognitive growth of specific training and formal education (Bruner, 1973) and of the genetic contribution to development (Flavell, 1977). Despite these reservations Piaget's major conclusions remain the most comprehensive and influential in the field of cognitive development.

Sigmund Freud and personality development

Having considered something of Piaget's views on the changes that occur in a child's perception and understanding of the world from birth to adolescence, we now turn to the development of personality – to the accompanying emotional and motivational changes. Again there is one theory, associated originally with one man, that has had a dominating influence on many disciplines concerned with child development (as well as more generally on Western thinking about the nature of man). We have already referred on several occasions to different aspects of Freud's psychoanalytic theory, but here we are specifically concerned with its application to personality development.

Before we begin an examination of psychoanalytic developmental theory, however, there are some general points to be considered. The first of these is that Freud's ideas, like those of Piaget, may be seen to be related to his training and interests. As a medical doctor specializing initially in neurology, where he first began to deal with neurotic patients, Freud derived his theory very largely from his clinical experience with such patients over a period of many years. In particular, he based it on data that he had gathered from individual patients during the lengthy procedure of psychoanalysis which he himself originated. His clients consisted for the most part of well-to-do, middle-class Viennese living in the early decades of this century, when social attitudes (especially towards sexual matters) and child-rearing practices differed in many respects from those of present-day society. It may therefore be questioned whether ideas about childhood development based largely on the recollections of Freud's patients in adult life are altogether applicable without modification today. Certainly there is much less social pressure requiring strict control of the expression of basic drives epitomized in the Victorian view that 'children should be seen and not heard', so that many have pointed to the shift of emphasis from conflicts within the mind (*intrapsychic*) to those between the individual and others (*interpersonal*). In fact, though we shall be unable to detail them all, several modifications have been made to so-called 'classical' psychoanalytic theory by later analysts, some of whom have been involved with the analysis of children (e.g. Melanie Klein and Anna Freud, a daughter of S. Freud).

A second feature of Freud's developmental theory, and one which again reflects his medical background, is that it is essentially biological. The stages of development are, like those of Piaget, held to be innate and related to maturation following an invariant sequence, though the extent to which progress occurs from one stage to the next may vary between individuals.

Another similarity may be observed between Piaget's equilibrium principle – the idea that in adapting to the environment there is a recurrent process of disequilibration resulting from external change followed by internal accommodation and a re-establishment of equilibrium – and Freud's so-called *pleasure principle*. This, to which we have previously referred in Chapter 9, assumes that, in the infant, failure to discharge instinctual energy arising from the *id* causes unpleasant tension, which then leads at this stage of development to internal 'hallucinatory' wish-fulfilment or satisfaction designed to relieve the tension and thus to reduce 'unpleasure', such phantasy being described as *primary process*. According to classical psychoanalytic theory, this infantile phantasy world has, however, to be given up during the course of development in order to allow effective adaptation to the environment, guided by the so-called *reality principle* – instinctual gratification now being sought from objects (usually persons) in the external world. This adaptation is made possible by the development of the *ego* – according to Freud a part of the id that is modified by the direct influence of the external world and which comes to exert a controlling influence over the id. Thus the pleasure principle is considered to be innate and primitive while the reality principle is acquired by learning during development associated with the problem-solving ability known as *secondary process*.

Because of the psychoanalytic assumption of a psychic split between the id and the ego, a distinction is also made between the development of each, though they are held to be linked. *Ego development* emphasizes the acquisition of functions which enable the individual to control his impulses, to become relatively independent and to cope with the environment. *Libidinal development* is the more fully worked-out in classical psychoanalytic theory and is concerned specifically with what happens during development to the *libido*, a form of 'mental energy' initially conceived by Freud to be associated with the sexual instinct and to have its source in the id, though later considered to be in part also possessed by the ego.

Libidinal development is held to progress through a series of stages from birth to adult life, each stage being characterized by a specific area of the body which, for that stage, is believed to be the site of libidinal pleasure when stimulated. The justification for the use of the term *infantile sexuality* in this context is that these so-called *erotogenic zones* (each associated with a bodily orifice) are to varying extents involved in both normal and deviant adult sexual behaviour, though clearly its use in childhood is not intended to indicate genital sexuality in the adult sense.

Another aspect of the psychoanalytic theory of libidinal development concerns the possibility of failure to progress satisfactorily owing to excessive frustration or gratification at any stage, so that an adult individual may be *fixated* at a particular early stage of development, resulting in a tendency to show outmoded patterns of behaviour or to *regress* to these under stress. Thus certain traits of adult personality are, according to the theory, attributable to libidinal fixations and to be labelled accordingly.

After these few introductory remarks we may now consider briefly the several stages of libidinal development.

Oral

The mouth is, of course, of vital importance to the infant's survival; but according to Freud it is also, for the first year of life, the main source of pleasure from local stimulation. The oral stage may be subdivided into two substages: oral sucking and oral biting, the latter also representing an early expression of the aggressive drive.

Fixation at this stage of development is believed to be associated in the adult with such character traits as optimism and pessimism and with a tendency to swings of mood to depression and elation. Fixation predominantly at the oral sucking stage results in a dependent personality, and at the biting stage an orally aggressive adult (sarcastic, cynical etc.). Ego development at the oral stage consists of an increasing awareness of the child's separateness from others, as we have already seen in Piaget's sensori-motor stage.

Anal

During the second year the anus becomes a more important focus for pleasurable sensation, brought about by the child's ability to control bowel movements. This ability is also important to ego development, since it indicates a degree of mastery of the body which can be of social significance in relation to pleasing or displeasing others in toilet training – the capacity to cause annoyance reflecting the operation of the aggressive drive. Again this stage may be subdivided into anal-expressive and anal-retentive substages, related to gratification from, respectively, eliminating and retaining faeces.

The so-called anal character in adulthood associated with fixation at the anal stage exhibits the obsessional traits of excessive cleanliness, fastidiousness, orderliness, meanness, etc., or the opposites (untidiness, messiness, generosity, etc.) – perhaps reflecting the conflict in infancy between holding back and expulsion of faeces and characteristic of each of the two substages.

Phallic

By the age of about three or four years the focus of attention has shifted to the genitals. The little boy becomes concerned with his penis, with its size and functions, and generally with the idea of potency, strength, manliness, etc. Thus the phallic character resulting from fixation at this stage considers sexual behaviour as a display of potency, rather than the more mature genital character which sees it as part of a relationship.

Oedipal

The stages of libidinal development considered so far may be said to be *narcissistic* in the sense that pleasure is derived from the child's own body. But now, at the age of about four or five years, he develops some largely unconscious sexual feelings about his parents – a desire to possess his mother and to eliminate his father, who is perceived as a feared rival who might inflict punishment by castration. This group or complex of feelings, the *Oedipus complex*, was so named by Freud after the classical Greek legend of Oedipus, whose fate was to kill his father and later marry his mother, both unknown to him as he was abandoned at birth. A similar triangular situation is also held to exist for the little girl, who sees her mother as a rival for the attention of her father – this is sometimes described as the *Electra complex* from another Greek legend.

In either case, resolution of the complex occurs through *identification* of the child with (as we shall see shortly, a wish to actually be, and therefore take on the characteristics of) the parent of the same sex and renunciation of the parent of the opposite sex as a sexual object – leading to the next stage of sexual quiescence. This identification is important for ego development and especially, according to classical psychoanalytic theory, for the creation of the *superego* – that part of the ego concerned with self-observation and self-criticism.

Fixation at the Oedipal stage results in adults who are said to be 'mother fixated' or 'father fixated', in the sense that they chose sexual partners with an obvious resemblance to the parent.

Latency

With the resolution of the Oedipal stage of development, the child is believed to enter a period of sexual quiescence during which attention is directed more to outside interests, such as school.

Genital

This, the final stage of libidinal development, is associated with the hormonal changes of puberty and the reawakening of the sexual drive. It represents, according to classical theory, full maturity. The genital character would be an ideal (probably non-existent) for whom no fixation at a pre-genital stage has occurred, the Oedipal complex has been satisfactorily resolved, and the individual attaches equal importance to his own and his sexual partner's satisfaction.

This then, in brief, is Freud's theory of child development (Freud, 1905, 1933, 1976); but what is its status today? It has certainly been subjected to much criticism both within and outside psychoanalytic circles. Some analysts hold that too much emphasis was placed on the sexual drive as the major determinant in personality development, and Jung and Adler were early dissenters from this view. Erikson, as we shall see shortly, has stressed the importance of the growth of the ego and describes a series of eight stages of psychosocial development, the first three of which correspond to the oral, anal and phallic stages of Freud. Others such as H.S. Sullivan, Karen Horney and Erich Fromm (so-called 'neo-Freudians') emphasize social and cultural rather than biological factors in personality development, and hold that, for example, the Oedipus complex is related to cultural attitudes and is not a universal phenomenon in all societies, while even the oral and anal phases, biologically based though they presumably are, may be influenced by socio-cultural factors.

Psychoanalytic views, even including those derived from the analysis of children, must depend upon the retrospective recollections of individuals – certainly as far as the pre-verbal phase of development is concerned. They may, however, be compared with direct observations of children and with studies of the long-term consequences of different child-rearing practices. The former confirm that obvious pleasure is derived from stimulation of the erotogenic zones by children, though these are less clearly related to the different stages of libidinal development of classical theory. The latency period, on the other hand, is far from being the period of sexual quiescence claimed by Freud; it is associated, in fact, with increasing sexual interest, though this is often concealed from adults (except in sexually permissive cultures where overt sexual activity may occur during middle childhood). At the same time studies of the effects on development of different methods of feeding and of toilet training have generally failed to show any marked effect on adult personality.

Experimental evidence in support of Freudian theory is sparse, largely owing to the untestable nature of many of its hypotheses; such attempts as have been made have met with only partial success (Kline, 1981; Eysenck, 1972; Eysenck and Wilson, 1973; Fonagy, 1986). Finally, the evaluation of psychoanalytic theory is complicated by the fact that, as psychoanalysis, it is applied as a particular form of treatment the effectiveness of which is also open to question. Success or failure of such attempts to bring about fundamental changes of personality in adults should not, however, necessarily be taken to indicate support or refutation of the theory as an explanation of how adult personality has developed.

It is clear that Freudian theory has had to be considerably modified and is likely to continue to be so. However, it would seem unwarranted to reject the whole of it, and many would acknowledge that it provides valuable insights into the world of the developing child.

Erik Erikson and psychosocial development

Erik Erikson, a psychoanalyst born in Germany in 1902 of Danish parents, studied psychological development in a variety of social and cultural settings. In contrast to classical Freudian theory, he places greater emphasis on ego development and resulting psychosocial gains, which he sees as occurring in eight stages or – following Shakespeare – 'ages'. He does not deny the importance of libidinal development but has developed his own interpretation of this biological process to include its relationship to social behaviour. The same three infantile stages based on the erogenous zones – oral, anal and phallic (though called genital) – are described. However, each is associated with other aspects of development, so that the first is called the *oral-sensory* stage because all the sensory surfaces are 'receptive' to stimulation, just as the mouth is to food; the second, *muscular-anal*, because not only the anal sphincters but all the musculature is increasingly involved in contraction and relaxation; the third, *locomotor-genital*, associated with independent movement and phallic sexual interest.

The individual stages are associated with various functions of the particular bodily orifice concerned which Erikson calls *organ modes* – incorporation, retention, elimination and intrusion – a single mode usually predominating at each stage. These are in turn accompanied by corresponding *social modalities* – patterns of interpersonal behaviour which represent a more general approach of the child to the social world. Thus the *first oral incorporative* mode (sucking) is associated with the general social modality of *getting*; the *second oral incorporative* mode (biting) with *taking*; the *anal retentive* mode with *holding on*; the *anal eliminative* mode with *letting go*; and finally the *phallic intrusive* mode with *making* (in the sense of 'being on the make', taking pleasure in attack or conquest).

This, very briefly, is Erikson's version of the theory of infantile sexuality which provides the basis for the first three of his eight ages of man. Each age is associated with a 'psychosocial crisis', a nuclear conflict between two contrasting 'senses' (positive and negative) which the developing ego has to resolve favourably (a 'favourable ratio' between the two senses) as another step in psychosocial adaptation, and as another contribution to the ultimate 'strengths' or 'virtues' of the adult personality. Our consideration of this sequence of stages must again necessarily be brief.

Oral-sensory: basic trust vs. *basic mistrust*

The individual is dependent largely on 'getting' the appropriate quality of caring from the mother, and this induces a sense of identity, of being 'all-right', and the 'virtue' of *hope*.

Muscular-anal: autonomy vs. *shame* and *doubt*

During this stage the sense of autonomy or self-control is fostered by well-guided encouragement to the child to 'stand on his own feet' as he becomes increasingly aware of his muscular maturation, thus gaining a degree of *will power*.

Locomotor-genital: initiative vs. *guilt*

Initiative is associated with successful accomplishment without the establishment of too oppressive a moral sense from the resolution of the Oedipal stage – a 'favourable ratio' resulting in an awareness of *purpose*.

Latency: industry vs. *inferiority*

This stage is associated with the experience of schooling and the world of skills and tools with its successes and failures – a favourable balance producing *competence*.

Puberty and adolescence: identity vs. *role confusion*

Identity is derived from the ego's integration of all the earlier identifications together with individual aptitudes and opportunities from social roles, all promoted by evidence from others of the adolescent's meaning to them – a favourable ratio leading to *fidelity*.

Young adulthood: intimacy vs. *isolation*

Intimacy is the willingness to fuse identity with that of others, to enter into and abide by affiliations and partnerships that may require sacrifices and compromises. Fear of such 'ego loss' may lead to an avoidance of intimacy and a sense of isolation, while *love* is the favourable outcome.

Adulthood: generativity vs. *stagnation*

Generativity is a concern with establishing and guiding the next generation, encouraged by social and religious institutions. It could also include productivity and creativity in the more general sense. *Care* is the favourable outcome.

Maturity: ego integrity vs. *despair*

The final stage is characterized by an acceptance by the individual of his particular life style and life cycle, which will end with his death. Failure of such ego integration leads to a sense of despair and a fear of death; success leads to *wisdom*.

Erikson's concept of eight stages of psychosocial development derives principally from the practice of psychoanalysis, but with the emphasis on the study of the ego and its relation to society. It receives cross-cultural support from his own field-work among Sioux and Yurok Indians and an examination of aspects of American, German and Russian character. Again, it is difficult to assess its scientific status in terms of testable hypotheses, but its influence has been considerable.

Development of language

This is clearly a most important feature of childhood development and will, therefore, receive separate attention. Not only is it vital for interpersonal communication, but it is also, of course, of great significance for the development of thought, as we saw in Chapter 8 and perhaps even for self-consciousness (Chapter 4).

As with all aspects of development the acquisition of the ability to communicate using a language of verbal symbols depends upon the two processes of maturation and learning. There is, in relation to the former, a view associated particularly with the linguistic theory of Noam Chomsky (1957) that there is an innate biologically based human predisposition to language – a so-called *language acquisitional device* (LAD). This supposes that there are some basic rules of language construction that are common to all languages and which are built into the LAD, so that the child applies these rules to what he hears in his particular environment to ultimately produce the appropriate language.

Obviously learning is also essential for the development of language, and the so-called learning theory approach stresses this aspect (e.g. Skinner, 1957), seeing language acquisition in terms of operant conditioning in which correct utterances of the child are rewarded. While this appears plausible for the learning of individual words, it does not adequately account for the production of sentences, although attempts have been made to provide an explanation in terms of stimulus–response chains, each word acting as a stimulus for the next word.

If we leave these theoretical positions and turn to observation of the actual process of language development, we find that, in general, the ability to understand develops at a faster rate than the ability to produce speech. In both cases, however, there is a fixed sequence of stages or milestones.

In terms of comprehension there is evidence for attention to the sound of the human voice by the age of two months (McCarthy, 1954), and this is followed by a progressive ability to discriminate and respond to tone of voice, words, phrases, commands, etc.

In speech there is a similar progress – from crying, through 'babbling' to words, and then to sentences with increasingly complex grammatical structure. Individual words are used for labelling, expressing emotion or indicating action, and even short strings of two or three words give evidence of patterning or rules of construction.

Two approaches to an understanding of this early grammar have stressed firstly the *position* of the words (Braine, 1963) – with a few *pivot* words (e.g. all, no, come, off, other) occupying a fixed position in the sequence and more common *open* words taking different positions (e.g. in relation to the above pivot words – all done, no more, mamma come, shoe off, other side); and secondly the *semantic* structure, i.e. in terms of the meaning of the words as agent, action, object, etc. (Brown, 1973). Even with two-word utterances there is an observance of the basic order rule that a sentence should consist of agent plus action plus object location – i.e. the two words, and later three or four words, will observe this order.

It is clear that language development is not piecemeal but involves the learning of rules. At first these are relatively simple and general but later they become more partial and limited. There is at first a tendency for these partial rules to be applied in an over generalized way so that grammatical mistakes occur, for example, with irregular plurals (e.g. sheeps instead of sheep) and past tenses (e.g. comed instead of came). Early development therefore includes learning to limit the application of such rules and to tolerate exceptions. All this can be seen as reflecting the child's general cognitive development in terms of understanding his environment.

Relationship of psychological to neural development

We have considered three major theories which make use of the concept of developmental stages assumed to be largely based on the process of physical maturation. Neuromotor development, as we saw earlier, is clearly dependent on the maturation of the nervous system, and Gesell (1954), on the basis of close observation of the behaviour of children, described the constant sequence of stages of motor behaviour – supporting the head, sitting, crawling, standing, walking, etc. Recent progress in neurobiology has led to more detailed attempts to integrate concepts of psychological development with what is known of neural organization and development (e.g. Meyersburg and Post, 1979).

Maturation of the nervous system has been found to progress at different rates within different segments, as shown particularly by their degree of myelination – the formation of the fatty myelin sheath round the nerve fibres which is important for rapid transmission of nerve impulses. An example of a parallelism between myelination and functional development is clearly shown by the optic nerve and tract, with completion of myelination by the fourth month being accompanied by evidence of increasing visual ability. More generally, from the psychological standpoint we may note that the oral period of Freud and the sensori-motor stage of Piaget evolve during the completion of myelination of the sensory and motor roots and pathways during the first eighteen months of life.

Maturation of other parts of the nervous system proceeds at a slower rate, so that the limbic system is only fully myelinated by the sixth year and the reticular formation in the second decade of life. Slowest in maturation is the cerebral cortex where myelination continues to increase beyond the fifth decade. A correspondence may be drawn between these delayed maturations and the age-related development of emotional differentiation and control and expression of cognitive abilities with, perhaps, the appearance of more complex cognitive processes and subtle personality features awaiting the still later expansion of cortical complexity.

Environmental influences on the process of development

Having considered the contribution of physical maturation to psychological development, we may now turn to the role of the environment and especially of learning in this process. As we have seen, maturation and learning are intimately related, and indeed environmental experience may even have a direct influence on neural development. Thus, for example, there is much experimental evidence to show that providing additional sensory stimulation to young animals or depriving them of normal stimulation may have long-term effects in increasing and reducing, respectively, their cognitive abilities (problem-solving, learning, etc.) as adults; but it has also been found that these early environmental experiences may affect corresponding limbic and cortical neuronal development. However, it is with learning from the social environment that we are particularly concerned here – with the development of the child as a new member of a society, the process to which we have previously referred as socialization.

Social learning

We have, of course, already considered the process of learning in some detail in Chapter 6, but here we are concerned with its special role in the acquisition of social behaviour by the developing individual. Of crucial importance to this process is the formation of a dependent relationship between the infant and an important adult or group of adults from whom he begins to learn. The formation of these social ties or *attachments* has been studied not only by psychologists but also by ethologists; for example, we have already considered (in

Chapter 6) Konrad Lorenz's studies of the *imprinting* of young birds to any moving object (normally the mother) during the short so-called *critical period* after hatching.

At the same time we also referred to H.F. Harlow's experiments with infant monkeys, which showed that their attachment to the mother depended upon 'contact comfort' obtained from clinging to her. The lasting effect of this early experience and (contrasting with other forms of learning) its independence of reinforcement (Harlow's infant monkeys preferred the cloth-covered 'surrogate mother' to a milk-supplying wire one) suggest an obvious similarity with Lorenz's imprinting of chicks, and both are clearly related to the development of fear and avoidance behaviour. Separation of the infant from the mother results in signs of fright and lack of exploratory behaviour.

Attachment of the human infant to the mother may likewise depend upon imprinting experiences, probably during a critical period of the first six months of life (Bowlby, 1969). Although the baby is unable to actively follow or cling to his mother, he is able to smile and to follow her with his eyes, which may be an equivalent behaviour.

An alternative, or perhaps complementary, view of the development of infantile dependency, at any rate in man, is derived from learning theory. It supposes that satisfaction of the baby's basic needs for food, etc., produces a sense of comfort which is associated with the presence of the provider – usually the mother. Anxiety, on the other hand, is evoked by parental absence, and the fear of such absence in the face of parental disapproval is crucial to the social learning theory view of the process of socialization.

Thus, in accordance with the principles of operant conditioning, the child's social behaviour is moulded by positive reinforcement and punishment (by fear) resulting from parental approval and disapproval respectively. Of course, parents may also use more obvious physical forms of reward and punishment, but the influence of their expressed approval and disapproval is an early example of the importance of *social reinforcement* during development, and indeed in adult life. Studies have shown an age effect, so that after the age of about five years children are increasingly affected by social reinforcers of the opposite sex and by adult strangers.

Learning in this way thus results in the child taking first the parents and then other adults as models for the acquisition of social behaviour. There are two further phenomena which are relevant to this process: imitation and identification. *Imitation* refers to the tendency of children to mimic the behaviour of other persons, sometimes in their presence and sometimes afterwards in their absence. Some psychologists hold that such behaviour is innate, but others suggest that the child's awareness of the 'appropriateness' of a piece of copied behaviour brings a feeling of satisfaction that is reinforcing. *Identification*, on the other hand, involves a more intensive and extensive, largely unconscious, modelling of the child on someone who is of particular significance to him in a relatively long-lasting relationship. The process results in the incorporation of aspects of that person's personality into the child himself, so that he takes over many of the model's characteristic attitudes and beliefs as well as his behaviour. We have already seen that identification plays an important part in Freudian theory, where resolution of the Oedipal phase of libidinal development is said to be achieved by the child's identification with the parent of the same sex, thus achieving sex-role identification as well as formation of the super-ego (we shall return to the latter shortly).

Both imitation and identification have been studied experimentally. Bandura (1962), for example, has shown that children will copy aggressive behaviour seen in a film, the more so if the model is seen being rewarded by an adult for the aggression than if he is seen being punished – an experiment of some significance in relation to possible effects on children of televised violence. Identification has also been investigated by comparing children's concepts of themselves and their models – similarity being assumed to indicate identification. It has been found that imitation and identification are most likely to occur in relation to parents who appear to show both dominance and warmth (Hetherington and Frankie, 1967; Bandura, 1969).

Moral development

An important aspect of the process of socialization is that the individual should come to accept a reasonable adherence to the norms and values of his society. This is achieved through the process of social controls, both external and internal. It is with the latter that we are chiefly concerned in moral development – with the way that the norms and values become internalized to form a *conscience* which exerts a controlling influence over behaviour.

Morality is, of course, a concept whose meaning is open to different interpretations, and there are many behaviours which in different societies and at different times in the same society may be regarded sometimes as moral and sometimes as immoral. Nevertheless, it may be argued that there is a 'true morality' of universal application based on a consideration of others' feelings, needs and rights. Even so, a differentiation must be made (Brown, 1965) between moral *knowledge*, moral *feeling* and moral *behaviour*, with a recognition that the three aspects do not necessarily coexist to the same extent nor develop at the same rate. Thus a feeling of guilt is not closely related to the ability to resist temptation, nor does moral knowledge always lead to moral behaviour.

The development of moral judgement was one of Piaget's interests. As a result of many interviews with children in which he led them to consider new moral problems, often in the form of short stories for them to judge (Piaget, 1932), he made a distinction between an early (between five and eight years of age) *immature* morality based on an acceptance of *rules* as fixed, unchangeable, emanating from adults and lasting for ever, and a later *mature* morality which sees rules as being determined, not by authority, but by members of a social group and alterable if agreed by all. These two concepts of morality influence the child's response to wrong-doing and to its consequences in terms of justice and punishment, and Piaget viewed the whole developmental process as a movement from *moral realism* based upon authoritarian external controls towards an internalized morality with internal controls – a *morality of cooperation*. He attributed the change to both cognitive development and the older child's increasing experience of cooperative behaviour with peers rather than his earlier dependency on adults.

Piaget's ideas have had a considerable influence, though later work has pointed to the need for some revision. While he concentrated on the acquisition of moral knowledge, others have combined this with moral feeling in their description of moral development. Thus Kay (1969) speaks of three stages: first an *amoral* stage in which behaviour is restrained by the fear of being caught by an authority figure who determines what is right and wrong; secondly a *premoral* stage when the child is influenced by social sanctions (approval and disapproval of friends); and finally the *moral* stage proper which depends upon personal sanctions from the child's moral feeling of right and wrong.

The development of moral feeling is a feature of psychoanalytic theory where it is attributed to that part of the individual's personality known as the *super-ego*. It is derived largely from the child's parents, especially with the resolution of the Oedipal phase of development. There are supposed to be two parts to the super-ego; a largely unconscious component, roughly equivalent to conscience, which exercises a restraining influence over unacceptable behaviour and causes feelings of self-punitive *guilt* if temptation is yielded to; and a more conscious *ego-ideal* which represents the individual's idea of how he wants to be – a source of aspirations which if not met may give rise to a feeling of *shame*. In terms of relationships with parents the super-ego is held to be largely derived from *identification with the aggressor* (a way of restoring the self-esteem experienced as lost at not being able to stand up to a powerful parent), the child behaving as if he were the aggressor and adopting the same punitive attitude towards himself; while the ego-ideal is thought to be due to *anaclitic identification* with a greatly loved parent (in order to restore to himself some of the love which he feels he has given up to the parent since there is only a limited total quantity of love available).

The learning theory approach to moral development sees resistance to temptation as resulting from inhibition of responses by conditioned anxiety learned from past punishment. In this process undesirable behaviour has to be 'verbally labelled' for the child (e.g. 'stealing a toy is wrong but not taking one with permission'), so that it is the label and the concept that is eventually anxiety provoking. Guilt is similarly explained as anxiety conditioned to the consequences of past transgressions, and the pursuit of 'good' behaviour as based on instrumental conditioning through parental reward of such behaviour.

The social learning approach lays more emphasis on the importance of the parent–child relationship in the learning process, and to this extent is closer to the psychoanalytic viewpoint.

Child rearing practices

It is clear that in the process of socialization it is generally the child's parents who, initially at least, play the most significant part. A major responsibility of parenthood in fact involves passing on to the child the values and norms of the society to which the family belongs, and individual parents are to a greater or lesser extent aware of that function. To achieve this they adopt varing patterns of child rearing practice, and attempts have been made to relate these, and especially the use of punishment, to the subsequent behaviour of the children.

Loevinger (1959) has defined three techniques by which parents might hope to bring about the behaviour which they desire in their children. One parent may use a reinforcement approach using rewards and punishments, often physical, for right- and wrong-doing respectively; a second parent might attempt to achieve the same end through insight – using explanation and pursuasion for this purpose; a third parent could concentrate on the process of identification and try to ensure that the child is not exposed to a 'bad' model of parental behaviour. In practice, of course, most parents' upbringing of their children will involve all three of these processes, though the children themselves may not always be aware of the parents' intentions; physical punishment by a parent, for example, may lead to 'identification with the aggressor'.

This raises the problem of variation between individual children in their response to the same child rearing practice, or indeed their roles in eliciting different behaviours from the same parent. Bell (1968) has stressed this interactive effect between parents and children, and has even questioned whether a correlation between parental treatment and child characteristics necessarily implies a causal association in the direction of parental behaviour causing child behaviour. This is one of the many methodological difficulties in the study of the effects of child rearing; others include the often retrospective nature of parents' reports of their own behaviour, the possible interference, on the other hand, in the behaviour if it is directly observed, and the likely inconsistency of parental behaviour.

Two principal approaches have been used to evaluate the child rearing antecedents of moral behaviour: comparison of families of delinquents and nondelinquents, and experimental studies using such measures as resistance to temptation, guilt responses to transgression and moral insight. Although there are discrepancies in the findings from these two sources, it is possible to make some generalizations about the factors likely to be associated with the internalization of social controls and moral behaviour. Probably the most important of these is the strength and quality of the relationship between parent and child, but others include use of the threat of withdrawal of love rather than physical punishment, and in any case consistency in whatever method of discipline is used.

The use of punishment in relation to the development of moral behaviour is one that has been the subject of much study, and although, once again, there is not complete unanimity, it does appear that on the whole physical punishment is not generally associated with development of a strong conscience but rather with the establishment of fear and techniques to avoid detection. 'Love withdrawal', on the other hand, seems to be more effective in producing guilt feelings, and there is some evidence of a greater use of this method of control by middle-class than by working-class parents, who tend to use more physical control. Reward of desirable behaviour appears to be particularly effective in small children while, as we mentioned earlier, clear labelling of what is and what is not approved is also important for learning by the child.

Clinical aspects

A knowledge of psychological development is clearly important for an understanding of psychological abnormality either in childhood or adult life. However, this is obviously too large a topic to be considered in any detail here, so that we shall concentrate on two aspects only: first, the possible ill-effects of deprivation of the mother–child relationship, and second, the question of psychological disturbance in adolescence and its causes.

Maternal deprivation

The importance of the relationship between the developing child and its mother has been stressed repeatedly, so that it is not surprising that much attention has been directed to possible consequences of any interference with that relationship.

Experimental evidence has come from animal studies, particularly those of H. F. Harlow with rhesus monkeys. We have already referred to this work in relation to infant monkeys' attachment behaviour, which showed that in the absence of the mother attachment could occur to an inanimate cloth-covered 'surrogate mother'. Such monkeys, deprived of normal mothering (Harlow *et al.*, 1966) were found to show behavioural abnormalities in adult life, especially sexual and maternal. These effects were, however, modified if the maternally deprived infants had been allowed to associate with other infant monkeys, and in any case their poor maternal care as mothers applied only to their first offspring – a second baby being cared for quite adequately.

The possible effect of disruption of the mother–child relationship in man has been extensively studied, but there are many methodological difficulties. A major problem has been the use of the term 'maternal deprivation' to cover a variety of conditions ranging from complete loss of the mother to poor quality of maternal care. At the same time the circumstances leading to separation of mother and child have often not been specified, nor even the age of the child or the length of separation.

An early study by Bowlby (1944) of forty-four juvenile thieves suggested that maternal separation of more than six months in the first five years of their lives had contributed to certain personality traits – especially deficiency in the ability to form adequate interpersonal relationships: 'affectionless psycho- pathy'. About the same time studies of children brought up in institutions (Goldfarb, 1943) and admitted to hospital (Spitz, 1945) examined the shorter- term effects of maternal deprivation. Spitz described a state of apathy in such children which he called *anaclitic depression*, and from which rapid recovery occurred if the child was reunited with the mother after a short separation but which tended to persist if this was delayed for more than three months.

These early studies led to a widespread review of institutional and hospital practices. In relation to the latter, admission of children is avoided whenever possible, and when this is unavoidable mothers are usually encouraged to main- tain maximum contact with their child, often being allowed to stay in the hospital if they wish.

However, the evidence for both short- and long-term effects of maternal deprivation has subsequently been critically reviewed (Ainsworth, 1962; Rutter, 1972), and it seems likely that the circumstances surrounding any sepa- ration may be more important than the separation itself – in particular, dis- tortion of relationships before, during and afterwards. An illustration of this is provided by the fact that when the connection between delinquency and a 'broken home' is examined it is found that, compared with a control group, the break-up of the future delinquents' homes was more often due to separation and divorce than death of a parent. Clearly any association between disruption of the mother–child relationship and disturbance of psychological develop- ment is a complex one and may involve both genetic and environmental variables.

Two other related aspects of early childhood experience that have attracted much interest are the possible effects of 'multiple mothering' and of mothers who go out to work. Studies (e.g. Bettelheim, 1971) of children in Israeli kibbutzim, who are raised with children from other families and who are looked after by both their natural mother and another adult, show that they appear to develop normally though showing less evidence of guilt than matched controls –

perhaps related to the less intense relationships with a number of adults.

Many have claimed that children of working mothers are more prone to delinquency or psychiatric disorder, but the evidence (e.g. Yudkin and Holme, 1963) is that this is not so provided there is a stable relationship with the mother and any other mother figures involved in caring for the child.

Adolescence

We have touched on this phase of development on several occasions so far, but since it is often held to be a period of great emotional difficulties it merits consideration in a little more detail.

The onset of adolescence is signalled by the physical changes of puberty – the development of secondary sexual characteristics such as facial and pubic hair and breasts – but its termination in adult maturity is much less clearly defined. The age at which puberty occurs may vary quite considerably from one child to another, and generally is earlier in girls than boys by about two years. Some studies have shown that early maturity confers a slight advantage for boys in terms of personality, whereas this is not the case for girls. This is, perhaps, not surprising in view of the social advantages to a boy of being large in comparison with his peers and probably being good at sports.

An obvious feature of adolescence is, of course, the increase in the sexual drive related to the rise in the levels of male hormones or androgens in both sexes. The expression of this sexuality is, however, very much influenced by socio-cultural factors, and especially by the restrictions imposed by family and society. It is this aspect of adolescence that is frequently held to be responsible for any emotional turbulence that is seen in Western societies, and which is contrasted with the relative tranquility of this period in so-called primitive cultures (Mead, 1958) where sexual freedom is much greater. This, however, is not the only problem that has to be faced by the adolescent in our culture. The gradual shift of emphasis from play to work occurs over a protracted period, often prolonged by further education before gainful employment can begin. Associated with this is a similarly slow transition from childhood to adulthood, in which the individual's view of his position may conflict with that of others – especially parents. Another characteristic of adolescence is a concern with moral values and standards, often leading to intense idealism and rebellion against prevailing norms and values of the society. However, society itself is not always consistent in its standards, and the adolescent is often faced with a bewildering variety of contrasting sets of beliefs, philosophies, religions, cults, etc.

Another aspect of adolescence which receives much comment is the question of alienation from parents – the so-called 'generation gap' – and the formation of a teenage sub-culture separate from the rest of society. Although such a belief is widespread, several studies have shown that, at least in the younger adolescent up to the age of sixteen years, only a small proportion hold materially different views from those of their parents with whom they also get on quite well. This is not to say that family disputes about clothing, length of hair, time of coming in at night, etc., are infrequent and do not cause much tension; but nevertheless fundamental differences between younger teenagers and their parents are less common than is often supposed (Rutter, 1979).

All these factors may contribute to emotional difficulties in some adolescents, but again the incidence has probably been exaggerated and most manage to pass through the period without too much trouble.

Further reading

Bel, H.L. and Mitchell, S.K. (1984) *The Developing Person: a Life-span Approach*. San Francisco: Harper & Row.

Bower, T.G.R. (1979) *Human Development*. San Francisco: Freeman.

Coleman, J.C. (1980) *Nature of Adolescence*. London: Methuen.

Dale, P.S. (1976) *Language Development: Structure and Function*, 2nd ed. Eastbourne: Holt, Rinehart & Winston.

Mussen, P., Conger, J. and Kagan, J. (1984) *Child Development and Personality*, 6th ed. London: Harper & Row.

Rutter, M. (1975) *Helping Troubled Children*. London: Cox & Wyman.

Turner, J. (1975) *Cognitive Development* (Essential Psychology Series). London: Methuen.

14
Psychological maturity, ageing and death

Having, in the last chapter, considered psychological development in the childhood years, we now turn our attention to the concept of psychological maturity, then to the changes associated with ageing and, finally, to death and the process of dying – together with its effect on others.

Psychological maturity

The concept of *maturity* implies that a final state of complete development is reached in which no further maturation occurs. From then on any further changes are the result of, on the one hand, acquisition of new knowledge learned from experience, and on the other hand, decline in abilities associated with the process of ageing. One of the difficulties in this area is that maturity may occur at different ages for different functions while, as we shall see, ageing likewise leads to different rates of decline in different functions.

As far as cognitive functions are concerned, general intellectual capacity (a concept which we shall be considering in some detail when we deal with intelligence in Chapter 17), having increased steadily during childhood, reaches its maximum in *intellectual maturity* between the ages of fifteen and twenty-five and declines thereafter. Failure to reach, at this stage, a level of intelligence within the 'normal' range is described as *intellectual retardation* or *mental handicap* and in its extreme form is generally associated with organic brain defect – a matter to which we shall also return in more detail in Chapter 17.

The term *psychological maturity* is generally applied to maturity of personality and is sometimes also referred to as *emotional maturity* to distinguish it from intellectual maturity. It is certainly a more difficult concept because of the risk of applying moral or value judgements to what constitutes 'mature' behaviour, attitudes, judgements, wishes, etc. It is also related to such ideas as 'mental health', 'psychological adjustment' – in general, 'normality'. Though we shall return to this for more detailed discussion in Chapter 20, we may note here that there are two main approaches to the problem of what is meant by normality. The first is to use an *ideal* concept which suggests a, probably unattainable, state judged against a set of criteria held to be desirable; the second employs a *statistical* notion of what is 'usual' or 'average', perhaps specifying a range of deviation on either side which would still be regarded as normal. Of course the latter approach, while avoiding value judgements, does require some means of measuring appropriate variables of individuals within a population to determine their means and distributions.

At the present time the approach to psychological maturity is still essentially clinical, with interest directed more to emotional immaturity and its manifestations – a matter of clinical judgement rather than objective measurement. Obviously, if the term 'immature' is to be applied to an individual with any validity it must be reserved for behaviour, attitudes, etc., inappropriate to an adult but characteristic of an earlier stage of development.

We have already seen that Freud's concept of maturity was concerned with an ideal state of complete libidinal (sexual) development to the final genital stage, with no fixation at any earlier pre-genital stages and with satisfactory resolution of the Oedipal complex. Erikson, on the other hand, reserves maturity of ego development to the eighth and final stage of psychosocial development which is only reached in old age.

A more widely held view would probably consider that psychological maturity is generally attained by early adult life with the achievement of a balance between extremes in certain areas of social behaviour. Thus:

Dependence/independence – successful development should see a progression from a state of complete dependence on others at birth to a position in which the individual is reasonably independent or autonomous yet able to relate to others in a social context.

Immediate/deferred gratification – a realistic seeking of gratification which acknowledges the frequent advantage and sometimes necessity of some deferment.

Emotional expression – appropriate expression of emotion that is neither under- nor over-controlled.

Acceptance of cultural norms – an acceptance of most of the values, beliefs, sanctions, etc., of the individual's culture, but with retention of a capacity for independent thought and action.

Response to change – an ability to adjust to changing circumstances in an appropriate way while at the same time being able to persist in the pursuit of particular goals without being deflected from them.

Self-valuation – a positive self regard with neither under- nor over-valuation of self in comparison with others.

As well as these aspects of social behaviour the mature person should have an overall sense of inner harmony or equilibrium.

Mental (ego-defence) mechanisms

The experience of equilibrium or mental stability just referred to may be threatened in various ways, both from within the individual (e.g. from pressure for expression of unacceptable impulses) or from the environment (e.g. from interpersonal conflict), leading to disturbance and unpleasant emotion, especially anxiety. There are, however, a number of mechanisms – described originally by psychoanalysts and especially by Freud's daughter, Anna (A. Freud, 1937), but widely accepted outside psychoanalytic circles – by which such threats can be minimized and the individual enabled to adapt to distressing or threatening circumstances. These *mental mechanisms* – which are also called *ego-defences* because they defend the ego against anxiety – are not in themselves pathological and are used to a greater or lesser extent by everyone, and especially in childhood. They may, however, if used excessively or inappropriately in adult life, become maladaptive. It is important to stress that they operate at an unconscious level so that a person using a defence mechanism is quite unaware of it, though it is often fairly apparent to others.

Individuals vary in their use of particular defence mechanisms, and the pattern of those that they use habitually contributes to the picture of their personality. A number of mental mechanisms have been described and we shall consider some of the more important of them.

Repression – rendering an unacceptable impulse or idea unconscious.

Denial – non-acceptance of an unpleasant or painful experience – common, as we shall see later, in the early stage of bereavement, for example.

Rationalization – substitution of acceptable explanations or justifications for behaviour in place of the true motives or reasons which would be too threatening. Thus failure in an examination is put down, not to insufficient study beforehand, but to ambiguity of the questions, failure of the examiners to confine themselves to the curriculum, or an unbelievable selection of questions covering just those few unimportant areas of which the candidate happens to be ignorant!

Displacement – shift of feelings and/or their expression from the appropriate object where they would be unacceptable, to another substitute object where they are less threatening (e.g. kicking the cat after being told off by the boss).

Projection – attribution of unacceptable aspects of the self to another person (preceded by their denial). Thus an individual who would find evidence of aggressive tendencies in himself objectionable and distressing, may deny his own hostile feelings and instead see them as belonging to others who then hate and persecute him. Patients may in this way feel that nursing and medical staff are hostile towards them when the origin really lies in their own resentment at being ill. Projection is one of the few aspects of psychoanalytic theory to have received some convincing experimental support from a classical study of Sears (1936). Members of a group of students rated each other and themselves on a number of undesirable traits – stinginess, obstinacy, etc. Those who were rated highest by their peers as possessing these characteristics but who lacked insight and rated themselves as low, were also most likely to rate many of their fellows as especially high on the traits. Since its function is to defend against awareness of ever-present basic drives such as sex and aggression, projection is liable to be used habitually by some individuals and to become, as a paranoid trait, a feature of their personality.

Reaction formation – another mechanism for dealing with unacceptable desires by first denying their existence and then developing strongly opposite attitudes. Thus a person with a fear of his own aggressive impulses may develop a strong attitude of pacifism, or a fear of sexual desires may lead to a very puritanical attitude to all sexual matters. Again, these are likely to become characteristic features of the personality. An interesting example of a kind of group use of reaction formation at a conscious level is shown by the organization Alcoholics Anonymous, which encourages strong attitudes against alcohol in those who have previously felt a strong desire for it.

Cognitive dissonance theory

We have already referred in Chapter 9 to this social psychological theory of L. Festinger (1957). There is an obvious similarity between its concern with the reduction of an unpleasant state of 'dissonance' between inconsistent attitudes, or attitudes and behaviour, and the analogous role of ego-defence mechanisms. Thus a person may hold views which conflict with the way he behaves (e.g. smoking and a realization of its harmful effects). According to the theory, which has experimental support, the state of dissonance motivates a change, either in attitudes or in behaviour (e.g. rejection of the medical evidence or giving up smoking) in order to bring about its reduction.

Clinical aspects

We have already noted that the concept of psychological maturity has been of greater interest to the clinician than to the psychologist because of the importance, in medical practice, of manifestations of immaturity. Not only may it present as a psychiatric problem when an individual is unable to deal adequately with the everyday responsibilities of adult life, but in general medicine it may create difficulties in terms of the patient being unable to cope with the effects of illness, especially if this is chronic and disabling – a matter to which we shall return in Chapter 20.

Ageing

It seems to be a fundamental feature of the human life cycle that it is divided into two phases – a period of development to biological maturity, followed by a falling-off in both physical and psychological capacities – a process described as *ageing* which, though most obvious in the later years of 'old age', in fact begins at the age of about twenty years. Just as the course of development is largely determined by the process of physical maturation, so ageing too reflects physical deterioration; this may in part be the result of an accumulation of damage from 'wear and tear' over the years, but it is also probably innate and 'built in' to the organism. As with psychological development, however, ageing is also subject to modification by psychosocial influences, so that the whole process represents a complex interaction between, on the one hand, deterioration of psychological functions, and on the other hand, a counterbalancing increasing knowledge gained through experience.

The study of ageing involves the assessment of various functions at different ages and two principal approaches have been used: *longitudinal* studies in which a sample of subjects is assessed for their performance on certain tests on two or more occasions separated by an interval of several years, the differences being referred to as *age-changes*; and *cross-sectional* studies in which comparisons are made between samples of subjects differing in chronological age but matched for other relevant variables such as social class, educational background, etc., the results being described as *age-differences*. Clearly, longitudinal studies offer the most direct approach to measuring the effect of ageing in the individual, and the findings may be generalized to the wider population provided the sample tested is representative and unbiased; but they require a considerable time to complete. Cross-sectional studies, though more economical of time, depend upon the adequacy of their matching procedures to ensure that any differences found between groups actually reflect the process of ageing. It is, however, possible to combine these two methods by selecting comparable samples of subjects at several age levels and then following them up over limited periods. By taking measurements at the beginning and end it is thus possible to obtain both age-changes and age-differences and to make comparisons between them.

Once again it is customary to make a distinction between the effects of ageing on cognitive functions and on personality.

Ageing and cognitive functions

We shall see, when we deal with intelligence in Chapter 17, that general intellectual ability as measured by intelligence tests increases in the childhood years but begins to level off in the early teens and reaches its maximum by the age of about twenty years. Thereafter, performance starts to decline, though at different rates for different mental abilities. Even with those that are affected in this way, the changes are usually not apparent in everyday life until the later years, but they can be detected earlier by tests that require maximum performance. Intellectual functions that tend to suffer from normal ageing, as well as with the accelerated changes associated with brain damage or degeneration, are those requiring rapidity and complexity of mental operations, particularly in unfamiliar situations. On the other hand, functions that require the use of words or the application of learned skills or knowledge are well maintained. This is shown by the changes with age in the performance on the various sub-tests of the Wechsler Intelligence test (Bromley, 1963). Thus 'vocabulary' and 'information', which depend upon past learning, show little or no decline, whereas others like 'object assembly' and 'block design', both measures of 'spatial reasoning', are adversely affected.

Another view of this distinction is provided by Cattell's (1963) concept of two types of intelligence – one consisting of *fluid* abilities which are likely to reflect the individual's innate potentialities and which are involved particularly in solving novel problems, and the other concerned with *crystallized* abilities which depend more upon education and experience and which are seen in such attainments as language and general knowledge which involve the largely routine application of learned skills. It is fluid intelligence that starts to decline in the twenties while the crystallized type may remain unaffected or even improve with further experience or practice.

Most tasks in life make demands on both types of intelligence, but the differential effects of ageing may explain the variation in age of the peak rate for *achievement* in different fields of endeavour – those requiring innate fluid ability being reached earlier than those dependent upon acquired skills and knowledge (Lehman, 1953). Despite these variations there is a general tendency for maximum intellectual achievement to occur in the years 30–34, and to fall off thereafter. Deterioration in intellectual ability is, however, not the only factor likely to be responsible for this decline; other age-related changes, such as diminishing energy and motivation, probably play their part, together with sociocultural influences including encroachment of administrative and other duties, changes in the nature of scientific activity with development of new research methods, etc.

Finally, we should note that there is evidence of differences between individuals in the effects of ageing on intellectual functions, so that people of originally high ability tend to retain their high verbal ability though declining in their performance on non-verbal tests, whereas people who were originally of low ability decline in both types of ability with ageing; individual differences in fact get larger with age.

Ageing and personality

As we have seen, personality as reflected in emotional responses, interests, attitudes, etc., is established by adulthood and these individual differences tend to remain fundamentally stable throughout the rest of life. Nevertheless, certain characteristic attitudinal and behavioural changes commonly occur in the later years, and, as with earlier personality development, these are usually seen as constituting stages of the life cycle – the traditional subdivision being into middle and old age.

Middle age

This segment of the life cycle is difficult to define with any precision. It is usually thought of as occupying the years between about 40 and 60, thus having an onset roughly mid-way between adolescence and old age and half way through a working life. There are, however, no reliable biological markers, and even though, in women, the menopause is obviously a significant feature, its age of onset is too variable to be used to identify the commencement of middle age which is, in fact, really a psychosocial concept defined largely by psychosocial criteria.

The stereotype of middle age includes such ideas as 'settled', 'comfortable', 'established', 'experienced', 'past one's best', 'out of the rat race' etc., and it may be that middle age is primarily a state of mind of the individual about himself and his position in the world. This involves the concept of *social age* – the individual's view of himself compared with others of the same chronological age and social background. Depending on whether he feels himself to be ahead of or behind the average, he will feel confidence or disappointment and inadequacy respectively.

A similar concept is the so-called *37-year-old crisis*, which implies that around this age the approach of middle age brings an awareness of the person's existing pattern of life and the lessening probability of being able to change it should he wish to do so. This in turn leads to a *changed view of the self*, including such aspects as sexual attractiveness, capacity to participate in certain recreations, to eat certain foods, etc., and an awareness of a predisposition to various bodily symptoms – stomach pains, headaches, backache, etc. Balancing these negative feelings, however, may be the fact of greater security of economic and social position, and in general there is what may be described as an *adaptation to disillusionment* – an acceptance of past failures of achievement. At the same time, there is an opportunity for *re-evaluation* of behaviour, relationships, interests, values, activities, etc. – in fact of personality – in the light of lessons learned from the past. The resignation involved in giving up unrealistic aims may then lead to a sense of contentment.

While the features just described may be characteristic of middle age in general, variations may arise owing to individual circumstances. For many people this is a period of major disruption of family relationships with the death of parents and the growing up and independence of children – the impact perhaps being greater on the woman than the man. Again, social class differences exist in the effect of age on occupational status; though economic circumstances generally improve through the working life, this tends to occur rapidly and early for the working class, while for the middle class or professional the pattern is usually one of delayed earning until completion of further education or training, followed by a gradually increasing earning capacity with promotion until a relatively high level is reached which can be maintained until, or even after, retirement. These economic differences are clearly likely to be reflected in more positive attitudes towards the middle years of life for the middle class person and family. The same factors are likely, of course, to have a persisting influence following retirement and into the next stage of old age.

Old age

Once again we are faced with a problem of definition, but the age of 60 years is generally taken as the onset of this final stage in the life cycle. Likewise, while the effects of biological ageing and often physical ill-health are obviously of great significance, social factors commonly play an important part in these years. *Retirement* from paid employment, usually at the age of 65 for men and 60 for women, poses a considerable challenge for many people, though, as we have just seen, there are social class differences in how this is likely to be perceived. It is, however, commonly preceded by a gradual reduction of activities and some withdrawal from social contacts – a process described as *disengagement* from the wider world with its responsibilities and obligations. For some this may bring a sense of relief and feeling of freedom to take up new, or to renew old, interests. For others there is a reluctance to so disengage and, where possible, a continuance of work for some years beyond the usual age of retirement – sometimes for the rest of life.

Another frequent loss in these years is the death of a spouse which, owing to the differential age at marriage and expectation of life between the sexes, is more often husband than wife.

Observation suggests that these behavioural changes and life experiences are associated with personality changes reflected in a tendency towards increasing introversion with decreased outwardly directed interests and increased self-awareness – especially a preoccupation with bodily functions. There is some support for this from the application of measures of personality (we shall be considering the measurement of personality in Chapter 16) in old age, though the shift to introversion (and also to neuroticism) is small and in general the relative stability of the pattern of measureable characteristics of personality is confirmed. Nevertheless, there is sometimes a tendency towards an exaggeration of previous personality traits in old age and, as with intellectual ability, there is an increase rather than a decrease of individual differences of personality. At the same time the frequent lessening in the elderly of such earlier characteristics as aggressiveness, competetiveness and sexuality, may be of advantage to their social role as grandparents in the family, or even as political leaders when they may provide a stabilizing influence (if this is seen as an advantage).

Perhaps the most obvious feature of old age is awareness of its limited duration and of the approach of death. Reactions to this vary between individuals, and though most seem to accept it with equanimity, for some the prospect of dying is hard to face and may bring feelings of anxiety over the unknown, anger over unfulfilled ambitions or guilt over past actions.

Clinical aspects

We are not here primarily interested in the obvious fact that advancing age is associated with an increasing incidence of physical illness, important though this is for the demands it places on the health services. From the behavioural point of view, as we have seen, ageing brings difficulties of adjustment, and these may be of sufficient severity to lead to pathological states of anxiety or depression which require treatment. More serious, perhaps, are the psychological consequences of progressive impairment of brain function which is most likely to occur in the elderly as *senile dementia* and to which we have already referred in Chapter 7.

In many respects, though not entirely, this may be considered as an accelerated form of ageing, but whereas the decline in performance on psychological tests is difficult to detect in normal ageing, it may be substantial with dementia – at least in the later stages. It is, however, in the earlier stages that diagnosis may be uncertain and when help may be sought from the clinical psychologist. The difficulty arises, however, that if a patient's performance on an intelligence test is poor, it could mean either that his intellectual ability has declined or that it has always been at this level. Occasionally results of earlier tests prior to the onset of the supposed illness may be available, but usually some estimate has to be made based on educational achievement or level of occupation.

An alternative approach is to try to make use of the differential impairment of cognitive functions such as we have seen occurring as part of normal ageing. If some functions are resistant to change then their measurement may be taken to indicate the level of premorbid intelligence. The evidence shows that, as with normal ageing, vocabulary scores usually hold up better than scores on other tests. Wechsler, in fact, made a distinction in terms of the subtests of his intelligence test, between those intellectual functions that 'hold' and those that 'don't hold'. Such indirect evidence of intellectual deterioration is, however, often not conclusive, and to confirm the diagnosis it may be necessary to repeat the assessment after an interval to see if further impairment has occurred.

Dying

The care of the dying and the comfort of the bereaved have always been major responsibilities of doctors and others in the caring professions, yet they are areas that have only in recent years been studied systematically. Perhaps one explanation for this is that (together with sex, but for different reasons) death has, at least in the present century, been a taboo subject – one which evokes fear and embarrassment among most people. This in turn may, paradoxically, reflect the fact that today death is not the ever-present threat that it was in the past when, from an early age, most people would have had first-hand experience of the loss of members of their own family – often their own brothers or sisters in childhood. Everyone then was familiar with the frequent curtailment of the life span, and this included the medical profession which, if it could not cure most serious diseases, was nevertheless able to offer help in easing the process of dying. With the improvement of life expectancy in this century, death has become less well known and therefore, perhaps, more frightening. For doctors it may also now evoke more of a sense of professional failure since the expectation is increasingly one of cure from life-threatening diseases – a fact which colours the doctor's attitude to the whole subject (we shall return to this later). At the same time, it may also tend to be seen as a matter only of 'common sense' – an area, therefore, not worthy of systematic examination. In fact, the results of such investigations have been of considerable value in understanding, and therefore helping, both the dying and the bereaved.

The ending of life may take a variety of forms – sometimes sudden and unexpected as with a fatal accident or heart attack, sometimes slow and expected following a period of 'terminal' illness. Many healthy elderly people die peacefully in their sleep without warning, death being simply due to 'old age'. There may, however, be a preceding period of increasing infirmity when it is clear that the old person is dying, and in any case most elderly people are aware of the shortness of their remaining life. Often, of course, life is cut short to a greater or lesser extent by 'incurable' disease, but awareness by the individual of this outcome is not always present – at any rate in the early stages of the illness. This is a matter to which we shall return when we consider the clinical aspects, but here we are concerned more generally with the way that people react to the knowledge of the approach of death.

Determinants of the psychological response to dying – like those in relation to illness generally as we shall see later in Chapter 20 – include those associated with its cause (e.g. whether it is due to ageing or disease, and if so its nature), with the individual and with his environment. Many people's fears are focussed less on the thought of death itself and more on the process of dying, which may be seen as likely to cause suffering reflected in the idea of the 'death agony'. While it is true that some terminal illnesses may result in physical distress, this is often not so and such widespread fears are based on a distorted picture.

When it comes to the individual there are clearly many factors influencing his response. One which might well be expected to be significant is the presence of religious faith, since this often holds out the promise of eternal life. Such an effect was indeed found by Hinton (1963) in a study of dying patients in hospital, among whom *anxiety* was least common in those who had a firm religious faith. However, anxiety was only slightly more common in the group with practically no faith, while the most anxious were the tepid believers who professed faith but did little to observe it. Another influential factor is age, with greater anxiety in the younger patient – often further aroused by parenthood with apprehension concerning dependent children.

In addition to anxiety, and rather more frequent, is the experience of *depression* among the dying. Again, while this may be partly related to physical discomfort in some illnesses, it may also stem from feelings of isolation resulting from a tendency to avoidance or emotional withdrawal on the part of others when a person is known to be dying. At the same time this disengagement may sometimes be a two-way process, with the dying person himself withdrawing – perhaps in anticipation of the final parting. Depression may additionally be explicable as part of a kind of anticipatory grief or mourning by the individual for the losses that he is experiencing or expecting – ultimately, of course, loss of life itself.

This analogy with mourning may also extend to the idea of stages in the psychological response to dying. Thus Hinton (1967) describes an initial phase of denial or of unawareness of the state of dying – not necessarily mutually exclusive since awareness may be only partial and accompanied by denial of the full significance of the threat to life. Once awareness has arrived, however, there may still be a struggle on the part of some against the inevitability of death, while others come to a peaceful acceptance, often associated with such socially desirable behaviour as kindness, generosity, courage, sensibility to others' feelings, etc. Kübler-Ross (1969) similarly describes a sequence of stages from initial denial, through anger (with the doctor, others who are healthy, etc.), bargaining (with God or the doctor for more time) and depression to final acceptance – the 'optimal death'.

Clinical aspects

The care of the dying has been a traditional responsibility of the doctor aided by others in the helping professions including, of course, the Church. Many people actually die in hospitals while others will be looked after at home by their general practitioners.

A great deal can be done to provide relief from physical discomfort, and especially pain; but care of the whole person includes consideration of his psychological welfare, and this is a matter which has received more systematic attention in recent years.

One of the most frequently discussed problems is how much information should be given to dying patients – in particular whether, and if so when, they should be made aware of the fact that their illness is fatal. This question is often put in relation to cancer – should the patient be told? – the implication being that this is tantamount to pronouncing a death sentence. In fact, of course, the matter is nowhere near as simple as this. By no means all patients diagnosed as having cancer will have their lives shortened by the disease, while there are obviously many other diseases that can threaten life. Nor, in the presence of a fatal disease, is the doctor usually able to predict with any degree of accuracy when death will occur. For their part, patients often suspect and sometimes are sure that they are dying before being told so. Doctors vary in their attitudes to telling patients the truth about fatal illness, ranging from those who consider it never right to do so to those who believe in always providing such information. Most, however, probably take a position somewhere between these two extremes and try to judge what is best for each individual patient.

Cicely Saunders (1959), based on her wide experience in this area, takes the view that most dying patients ultimately come to an awareness of the truth whether or not they ask for and are given it, and she lays greater stress on listening to what patients have to say and ask than on what should be said to them. If they are given the opportunity to talk about their situation, to voice their concerns and to express their wishes, it is usually possible to judge the best response to any question about prognosis. Some indicate quite openly that they do not want to know if their illness is fatal, and this wish should be respected. Others ask the question in such a way that it indicates the need for reassurance, or at least hope ('It's not cancer is it doctor?'). In this event, rather than giving an immediate denial and perhaps untruthful reassurance, the patient should be encouraged to describe his anxieties more fully to discover their basis – such as a fear of physical suffering which may be unwarranted. It may then be possible to give a considered and truthful reply which will be of more lasting value to the patient than a consoling but false picture of the future. By allowing him to talk freely and repeatedly in this way, and by giving simple explanations of his disease, the patient's awareness of dying may gradually grow in an atmosphere of sympathetic understanding.

All of this is, of course, very much concerned with the relationship between the patient and the doctor and other staff – a matter to which we shall return again in more detail in Chapter 19. One of the difficulties here stems from the attitudes towards death to which we have already referred – namely the sense of failure felt by medical and other staff in the face of a fatal illness. This may sometimes lead to a tendency to withdraw from contact with the dying – a fact of which the staff themselves may be unaware but which may be perceived by the patient. Many patients are sensitive to this difficulty on the part of some doctors and feel unable to talk openly to them about their illness for fear of causing embarrassment. It appears, however, that a shift may be occurring in the climate of opinion within the medical profession towards greater frankness, and this is associated with an increasing emphasis on the care of the dying in medical education.

Bereavement

The effect of death on those who are still alive has also received systematic investigation in recent years and a fairly consistent pattern of mourning identified (Lindemann, 1944; Parkes, 1965).

Typical or uncomplicated grief is usually seen following the death of a first-degree relative with whom there has been at least a moderate amount of social contact within the preceding year. It involves several stages.

The first response to an unexpected death is one of shock and disbelief – a period of *denial* which may last from a few hours to a fortnight, and during which the bereaved person feels numbed but is able to carry on with the usual routine as well as coping with arrangements for the funeral.

Gradually, however, this protective denial begins to give way to a full realization of the loss – often in short bursts at first and associated with feelings of *despair*. Attacks of *yearning* may be accompanied by great distress, with physical symptoms due to autonomic disturbance – often precipitated by reminders of the deceased (such symptoms may include feelings of tightness in the throat, emptiness in the abdomen, lack of strength, sighing respiration, etc.). Between these waves of distress there is a general state of depression, apathy and sense of futility. Sleep is disturbed and appetite poor. There is a preoccupation with thoughts of the deceased and often a characteristic restlessness which may appear aimless but probably represents a *searching* for the dead – sometimes acknowledged by the bereaved person who consciously looks in places previously frequented by the dead person. Irritability and anger are not unusual, stemming from the feeling of desertion but directed at others seen as responsible for the death – sometimes including the medical staff. On the other hand there may be feelings of *guilt* and self blame for past behaviour towards the deceased, whose memory tends to be idealized. In the earlier part of this stage, however, there is a tendency to think of the dead person as still alive – to feel his presence or to actually see or hear him – but gradually this is replaced by full realization of the loss. Another frequent characteristic is the appearance of traits of the deceased in the behaviour of the bereaved – including often the symptoms of the last illness. Finally the intensity of this stage begins to decline after a few weeks and is generally minimal by about six months, with full *acceptance* of the death. For several years thereafter, however, there may be occasional brief periods of depression and yearning, usually precipitated by reminders of the loss and especially by anniversaries.

We have seen, then, that the process of grieving involves a great deal of mental activity which Freud (1917) described as *grief work* and which Lindemann (1944) subdivided into three components: first, emancipation from bondage to the deceased; second, readjustment to the environment from which the deceased is missing; and third, formation of new relationships. The first of these tasks is the most crucial and depends upon the bereaved person remembering, often repeatedly, the many shared experiences that formed the basis of the relationship with the deceased – a process initially extremely distressing but becoming progressively less so, until the final goal is reached in which such recollections bring not pain but pleasure.

A person's mourning does not, of course, take place in isolation but within a socio-cultural context which includes the particular beliefs and rituals of his culture. Anthropological studies have shown that these vary widely between different societies, each of which seems to have developed its own beliefs about the meaning of death together with a set of rituals concerning the disposal of the body and the appropriate behaviour, including expression of emotion, of the bereaved. Thus in Western cultures the funeral within a few days of death with burial or cremation of the body is followed by a period of mourning which may be signified by the wearing of a black armband, black tie, etc. – residual tokens of the black mourning of the Victorian era. Yet even this ritual has declined in recent years and Gorer (1965) claims that this loss of recognition and support for the expression of grief is responsible for increased psychological disturbance among bereaved people today. In this respect the Orthodox Jewish 'shivah' or seven-day period of ritual mourning appears to provide a more favourable environment, though Parkes (1975) formed the impression from talking to intelligent middle-class Jews that there was, even here, a tendency to encourage the strict control of feelings on the part of the mourner. An Irish custom which is also disappearing is 'keening' or lamenting for the dead, when the relatives' weeping was accompanied by the chanting of dirges and artificial wailing by others hired for the purpose.

As well as these ritual influences on the bereaved's grief, religious beliefs are also clearly important. Just as belief in an 'after-life' can colour the attitudes of the dying to their condition, so too it affects those who are left behind. The idea of ultimate reunion can be a great comfort to the bereaved, though it sometimes leads to suicide in order to hasten the process.

Clinical aspects

An awareness of the normal sequence of events in typical grief, together with an understanding of the psychological processes involved, should be of assistance to those who are concerned with advising and helping the bereaved, and indeed it has become recognized that bereavement counselling requires more than common sense if it is to be effective.

During the early stage of numbness the bereaved person needs a certain amount of assistance with simple decisions and practical matters to do with the registration of the death, funeral arrangements, etc. Once the initial phase of shock has passed, sharing of the feelings of grief may be most helpful, while advice to 'stop thinking about it' can be positively harmful. Expression of emotions should be allowed but not forced by insensitive probing. Individuals will vary in the degree to which they actually express their grief – what is important is that they should be able to feel it. This means rejecting the customary social attitude which seems to imply that grief can be avoided by not talking about it, and by restricting conversation to trivialities instead. The bereaved person needs sympathetic understanding but not pity, and recognition of this fact has led to the setting up of organizations for the purpose. Since husbands are likely to die before their wives, the largest group of bereaved people consists of widows, and in the United Kingdom a self-help organization for widows called Cruse was founded in 1959 by Mrs Margaret Torrie when she herself was widowed. A similar organization designed especially for bereaved parents, the Society of Compassionate Friends, was set up in 1969 by a hospital chaplain, Father Simon Stephens, who had discovered that parents whose children had died were frequently avoided by their friends and experienced difficulties in their marriages and with their other children.

So far we have spoken of typical or uncomplicated grief, but bereavement sometimes leads to abnormal reactions which may be of clinical importance both physically and psychologically. There is evidence for an increased incidence of both morbidity and mortality from organic disease following bereavement, but we shall defer further consideration of this aspect until Chapter 20 when we examine the role of psychosocial factors in the aetiology of disease in general.

In the same way bereavement may also result in a psychiatric illness such as may be met with in other circumstances – a neurotic illness, schizophrenia, depression or mania for example. In this case the actual nature of the psychological disturbance is probably not determined by the bereavement, which simply acts as a non-specific precipitating stress.

Other individuals may, however, develop abnormal grief reactions which may be seen as variants of the normal process and are thus 'stress-specific' – i.e. they only occur following a loss. Parkes (1965) describes three types of abnormal grief. *Chronic* grief represents an intensification and prolongation of the typical form and is frequently associated with recurrent ideas of guilt and self blame and with physical symptoms similar to those of the final illness of the deceased. *Inhibited* grief tends to occur in the very young or the very old, and is characterized by the prolonged inhibition of a large part of the total picture of typical grief with substitution of other symptoms instead. *Delayed* grief is typical or chronic grief occurring after a delay of months or years.

Parkes reviewed the evidence, mostly from studies of bereaved women, concerning the determinants of severe grief reactions, and concluded that the high-risk case would have the following characteristics: a young widow with children still at home and no close relatives nearby; a timid, dependent personality who had reacted badly to previous separations; a past history of depressive illness; a relationship with her husband which was closely dependent or ambivalent with no preparedness for his unexpected death; finally a family and cultural tradition which inhibits the expression of grief.

Further reading

Bromley, D.B. (1974) *The Psychology of Human Ageing*, 2nd ed. Harmondsworth: Penguin.

Hinton, J. (1974) *Dying*, 2nd ed. Harmondsworth: Penguin.

Kimmel, D.C. (1980) *Adulthood and Ageing: an Interdisciplinary Developmental View*, 2nd ed. London: Wiley.

Parkes, C.M. (1975) *Bereavement*. Harmondsworth: Penguin.

Kübler-Ross, E. (1982) *Living with Death and Dying*. New York: Macmillan.

Part 4
The differential (holistic) perspective

How do individuals and societies differ one from another in terms of their behaviour? It is to these questions that this section is addressed.

Chapter 15 takes a brief look at the discipline of social anthropology – a relatively recent offshoot of the older science of anthropology – and at some of its comparative studies of social institutions and cultures of different societies. In preparation for the following chapter the nature of the relationship between personality and culture is also examined.

Chapter 16 considers the psychological concept of personality and reviews various approaches to its understanding and measurement. The major theories of personality are introduced, together with their associated techniques of individual measurement and possible applications to psychological treatment. Finally there is some discussion of the possible influences, both innate and environmental, that go to make up the nature of the individual adult personality.

Chapter 17 deals in a similar manner with intelligence – its definition, theories, methods of measurement and determinants. Situational factors that may affect individuals' performance on intelligence tests are also described.

There is again reference to relevant clinical aspects in each of these chapters.

15

Differences between societies

Although the practice of medicine is concerned primarily with patients as individuals, the importance of considering any person within a social context has been stressed in previous chapters. In our own society we may observe differences, for example, between those of different occupational groups and social classes, but we are also increasingly aware, especially through immigration, of the wide variety of social institutions and cultures possessed by peoples of other lands.

The comparative study of these aspects of different societies has been of relatively recent origin and is generally described as *social anthropology* or sometimes *cultural anthropology* – the former perhaps emphasizing differences of social structure and the latter of culture, though there is much overlap between them.

The older science of *anthropology* dealt essentially with the study of mankind and its evolution. The subject now covers several distinct branches including, in addition to social anthropology, *prehistoric archaeology* (investigation of relics of early human activity), *physical anthropology* (evolution of man as a physical organism with classification of early human forms, examination of physical differences between races, etc.), *ethnography* (first-hand accounts of the cultures and social life of individual societies – basic material for the comparative analyses of social anthropology), and *ethnology* (racial and cultural classification of peoples related to their historical or prehistorical origins).

We saw in Chapter 12 that, in the nineteenth century, societies were generally considered to evolve (by analogy with biological evolution) from an inferior, simple form to a superior, more complex state – a process of so-called development or evolution. Comparison between societies then tended to be made in terms of their supposed relative levels of development or evolution, and explanation of their current social institutions was sought in their *historical* origins.

Later, however, in the early years of this century, Durkheim, with his views of society as a dynamic organism – a holistic approach stressing the importance to the whole society of the functional relationships of its component parts – came to have a profound influence on the so-called *functionalist* school of social anthropology in Great Britain through its founding fathers, Bronislaw Malinowski (1884–1942) and Alfred Radcliffe-Brown (1881–1955). They emphasized the social nature of man and concentrated on the empirical study of contemporary societies by *fieldwork*, which entailed living with the people being studied (a form of *participant observation*); and in the years between the two world wars many societies, mostly in Africa and New Guinea, were studied in this way. Everything that was observed, however apparently bizarre or irrational, was assumed to have some social function in relation to the structure of the society – a viewpoint similar to that of Talcott Parson's structural-functional school of sociology discussed in earlier chapters. It was hoped by the social anthropologists that such observations would lead to an understanding of social institutions in terms of their functional interconnections, and ultimately to the establishment of causal laws governing social phenemena.

An alternative approach to understanding contemporary cultural and social phenomena, but now associated more with archaeology and history, is known as *diffusionism*. Rather than seeking an evolutionary origin of the present in the remote past, it looks to the geographical spread of ideas and cultural artefacts (man-made objects) associated with trade and migration from one continent to another. A recent diffusionist, Thor Heyerdal, achieved popular fame with his Kon-Tiki expedition designed to prove the feasibility of supposed ancient migration routes.

Considering, then, these three viewpoints – historical/evolutionary, functional and diffusionist – it seems unlikely that they are mutually exclusive but rather that they all contribute to an understanding of the features of a particular society and culture. Domination of British social anthropology by the functional approach was, however, challenged after the Second World War, especially by E. Evans-Pritchard. Among other things the functionalists, with their insistence on empirical objectivity, were held to have concentrated on societies as systems of action at the expense of considering peoples' ideas and values – their culture – and this has led to a shift of interest from function to *meaning* so that the modern emphasis is on understanding what social phenomena actually mean to the people themselves. In the USA some anthropologists – notably Ruth Benedict and Margaret Mead – adopted an even more psychological approach and focussed on the effects of different cultures on the individual.

Finally, mention should be made of the contemporary French school of social anthropology of Claude Levi-Strass. Described as *structuralism*, this differs from other approaches in that it minimizes differences and takes the view that social phenomena in all societies have a universal structure because they reflect, and indeed are the result of, the way the human mind/brain functions.

These several social anthropological schools of thought are much more complex than has been conveyed in this brief introduction, but we can see that in examining different societies, emphasis may be placed on their social structure or their culture. In this chapter we cannot consider either aspect in any detail in relation to individual societies, but we can at least draw attention to the wide variation that exists throughout the world – an awareness of which may reduce the tendency to *ethnocentrism* or the belief that one's own culture is obviously the norm.

Classification of societies

While social anthropology is concerned with the study of social institutions and cultures of different societies, it does not generally make comparison between whole societies. Nevertheless, attempts have been made to compare – and indeed to categorize – societies on a world-wide scale from a sociological standpoint. Perhaps the simplest contemporary classification of societies depends upon two criteria: their level of *economic development* (developed versus under-developed), and their type of *social ideology* (capitalist versus communist). Thus the USSR and the countries of Eastern Europe are classified as advanced industrial communist societies, contrasted with advanced capitalist societies such as the USA, the EEC and Japan. Under-developed communist societies include China, Viet-Nam and Cuba, while the Third World constitutes the fourth category – under-developed and capitalist. Such a classification is obviously an over-simplification, but it does illustrate the very considerable social contrasts existing between nations – differences which are clearly of great significance for their inhabitants in terms of their way of life and probably their health; certainly as regards level of health care facilities.

Social institutions

In Chapter 7 we noted the variety of patterns of kinship and of types of marriage that can exist in different societies. To modern Western eyes some of these may appear quite bizarre and incomprehensible, but when considered within their own cultural and social contexts they may be seen to be perfectly reasonable and understandable.

Kinship systems – the patterns made up of various categories of blood relationship (kinship) and of marriage relationships (affinity) – have been a major concern of social anthropologists. One reason for this is that in small-scale societies, in contrast to modern Western European countries where it is of very limited significance in a person's social life, kinship provides a simple means of categorizing people and of defining social relationships. Different kinship relations may then be associated with different types of social behaviour – determining, for example, who is subordinate to whom. In addition, kinship provides a means of passing on status and property from one generation to the next, and it also helps to establish social groups within the total society.

To take these latter aspects first, although we are not particularly concerned here with inheritance we may note that most societies have adopted the patrilineal mode, in which name and title and usually property pass down the male line. Less commonly, inheritance is matrilineal, but even then it is usually to males only so that a man's inheritance passes to his sister's son. Sometimes one line of descent is important for one purpose and the other has a different significance, while in yet other societies inheritance can be from both sides of the family; whatever the mode it serves the purpose of providing a set of rules governing an aspect of social life important to all societies.

The role of kinship in defining social groups can be easily understood in relatively small, 'primitive' societies which lack a centralized government and a large-scale political and economic organization. Survival in such conditions depends upon belonging to a cooperative group of sufficient size – certainly larger than the nuclear family of parents and siblings. Thus unilineal descent through the father or the mother provides an individual with a large group to which he belongs by descent through that parent, but at the same time he is also linked through the other parent to his or her lineage group – such links helping to bind separate descent groups into one total society. A feature of such societies which at first sight seems curious is the terminology used for relatives. Thus in a patrilineal society a father's sister may be called 'father', though qualified by the word 'female', while what in our society would be called a 'third cousin' may be termed, if related through the male side, 'brother'. Of course, the true relationship is understood but the use of such terms helps to underline membership of the same lineage and to determine the same general type of behaviour to all members.

If we now turn to more specific relationships within kinships, we find that social behaviour is often governed by formal rules. To take just one example, the relationship between father and son will often be subject to very strict rules within a patrilineal society where the son will inherit his father's status and property, whereas in a matrilineal society where a man inherits from his mother's brother, it is the relationship with his maternal uncle that is more formal and authoritarian and his relationship with his father far less so. Other parent–child relationships such as mother–son and father–daughter, though they may be emotionally significant, have little social importance owing to the generally lower status of women in most non-Western societies with inheritance passing only to males. An observation by Radcliffe-Brown that seems to have a more universal application to our own as well as more 'primitive' societies is that an easier relationship often exists between grandparents and grandchildren than between parents and their children – a 'merging of alternate generations' compared with an 'opposition of adjoining generations'.

Leaving this brief discussion of blood relationships we must now consider the universal institution of *marriage*. In almost all societies an important function of marriage is legitimization and conferment of an acknowledged social status on any offspring of the union – vital for inheritance and succession. Beyond this, however, there is a wide variety of forms of marriage between different cultures. Again they may be understood in relation to other aspects of the society, and especially the kinship system. Thus in patrilineal societies such as the Nuer of the Sudan studied by Evans-Pritchard (1940), a form of marriage known as the *levirate* is found in which, when a married man dies, his widow may be taken over by his brother or sometimes his son, provided the latter is by another wife. Consistent with the idea of the kinship group she becomes a 'wife' to the group as a whole, while any children she may bear by her new spouse are considered not to be his but to be those of her dead husband. This will, of course, allow succession to continue even if a man dies without a son of his own.

Even more extraordinary to Western eyes is the idea of *ghost marriage*. Among the Nuer, if a man dies before he has married and had sons it is a responsibility of a younger brother to marry a wife for him. She will then not be this man's wife but the wife of his deceased older brother, and any children from the union will belong to the latter and succeed him. Thus both the levirate and ghost marriage serve to maintain the idea of the kinship group based on unilineal descent – a matter of great social importance in such societies.

Of major concern in marriage is, of course, the nature of the relationship between the partners, including their respective status and roles. Again, anthropologists are interested in the comparative aspects but have found that in all societies there is a division of labour between the sexes generally related to the man's greater physical strength and the woman's child-bearing capacity, though the details may vary greatly from one culture to another. The status of the wife is almost always regarded as inferior to that of her husband, who expects her to be submissive and obedient – though female emancipation is emerging under the spreading influence of Western ideas.

A fascinating account of contrasting patterns of marital relationships and gender roles has been provided by Margaret Mead's classic studies of four racially similar tribes in New Guinea (Mead, 1962). As an anthropologist she was concerned with the cultural patterns and social institutions of the tribes, but at the same time she was interested in the way these related to the behaviour of their members. In particular she pointed to differences of child-rearing practices which could be of significance in terms of the contrasting adult personalities (a matter to which we shall return again later in this chapter).

The *Iatmul* were a tribe of head hunters living by a slow-moving river and well supplied with food in the form of sago and fish. They were dominant over their neighbours and intensely proud, living in large and impressive villages. As children boys and girls were treated alike, sharing in the life of the women – even in ceremonies from which men were excluded. Little boys thus tended to identify first with the women and were rather feminine in manner. In their early teens, however, they were taken away to be initiated by an elaborate ritual into adult manhood, when they were encouraged to behave, within the society, in an exaggeratedly masculine way. The earlier passivity often appeared, however, in homosexual behaviour outside the tribe. Sexual relations with women were vigorous and often provoked by taunts about the man's virility, while in their own houses the men had no special role and would frequently quarrel with their wives. In the special men's house, however, which was taboo to women, the men maintained a precarious myth of masculine superiority using various mysterious noise-making instruments unseen and unknown to the women and children.

The *Tchambuli* were a small tribe, numbering only about six hundred members, living on the edge of a lake in villages superficially like those of the Iatmul. They also had an initiation ceremony for the young boys but a much less ruthless one, and the men themselves were unwarlike and generally feminine by Western standards in their behaviour and manner. They wore ornaments, carved, painted and danced while the women had shaven heads, no ornaments and were hard working, making mats, baskets, etc.

Living on the banks of a fast-flowing river were the cannibal *Mundugamur*. Boys and girls were brought up within an elaborate kinship system with many taboos including, for example, one that divided brothers so that they should not eat from the same dish and might only speak to each other in anger. The two sexes grew up to have similar personalities, vigorous and hostile and, by Western standards, masculine. The women were as assertive as the men and hated pregnancy and nursing, so that they treated their children roughly and often deliberately kept them hungry.

Finally, the *Arapesh* lived in an unproductive mountainous district where they were always short of food. Their great interest was in growing things – children, coconut trees, pigs – and they had a great fear that each generation might become shorter in stature until the tribe would eventually die out altogether. Both sexes were mild, unaggressive and 'maternal' in behaviour. Children were brought up together in a protective atmosphere, though they modelled themselves on the parent of the same sex and learned that they would have different duties as adults.

Thus we have here a striking example of the variety of roles and relationships that may exist between men and women in different societies: the superficially Western type masculine–feminine roles of the Iatmul though with an underlying passive homosexuality in the males; the reversal of this pattern within the

Tchambuli; the masculine behaviour of both sexes in the Mundugamur; and the contrasting 'feminine' behaviour of Arapesh men and women.

Behavioural differences of these kinds between societies raise the fundamental question of the relationship between individual personality and culture to which we have previously alluded and to which we shall return again later. Before doing so, however, we must turn from primarily a consideration of social institutions to that of the beliefs and values of a society.

Culture

In our examination of kinship and marriage it will have been apparent that such social institutions cannot be properly understood without some reference to the values and beliefs that they involve – the ideas that the people themselves have about them. Only in relatively recent times, however, have anthropologists undertaken the systematic study of the shared beliefs and values of societies – their culture. Earlier workers tended to assume that what was referred to as 'primitive thought' was of a very simple and inferior kind, and it was only with the later development of intensive fieldwork that anthropologists who lived among the people they studied and communicated with them in their own tongue realized the complexity of the ways of thought of even preliterate peoples. Thus in his classic studies of the Azande of the southern Sudan, Evans-Pritchard (1937) showed that their system of beliefs in magic and witchcraft, strange and irrational though it might seem to Western thought, provided a very practical answer to the problem of explaining the occurrence of misfortune and how to deal with it. Illness is, of course, a common example of a misfortune that may befall an individual, and in many parts of Africa and elsewhere it is attributed to the activities of ghosts or spirits or of a living witch or sorcerer. This provides not only an acceptable (even though incorrect) explanation of the illness, but also a way of dealing with it by conciliation of the ghost or spirit or appeals to the witch or sorcerer to remove the evil influence.

Beliefs about the origin and significance of misfortunes, the meaning of life, of man's position in the universe, such ideas whether based on 'primitive' witchcraft and sorcery or the more 'advanced' monotheistic religions of Judaism, Christianity or Islam, may be seen as part of a need for man to make sense of the world and his existence in it. Indeed Levi-Strauss conceives this desire for meaning and for the imposition of order in the universe through the use of classificatory systems to be a fundamental human propensity and not dictated solely by practical considerations; in short, man is a 'meaning-maker' as well as a 'tool-maker' and a 'weapon-maker'. The nature of the meanings will, of course, differ between societies. What may be held to be important within one culture may be considered of little significance in another, and this may even determine the perception of the world by their members – a question once more of the interaction between the individual and society which we shall now examine in a little more detail.

Personality and culture

In Chapter 11 we considered this topic and recognized two approaches to the relationship between man and society – one seeing the individual's behaviour as derived from the social system of which he is a member, and the other taking the view that society itself is a reflection of characteristics of the human mind. Both presuppose the existence of certain regularities of behaviour within a society, but the former explains these in terms of its institutions and the latter on the basis of a so-called *modal personality* type. Thus if certain forms of behaviour can be recognized as typical of a particular society, it may be argued that they are determined by the practices and social roles prescribed by the social institutions of that society, or it may be claimed that they are due to the fact that, despite the existence of a range of individual differences of personality, a particular type predominates within the society – its modal personality.

A difficulty with the concept of a modal personality is that it sounds suspiciously like the generally discredited notion of national stereotypes – the basis of 'a Scotsman, an Irishman and an Englishman' type jokes. Such stereotypes are, of course, exaggerated and frequently pejorative caricatures, but it may be that there is, nevertheless, a germ of truth in some of them and that there is indeed a modal personality which can be discovered through the careful observations of the anthropologist.

The study of the relationship between culture and personality has been of interest to psychologically minded social anthropologists and sociologists, but particularly to social psychologists. Despite all this interest, however, it must be admitted that many questions remain unanswered. We have already met with the process of socialization in relation to child development, and here again (as we saw with Margaret Mead's studies in New Guinea) major importance is usually attached to child-rearing practices as providing the link between culture and personality – often within a framework of psychoanalytic theory. Thus the American psychoanalyst, Abram Kardiner (1945), working with anthropologists studying a wide range of cultures, developed the concept of a *basic personality structure* (similar to the modal personality) characteristic of a particular culture and derived from a set of *primary institutions* including child-rearing practices and the family. This personality in turn was held to give rise to appropriate *secondary institutions* such as art and religion. A weakness of this schema, however, is that it depended largely upon the use of the Rorschach test (considered in more detail in the next chapter) to confirm basic personality structures predicted by Kardiner, though some doubt has been cast on the cross-cultural validity of the test.

Whiting, in a series of studies (1963), used a more objective approach based mainly on anthropological data recorded in the Human Relations Area Files at Harvard University. These contained ethnographic descriptions of a large number of societies in different parts of the world, and information was extracted on child-rearing practices and adult behaviour, including customs related to illness. The theoretical model proposed that the nature of a society's physical environment determines its maintenance systems, such as the economy and social structure, which in turn influence child-rearing practices. These then result in a modal personality among the people who create their particular cultural products such as religion and theory of disease. Significant correlations were found between child-rearing practices, adult personality and cultural products; but unfortunately this does not indicate anything more than a relationship which could have causal significance in either direction (child-rearing practices producing cultural products via adult personality, or the cultural products determining the child-rearing practices), or be due to a causal factor such as the environment, which is common to both. It may well be, of course, that the culture–personality relationship is a two-way process, but further studies are needed to elucidate the whole system of interacting variables.

Clinical aspects

Given the wide variation between societies in their social institutions, customs and beliefs, it is not surprising to find differences between them in the manifestation of disease and in their understanding and response to it.

We have already seen that illness is often attributed to supernatural agencies, as illustrated by the Azande who place responsibility for such misfortune on the operation of witchcraft and ultimately to a rather vague entity that they call 'mbori'. This is not to say that such beliefs exclude the existence of more proximate, non-mystical causation – tripping over a stone causing a broken leg for example, or the use in the first place of suitable remedies based on accumulated experience. The Azande, indeed, have an enormous pharmacopoeia according to Evans-Pritchard. It is only when their traditional medication fails to cure the symptoms of an illness that they turn to oracles to discover who is bewitching them – providing an explanation of why they should have become ill or injured themselves at this particular time as well as a means of dealing with it.

Western medicine has scientific theories of the aetiology of disease and remedies for it, but when it comes to explaining why it should afflict us we may also turn to some ultimate cause, be it 'God' or 'fate'. We shall return in Chapter 20 to a more detailed consideration of the concept of disease, but here our main concern has been to note the variation that may occur between different cultures and which may sometimes be found among non-Western immigrant groups such as Africans, Asians and West Indians in the UK. Within their own countries, too, the place of scientific medicine has also sometimes been a matter of some concern. The attempt to introduce such medical practices without taking sufficient account of the local culture has not always been free from difficulties, and many of the recently independent African societies are now acknowledging and encouraging the coexistence of traditional healing alongside Western medicine.

If we turn to the prevalence of disease in different populations, it is obvious that social customs – including such aspects as standards of hygiene and dietary habits – will have a profound influence on certain medical conditions. (We do not have to look further than the effects of tobacco smoking in our own country.) Durkheim's studies of suicide, to which we referred in Chapter 12, provide an example of the correlation of behavioural disturbance with socio-cultural factors, but the latter are also of importance in affecting the prevalence rates of other conditions such as alcoholism and various forms of psychiatric disorder. The actual content of particular psychiatric illnesses may also be influenced by culture so that, for example, the delusions held by a schizophrenic patient may reflect the values and beliefs of his country, and there are certain patterns of behaviour, probably variants of hysteria, restricted to particular cultures (e.g. the well-known Amok (running amok) found among Malayan men).

Further reading

Beattie, J. (1966) *Other Cultures*. London: Routledge & Kegan Paul.

Frank, J.D. (1973) *Persuasion and Healing*. Baltimore: The Johns Hopkins University Press.

Munroe, R.L. and Munroe, R.H. (1975) *Cross-Cultural Human Development*. California: Brooks-Cole.

Lewis, I.M. (1981) *Social Anthropology in Perspective*. Harmondsworth: Penguin.

16

Individual differences
I – Personality

Having, in earlier chapters, examined the separate component psychological functions into which human behaviour and experience may be subdivided, and looked at the process of psychological development and the variety of social environments in which it may occur, we are now in a position to consider from a psychological standpoint the adult individual as a whole. In particular, we are concerned to find out how and why one person differs from another.

In our everyday lives we are accustomed to making some kind of assessment of other people. If we are asked to describe someone whom we know fairly well we are likely to say something about their physical appearance, but we may also comment, perhaps, on how clever we think they are and on other aspects of their behaviour which characterize them as an individual different from anyone else.

We shall deal with intelligence in the next chapter, but it is with the complementary affective and motivational aspects of a person revealed in their attitudes, beliefs, habits, emotional responses, etc., that we are concerned here – with their *personality*.

Personality is another concept that is difficult to define and, indeed, there is a general lack of agreement among psychologists on the use of the term. R.B. Cattell, whose theory of personality we shall consider shortly, defines it as 'what determines behaviour in a defined situation and a defined mood' (Cattell, 1965). The assumption here is that the way an individual behaves at a particular moment will depend, not only on the situation in which he finds himself and on his emotional state at the time, both of which may vary, but also on the relatively constant and enduring characteristics of his individual personality – and it is this stability of personality which allows behaviour to be predictable within limits. We should note, however, that there has been a tendency among some personality theorists to under-estimate the importance in behaviour of situational factors, including the social context and the playing of social roles.

So far we have spoken of personality, but reference must be made to two other terms used to describe people which are sometimes thought to be synonymous with personality but which should be distinguished as really representing only facets of it. *Character* is a word that tends to be used in a morally judgemental way, the individual being evaluated in terms of cultural norms against which he is seen as 'good' or 'bad' (e.g. generous or mean, honest or dishonest). *Temperament* refers to the emotional aspects of a person – particularly emotional responsiveness such as hot-tempered or placid, fearful or unworried. Both terms, however, though common in everyday parlance, have generally passed out of use within psychology.

Methodology

Before we proceed with a consideration of the various theories which have been advanced to explain the nature of personality as a whole, or of particular aspects of it, we should mention briefly the different techniques employed in its study since, as we shall see, the former are often related to the latter.

First we should note the two fundamentally different approaches to which we referred in Chapter 2, the *ideographic* and the *nomothetic* – the former emphasizing the uniqueness of the individual with the intensive and extensive investigation of single cases, and the latter concerned with generalization in the form of universal laws applicable to populations of individuals and derived from the study of representative samples. It is obvious that theories associated with the ideographic approach are likely to be more complex and compre-hensive, but often more subjective and therefore less reliable and certainly more questionable in their general applicability, than those based on the nomothetic approach; these, by contrast, though more scientifically acceptable, may some-times be rather simplistic in their view of personality.

To take this last point, however, if comparisons are to be made between individuals beyond stating that each is unique, it is necessary to reduce to a manageable size the enormous number of features of personality that could be considered. There are said to be some 18,000 words in the English language which can be used to describe human behaviour (e.g. shy, aggressive, cautious, domineering), and each of these could be regarded as a *trait* of personality – meaning a predisposition to respond in a particular way. It is a common observation, however, that many of these tend to 'go together' (aggre-ssive, quick-tempered, domineering, for example) thus forming groups of related traits, each group being independent of others and comprising a person-ality *type*. We shall return to a consideration of this way of describing person-ality when we deal with the theories of two psychologists influential in the field of personality, R.B. Cattell and H.J. Eysenck. Here, however, we must take a brief look at the statistical technique of factor anaylsis that forms the basis of this approach and which we shall meet again when we come to consider intelligence.

In Chapter 1 we saw that a linear relationship between two variables A and B may be assessed by the correlation coefficient which provides a measure of association, ranging from 0 for no association at all to 1 for perfect correspon-dence (and minus 1 for an exact inverse relationship). Of course, this measure tells us nothing of the nature of the association. It might be one of dependence such that A actually causes B or vice versa, like an increasing voltage across an electric heating element producing an increasing temperature; or it may be a matter of interdependence so that A_1 and A_2 are related because they reflect changes in another and common variable A which is associated with each of them (e.g. the total volume and weight of an increasing number of ball bearings). It may be, indeed, that several variables A_1, A_2, A_3, A_4, etc., are all related to another and common variable A.

Suppose now that we take a group of individuals and apply some kind of measure to a number of variables for each person, such as the traits of per-sonality that we have been discussing. Each person will have a score for each variable, and each variable will have a set of scores – one for each person. From the latter a correlation coefficient can be calculated for any pair of variables – A and B, A and C, B and D, etc. The correlations for all the possible pairs of variables can be set out in a table as a 'correlation matrix', and if there are a sufficient number of high values it may be supposed that some of these variables could be grouped together because they might reflect common underlying *factors* to which they are related.

There may be several of these factors, and the purpose of factor analysis is to identify or 'extract' those which will best account for the associations between variables present in the matrix of correlations, thus reducing the complex information contained in the original data to a relatively small number of underlying factors. The extent to which a particular variable is related to a particular factor is itself expressed by a correlation between them called the *factor loading* of the variable on the factor. The factors themselves are defined by the loadings of the variables on them, and each may be given a name appropriate to the pattern of high loading variables, i.e. the variables to which it is most related and which it may be considered to largely determine.

There is no need here to go into the mathematics of the technique of factor analysis, but it should be noted that there are certain decisions that can be taken which affect the factors extracted from the correlation matrix. Thus they may be determined in such a way that they are independent of each other, i.e. uncorrelated. If this is expressed graphically the axes of any pair of factors would be at right angles, so that they are described as *orthogonal*. Alternatively, it may be assumed that any underlying factors determining the scores on the variables are themselves likely to be correlated to some degree, so that the resulting factors are not independent, in which case, again based on their graphical representation, they are described as *oblique* (i.e. with an angle of less than 90° between the axes). In these circumstances it is possible to construct another correlation matrix of the correlations between the various pairs of factors and to carry out a further factor analysis to produce what are called 'second-order factors' – thus reducing the information in the original data to an even smaller number of factors.

There are further refinements of the technique which we cannot pursue, but we have examined factor analysis to this extent because it has proved to be probably the most frequently used of a number of important tools in the behavioural sciences concerned with the analysis of large numbers of variables. We shall shortly consider its application to personality theory and measurement.

Finally in relation to methodology, the various methods of study, including measurement of personality, will be detailed with each of the theoretical approaches, but here we can note that the three major techniques employed, which were described in Chapter 2, are the interview (structured or unstructured), questionnaires and projective tests.

Theories of personality

We can now turn to a consideration of some of the principal theories of personality. Although we have seen that there are different schools of psychological thought about particular psychological functions, development, etc., it is in relation to personality – to the whole person – that we find the most striking contrasts in approach.

Cattell (1965) describes three historical phases in the understanding of personality. The oldest, though still continuing to the present day, is the *pre-scientific* or literary and philosophical phase. Many of the great poets, novelists and playwrights have, in their writings and especially in the characters they created, conveyed seemingly brilliant insights into the complexities of human nature. Together with the speculations of philosophers, however, their views have not been subjected to any kind of scientific verification, so that while they may be judged aesthetically satisfying, their truth as statements about personality are untested.

The second historical stage is called by Cattell the *proto-clinical*, since it was based largely on observation of psychiatrically sick people by doctors and others working in the latter part of the last century and into the present one. These included 'founding fathers' of psychiatry like Emil Kraepelin in Germany and Pierre Janet in France, but more especially Sigmund Freud and his early associates Carl Jung and Alfred Adler. Among the personality theories we shall be considering the so-called psychodynamic approach of these latter theorists, but here we must recognize more generally two major limitations to this essentially descriptive historical phase in psychology: first, the fact that it was derived from the study of psychological abnormality rather than the 'normal'; and second, the virtual absence of any attempt at measurement. We may, of course, recognize an equivalent phase in the history of human physiology when the early contributions came from the study of abnormalities of function in disease and similar descriptive phases in other sciences before the technical developments necessary for quantitative measurement. Thus, despite the obvious criticisms, some at least of the insights and concepts of clinicians have proved valuable and have persisted, perhaps in modified form, within the framework of the succeeding stage.

The characteristics of the third stage, which began at the turn of the century, are evident from Cattell's description of it as *quantitative and experimental* – in other words, the scientific study of personality based on actual behavioural measurements. This at least is what is claimed for it though, as we shall see, it sometimes involves explicit assumptions about personality, such as the cross-situational consistency of behaviour, which may be open to challenge; even then the assumptions are usually such that they can be put to empirical verification or refutation, which cannot be said of many of those of the earlier clinical phase.

We shall now examine each of the major personality theories together with the techniques of personality assessment associated with them. We shall also refer, where appropriate, to clinical applications, including those in the form of techniques for attempting to bring about changes of personality – usually referred to as 'psychotherapy'.

Psychodynamic theories

Clearly ideographic and arising in the clinical phase largely from observations made during the course of treatment of psychologically disturbed patients, these theories, though differing among themselves, are all ultimately traceable to Freud's original psychoanalytic theory to which we have made several references already (particularly in the chapter on psychological development). We need only summarize the main features of the theory. Structurally, the mind is seen as functionally differentiated into three parts: the unconscious *id* with its energizing primitive instincts or drives which it can only satisfy, according to the pleasure principle, by wish-fulfilling fantasies; the largely conscious *ego* which gradually develops in order to mediate between the demands of the id and the constraints of the outside world in accordance with the reality principle and guided by the third structure, the *super-ego*, which represents the values and controls of society through early identification with the parents and other figures of authority. Inadequate control of the id impulses by the ego leads to anxiety, as does perception of an actual threat from the outside world.

The instinctual energy of the id, mainly in the form of the *libido* concerned with sex and self-preservation, is in the early years, largely narcissistic and attached to different erogenous areas of the body in turn – oral, anal and phallic – though as a result of excessive gratification or frustration it may become fixated at a particular stage. Later the libido becomes more outwardly directed as erotic feelings towards the parent of the opposite sex, with rivalry and fear of the parent of the same sex – the *Oedipus* or *Electra* conflict – which should be successfully resolved by identification with the same-sexed parent and repression of the sexual drive during the latency period, until its reawakening at puberty in the final genital stage of development.

Another important aspect of psychoanalytic theory, though developed principally by Freud's daughter Anna, concerns the defence mechanisms used by the ego to reduce or avoid anxiety, including repression, denial, rationalization, displacement, projection and reaction-formation (see Chapter 14).

Adult personality is, then, according to classical psychoanalytic theory, biologically determined by the outcome of libidinal development with, as we saw in Chapter 13, certain personality traits and aspects of sexual behaviour resulting from fixation at particular developmental stages or failure of resolution of the Oedipal or Electra conflicts. More emphasis was later placed on the role of the ego-defence mechanisms – especially those like reaction-formation and projection which may be used habitually to deal with threatening sexual and aggressive impulses – in determining certain characteristics of personality (suspiciousness and a tendency to feelings of persecution, with projection, for example, and prudishness or submissiveness with reaction-formation).

Early splits with Freudian psychoanalysis, particularly over its emphasis on sexuality, resulted in Alfred Adler's school of individual psychology and Carl Jung's analytical psychology. *Adler* (1870–1937), starting from the well-known observation that the body can compensate for organic damage, applied the same notion to the psychological sphere. He claimed that even in normal circumstances a child feels helpless and begins to develop a particular strategy or *life style*, to compensate for feelings of inferiority and to reach the goal of superiority – 'to be a human being means the possession of a feeling of inferiority that is constantly pressing on towards its own conquest'. Ideally this compensation leads to a good adjustment to the three major challenges in life – society, work and sex – but sometimes there is over-compensation or, alternatively, a retreat into neurotic illness to gain a feeling of superiority. Thus in contrast to Freudian theory, Adler drew attention to the importance of the ego and of non-sexual factors in the personality, and this had influences beyond his own school, though the latter itself has now largely disappeared.

Jung (1875–1961) also reacted against Freud's emphasis on sex. He developed a complex theory based as much on his knowledge of the religions and philosophies of different cultures as on his clinical experience, though here we can only refer to a few of his concepts. The motivating force in Jung's view, although still called the libido, was non-sexual and more in the nature of a life-force, with sexuality only beginning during what for Freud was the latency period as a pre-pubertal phase before sexual maturity, and following the Oedipal conflict based primarily on a primitive love of the food-giving mother. From the mental structural point of view, Jung postulated not only a conscious mind and a *personal* unconscious, but in addition a much larger *collective* or *racial* unconscious containing the beliefs and myths of the individual's race and, at a still deeper level, a *universal* unconscious shared with all humanity. Jung called the frequently recurring themes (present in dreams and myths) of the collective unconscious *archetypes*, and he believed that they were inherited with the physical structure of the brain. While the existence of such widespread myths is not denied by anthropologists, they and psychologists would generally see them not as innate but as the product of shared experiences common to all mankind (e.g. having a mother and father giving rise to the myths of 'the Great Mother of All Living', 'the Great Father' etc.).

At the most superficial level of the personality was the conscious *persona*, named after the mask which in Roman plays hid the face of the actor. Rather like the sociological concept of role, it was concerned with the image of the person presented to the world. Behind the persona, however, was an unconscious mirror image – the *anima* in the man or *animus* in the woman – a 'feminine' unconscious in the male and vice versa. The personal unconscious thus provided a compensation for the conscious – a very masculine man having a strongly feminine anima and a cowardly man being unconsciously brave. This notion of a duality of personality with a balance between different trends has probably gained some general acceptance, but perhaps the most lasting of Jung's concepts has been that of *introversion* and *extraversion*, either of which was held to predominate in an individual – again with the opposite in the unconscious. We shall be considering the more recent applications of this concept shortly.

A feature of these early psychoanalytical views of personality was that they tended to be centred on the individual and his gratifications and to neglect, relatively, the social dimension. We have already (in Chapter 13) referred to the psychosocial developmental theory of Eric Erikson who, with Erich Fromm, Karen Horney and Harry Stack Sullivan, comprised the sociologically oriented group known as the neo-Freudians that developed in the USA in the 1930s. Emphasis was placed on the interpersonal rather than the intrapsychic dimension and on the conflicts which may arise in relationships between the individual and others as well as within himself.

More recently *object relations theory* – developed particularly by W.R.D. Fairbairn and H. Guntrip – and using 'object' in the sense of a psychologically significant person or part of a person, has stressed the relationship of the individual to such objects, the seeking of which is in fact considered to be the primary motivational drive. The stages of development are then seen as different means of achieving such relationships (e.g. through feeding at the oral stage), and adult personality as being much influenced by the nature of these early relationships – evidence for which, as we have seen earlier, came additionally from the work of Harlow on non-human primates.

Assessment

The assessment of personality according to psychoanalytic theory is, of course, involved in the technique of psychoanalysis itself – each personal analysis comprising, in a sense, a prolonged intensive and extensive assessment of that individual's personality. However, other techniques have been developed which are closely linked to psychoanalytic theory and which are intended to reveal unconscious aspects of the personality. We have already referred to these so-called *projective* tests in an introductory way in Chapter 2 and in relation to motivated perception in Chapter 5. In essence the subject is presented with an ambiguous stimulus to which he has to respond, though without awareness of the full significance of the test, and it is from these responses that deductions are made about the personality dynamics, including underlying conflicts and ego defences. The *Rorschach* technique, named after its originator, a Swiss psychiatrist, consists of ten symmetrically shaped 'ink-blots' such as would result from folding within a piece of paper some spilt ink and then opening it up again. Five of the ink-blots are in shades of grey only, while two are grey and red and three are multicoloured. The subject is shown each card in turn and asked to say what he sees in it, following which it is usual for the Rorschach tester to question the subject further. The whole material is then scored and interpreted by the tester who requires special training for the purpose. Some responses are common or 'popular' and of little significance ('a bat', 'two clowns', etc.), but others are unusual and may suggest unresolved conflicts (e.g. 'death', 'male genitals'). Other formal aspects of the responses are considered, including whether the whole area or only part of it is chosen as the stimulus and what other specific properties of the blot, such as form, colour or shading, prompt the subject's response.

The *thematic apperception test* (TAT) of the American psychiatrist H.A. Murray consists of a series of black and white pictures depicting scenes varying in their degree of explicitness and detail. The subject is shown each card in turn and asked to make up a story describing the events at the time of the picture, what preceded them and the likely outcome. Interpretations of the stories, depending mainly on the recognition of recurring themes, were originally made in terms of psychoanalytic concepts (e.g. frequent reference to violence suggesting projection of repressed hostility), but other interpretative systems have subsequently been used. In particular McClelland, as we shall see later, has used the TAT as a measure of achievement motivation and has applied it cross-culturally for this purpose.

The Rorschach and the TAT are the two most widely used projective tests, but others involve similarly ambiguous situations into which the subject is supposed to project his unconscious processes (e.g. completion of incomplete sentences, drawing a person). Apart, however, from attempts to apply objective scoring procedures to some aspects of the subject's response, it is obvious that interpretation of projective tests must involve a large subjective element, and studies of their reliability and validity (see Chapter 2) have revealed disappointingly poor scores (of the order of 0.2). This has obviously cast serious doubt on their value in the assessment of personality in general, though in clinical situations an experienced interpreter may be able to obtain useful information about the dynamics of an individual patient.

Applications

The impact of psychoanalytic theory on Western thought has been enormous, but here we are only concerned, however briefly, with its clinical applications in the treatment of psychiatric patients. Psychodynamic psychotherapy – meaning psychological (non-physical) treatment based ultimately on psychoanalytic theory or its derivatives – includes psychoanalysis itself (usually occupying an hour a day, five days a week for several years), together with various modifications such as group psychoanalytic psychotherapy (a group of patients instead of one individual) and brief individual interpretative psychotherapy (usually an hour a week for a few weeks or months).

Common to all, however, is a belief in the importance of unconscious conflicts in causing psychological distress, especially anxiety. These conflicts relate back to early childhood experiences and relationships of which the patient is largely unconscious, and a major aim of treatment is to bring about greater awareness within the therapeutic relationship (between the therapist and patient). This is facilitated by the process of *free-association* – the patient verbalizing whatever thoughts enter consciousness, however embarrassing or frightening. At the same time feelings about significant objects (i.e. people) in childhood, especially parents, become 'transferred' on to the analyst, so that he may be loved (positive *transference*) or hated (negative transference). The inappropriateness of these feelings is pointed out or *interpreted* by the analyst, together with their likely origin in earlier relationships, thereby helping the patient to gain *insight* into the irrational nature and causes of some of his attitudes and behaviour towards others. Such understanding is not, however, easily achieved, and there may be much *resistance* to the development of insight in the early stages of treatment, which must also involve interpretation and consequent weakening of defence mechanisms which have been providing an alternative way of dealing with anxiety.

The effectiveness of psychodynamic psychotherapy has been difficult to establish in any rigorously scientific way, but there have been a number of studies in which a comparison was made with some kind of control group, the majority showing a more favourable outcome for the treated patients (Meltzoff and Kornreich, 1970). An interesting observation is that improvement often continues after cessation of treatment, and in general it seems that psychotherapy may have two beneficial effects – a relatively rapid relief of distress followed by a more gradual and continuing improvement in personal functioning.

Type and trait theories

We now turn to a very different and nomothetic approach to the study of personality – the attempt to identify quantifiable aspects using mathematical techniques of multivariate analysis like factor analysis to which we have already referred. Although this is clearly located in Cattell's 'quantitative and experimental' historical phase, it has an ancient origin in the third century BC in Hippocrates' classification of the four temperaments depending upon the predominance of each of the four 'humours' in the body. An excess of 'black bile' resulted in the *melancholic* temperature prone to sadness; of 'yellow bile', the bad-tempered *choleric*; of 'phlegm', the stable *phlegmatic*; and of blood, the optimistic *sanguine*. Here we have the concept of individuals being classified qualitatively according to constellations of characteristic behaviours into four categories that are mutually exclusive – a person is melancholic or sanguine or choleric or phlegmatic. Later, however, a quantitative approach was applied to this notion of temperaments by Wilhelm Wundt (whom we met in Chapter 5 as one of the Gestalt school of psychologists), who suggested that

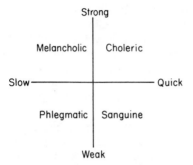

Fig.16.1   The four personality types of Hippocrates and the two emotional dimensions of Wundt

the four types might be explained by different combinations of two underlying emotional continua – one concerned with the strength of the emotions from weak to strong and the other with their speed of change, running from slow stable to quick changeable (Fig. 16.1). This represents a move to a quantitative, continuous or dimensional approach, with an individual's personality being described in terms of his position on the two scales. A person with very strong and highly volatile emotions may be described as choleric, but most people will not be so extreme and will cluster near the point of intersection of the dimensions, so that they are not easily characterized as belonging to any one of the four categorical types.

There are thus two ways of looking at the concept of *type*: either as a discontinuous *category* made up from a particular pattern of personality traits and to which an individual may or may not belong; or as a continuous *dimension* – again determined by a number of continuous traits – which a person may possess in any degree from one extreme to the other, though it will be unrelated to any other dimension or dimensions. Both of the principal modern exponents of the trait and type approach to personality, whom we are about to consider, adopt a dimensional approach using factor analysis; but they differ, as we shall see, in the method used and therefore in their structural concept.

R.B. Cattell

Cattell, an English psychologist who went to the USA, used oblique factor analysis of a large number of questionnaire items. He obtained sixteen first-order factors, or 'primary' factors, which he considered to represent underlying *source traits* (including one of intelligence) of major importance in influencing the behaviour of the individual, though what is more easily observed is their interaction reflected as so-called *surface traits* (Cattell, 1965). In fact a second-order factor analysis of these oblique, and therefore to varying extents correlated, primary factors results in several second-order factors, the two most important of which Cattell calls 'anxiety' and 'exvia–invia' (which correspond quite closely to Eysenck's dimensions of neuroticism and extraversion-introversion respectively that we shall be considering shortly). Fig. 16.2 shows diagrammatically the hierarchical relationships of these factors.

For Cattell, though, it is the source traits that are most significant in describing and predicting behaviour. His is essentially a 'trait' theory of personality. He himself sees the term 'type' as describing a discontinuous category

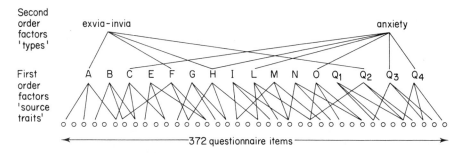

Fig.16.2 The hierarchical organization of questionnaire-derived personality factors according to Cattell's theory (after Cattell, 1965, p. 118)

and therefore as generally unsuitable for use in personality description, except in so far as certain patterns of trait measures may sometimes be associated with particular groups of people (e.g. related to age, sex, occupation, culture etc.), thus defining types which may have behavioural predictive value.

Assessment

The most widely used instrument for measuring personality designed by Cattell is the 16PF questionnaire – so-called because it provides a set of scores, each ranging from one to ten, on the sixteen factors or source traits just discussed. Each trait represents a continuum between contrasting extremes – the low score and high score descriptions (in the popular rather than technical versions) for the sixteen factors being respectively: A – reserved vs. outgoing; B – less intelligent vs. more intelligent; C – emotional vs. stable; E – humble vs. assertive; F – sober vs. happy-go-lucky; G – expedient vs. conscientious; H – shy vs. venturesome; I – tough-minded vs. tender-minded; L – trusting vs. suspicious; M – practical vs. imaginative; N – forthright vs. shrewd; O – placid vs. apprehensive; Q_1 – conservative vs. experimenting; Q_2 – group-tied vs. self-sufficient; Q_3 – casual vs. controlling; Q_4 – relaxed vs. tense. A subject's scores on each of the sixteen traits can then be represented graphically as points above or below the mean of 5.5 to give a personality 'profile' for that individual.

Despite the widespread use of the 16PF questionnaire its reliability and validity have been questioned. Cattell himself seems to have assumed that measures of temporal reliability are inappropriate since normal variations in the traits may be expected to occur over time, while factor analysis of 16PF data by other workers has not revealed the same factor structure except for the second-order factors, which may therefore be of greater importance than in Cattell's view.

Applications

On the whole, Cattell's 16PF test has not proved to be of great clinical value in terms of diagnosis or management of patients, though from a research point of view a low score on factor C (emotional stability or 'ego-strength') has generally been found with both neurotic and psychotic groups.

H.J. Eysenck

Lately professor of psychology at the Institute of Psychiatry, University of London, Eysenck also employs factor analysis of questionnaire data. He differs from Cattell in making greater use of pathological as well as normal groups of subjects, and in extracting unrelated or orthogonal factors (Eysenck, 1953). In a large sample of normal and neurotic soldiers, Eysenck found two orthogonal factors, or *dimensions* as he called them, of personality – 'extraversion-introversion' and 'neuroticism–stability'. A great deal of subsequent work on normal subjects and psychiatric patients led to the construction of question-naires designed to measure these two dimensions together, later, with a third named 'psychoticism'. *Extraversion-introversion* is a bipolar factor, the extremes of which resemble the concepts of the extravert and introvert of Jung. The introvert tends to be inward-looking or introspective, shy, reserved, more interested in books than people, and with well-controlled emotions, whereas the extravert is outgoing, sociable, fond of parties, craving excitement and generally impulsive. The dimension of *neuroticism* has roughly the same meaning as emotional instability, with individuals at the extreme prone to anxiety and other emotional difficulties. Although *psychoticism*, characterized by emotional coldness, is claimed to be a normal personality dimension related, in an extreme form, to the severe forms of psychiatric disorder described by psychiatrists as psychoses, its status is more controversial and we shall not consider it further here.

Figure 16.3 shows the relationship between the various levels of personality organization according to Eysenck's theory. At the lowest level specific respon-ses are acts, such as those in response to an experimental test or an everyday life experience, that may be observed on one occasion but may or may not be characteristic of the individual. At the next level, habitual responses are specific responses tending to recur in similar circumstances. The third level represents the organization of habitual acts, based on their intercorrelations, into traits. Finally, at the highest level, intercorrelated traits are organized into the general type or dimension of personality – such as introversion or neuroticism.

Underlying these descriptive personality dimensions, Eysenck postulates a biological basis in terms of central and autonomic nervous system functioning which is largely genetically determined. Thus an individual's degree of intro-version is held to be related to ease of conditioning, which in turn is dependent upon the balance of cortical excitation (or arousal) and inhibition (postulated

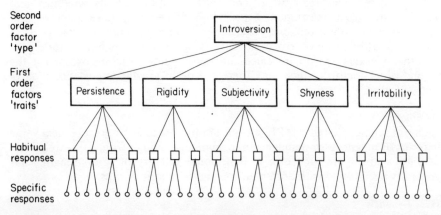

Fig.16.3   The hierarchical organization of the personality dimension of introversion according to Eysenck's theory (after Eysenck, 1953, p. 13)

originally by Pavlov). Establishment of stimulus–response connections in learning is encouraged by rapid excitation with a slow development of inhibition in introverts, while extraverts are slow to condition owing to an excess of cortical inhibition. The reticular activating system (RAS), which we discussed in Chapter 4, is thought to be the neural substrate since it is involved in the process of cortical arousal. Neuroticism or emotionality is considered to be related to the lability or reactivity of the autonomic nervous system, governed by the limbic system, and evidenced by the degree to which strong, painful or sudden stimuli evoke strong and lasting increases in heart rate, blood pressure, sweating, etc. As we saw in Chapter 10, however, activation of the limbic system may also stimulate the RAS, so that individuals scoring highly on both introversion and neuroticism may be more aroused than those with low scores.

Evidence in support of these postulated neurophysiological bases for Eysenck's dimensions of personality has been considerable but not, however, unequivocal, and certainly the relationship between introversion and ease of conditioning has been questioned by some studies.

Assessment

The measurement of Eysenck's personality dimensions involves the use of questionnaires. The original and best known of these was the *Maudsley personality inventory* (MPI) published in 1959, though this has largely been replaced by the *Eysenck personality inventory* (EPI) and the *Eysenck personality questionnaire* (EPQ) which appeared in 1964 and 1975 respectively. The contents are similar except that included in the EPI is a so-called 'lie scale' consisting of items which are intended to reveal subjects who are making 'socially desirable responses' rather than strictly honest ones whilst the EPQ includes the dimension of psychoticism already referred to.

Validation of these questionnaires has been largely in terms of their success in differentiating various groups of individuals some of whom were predicted to differ widely on a particular dimension.

Applications

Eysenck used the concept of personality dimensions in an attempt to understand a wide range of human behaviours, including both psychiatric disturbance and criminality. In relation to the former he challenges the traditional psychiatric approach to diagnosis which tends to place individuals into distinct diagnostic categories – an 'either–or' phenomenon – so that they either have, or do not have, a particular condition. Eysenck argues (see Fig. 16.4) for a dimensional approach in which an individual whose position on the dimension of neuroticism or of psychoticism is extreme is likely to have psychological difficulties or manifestations which lead him to be diagnosed as suffering from a neurotic or psychotic illness respectively. There is, however, in Eysenck's view no clear-cut demarcation but a continuum between 'normal' and 'abnormal'.

The third dimension of introversion–extraversion is held to explain the distinction, within the neurotic disorders, between dysthymics (depressives, obsessionals and phobics) characterized by high neuroticism and high introversion, and hysterics who are high on neuroticism but about average on the introversion–extraversion dimension. The combination of emotional instability and strong conditionability in dysthymics supposedly results in the easy formation of inappropriate conditioned emotional responses, especially of

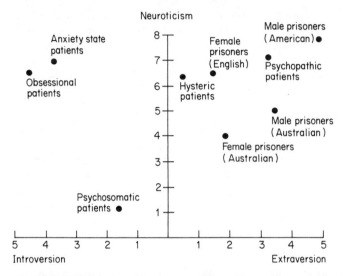

Fig.16.4 Positions of various patient and criminal groups on the two personality dimensions of neuroticism and introversion–extraversion (after Eysenck and Rachman, 1965)

phobias. We have already considered (in Chapter 6) the therapeutic applications of this theory in the form of deconditioning procedures, but, generally speaking, measurement of neuroticism and extraversion has not been an important adjunct of treatment.

Psychopaths (individuals whose antisocial behaviour is attributable to their abnormal personality) score highly on neuroticism and extraversion, as indeed do others convicted of criminal offences. Eysenck, in fact, seeks to explain antisocial behaviour and criminality in terms of weak conditionability (associated with extraversion) which results in under-socialization and thus less highly developed internalized controls or 'conscience'. Again, however, evidence in support of this hypothesis from other studies of criminals has been somewhat conflicting, and the emphasis on the role of classical conditioning in socialization can be criticized as neglecting social learning variables.

Cognitive/phenomenological theories

The assumption common to the two theories to be discussed under this heading is that behaviour is determined by an individual's perception of himself and his surroundings rather than objective reality. They are concerned with understanding the totality of his experience at any moment – the so-called *phenomenal field*. They also share a view of man as a more rational being than is suggested by most other theories yet, paradoxically, they are derived from clinical experience since their originators have both been practitioners of some form of therapy.

Carl Rogers

An American evangelist who became an academic psychologist, Rogers focussed on the concept of the *self* – meaning the organized totality of perceptions, feelings, values, etc., that the individual considers to be unique to himself (Rogers, 1959). This represents a holistic approach to personality in which the 'whole' person reacts with the field of experience in such a way as to satisfy the basic psychological need to be accepted, respected and loved by important people in his life, as well as to achieve increased independence and greater self-expression. The basic motivating force behind all behaviour is the tendency to this *self-actualization* – towards the maintenance and enhancement of the self.

In the early years of life the child's experience of his parents' positive feelings for him, whatever his behaviour, encourages him to engage in self-actualizing activities rather than behaviour solely to satisfy others – he is then said to experience *unconditional positive self-regard*. Gradually, however, he finds that most other people in his life make positive regard for him conditional upon his behaviour – liking him when he behaves as they wish but not so when his behaviour is disapproved of. This may lead him to engage in experiences according to the wishes of others and at the expense of maintaining or enhancing his self. This lack of 'congruity' between his experiences and his perceived self is felt by the individual to be threatening and causes anxiety and tension. This may be dealt with by a change of behaviour in order to be consistent with the self concept, or a modification of the latter to accommodate the incongruent behaviour. Ultimately the self may be considerably changed in order to meet the individual's need for positive regard – a condition which Rogers sees as 'the basic estrangement in man' in the sense that he is not true to himself for the sake of preserving the positive regard of others.

At the same time, two basic defence mechanisms of distortion and denial may be used to reduce anxiety by preventing incongruent experiences of reality entering consciousness. Used frequently, this prevents the self concept from being moulded by reality, so that it becomes increasingly incongruent with it, thus causing further anxiety and use of the defence mechanisms – a state which may considered to be a 'neurosis'. If the denial of experiences is sufficiently great, contact with reality may be lost and a 'psychosis' results. The bizarre behaviour of the psychotic may, however, simply be congruent with previously denied experience. Another of Rogers' concepts that is related to psychological adjustment is that of the *ideal self* – the person as he would like to be in contrast to the self which is as he is. The better the adjustment the closer the correspondence between the self and the ideal self.

Assessment

A technique that may be used for measuring the degree of correspondence between the self and the ideal self is the *Q-sort*. The subject first places, in turn, a series of cards with statements concerning various personality characteristics into one of ten piles indicating how much each is characteristic of him – ranging from 'very characteristic' to 'not at all characteristic'. On completion the cards are sorted again but this time in terms of his ideal self or how he would like to be. Correlation between the two Q-sorts then provides a measure of correspondence between the two concepts. Repeated Q-sorts have been used to determine change – for example in the course of therapy. Theoretically, improvement in adjustment should be reflected in a decreasing discrepancy between self and ideal self, but in practice this has not always been found to correlate well with other measures of psychological improvement. Furthermore it appears that the mere readministration of the Q-sort may result in change which brings into question, of course, its temporal reliability.

Applications

Rogers put his theory into practice in the form of *client-centred therapy* (1951), aimed at producing personality change towards greater self-actualization. Increased unconditional self-regard and congruence, with reduced anxiety and use of defences, is achieved by the therapist providing the appropriate conditions for change. These include non-judgemental acceptance of whatever the client says (unconditional positive regard) with, in a non-directive role, minimal intervention by the therapist, and then only to help to clarify and reflect back to the client his ideas and feelings – rather as a mirror reflects back an image of a person's face which would not otherwise be visible to him.

Studies by Truax and Carkhuff (1967) suggested that successful therapy is related to three qualities on the part of the therapist – accurate empathy, non-possessive warmth and genuineness – all of which could be expected to encourage the process of self-actualization in the client. Subsequent evidence has proved equivocal, but in general has confirmed some relationship of these qualities to client change (Parloff *et al.*, 1978).

In more recent years Rogers (1970) has been involved in the *Encounter movement*, in which people meet in groups (encounter groups) of between eight and eighteen members with the aim, again, of discarding their social facade and getting in touch with their true selves. Gradually, in the supportive environment of the group and with the experience and acceptance of positive and negative feelings, a climate of trust develops in which the individual receives unconditional positive regard from the other members and can therefore increase his own positive self regard.

George Kelly

Another American academic psychologist, Kelly takes a similar view of the individual as essentially a rational being whose behaviour is determined by his experience of the world in which he lives (Kelly, 1955). Man is seen as a 'scientist' who is engaged in trying to make sense of the world in order to be able to succeed in it. To achieve this understanding he sets up hypotheses from which he makes predictions that can be tested. If events prove the hypotheses to be false, the latter can be changed to take account of this so that, it is hoped, better predictions can henceforth be made. These 'hypotheses' are essentially concerned with the way that the individual interprets events – with the *construction* that he places on them. The way he *construes* them will be unique to him, there being no absolute truth about them; hence Kelly's description of this approach to personality as *personal construct theory* (PCT). It is in terms of their usefulness in predicting future events that constructs are evaluated by the individual and retained or modified. A fundamental postulate of Kelly's theory is that 'a person's processes are psychologically channelized by the ways in which he anticipates events' – anticipation of, and not simply reaction to, events is the basis of human behaviour.

Constructs consist of bipolar interpretations or judgements (e.g. tall–short, honest–dishonest) that vary in the range of objects or situations (*elements*) to which they can be applied – their *range of convenience* – and are commonly organized in a hierarchical or pyramidal fashion with those of limited range in a *subordinate* position to those at the top (*superordinate*) that are applicable to a wide range of situations (e.g. good–bad).

Constructs are constantly being *validated* by the accuracy of their predictions of the behaviour of elements within their range of convenience. Consistent validation results in strengthening of constructs, while frequent invalidation leads to their disuse. Another important feature of constructs is that, like personality traits, they may 'go together' or correlate with each other (e.g. the construct loving–unloving with trustworthy–untrustworthy). The degree to which they correlate will, however, vary from one person to another. Those individuals in whom a large proportion of their constructs tend to be highly correlated are said to have a *tight* construct system. This means that they have strong and unvarying predictions but about a rather limited world so that, lacking flexibility, they run the risk of having their constructs invalidated at times by major failures of prediction. The *loose* construer, on the other hand, while less likely to meet with such invalidations, faces a much more confusing and unpredictable world so that the ideal construct system should obviously avoid both extremes.

We see, then, that individuals differ in the nature of their constructs and the way these are organized into a unique construct system which, according to Kelly's theory, constitutes their personality.

Assessment

A technique for discovering a person's basic constructs and the relationships between them, originally devised by Kelly as the *role construct repertory test* and later modified as the *repertory grid*, has been used extensively in many research applications both within and outside the field of personal construct theory. Its particular attraction is that it brings measurability to the ideographic approach (i.e. to the study of the unique personality of the individual).

The technique itself is flexible and may be applied in various ways, but here we can only briefly look at the traditional method. The subject is first asked to choose a number of people who are or have been important to him (e.g. father, mother, wife, son, employer). These provide the elements he is to construe. Next he is given (usually at random) three of these names and asked to say in what way two of them are alike and differ from the third. If he says, for example, that two are considerate in contrast to the third, then the construct 'considerate–inconsiderate' has been elicited. All the elements are now ranked according to this construct – i.e. from the most to the least considerate. The process is then repeated using different triads of elements and obtaining new constructs, until no more can be elicited. With each construct the elements are again ranked according to it, so that finally a matrix can be created consisting of the list of elements on the left of a series of columns of figures, one column for each construct and each figure indicating the rank position of each element on that construct (e.g. from 1 to 10 if there are 10 elements).

The data can then be analysed in various ways. Correspondence between constructs may be examined by calculating the correlation coefficients between them, and from the matrix of such correlations a factor analysis may be performed to extract factors which may indicate whether there is a loose system with a wide variety of constructs or a tight system with a small number of superordinate constructs. As well as elicited constructs it is possible to use some supplied by the investigator. Thus the constructs 'like me' and 'like I would like to be' may provide information about the individual which may be analogous to the 'self' and 'ideal self' of Rogers.

The repertory grid has been put to many uses, but its validity and reliability have not gone unchallenged, poor equivalent form and test–retest reliabilities (see Chapter 2) being found in at least one study. However, it may be argued that such concepts are not strictly applicable to the technique of the repertory grid since it is not intended as a standardized test.

Applications

If personality change is to be achieved by psychotherapy, then according to PCT it must involve a modification of the individual's particular construct system. If this is too 'tight' an attempt is made to weaken the association between constructs by a variety of means derived from other forms of psycho-therapy (e.g. free-association, dream interpretaion, reflective listening (Rogers)). On the other hand, 'tightening' in a loose construer may involve the use of behavioural techniques. A particular technique devised by Kelly for encouraging the person to see the possibility of changing his construct system is known as *fixed role therapy* (FRT). Briefly, this requires him to write a self description, following which the therapist prepares a 'fixed role sketch' for him to play in his daily life for three weeks. The new role must differ in terms of its constructs from his own, but not so much that he is unable to play the part without arousing the suspicions of others that he is doing so. The purpose is to enable him to see that he can behave, think and feel differently and that this will evoke different responses in others – he can thus be a 'different person'. Whether it is necessary to explain such a change in terms of PCT is, however, debatable.

Narrow band theories

A distinction has been made between the types of personality theory we have discussed so far – which are called *comprehensive* in that they encompass the whole of personality – and some others, described as *narrow band*, that are more specific and restricted in their content and relate only to particular aspects of behaviour (Hall and Lindzey, 1957; Peck and Whitlow, 1975). It could be argued that, with their limited applicability, such theories are not really per-sonality theories, but four examples will be considered briefly here since they have attracted considerable attention in recent years. The first two may be regarded as motivational and the others as cognitive theories.

Achievement motivation

In Chapter 9, when we were considering motivation, reference was made to a number of social 'needs' described by the American psychiatrist Henry A. Murray. Among these was a *need for achievement* (nAch), and this has been extensively studied as a personality characteristic, especially by McClelland (1953) and his associates in the USA. Attainment of success by the individual is related to a combination of this achievement motivation with two other factors: *fear of failure* (FF), and the *incentive* attaching to the particular desired goal. The motive itself is held to be learned, mainly in childhood, as a result of positive reinforcement of accomplishments. Fear of failure, on the other hand, follows frequent punishment for past failures. A person with high *nAch* is prone to tackle difficult tasks, while those that are too easy appear unattractive to him; very difficult ones may also be avoided though, if there is little chance of success. High FF is, of course, associated with a lack of self-confidence and low self-esteem, leading to avoidance of moderately difficult tasks but, para-doxically, attempts at those that are impossibly difficult where failure can be attributed to this and not to personal inadequacy. Studies relating *nAch* to both economic advancement and upward social mobility have provided evidence for the validity of the concept.

Measurement is most commonly obtained from the *thematic apperception test* (TAT), to which we have already referred as one of the projective tech-niques involved in psychodynamic assessment. Here it is phantasies of achieve-ment that are rated, using specific criteria, with a high inter-rater, though poor temporal, reliability.

Applications of the concept have mainly been in the educational field.

Sensation seeking

Another drive to which we referred in Chapter 9, probably biological or innate rather than learned, is concerned with stimulus seeking. Considered as an aspect of personality, this 'sensation seeking' is viewed as a continuum from the individual with a high sensation-seeking tendency who looks for new, unusual or unexpected situations, to the opposite extreme of the low-sensation seeker who prefers a routine, unvaried environment.

Individual differences in sensation seeking may be related to differences in the ability to tolerate sensory deprivation experiences such as were described in Chapter 4, as well as to behaviour in other situations where seeking or avoiding sensations may be important; findings have, however, tended to be incon-sistent. It was, in fact, in order to predict the response to sensory deprivation that a *sensation seeking scale* (SSS) was designed, and this has been used in modified form to measure the level of sensation seeking tendency (Zuckerman *et al.*, 1964). One clinical application has been the demonstration that drug abusers who take stimulant drugs like amphetamines have high SSS scores, while those who prefer depressants such as heroin tend to be low sensation seekers (Zuckerman *et al.*, 1972).

Internal–external locus of control

This concept was introduced originally by J.B. Rotter, but it has sub-sequently been developed as a cognitive personality dimension largely by other psychologists. In this sense it postulates a continuum at one end of which are individuals who believe their actions and experiences to be under their own control, while at the other end are those who believe themselves to be largely under the influence of external events that are outside their control. The 'internals' tend to feel confident in their ability to direct their lives; the 'exter-nals' feel relatively powerless in this respect.

The development of such differences in the position or 'locus' of control is held to be related to the past experiences of the individual in terms of repeated consequences of particular behaviours. These lead to expectancies as to whether what happens is generally the result of his own actions or due to some other factors.

There is some evidence to support the prediction that internals will be more independent and successful than externals, who would be expected to feel vulnerable and anxious since their actions are seen by them as ineffective. A similarity may be noted here with Seligman's concept of 'learned helplessness' to which we referred in Chapter 10. A twenty-nine item questionnaire to measure the internal–external orientation has been designed by Rotter (1966), and this appears to have good reliability though more questionable validity.

Application of the scale in the field of psychiatry suggests that psychological abnormality is associated with externality but also possibly with extreme internality.

Field dependence–independence

In Chapter 5 where the active nature of perception was stressed, reference was made to the influence of personality on this cognitive function. It has been suggested that differences in perception might thus be used as a measure of individual differences of personality, and one of the most popular of these theories has been developed by H.A. Witkin and his colleagues (1962). This was originally concerned with the ability to perceive an object when it is in relation to, and separated from, its background. Thus for the so-called *field-dependent* individual, perception is very much influenced by the surroundings of the perceived object; for the *field-independent* person the object can more easily be differentiated from its surrounding environment, illustrated for example, in the ability to recognize figures 'embedded' or hidden in a complex background. Later work suggested that such differences between people were not confined to perception, but also extended to other intellectual and social activities, reflected in differences of *cognitive style* ranging along a continuum between two extremes: at one end viewing events in an undifferentiated holistic manner, and at the other end seeing them in terms of their constituent parts – called *global* and *articulated* cognitive styles respectively. Thus, just as the global, undifferentiated, field-dependent person's perception is influenced by the physical background, so his behaviour is affected by the social background in the sense of being more conforming than that of the more articulated, differentiated, field-independent individual.

The differentiation of a simple figure within a more complex design, to which we have just referred, has been used in the *embedded figures test* (EFT) as a measure of field-independent perception. Another well-known technique is the *rod and frame test* (RFT) in which the subject, in a darkened room, is shown a luminous rod within a luminous square frame, both of which can be independently tilted. The ability to adjust the rod to the true vertical, whatever the position of the frame, provides a measure of field-independence or differentiation. The reliability of these and other measures has been shown to be quite high, though agreement between them is less satisfactory, suggesting that they may not be dealing with a unitary concept. It has been demonstrated, too, that field-dependence measures also correlate with at least some aspects of intelligence, and it has been suggested that they should really be regarded as intellectual rather than personality measures.

Application of the concept in psychiatry has, however, shown some relationship between field-dependence and other kinds of 'dependent' behaviour such as alcoholism.

Behavioural or social learning theories

This approach should, perhaps, be seen as an alternative to personality theories rather than as a theory of personality itself, since it challenges many of the traditional assumptions in the study of personality. In particular, it takes the view that the determinants of behaviour should be sought, not within the individual in the form, for example, of innate traits of personality, but rather in the environment to which a person responds in ways that have been learned from his unique past experience.

Clearly, in examining a particular piece of behaviour it is necessary to look at both the individual and the situation with which he is confronted; the same person will behave in different ways in different situations and different people will react differently to the same situation – it is not just the situation itself so much as the particular meaning to the individual that is important. Thus what may be termed *person* variables and *situation* variables have both to be considered; but it may well be that the interaction between them is even more significant, as has been demonstrated by several studies that have examined the separate effects on behaviour of the person, the situation and the interaction between them. Nevertheless, we are here primarily concerned with the contribution of person variables to behaviour.

The approach adopted is that each person possesses a unique organization of relatively stable tendencies to behave in particular ways based on their learning experience, and which may be described as traits of personality; but these are not universal in the sense of being present in everyone – as is held to be the case with 'type' and 'trait' theories. The fact that, despite the importance of interaction with situations, behaviour does generally tend to be stable and predictable for an individual, as implied by the concept of personality, is then attributed to previous social learning together with the fact that there is a tendency for situations themselves to remain consistent over time, while an additional contribution may come from the influence of the individual's physical appearance.

Assessment within the framework of social learning theory, stressing as it does the uniqueness of the individual, cannot make use of the traditional nomothetic methods such as questionnaires. Rather, it generally involves such techniques as direct observation of behaviour in different settings, or behavioural interviews.

The clinical applications of this approach lie mainly in the field of behaviour therapy to which we have already referred in Chapter 6. There we saw that learning theory provides a theoretical basis for attempts to effect psychological changes such as the removal of phobias, or habitual maladaptive behaviours like 'pathological' gambling. In these examples particular behavioural methods of treatment are applied to particular categories of psychological problem, but another technique, more allied to the social learning theory approach we have been discussing, and sometimes distinguished as 'behavioural psychotherapy', focusses on the individual in his own right rather than allotting him to a particular diagnostic category which then dictates the appropriate treatment. This more individual approach involves carrying out a *behavioural analysis* to take account of both person and situation variables as determinants of the problem behaviour. In particular, attention is directed to social reinforcers that may be maintaining the behaviour (e.g. the increased attention which a phobic wife may receive from her husband as a result of her fears). The behavioural treatment is then tailored to meet the particular conditions and continually monitored and revised if necessary (Mackay, 1975).

Social role theory

We have referred in earlier chapters to the social psychological concept of social roles that determine the ways in which an individual may 'act' or behave in different positions, according to the norms and expectations of his society as to what is appropriate conduct (e.g. as a husband and father at home, or as a doctor at work). They allow behaviour to be predicted within limits in given situations, though there will still be considerable variation owing to the ways in which different individuals interpret their roles. This means that each person has a reasonably stable pattern of social behaviour which has some similarity to the concept of personality. It does, however, place greater emphasis on situation variables as determinants of behaviour, and it is probably better to view the relationship between personality and social roles as an interactive one, with personality influencing the way particular roles are 'played', and some long-standing roles coming to modify some aspects of personality. Of course roles, like any other social behaviour, have to be learned, though the amount of learning required will vary between roles from the simplest (e.g. the role of train passenger) to the highly complex (e.g. the role of doctor or nurse).

An important aspect of role theory concerns the various types of conflict that may arise. Hargreaves (1972) describes six varieties:

(1) Incompatibility between two or more roles with conflicting demands on the individual, justifying, for example, the usual prohibition on doctors treating members of their own family owing to the possible conflict between their roles as a relative and a doctor.

(2) Disagreement between occupants of the same position on the nature of their role, exemplified by differences among doctors over certain clinical matters, especially where they involve social or moral issues such as abortion or euthanasia.

(3) Disagreement between occupants of complementary positions – those whose roles are complementary or reciprocal to the subject's role (e.g. parent-child, teacher–pupil), such as patients who have different expectations of the same doctor or nurse.

(4) Disagreement between role partners over the definition of their roles, a situation that may arise, for example, when doctors and patients differ in their perception of what their roles should be – the doctor perhaps seeing himself as trained to deal with serious physical disease while the patient may expect to find someone who will meet his need for a wise counsellor on domestic problems.

(5) Conflict between the expectations of different role partners, typified by the 'man-in-the-middle' whose role is perceived differently by his 'superiors' and his 'inferiors' or by two or more 'superiors' within a hierarchical system – a nurse, for example, given conflicting instructions by a doctor and a senior nurse, or caught between them and the patient who, in the hospital environment, may be considered to be in a position inferior to the nurse.

(6) A single role partner with conflicting expectations of another, found particularly within the family setting in relation to parents' contradictory

expectations of their adolescent child to be both conforming and independent, but which may occur in a similar way in clinical situations between staff and patients with chronic conditions on long-term treatment.

Finally, there may also be a conflict in the interaction, to which we have already referred, between the personality of an individual and the role he is expected to play. This may give rise to great difficulties for some patients, especially if normally 'dominant', in accepting the 'sick role' with its restrictions and its dependence on others.

We have considered several clinical aspects of the concept of role conflict, but role theory itself has more general applications in medicine in relation to the so-called 'sick role', to which we have just referred, and to the roles of the various staff disciplines. This is a matter which will receive more detailed consideration in Chapter 20, though we shall also refer to the reciprocal role relationships between patients and staff in Chapter 19.

Determinants of personality

We have, in our consideration of the various personality theories, touched on the determinants of individual differences of personality as viewed from their different perspectives. In general, the major distinction is drawn between those influences that are biological, physical, 'innate' and therefore most likely to be genetically determined at conception, and those that are environmental leading to the 'moulding' of the personality thereafter from life experience through the process of learning.

Heredity
The relative contributions of 'nature' and 'nurture' to the formation of adult personality are difficult to determine, not least because of the uncertainties surrounding the concept of personality itself. However, individual traits or dimensions of personality are reasonably satisfactory for study in this way, and Cattell developed a statistical technique called *multiple abstract variance analysis* (MAVA) in an attempt to measure the influence of environment and heredity in producing personality differences both within and between families. Applying the technique to a large population of children of varied environment and genetic relationship, he found that some aspects of personality were more likely to be determined by environment and others by heredity, though in some cases, for example with general neuroticism, differences between families were mostly due to genetic factors while those within families seemed to be due to environmental influences.

The importance of heredity to Eysenck's personality dimensions was shown by a study by Shields (1962) of the adult personalities of 44 pairs of identical twins separated shortly after birth and brought up apart, 44 pairs of identical twins brought up together and 28 pairs of non-identical twins. Scores on the dimensions of extraversion and neuroticism showed no significant correlations between the non-identical twins but were quite closely related for the identical twins – rather surprisingly even more so for those separated than for those reared together (correlations of 0.61 and 0.42 respectively for extraversion and 0.53 and 0.38 for neuroticism). This latter finding would seem to refute the environmentalist argument that identical twins may be more alike because they are more likely to be treated in similar ways than non-identical twins or siblings.

Physique

Further evidence for the part played by biological factors in personality has been sought in attempts to relate individual differences to variation of physique. An early example of this approach was that of the German psychiatrist E. Kretschmer (1925), whose concept of personality types was not included in our discussion of personality theories as it was very much a clinical one – being based on the view that the two types, the *schizothymic* and the *cyclothymic* personalities, were the normal counterparts of the major psychiatric disorders, schizophrenia and manic–depressive psychosis respectively. The schizothyme – shy, inward looking (similar to Jung's introvert) – was likely to be of *asthenic* or *leptosomatic* body build (long and narrow), while the cyclothyme – sociable, outward looking but liable to swings of mood (similar to the extravert) – tended to have a *pyknic* physique (thick-set, 'John Bull').

A more sophisticated elaboration of Kretschmer's ideas was developed by W.H. Sheldon, who identified three types of physique from a large number of photographs of male college students. Each of these physiques was considered to be determined by predominance of one of the three primitive embryonic layers (endoderm, mesoderm and ectoderm), and consequently to be associated with a particular type of personality reflecting dominance by the functions of the body organs and systems developed from that layer (Sheldon and Stevens, 1942). Thus the *endomorphic* (similar to Kretschmer's pyknic) physique is associated with the *viscerotonic* personality characterized by a love of comfort and of food – 'the digestive tract is king'; the *mesomorphic*, muscular build individual with a *somatotonic* personality, vigorous, active and assertive; the *ectomorphic* (similar to the asthenic of Kretschmer) physique with the *cerebrotonic* personality dominated by the central nervous system with inhibition, restraint and little social contact. These physical and personality types as described represent, however, the extremes of dimensions rather than categories, and any individual's physique or *somatotype* can be described by a three digit number – each digit being a score on a seven-point scale for each component. Sheldon found correlations of the order of 0.8 between scores on each of the three physical components and the three corresponding personality dimensions, though later workers have been unable to confirm such high values. Whether such associations between physique and personality are attributable to underlying genetic or environmental factors is, in any case, uncertain, and an alternative explanation would be that different physiques lead to different personalities through a process of selective experience.

Culture

In the last chapter we referred to the possible influence of culture on personality, though from a social anthropological point of view. This has, of course, also been a matter of considerable interest to psychologists, and Cattell and Warburton (1961) looked at the results of the 16PF test in comparable groups of American and British students. They were able to compare the scores on the second-order factors of anxiety and extraversion, on both of which the Americans had higher scores. These differences, together with others in relation to some of the first-order factors suggestive of greater conservatism among the American students, were interpreted as being due to cultural factors – distinguishing the moral attitudes of the two countries as being rationalist in Britain and fundamentalist religious in the USA.

Other cross-cultural studies have included those of achievement motivation and field-dependency in different societies. Thus McClelland (1961) found differences between ratings of achievement imagery in TAT stories of school-boys in Japan, Germany, Brazil and India and of business executives in Italy, Turkey and Poland, and in comparison with American subjects, though his interpretations of these differences are open to question. Le Vine (1966), scoring reports of dreams for achievement imagery, found differences between the Hausas and Ibos of Nigeria in the direction predicted by their status mobility systems, though whether this really reflects differences in personality is again questionable.

Measures of field-dependence have also shown cross-cultural variation in many studies, though there have been three main theories advanced to explain the differences. The first attributes differences of cognitive style to different child-rearing practices; the second takes a more Gestalt view and considers that performance on the RFT, EFT, etc., is essentially a perceptual skill which depends upon past experience of similar tasks and which will vary from one culture to another; the third represents an intermediate position which supposes that the two tests, the RFT and the EFT, are measuring different characteristics in different ways in different cultures. We may note that this last point of view raises a more general problem of the rather frequent 'ethnocentric' bias of cross-cultural researchers – usually with the application of established 'Western' tests to people of non-Western cultural background, leading to con-clusions that may not always be valid.

Clinical importance of personality

Several references have been made to clinical applications of the various theories of personality, but here we shall look more generally at the significance of personality for medical practice. This takes us back to the opening of this chapter, and indeed of the book, where attention was drawn to the differences in the behaviour of patients – even when they are suffering from the same disease. The explanation for such variation in patient behaviour lies, of course, very largely in their personalities. We can understand that an extravert and an introvert may react differently to the restrictions imposed by illness; that someone who habitually uses the defence mechanism of projection may tend to blame others for his predicament; that a person with poor self regard may have his self image further threatened by a feeling of failure to meet the demands of coping with illness; that the way a patient construes illness in general, and his own in particular, in relation to other aspects of life, will determine his response to it; that an individual's strength of achievement motivation may be significant in relation to any disability threatening his career; that a sensation seeker would find any degree of sensory deprivation from illness particularly stressful; that those whose locus of control is internal may be vulnerable to the dependence on others often entailed by illness; that the global, field-dependent cognitive style may be associated with greater compliance with the requirements of medical treatment. This is not to suggest, of course, that every patient should be assessed in terms of all these approaches to personality – the way a patient responds to illness is determined by factors related not only to his personality or his intelligence, but also to the nature of the illness and of the environment (Lipowski, 1970). This is a subject which has received greater attention in recent years as part of the attempt to practice comprehensive or 'whole person' medicine. It is also a matter which will be dealt with in greater detail in Chapter 20.

From a more psychiatric standpoint, some knowledge of a person's 'normal' or 'previous' personality can be important in order to detect changes which may have occurred as a consequence of disease – either organic or psychological – and also to assess the degree of recovery from such illness. An individual's personality will also 'colour' the clinical picture of any psychiatric disorder that he develops, so that it will never be identical with that of another patient.

So far, we have been concerned with differences of personality between people that would generally be regarded as falling within the normal variation in a society. Of course, it is difficult, if we are talking of a range of variation, to define what is 'normal' and what is 'abnormal' – a matter to which we referred in Chapter 14 when considering the concept of psychological maturity; but let us take as an operational definition that the individual with a 'normal' personality does not himself suffer because of it, nor does he cause suffering to others.

There are, then, some people whose personalities depart, in various ways, from the norm to such an extent that they experience difficulties themselves, resulting in anxiety or depression, or cause difficulties to others in their attempts to cope with the normal pressures and responsibilities of life; they may therefore be diagnosed as having a *personality disorder*.

Personality disorders themselves are classified into a number of types in a way that is generally quite different from that of the personality theories we have been considering. The definitions of the various personality disorders are essentially derived from clinical experience – often being seen as personality 'equivalents' of particular psychiatric disorders (e.g. the 'schizoid' personality and schizophrenia, the 'hysterical' personality and hysteria), though the association between the personality and the disorder is, in practice, far from complete.

Personality disorders that often result in problems for society at large as well as for those close to the individual are described as *psychopathy* (or sociopathy in the USA), sometimes with the qualifying adjectives 'inadequate' or 'aggressive' indicating the nature of the abnormality of behaviour. This is not, however, the place to discuss in further detail the clinical aspects of personality disorders, except to refer to a very well known and widely used personality questionnaire which is largely based on the clinical approach. The *Minnesota multiphasic personality inventory*, or MMPI (Hathaway and McKinley, 1943), is made up from nine clinical scales which cover most of the various neurotic and psychotic disorders: Hs for hypochondriasis, D for depression, Hy for hysteria, Pd for psychopathic deviate, Mf for masculinity–femininity, Pa for paranoia, Pt for psychasthenia, Sc for schizophrenia, and Ma for hypomania. Despite evidence of high reliability and of validity in terms of predicting ultimate diagnosis in new psychiatric admissions, a major criticism of the MMPI is the fact that it tends to perpetuate the confusion of psychiatric conditions with personality.

Finally we shall consider more generally the question of the deliberate attempt to bring about personality change by psychological means – usually referred to as *psychotherapy*. We have mentioned several varieties in relation to the various personality theories, but it may well be that the effectiveness of each treatment approach lies in those factors that are common to all. From a theoretical standpoint we may consider another model, that of the computer, and take the view that an individual's social behaviour will depend in part on his biological constitution (equivalent roughly to the 'hardware' of a computer) and in part on what he has learned (the programs or 'software' of the computer). Malfunctioning may be due first to defects within the 'machine' (chiefly the central nervous system) which may be corrected by physical means (drugs, ECT, etc.); secondly to problems or tasks being presented that are outside its (his) capabilities (for which the hardware or software is inappropriate), such as promotion to a more responsible position, and which may best be dealt with by 'environmental manipulation' (e.g. arranging for a less demanding job); and thirdly to inappropriate or faulty programming.

It is, of course, the programs with which it has previously been fed that instruct the computer how to tackle problems with which it is currently being presented. Similarly, it is with what has been learnt of social behaviour, particularly in the early years of childhood, that the adult knows how to relate to others. Unfortunately these early 'programs' may not always be appropriate to adult life – the little boy who has learned to be submissive to a dominating father may, without full awareness of the fact, continue to show the same response in adulthood to anyone in authority, even though this is not always to his advantage; in this case what may be required is some form 'reprogramming'. But just as a computer requires a particular mode of input (punch card, punched tape, keyboard) for inserting a program, so human 'programming', at least of social behaviour, takes place not by formal instructions but via social relationships – especially with parents during childhood. Reprogramming would then require the same input format – namely a relationship – and it seems probable that it is this relationship with a therapist that is of crucial importance to all forms of psychotherapy. At the same time it may be noted that the model allows for some reprogramming within other significant relationships in adult life, especially if stable and long lasting – perhaps most commonly in our society within a marriage.

Further reading

Bloch, S. (ed.) (1979) *An Introduction to the Psychotherapies*. Oxford: Oxford University Press.

Brown, J.A.C. (1961) *Freud and the Post-Freudians*. Harmondsworth: Penguin.

Fonagy, P. and Higgitt, A. (1984) *Personality-Theory and Clinical Practice* (New Essential Psychology Series). London: Methuen.

Fransella, F. (ed.) (1986) *Personality: Theory, Measurement and Research*, 2nd ed. London: Methuen.

Peck, D. and Whitlow, D.A. (1975) *Approaches to Personality Theory* (Essential Psychology Series). London: Methuen.

17
Individual differences
II – Intelligence

In this chapter we shall be looking at the ways in which people may differ in terms of their so-called intelligence. This is a concept that, once again, is difficult to define in any precise way. Of course, everyday experience suggests that individuals do vary, one from another, in those mental functions – thinking, remembering, learning and perceiving – that we have earlier considered as the 'higher mental' or cognitive processes. Some people are clearly much better than others at such tasks as solving problems, learning new facts and remembering them or perceiving spatial relationships, and they are usually regarded as being 'clever' in these respects. In fact the notion of intelligence has generally implied that the intelligent person will be more able in all these processes – will show greater 'all-round' cognitive ability and be generally more 'successful' than others. This, of course, begs the question of how success may be defined and measured.

One way of attempting to assess intelligence might be to devise some form of measurement of the various cognitive processes that have received so much attention from experimental and developmental psychologists. In practice, however, such an approach has, until recent times, seldom been applied to the study of individual differences. The emphasis, instead, has been 'psychometric' with the construction of tests designed to differentiate between people in terms of their individual performances on a series of intellectual tasks. Indeed, one way of dealing with the difficulty of defining what is meant by intelligence has been to take an operational view and simply to regard it as whatever it is that is measured by intelligence tests. This may seem, at first sight, to be very much putting the cart before the horse, but it is an approach that has worked well enough in the development of the physical sciences; consider, for example, the concept of temperature and its measurement by thermometers long before any fundamental understanding of its nature. One difficulty, however, is that a variety of intelligence tests may give different results in the same subject, suggesting that they may be measuring different kinds or aspects of intelligence. Furthermore, the idea that individual differences on intelligence scores can be satisfactorily explained in quantitative terms with 'higher' meaning 'more' (of the same thing) has recently been challenged with evidence of qualitative explanations of differences in test results between less and more intelligent people.

A distinction has also to be made between an individual's supposed intellectual *capacity* and the way this is expressed as *ability* – the latter depending upon such factors as past experience, current situation and degree of motivation. Measurement, of course, can be directly applied only to the observable ability or abilities, while it is the underlying capacity or potential that has generally been identified with the concept of intelligence. Obviously, assessment of those abilities that are least dependent on learning, and which are therefore less prone to variation from inequalities of educational experience, will give the best indication of innate differences of intellectual capacity between individuals.

There remains, however, a philosophical objection to the whole notion of intelligence as an entity – as something that a person possesses even if to a varying degree. While certain forms of behaviour may be described as intelligent, using the word in an adjectival sense, to explain such behaviour as due to some kind of energy or force called intelligence is open to criticism as being tautological – involving a circular cause and effect relationship with intelligence being inferred from intelligent behaviour while the latter in turn is attributed to that same intelligence. It is important, therefore, to recognize that what we observe in individuals is their intelligent behaviour, and that the so-called intelligence that we infer from this is no more than an abstraction or a hypothetical construct. It may perhaps, as suggested earlier, best be regarded as a set of highly developed cognitive processes or skills which show individual variation. Measurement of differences in these terms requires a new approach – looking, for example, at processes of memory or strategies for problem-solving used by different individuals (Resnick, 1976).

Methodology of measurement

It is clear that, as with studies of individual cognitive processes, the psychometric approach to intelligence has been essentially nomothetic with its emphasis on establishing universal measures that can be applied to all individuals – though more recently a more ideographic approach may be seen in the studies of, for example, individual strategies of problem-solving to which reference has just been made.

The psychometric approach has, to date, generally dominated the study of individual differences of intelligence, and we must consider, briefly, the methodological principles involved before we begin an examination of the various models or theories of intelligence together with their associated techniques of measurement. Remembering, then, that intelligence in this sense is defined by performance on 'intelligence tests', we have to go back to the early years of the present century for the beginnings of such measurement. After some rather unsuccessful attempts prior to this, for example involving the measurement of reaction times or the learning of nonsense syllables, it fell to a Frenchman, Alfred Binet (1875–1911), to devise the first true intelligence test aimed at measuring the ability 'to judge well, to comprehend well, to reason well'. In 1904, Binet was given official support in this task by the French government when he was asked to identify children in Paris schools who were mentally retarded and therefore unable to benefit from a normal education.

Starting from the observation that intellectual abilities in childhood increase with age, Binet, in collaboration with T. Simon, set about developing a scale with items of increasing difficulty with which he could measure a child's intellectual level. This entailed, in the first place, testing a group of children of different ages with tasks of varying difficulty and finding which of the latter could be successfully accomplished by a majority in each age group. Each such test could thus be designated as appropriate for a particular age and the complete scale constructed by ranking the tests according to their age levels. This could then be applied to the measurement of the *mental age* (MA) of an individual child by finding up to which level of difficulty he could perform correctly. This mental age would, of course, in the child of average intelligence, correspond to his actual or chronological age (CA), but lesser intelligence would result in his being developmentally behind his peers, reflected in a mental age less than his chronological age.

The first Binet–Simon scale was published in 1905, followed by two revisions in 1908 and 1911; but further versions have been produced in the years since then – in 1916 by Terman at Stanford University in the USA, and therefore referred to as the 'Stanford Binet', in 1937 by Terman and Merrill as two equivalent forms of the scale, L and M, and lastly in 1960 with a combination of the best of the L and M tests in one 'Terman–Merrill Form L-M'. These tests are still used quite extensively for the measurement of intelligence in children.

In 1912, W. Stern suggested the use of the *ratio* or quotient of mental age to chronological age in order to show what proportion of the intelligence that would be normal for his age is possessed by a 'feeble-minded' (mentally handi-capped) child. Thus was born the concept of the *intelligence quotient* (IQ) expressed as a percentage and calculated by the formula:

$$\text{Intelligence Quotient (IQ)} = \frac{\text{Mental age (MA)}}{\text{Chronological age (CA)}} \times 100$$

Clearly, the child of average intelligence whose mental age corresponds with his chronological age will have an IQ of 100. If, however, a child aged 10 years is more developmentally advanced than average with, say, a mental age of 12, he will have an IQ of 120. Similarly, a less intelligent 10-year-old with a mental age of 8 will have an IQ of 80.

The concept of the IQ has proved to be very popular and the term has come to be used almost as a synonym for intelligence, despite the fact that other mea-sures of intelligence, especially in adults, have nothing to do with the calcula-tion of a ratio or quotient. It also has other disadvantages – even in its original conception. It tends to suggest, for example, that intelligence is fixed early in childhood and will remain constant thereafter, whereas, although studies of large samples of children have shown a fairly high degree of stability through childhood, individual children may have scores that fluctuate quite widely. Another problem is that the improvement in intellectual performance with age, on which depends the concept of MA and therefore of IQ, reaches a maximum at different ages for different tests (but in any case mostly around 14–15 years), making the whole notion inappropriate for use in adulthood.

In the measurement of intelligence at ages beyond the period of childhood mental development some alternative means is therefore required to quantify individual differences. The psychometric approach here is, first, to apply to a sample population a test that includes items covering a wide range of difficulty. If the frequency of individual scores is now plotted it is likely to produce a normal distribution curve, with the majority of the sample scoring somewhere in the middle of the range and fewer and fewer above and below this. In fact psychologists have generally assumed that the distribution of intelligence will be normal like that of other continuously distributed biological variables such as adult height, and scores on intelligence test items can be weighted to ensure that this is so.

Given such a distribution it is then possible to see individual intelligence scores as *deviations* from the mean and to express them in terms of standard deviations. The actual figure can be quite arbitrary, and indeed in the 1966 revision of the 'Stanford Binet', to which reference has already been made, this approach was employed so that instead of using the ratio of mental age to chronological age to calculate the IQ, the distribution of mental ages for each chronological age was determined and the mental ages falling one standard deviation above and below the chronological age were designated as IQs of 116 and 84 respectively; a distribution with a mean of 100 and a standard deviation of 16 whatever the chronological age.

The most popular adult intelligence test, the *Wechsler adult intelligence scale* (WAIS), named after its developer David Wechsler, is similarly based on the notion of deviation IQs with, in this case, a mean of 100 and a standard deviation of 15. It differs, however, from the Binet type of test in estimating two categories of mental ability – verbal and non-verbal (or performance). The *verbal* IQ depends upon previously learned verbal material and is measured by totalling the scores on six subtests: information (covering a range of general knowledge), comprehension (the ability to understand and deal with various situations), arithmetic (computation and reasoning with figures), similarities (recognition of similarities and differences of pairs of words), vocabulary (definition of meanings of words), and digit span (the number of digits that can be remembered and repeated both forwards and backwards immediately after hearing). The *performance* IQ is similarly derived from the scores on five subtests: picture completion (identifying the missing parts of incomplete pictures), picture arrangement (arranging sets of pictures into a meaningful sequence), block design (arranging painted wooden blocks to copy designs of varying difficulty), object assembly (building up shapes from pieces of cardboard), and digit symbol (filling in the appropriate symbol against a series of numbers according to a code). The time taken to complete these items is taken into account in scoring, in contrast to the verbal tests which are untimed.

In addition to the separate verbal and performance IQs, the WAIS provides a combined or *full scale* IQ. A version for children aged 6 to 16 is also available, known as the *Wechsler intelligence scale for children* (WISC). Individual raw scores have to be differentially weighted according to chronological age, so that once again the comparison is with the mean for the child's age group.

A criticism of the psychometric approach to intelligence is that, however reliable or valid (often in terms of agreement with school attainment) the tests, they do not have their origin in any sound theoretical framework but are built up purely from items chosen for their ability to discriminate between age groups and/or individuals. There have recently been some attempts to remedy this situation, and we shall look at these briefly; but first we must consider some of the earlier theories or models of intelligence – mostly based on multivariate analysis of intelligence test data.

Theories of intelligence

In the last chapter we saw how factor analysis may be applied to the study of personality, but the technique was in fact developed in the early years of this century by Charles Spearman in connection with his investigation of intelligence in children. At the time that Binet was constructing his test and formulating the concept of mental age, Spearman (1904) gave a variety of tests of mental ability to large numbers of children and then examined the degree of agreement (i.e. correlation) between the scores on the different tests. Since there was a positive correlation between the tests he assumed that they were to some extent measuring a common or underlying 'factor', which he called 'g' for 'general intelligence'. However, since the correlations between tests were only partial, they must also each be measuring some 'specific ability' or 's'. This, then, was a *'two-factor'* theory which proposed that there is a general intellectual ability which varies between individuals and which has a general influence on a number of more specific abilities, the levels of which, however, will show some differences within the individual. A person will thus have a particular pattern of intellectual abilities differing from others, as well as having a certain level of general intelligence.

Later, however, applying Spearman's own technique of factor analysis, other psychologists including Philip Vernon (1950) failed to confirm the existence of only one factor common to a number of tests, and this led to a *'hierarchical'* theory of mental abilities analogous to the personality theories of Cattell and Eysenck. It still includes, at the highest level of organization, a general factor of intelligence, but between this and the specific or *special* abilities there are a number of *group* factors. These fall into two categories, 'verbal' and 'practical', the former including those labelled 'creative', 'verbal' and 'numerical' and the latter comprising 'spatial' and 'mechanical'.

These British theories with their concept of a factor of general intelligence were challenged by the American psychologist, L.L. Thurstone, who also made his own contribution to the development of factor analysis but in a way different from that used by Spearman. This aims at achieving as much separation as possible of the individual factors, which therefore minimize the likelihood of revealing a general factor. In the related *multiple factors theory* of intelligence (Thurstone, 1938), the seven individual factors (all of equal status) are called 'primary mental abilities': numerical, verbal comprehension, memory, word fluency, spatial, reasoning and perceptual speed. It will be apparent, however, that the difference between the British and the American approaches was, in part, simply a reflection of the different type of factor analysis employed, and in fact if a 'second-order' analysis is performed on Thurstone's primary factors (which are to some extent positively correlated – i.e. are oblique) a general factor once again emerges. The argument then becomes a matter of whether it is of greater use to consider an individual's overall general intelligence or his profile of specific abilities.

An even more atomistic or reductionist view of intelligence, but still derived from test measurements, has been advanced by another American psychologist, J.P. Guilford (1967). This involves a logical analysis of intellectual activities into three main categories: four types of *content* of information (figural, symbolic, semantic, behavioural), five mental *operations* which may be carried out on these contents (thinking, remembering, divergent production, convergent production and evaluating), and six types of *product* or ways of understanding resulting from these operations on the contents (units, classes, relations, systems, transformations and implications). It is obviously not possible here to consider all these terms, but it can be seen that such a system generates 120 separate abilities – such as to be able to recognize (operation) letters (symbols) as a word (product = unit). This may seem an absurdly large number of distinct abilities, but Guilford's model is at least based on concepts derived from experimental work and may also be truer to the complex nature of human intelligence than other more simple versions.

Cattell and Eysenck have both also contributed to the study of intelligence. Cattell (1971), on the basis of factor analytic studies, splits the general factor of intelligence (or g) into two parts which he terms *fluid* intelligence (g_f) and *crystallized* intelligence (g_c) – the former being biologically or genetically determined (i.e. innate ability) and the latter based on cultural and educational experience. Eysenck (1973) makes a distinction between *speed* and *power* components of intelligence – the first measured by tasks requiring quick and accurate performance (like the digit symbol test of the WAIS) and the second by untimed tests of complex reasoning, some of which could never be solved by the less intelligent subject however much time is allowed (e.g. Raven's matrices – a set of tests of increasing difficulty requiring choice of the correct design to fit the missing part of a larger pattern).

Yet another splitting of intelligence, but this time in terms of two *levels*, has been suggested by Arthur Jensen. The levels actually represent extremes of a continuum, with the lower level (I), *associative* ability, being the capacity to learn, remember and recall information, whereas *cognitive* ability (level II) is concerned with making use of such information in reasoning. Level II thus depends upon level I but not vice versa.

In Chapter 8 we considered two types of thinking, named by Guilford *convergent* and *divergent*, and forming, as we have just seen, two of the 'operations' within his analysis of mental activities. This notion has been developed (Hudson, 1966) in the field of individual differences as a personality trait, so that some people are predominantly 'convergers' and others 'divergers'. The former are likely to perform well on conventional tests of intelligence since these mostly require focussing down on to one correct answer to each question, whereas problems requiring as many appropriate responses as possible to one item – sometimes considered to be a measure of 'creativity' – will be more easily performed by divergers.

D.O. Hebb (1966), whose neurological basis of learning in terms of cell assemblies and phase sequences was also described in Chapter 6, has distinguished two meanings of intelligence. Intelligence A is the innate potential and is based on the brain which is capable, during the course of development, of acquiring intelligent performance by building up networks of assemblies and 'schemata' concerned with particular activities. In this way good intelligence A depends upon 'the possession of a good brain and a good neural metabolism' – but it is not directly observable or measurable. Intelligence B involves the actual functioning of the brain, is observable indirectly in the individual's behaviour and can be measured by tests. It depends upon interaction between intelligence A and the environment through which various intellectual abilities have been acquired, especially in the early years of development.

We have seen that most of the theories of intelligence discussed so far are based on the psychometric approach, which in turn makes use of the concept of deviance from an average or norm, whether this is in terms of rate of development or the mean of a population of the same age. We have also seen that criticisms can be levelled at this view of intelligence and what can be called the *norm-referenced* tests associated with it. An alternative view is emerging which sees intelligence as a range of hierarchically organized intellectual skills with measurement concerned with finding out whether particular tasks – so-called criterion tasks – can be achieved. Such a *criterion-referenced* measure of intelligence for children aged 2 to 17, and known as the *British ability scales* (BAS), has been under development for several years at the University of Manchester (Elliott *et al.*, 1978). The twenty-four scales cover a range of cognitive processes and abilities which can be estimated directly rather than by comparison with population norms; they are also based to some extent on theories of development, including that of Piaget on concept formation (discussed in Chapter 13). Whether this method of measurement of intelligence will prove to be more useful than the more traditional psychometric approach exemplified by the Wechsler scales remains to be seen.

Determinants of intelligence

With so much uncertainty about the very nature of intelligence it is perhaps not surprising to find some confusion surrounding the issue of what factors may affect it. Just as with personality, it is obvious that adult intelligence, at least as revealed in intellectual performance, must depend upon an interaction between internal 'biological' and external environmental influences. Difficulties arise, however, when questions are posed as to the relative importance of 'nature' and 'nurture' in this context, for the answers may have great educational, social and political significance. Consider, for example, the possible implications if it could be shown that intelligence is entirely determined by inheritance, being fixed at birth and unalterable thereafter, or on the other hand that it is completely dependent on education and other environmental experience.

This issue has for many years given rise to much vigorous debate. Attention has also been directed to apparent differences of intelligence between ethnic groups – a matter to which we shall return shortly. It is important to stress, once again, that it is the interaction, not the simple addition or combination, of internal and external factors that ultimately determines the intellectual abilities of the individual, but we shall now examine these two aspects separately – looking first at heredity and then at the environment. (There are some additional 'internal' influences that we shall consider later in relation to retardation of intellectual development, but here we shall confine our attention to 'normal' genetic factors.)

Genetic factors

Before considering human intelligence we may briefly note that animal studies have shown that it is possible to breed strains that differ in their 'intelligence' – for example with rats as reflected in their ability to learn to negotiate mazes ('maze bright' and 'maze dull' rats).

In man, evidence pointing to the influence of heredity within the normal range of intelligence comes mainly from family and twin studies. Generally, the more closely related any two individuals are the more similar will be their IQ scores. Unfortunately from the genetic point of view this could, in part at least, be explained in terms of environment, since the latter is also likely to be more similar the closer the relationship. As with personality, the most convincing genetic evidence comes from twin studies which compare the closeness of scores of monozygotic with dizygotic pairs – the correlation for the former being greater (usually about 0.8) than for the latter (0.5–0.6). Once again it may be argued that monozygotic twins, being 'identical' in appearance, are more likely to have an 'identical' environment (i.e. be treated alike) than are dizygotic, dissimilar twins. This, however, may be countered by studies of identical twins separated at, or soon after, birth and reared apart, who have still shown a high correlation of intelligence scores (though it has been suggested by critics that the environments of separated twins may often be quite similar, and the previously accepted findings of the late Sir Cyril Burt (1966) in his studies of separated twins has been largely discredited (Kamin, 1974)). Additional support for the influence of heredity comes from comparisons of parent–child with foster parent–child correlations – the former being higher, though only slightly so, than the latter. In general, the evidence supports a polygenic mode of inheritance through the combined action of a number of genes of small effect, rather than the effect of a single major gene (which can, however, be of importance, as we shall see, in causing some forms of mental handicap).

The contribution of the genetic component to the determination of intelligence is probably to set an upper limit to intellectual development, with the extent to which this is reached being influenced by other, largely environmental, factors. From the correlation of IQ scores, especially in twins, a so-called index of heritability may be calculated. This compares the ratio, within a particular population, of the variance of test scores attributable to inheritance to the total variance. It is important to stress that such an index of heritability is specific to a particular population at a particular time – in other environmental circumstances the ratio might be quite different. It also applies to a group and not to an individual; it is quite impossible to apportion how much of a person's intelligence is due to heredity, and indeed it is a meaningless exercise in view of the interaction between heredity and environment to which we have repeatedly referred.

Environmental factors

The influence of the environment may be said to begin from the moment of conception. The development of the fetus, especially at critical times, may be affected by various physical factors, including the diet of the mother, her cigarette smoking, alcohol drinking and drug-taking habits, or by disease such as rubella (German measles), and damage to the brain may occur during the birth process. All these aspects are, of course, of clinical importance and may lead to degrees of mental handicap. We are more concerned here, however, with subsequent environment, especially during childhood and including sociocultural, family and educational influences.

It has long been recognized that children from social class 5 families generally perform less well on intelligence tests than those from higher social classes, though within each social class the complete range of intelligence scores is represented. The explanation of these social class differences is still uncertain, but lack of sufficient stimulation and variety of experience is likely to play a part. Differences in the patterns of intellectual abilities have also been found between children of different ethnic groups, both within the same city (Lesser *et al.*, 1965) and in different parts of the world (Vernon, 1969), indicating the importance of cultural factors. Studies of family influences suggest that greater parental attention such as may be received by children of smaller families and those that are first born may result in higher IQ scores. The question of the effect of education on IQ is obviously of importance, and studies suggest that not only does the sheer amount of schooling have a positive influence on test scores but, within a school, factors such as teacher expectations may speed up or slow down the development of individual children.

Some of the most convincing evidence for the influence of the environment comes from successful attempts, through intensive stimulation and education, to improve the IQs in children who were at risk of some degree of mental retardation because they were born to mothers of low IQ or because they came from 'deprived' backgrounds. Similar increases of IQ scores have been found when children are transferred from poor institutions to good foster homes.

The ethnic controversy

In recent years the nature–nurture dispute in relation to intelligence has received wider publicity because it has become a key part of the controversy over the existence of, and explanation for, differences of average intelligence between races. There seems to be no dispute over the fact that in the USA black children and adults, when given IQ tests, score on average significantly lower than whites. There is also a north–south difference, with both blacks and whites in the north scoring higher than their counterparts in the south. In the UK, too, below-average attainment and IQ measurements have been demonstrated in school children of West Indian origin.

The issue, of course, is whether these findings represent true differences of 'intelligence' (raising once again the problems of the concept itself and of its measurement), and if so whether or how much this is due to genetic or environmental factors. As far as the first question is concerned, it has been suggested that tests have been designed for white people and are therefore not appropriate for other cultures. There is certainly some truth in this, but the likely extent of the effect is reduced by the fact that other minority groups in the USA (American Indians, Mexican Americans, Japanese Americans) and in the UK (Irish, Asian, African) have similar scores to the white population. Poor motivation and low self-esteem felt by US blacks and UK West Indians may affect their performance on intelligence tests, as may the colour of the tester, but the evidence for this is equivocal.

This leaves a major and often bitter controversy, which was re-opened in 1969 by Jensen to whose concept of two levels of intelligence we have already referred. One obvious explanation of the poor intellectual performance of negroes in the USA was their inferior environment, but Jensen challenged this and claimed an 80 per cent genetic determination of the differences in IQ between the black and white populations. However, we have already seen that any estimate of heritability is specific to a particular population, so that Jensen's claim has been rejected by many psychologists.

Unfortunately, the suggestion of apparent racial inferiority has been so inflammatory that some have urged a taboo on the whole subject of heritability. At present the matter is not settled, and it seems likely that neither extreme view – genetic or environmental – will prove to be correct. In any event, it is important to stress that inter-ethnic differences of average intelligence or of the pattern of abilities, even if they do exist, tell us nothing about the intelligence of any *individual* of whatever race.

Clinical aspects

With the many difficulties surrounding the concept of intelligence and its measurement, it might be supposed that it has little importance in clinical medicine. This would be rather ironic since, in its early days, a major concern of clinical psychology was in fact the measurement of intelligence in psychiatric patients. Since then the role of the clinical psychologist has broadened considerably while attitudes to the measurement of intelligence have become, as we have seen, more critical if not actually sceptical. Nevertheless, provided its limitations are recognized, intelligence testing can make a useful contribution in certain areas of clinical practice. Before considering these, however, we must refer briefly to the possible influence on test performance of certain situational factors which have to be taken into account by the psychologist.

Situational factors affecting performance in intelligence tests

Physical and/or mental ill-health may temporarily impair intellectual performance. Distressing physical symptoms may obviously interfere with mental concentration, while great anxiety, deep depression or the thought disorder of schizophrenia may make it extremely difficult for a patient to respond adequately to test material.

Again, as we have mentioned in relation to the question of racial differences of intelligence, there may be problems of communication and understanding between a subject of one race or culture and a tester of another.

The influence of motivation may also be quite profound. If the individual sees no relevance of the intelligence testing to his current situation or problems, he may make little attempt to cooperate with the tasks involved, and may then achieve a much lower score than would have been the case if he had been more highly motivated.

Finally, the effect of 'practice' on test performance has to be avoided or allowed for – in other words, improvement in performance due to previous exposure to the test material has to be minimized by either ensuring a sufficient interval of time between performances on the same test or, preferably, employing 'parallel' forms of the test which allow the use of different material for retesting.

It is particularly in recognizing and making allowance for all these various influences that the skill and experience of the clinical psychologist lies.

Applications in clinical practice

Apart from the situational influences just discussed, it is generally organic disease affecting the functioning of the brain that is likely to impair intellectual performance, so that it is in the field of neuropsychiatry particularly that intelligence testing may be of greatest assistance. Not only may there be evidence of a general falling off in intellectual functioning compared with an actual previous measurement, or an estimate based on past educational or occupational history, but more specific cognitive impairments may indicate lesions of particular parts of the brain.

As well as this diagnostic and monitoring (measuring change over time in a progressive dementing process) role, the assessment of an individual's intellectual abilities can be of value in other clinical situations where psychological problems may be arising in an educational or vocational context.

Mental handicap

We have seen earlier that there has generally been an underlying assumption that the distribution of levels of intelligence among the members of a population will tend to follow a normal distribution curve. Indeed, intelligence tests may be designed to achieve just this – a symmetrical inverted U-shaped curve about a mean score of 100. Such a distribution will then be found in 'normal' populations similar to that on which the test was standardized, but if a truly representative sample of a total population is tested a curve is found which is slightly 'skewed' to the left or lower end of the intelligence range. This means that there are, in fact, more individuals with low intelligence scores than would be theoretically expected from a normal distribution. The explanation for this lies in the pathological causes of low intelligence – what is now called 'mental handicap'.

While some people of limited intelligence simply represent the lower end of the normal distribution – balancing those of high intelligence at the opposite end – there are others, particularly those of very low intelligence, who have abnormalities of various kinds that have affected the normal development of their brains. These abnormalities may be genetically determined. For example, in the condition known as phenylketonuria, owing to the inheritance of a recessive gene from each parent the newborn child is unable to metabolize the amino acid phenylalanine. This results in mental retardation unless prevented by the prescription of a special diet largely free from the amino acid. Some chromosomal abnormalities, including that causing Down's syndrome, provide another cause of mental handicap. Finally, a wide range of injuries or infections can damage the developing brain before, during or after birth.

A rough distinction may be made between milder degrees of mental handicap within an IQ range of 50–70, and more severe degrees with scores below 50, the latter more than the former tending to be associated with brain pathology.

Further reading

Anastasi, A. (1982) *Psychological Testing*, 5th ed. New York: Macmillan.
Butcher, H.J. (1970) *Human Intelligence: Its Nature and Assessment*. London: Methuen.
Heim, A. (1970) *Intelligence and Personality*. Harmondsworth: Penguin.
Richardson, K. and Spears, D. (eds.) (1972) *Race, Culture and Intelligence*. Harmondsworth: Penguin.

Part 5
The interactional perspective

This section is concerned with social behaviour. Chapter 18 offers a brief introduction to the discipline of social psychology – a bridge between the two major behavioural sciences of sociology and psychology. Areas relevant to medicine and reviewed here include attitudes, social perception, social influence, interpersonal relationships, communication and social roles.

Chapter 19 deals with particular clinical applications: marriage and its breakdown, including sexual behaviour and interpersonal aspects generally; and professional relationships, especially that between doctor and patient with emphasis on the two-way communication involved, but including relationships between different health service staff and the concept of the multidisciplinary team.

18
Social interaction
I – Social psychology

'No man is an island entire of itself'. John Donne's graphic description of the essentially social nature of human existence provides the theme of this chapter.

We have looked at man as an individual as well as at the social groups of which he may be a member, and in so doing we have necessarily touched upon some aspects of their interrelationship. Now we turn to the discipline of social psychology itself whose basic concern is with social behaviour or the way in which people behave in relation to others – to their so-called 'social environment'. An interest in social behaviour is not of course confined to social psychology but is shared in varying degrees by other disciplines, and especially by its 'parents', psychology and sociology.

It will also be apparent that the subject must encompass a very wide area, with boundaries that are difficult to define. Indeed, although of comparatively recent origin as an experimental science, social psychology's interests have been identified with such varied and fundamental human concerns as knowledge, power, freedom, work and play, identity, love, justice and happiness – issues that have been of great moment to Western culture for at least two thousand years and reflected in the writings of the Greek philosophers and of the Old and New Testaments, in the ideals of the Reformation and Enlightenment, and in works of literature and art generally (Brickman, 1980). Clearly this chapter will have to be somewhat less ambitious.

Social behaviour and its study

It is difficult to give a precise definition of social behaviour. The most obvious examples of behaviour that may be classed as social must be the everyday face-to-face interactions that take place between individual people. Social psychologists are, however, also interested in the wider social context – in those aspects of society that may influence such behaviour – and we have already in previous chapters looked at some of these.

The *research methods* used by social psychologists include, as might be expected, those described in earlier chapters as employed within both sociology and psychology. They range from relatively uncontrolled observations by individuals attached to particular social groups (participant observation), through more controlled observations (focussed, for example, on the behaviour of selected individuals), surveys (often of large populations using questionnaires), natural experiments (making use of natural events which allow a comparison of the behaviour of groups differing in one characteristic), field experiments (observation of the effect on behaviour of experimental manipulation of particular variables but within as natural a setting as possible), to laboratory experiments (an artificial environment but more easily arranged and allowing greater control over all variables).

The use of the laboratory experiment is in fact a rather distinctive feature of social psychology when compared with other social sciences such as sociology and social anthropology – being closer in this respect to psychology. It is necessary, however, to note some special difficulties associated with this type of experiment arising from the fact that the procedure itself involves a social interaction between experimenter and subject, so that there is what can be described as a social psychology of the experiment. This is particularly concerned with the social influences on the behaviour of the individual who is aware of taking part in an experiment. Such an awareness is liable to alter behaviour in ways that are difficult to predict; subjects frequently attempt to guess the purpose of the experiment and may then try to behave in ways that they think are required of them. In an effort to minimize these so-called *demand characteristics* of the experimental situation (Orne, 1962), attempts have been made to hide the true purpose of experiments from subjects; but in addition to its questionable ethics, this has become so well known among the student population, from whom most of the experimental subjects are obtained, that it has led to a great suspicion and mistrust of the experimental psychologist.

The latter is also, however, himself a potential source of bias in such experiments owing to what may be termed *expectancy effects* (Rosenthal, 1966) – the experimenter may unwittingly influence the outcome of the experiment in such a way as to confirm his predictions. This risk is, of course, not confined to social psychology and is the reason for the 'double blind' technique in clinical trials; but it is a more potent influence here owing to the social nature of the experiment. It has been found, for example, that the sex of the experimenter is important in influencing behaviour of subjects – male experimenters tending to be friendlier, especially towards female subjects. The use of written instructions to subjects, or ensuring that the experimenter is unaware of the details of the experiment and of the subjects being used, are ways of trying to circumvent this problem.

Determinants of social behaviour

As always when we attempt to understand why a person behaves in a particular way, we must look at factors within the individual and within his, in the present context, social situation. In relation to the former we have already (in Chapter 9) noted the several so-called social drives and concluded that, although these may be in some cases partly biological and innate, they are more generally considered to be secondary and learned from experience during the process of development.

We should, however, take some note here of the alternative view of the relatively new and controversial discipline of sociobiology which seeks a biological basis for all social behaviour (Wilson, 1975). It claims in short that social behaviour in animals, including to a large extent humans, is not learned but is genetically determined and has evolved from the process of natural selection. It is well known that many animal species, especially insects, live in colonies and exhibit 'social' behaviour, with clearly defined roles for the members of different groups. From an evolutionary standpoint this posed a problem for

Charles Darwin, who was unable to explain how a 'worker' caste of insects had evolved since they are sterile and leave no offspring – nor could he account for altruistic behaviour in which an individual may help another to survive though putting itself at risk of death.

The sociobiological answer to this dilemma starts from the assumption that evolution is concerned solely with the survival of genes. Since an individual shares many genes with his kin the existence of a kinship group, for whose defence he is willing to sacrifice himself, is likely to ensure the survival of 'his' genes to be passed on to further generations. Furthermore, if there are genes that are responsible for such altruistic behaviour, and these are shared by two organisms through common descent, then if an altruistic act by one allows the survival of the other, so increasing their gene contribution to the next genera-tion, the tendency to altruistic behaviour within the species will also be increased. Studies of animal behaviour over a wide range of species, including primates, have, it is claimed, provided support for this hypothesis of the evolu-tion of social behaviour.

Whether this holds true for human behaviour is, however, a matter of dis-pute. It may be argued, for example, that a pattern of altruistic behaviour such as that shown by eskimo grandparents, who remain behind when the family has to move on in search of food in times of scarcity, is not due to an altruistic gene but represents an adaptive behavioural response that has been learned and passed on within the culture; families who do not conform to the tradition are not likely to survive for many generations. At present the dispute is unresolved, and for the rest of this chapter we shall restrict ourselves to essentially psychological and social rather than biological influences on behaviour.

Areas of social psychology

It has been customary for social psychologists to consider behaviour in relation to three social settings: dyadic (one-to-one relationships), small groups and larger social groups such as institutions and organizations. We can assume, though, that in any social encounter peoples' behaviour will be guided by their mutual expectation of each other. Clearly these expectations must encompass a range of behaviours, stretching from those of a fairly basic nature and shared by all of mankind, to those found within recognized social groupings, and finally to that of individuals well known to each other. Thus we carry with us a set of symbolic representations of our social world based on past experience and manifested as *attitudes* which largely determine our behaviour towards others. At the same time we have to be able to evaluate the other person – a process of *social perception* through which we attempt to make an *attribution* to them of those personal characteristics which will supposedly determine how they will behave to us, and thus in turn how we will behave to them within a particular *interpersonal relationship*.

Such social interaction will, of course, depend very much on the process of *communication* between the individuals involved, while another important aspect – especially in the small group setting – is the extent to which individual behaviour may be modified by the *social influence* of others.

Finally, social behaviour may be considered in the wider social context where it is influenced by the various *roles* which a person may play within particular social institutions and organizations.

This brief overview has emphasized some topics which, because of their relevance to medicine and the health professions, we shall be considering in more detail in this chapter. It is clear that they are highly interrelated, and there will be a degree of arbitrariness about the order in which they will be discussed.

Attitudes

Opinion polls have become a prominent feature of our society. Opinions are statements of peoples' beliefs, values and attitudes, and from these the pollster hopes to be able to make predictions about their behaviour.

An *attitude of mind* (as distinct from the older usage of a bodily attitude – a posture of the body proper to or implying some action or mental state) represents a positive or negative *orientation* towards, and with it a *predisposition* to behave in a particular way in response to, an object or class of objects (stimulus). There are several theoretical conceptualizations of attitudes, including the behaviourist, learning theory and cognitive.

The *behaviourist* approach avoids any speculation about processes intervening between the stimulus and the response, and sees attitudes as simply the individual's self description of his behavioural tendencies, which can then become a self instruction to guide behaviour (Bem, 1968). Thus behaviour originally carried out at the behest of others (e.g. parents) is self-perceived by the individual as a behavioural tendency (an example of the process of self attribution which we shall shortly be considering in more detail), and is perpetuated by self instruction. However, most social psychologists see attitudes as intervening variables or hypothetical constructs interposed between the stimulus and the response.

The *learning theory* approach defines it as an implicit response, stressing the efferent or outgoing part of the intervening process, while *cognitive theory* emphasizes the incoming afferent perceptual part – a 'set' which influences perception of the stimulus object.

Perhaps the most popular view of the intervening process, however, is that it has a *three-component* structure. First there is a *cognitive* evaluation of the object – what the individual knows of it and his *belief* about it; is it good or bad, true or false, etc? Second, there is an *affective* response – how he feels about it, whether he likes or dislikes it, approves or disapproves of it – and this will be influenced by his *personal system of values* reflected in the relative importance he attaches to such ideals as freedom, order and truth. Finally, with the *conative* component there is his behavioural tendency, both verbal and non-verbal, towards the object. Some have argued that actual behaviour is not an essential part of attitude – that it can exist without overt expression in behaviour. In any case it is clear that there may be discrepancies between the three components; the saying 'it's naughty but it's nice' exemplifies conflicting cognitive and affective evaluations – the actual behaviour in this instance tending usually to be determined by the latter rather than the former! This inconsistency also emphasizes the fact that an attitude is only a predisposition to respond in a particular way – not a fixed response. Thus behaviour towards any object or class of objects is likely to be influenced by a number of different attitudes which themselves have different relative strengths of their cognitive and affective components, so that it is not surprising that trying to predict behaviour from attitudes is a very uncertain exercise (Wicker, 1969).

Attempts at measurement of attitudes reflect the different emphases attached by learning and cognitive theorists to the response and stimulus aspects respectively. The view held by learning theorists that an attitude is an implicit behavioural response would require direct observation of behaviour, in the natural setting and in response to a variety of stimuli, as the ideal means of determining a person's attitudes. However, practical difficulties have limited such studies, and most attitude measurement has used peoples' verbal responses to verbal statements about an object. The learning theory approach here emphasizes the response aspect (e.g. 'Would you accept (members of a particular race) as workmates?') and is described as a *response-centred* approach (Torgerson, 1958). The cognitive view emphasizes the perception of the stimulus and is a *stimulus-centred* approach (Thurstone and Chave, 1929). It involves subjects choosing, from a number of evaluative statements about the stimulus/object, those which best represent their views. A third, and probably the commonest, *subject-centred* approach (Likert, 1932) uses statements of attitudes chosen primarily for their ability to discriminate between different subjects – the emphasis here being on individual differences.

Attitudes do of course, differ, between people (in terms of how extreme they are, their cognitive basis and degree of sophistication, the firmness with which they are held), and as we saw in Chapter 16 they contribute to that major aspect of individual differences called personality. It is important, however, to differentiate between the specificity of an attitude – which as we have seen is oriented towards, and may result in behaviour to, an object (e.g. aggression towards a particular person) – and the generality of a personality trait which indicates a persistent predisposition towards a particular type of behaviour (e.g. aggression). Of course such a personality trait is likely to be reflected in the behavioural component of many of that person's attitudes.

We also saw in earlier chapters that the concept of culture includes the sharing of a set of beliefs and values which transcend differences between individuals, though they will clearly influence each member's particular attitudes; an example of such a widespread influence might be the effect of the so-called protestant ethic to which we referred in Chapter 12. Other shared attitudes, often negative, about a class of people, involving a simplified, superficial and usually biased cognitive evaluation, can form a *stereotype*. The tendency to use such stereotypes is greater in people who can be described as prejudiced in their *social* attitudes – attitudes concerned with the way that society is organized and therefore in some senses political.

The study of social attitudes has in fact largely been concerned with the concepts of *prejudice* and *authoritarianism*, and Adorno *et al.* (1950) described a so-called authoritarian personality associated with attitudes that would generally be called fascist and be associated with extreme right-wing views. A measure of *dogmatism* (Rokeach, 1960) which correlates with that of authoritarianism is, however, associated with extremes of political views rather than their direction; it can be seen as a state of 'closed-mindedness' with an extremely resistant set of attitudes.

If attitudes are such a universal feature of human existence what can we say about their purpose, and how they are acquired? It is clear that a meaningful evaluation of the environment, both physical and social, would be impossible without some means of ordering and classifying the information that we receive, and we considered this as a cognitive function when we looked at the process of concept formation in Chapter 8. Having defined classes or categories of objects, however, we need in addition to know how to respond to them, and this is where attitudes provide us with a guiding framework. The attitudes themselves must have been based on past experience, though it is possible that there may be a genetic contribution exerting an influence on general orientations (e.g. towards aggression, altruism, ethnocentrism). Learning, however, clearly plays a major part in determining our attitudes – sometimes from direct experience of particular objects and events but often, especially in relation to cultural beliefs, values and attitudes, indirectly from parents and immediate family in the process of *socialization*. While both classical and operant conditioning may play a part in such learning, imitation is probably the most significant means by which attitudes are acquired. Parents when they express a particular attitude provide a model for the child to copy, and may then positively reinforce the imitation. Similar influences occur later within the child's peer groups, etc.

Attitude change

If the major determinant of social attitudes is the social environment – the social influence of the various groups of which the individual is a member – attitude *change* may also be seen as a result of further social communication. This in turn may be broken down into three parts: the source, the message (and its channel) and the receiver. Not surprisingly in view of its practical importance for various aspects of social, political and commercial life, much research has been carried out in the area of attitude change, most of it in relation to the variables just listed. The *source* (an individual) has, as might be expected, generally been shown to produce more attitude change if he has expertise, attraction and reward or coercive power over the receiver. The greater the discrepancy between the attitude of the source as indicated in the *content* of the *message* and the attitude initially held by the receiver, the greater the attitude change produced in the latter. But the extent to which the advocated change in attitude is seen as consistent with existing value systems is also important in relation to its acceptance. We have already (in Chapters 9 and 14) referred to Festinger's theory of cognitive dissonance, which postulates a drive towards a balance or consonance of attitudes and attitude components such that any state of dissonance creates tension until the balance is redressed by a change of attitude or attitude component to bring it into line with the rest of the system (e.g. a disbelief in the evidence of harmful effects of cigarettes in order to reduce dissonance with liking for and indulgence in smoking).

Findings in relation to the *form* of the message have, however, been inconsistent, and such effects on attitude change as the arousal of fear in the receiver, the use of an emotional appeal, and repetition of the message can all be seen as increasing the power of the source over the receiver. Another message variable, the refutation of counter-arguments, has been shown to strengthen the changed attitude of the receiver against subsequent attempts to change it once more.

Most of these results have been obtained from laboratory studies, but a related field of interest has been the study of the mass media as a communication channel and their effectiveness in changing attitudes. In general the results have shown surprisingly little evidence of much influence on attitudes or behaviour (McGuire, 1969). Instead it seems that the mass media are involved primarily in controlling the *flow of information*, while face-to-face communication within interpersonal relations is more important for the *flow of influence*, especially from certain persons – *opinion leaders* – who tend themselves to derive at least some of their 'expert' knowledge from the media.

Completing the model of the communication process in attitude change, we come to the *resistance of the receiver*. Although we have seen that an important factor for change is the discrepancy at the start between the attitudes of source and receiver, it does not hold unless the latter begins with an attitude that is fairly neutral. He is likely to be more resistant if he already holds an extreme attitude. The receiver has first, of course, to perceive the attitude of the source – to attend to and comprehend the message – before he may yield to it. McGuire (1969) pointed out that these two stages in the process of message receipt may be differentially affected by personality characteristics of the receiver. Thus to take an example, low self esteem tends to be associated with lesser understanding of the message but weaker resistance to change if it is comprehended. This is associated with the finding that self esteem is negatively related to attitude change if the message is fairly simple to understand but positively with a complex message.

Social perception

In Chapter 5 we saw the importance of perception as an active psychological process concerned with providing a meaningful interpretation of the external world. In an analogous way we can see the attempt to make sense of, understand and perhaps even predict the behaviour of other people as a process of social perception. From observation of another's behaviour the individual draws inferences about his habitual dispositions, motives, intentions, abilities and responsibilities – in fact his personality – and this process of judgement about another person is termed *interpersonal attribution*.

So called 'attribution theory' has its origin in the work of Fritz Heider (1958), who started from the assumption that people need to see their social world as predictable and therefore controllable. To do this they have to be able to determine the causes of others' behaviour, and in the first place to distinguish between behaviour that is *intended* by the other (*personal*) and that which is caused by outside factors (*impersonal*), and if the former whether it is due to an enduring disposition to behave in that way. This means that the behaviour has to be judged within its particular physical environment and social context and set against some idea of a norm for behaviour in those circumstances. Obviously the more a person's behaviour deviates from that norm, the more we are likely to make an inference about his particular personality, and there is experimental evidence to support this (Jones and Davis, 1965).

It is nevertheless not a simple matter to make such judgements from behavioural observations. McArthur (1972) has looked at differences of attribution arising out of different 'data patterns'; given contrasting sets of information concerning a person's behaviour in response to a particular stimulus, how do these influence the subject's judgement of that behaviour as due to something about the person (person attribution), something about the stimulus (stimulus attribution), something about the circumstances at the time (circumstance attribution), or some combination of two or more of these – especially of person and stimulus (person–stimulus attribution)? Without detailing the full results here, we may note that the last type of attribution, person–stimulus, was found to be common and that this resembles the interactionist viewpoint within personality theory to which reference was made in the last chapter.

Another resemblance to personality theory of psychology is the way in which the 'man in the street' also has ideas about the way personality traits cluster together – his own theory of personality structure – and this is known as *implicit personality theory*. As well as those that are held by each individual, there are other implicit personality theories that are shared by a group or even an entire culture. These contribute to the concept of *stereotypes* to which we have just referred in relation to attitudes, and previously in Chapter 15 when we considered the notion of a modal personality within a culture. The particular dimensions of personality used in individual implicit personality theories will, of course, differ between individuals; or put another way, they will have their own personal construct systems for construing others. Indeed, we saw in Chapter 16 that Kelly has developed a comprehensive theory of personality based on the individual's construct system and measured by the repertory grid test.

So far we have considered attribution as applied to others, but it is possible to see a similar process of *self-attribution* involved in inferring one's own feelings, attitudes and dispositions. The experiment of Schachter and Singer (1962), for example, to which we referred when discussing cognitive labelling of emotions in Chapter 10, demonstrated that the subjects attributed to themselves emotions of anger or amusement – increased by the arousal resulting from an injection of adrenalin (if they were uninformed of its effects) – on the basis of their reaction to the angry or euphoric stooge. Further studies of self-attribution (Jones and Nisbett, 1971) have shown that, although the individual (actor) makes inferences about his own attitudes and feelings from observation of his own behaviour, these may not agree with those of an outside observer. The individual tends to attribute his actions to situational requirements, whereas observers will be more likely to attribute them to his personal dispositions.

However, Storms (1973) demonstrated that these differences can be reversed by allowing the actor to observe his own behaviour within a two-person conversation on videotape recorded from the same position as the observer and, in the same way, allowing the latter to see the exchange from the actor's viewpoint. In this situation the actor becomes more 'internal' or personal in his self-attributions, while the observer attaches more importance to the situation – a finding which seems to suggest that anything different about self-attribution may simply reflect the fact that the individual literally cannot see himself as others can. (Remember Robert Burns: 'O wad some Pow'r the giftie gie us. To see oursels as others see us! It wad frae mony a blunder free us, And foolish notion.')

To return to the subject of interpersonal attribution, it is clear that behaviour within a social interaction is much influenced by the way each sees the other and expects him to behave. It is, of course, a two-way process: one's own behaviour is based in part on one's interpersonal attributions, but in turn that behaviour may exert a controlling effect on the other's behaviour even to the extent that he is compelled to behave in a way that confirms one's expectations – a self-fulfilling prophesy. This is particularly important in relation to attribution of ability; as we saw briefly in the last chapter, teachers' expectations of their pupils may have an effect on their scholastic achievement (Rosenthal and Jacobson, 1968). In a similar way self-attribution can influence performance;

Meichenbaum and Smart (1971) showed that students not only reported greater self-confidence and a more positive evaluation of their course after being given an encouraging assessment of their future performance on the basis of ability interest tests, but also showed significant improvement in the course. This may also be seen as supporting the notion that a person's self concept – the way he thinks about himself – is an internalization of what he sees as others' views of him.

Social influence

We have already referred to the role of social influence (i.e. of other persons) in determining attitudes or in changing them, but this is only one example of the effect of such influences on social behaviour. We all know, of course, that we tend to behave differently when we are 'in company', and the effect on individual behavior of the presence of and interaction with others has been an important area of psychological study. Experiments have mostly been carried out within the small group setting, and particularly in terms of conformity of the individual to the norms of the group; but before considering this aspect, we shall look briefly at the notion of social power and obedience.

Social power

This has also tended to be studied in small groups and in relation to their power structure, the term being used to describe the potential influence of an influencing agent (individual or position) over a particular person which can result in a change in their cognition, attitudes, behaviour or emotion. Collins and Raven (1969) have distinguished six types of power, of which the first five are dependent on the nature of the influencing agent while the sixth is independent:

(1) *Reward* power depends upon the recognition of the agent's power to reward; an obvious example of which would be the child's view of the mother.

(2) *Coercive* power – through punishment – exemplified perhaps by the father–child relationship.

(3) *Referent* power through the person wishing to identify with, and therefore to copy, the agent (e.g. fan and popstar).

(4) *Expert* power – where the agent is seen as possessing greater knowledge, such as in a pupil–teacher relationship.

(5) *Legitimate* power – exercised, for example, by the judiciary when a person accepts the authority of a judge in court.

(6) *Informational* power – independent of the social nature of the source, which may not even be remembered but where change is brought about by force of argument.

Obedience

The other side of the coin from social power or authority is, of course, the obedience of the individual to that authority. The notion of 'blind' obedience which avoids any other consideration is one which is generally decried, though it may be encouraged in certain organizations such as the armed forces, on the grounds that it is necessary in the interests of the group, and that the person giving the orders is capable of making a better decision than his subordinates.

Problems arise, of course, when the required behaviour contravenes what others, and perhaps the individual himself, perceive to be significant social norms or even moral injunctions; the defence that they were 'simply carrying out orders' as advanced, for example, by those involved in the extermination of Jews in Nazi Germany, may not be accepted by society at large or even by international law. There are obviously many situations which can pose a moral dilemma for the individual caught between conflicting loyalties (e.g. the civil servant to his 'conscience' and the Official Secrets Act), but most people would probably like to think that they would not themselves obey an instruction to, for example, deliberately inflict pain on another person against that person's wishes.

A series of experiments by Stanley Milgram (1974) appeared, however, to show that a disturbingly high proportion of normal people from all walks of life were prepared to do just this. The experiments also demonstrated very well the kind of deception to which we have already referred as employed in much social psychological research, though in this case not using students as the deceived! Milgram informed his subjects that they would be taking part in an experiment to investigate the effect of punishment by electric shock on the rate of learning of pairs of words. Although they thought they were being recruited as either 'teachers' or 'learners' and that the choice would be dependent on chance, they were in fact all employed as 'teachers' while the 'learners' were accomplices of the experimenter who had been trained to simulate the behaviour of someone in pain. The teacher's task was supposedly to administer successively higher voltage shocks each time the learner made mistakes in learning, though in reality of course (unknown to the experimental subjects) no current was actually administered.

The results, which understandably caused a considerable stir both within and without social psychological circles and which went against prior expectations, were that despite hearing the protestations and appeals from the 'learner', including shouting and screaming and finally silence, 'teachers' continued to apply increasingly strong 'shocks'. In fact 62 per cent of the subjects continued to obey the experimenter's admittedly increasingly forceful instructions (finally 'You have no choice but to go on') up to '450 volts' – described as *Danger! severe shock* on the machine. It is perhaps some small consolation that when the experiment was repeated with various modifications, the level of obedience was found to fall with increased contact between 'teacher' and 'learner' (e.g. in the same room, and the 'learner' visible as well as audible to the 'teacher') and with decreased contact with the experimenter (e.g. when orders were given only by telephone). It should also be noted that many subjects who carried out the procedure to the full were deeply upset by it and repeatedly questioned the experimenter and his authority. It has even been claimed that Milgram himself was submitting to the 'authority of science' by being prepared to inflict such psychological pain on his subjects (though they were, of course, reassured after the experiment by their 'learners' that they had not actually caused them any pain).

Milgram's explanation of his findings is that the subjects were influenced by the whole setting of the experiment – a prestigious university and an experimenter who introduced himself as a professor – in such a way that this could override their belief in the immorality of inflicting harm on others. This view received some support from results of further experiments when less obedience was found in the less impressive setting of an unknown commercial research organization as the supposed sponsor of the research, and similarly when an accomplice acted as co-teacher and defied the experimenter by refusing to give further shocks – the subjects then following suit, and subsequently explaining that until then they had not realized that it was possible to refuse the instructions!

Social facilitation

Some early studies of social influence showed that the mere presence of other people, either as an audience or as fellow performers, produced a quantitative improvement in performance on simple tasks – a process known as *social facilitation*. The fact that with more complex tasks this influence was reversed, the performance being disrupted by the same influences, was explained later by Zajonc (1966) in terms of the arousing effect of the presence of others. This was considered to improve performance of previously learned behaviour up to a certain level of arousal, resulting in improvement for simple tasks; with complex tasks, however, enhanced performance of mostly incorrect responses would interfere with overall performance. An alternative explanation more in line with the evidence on the relationship of performance to arousal which we have already considered (in Chapter 9) is that the complex task is itself arousing, and that this summates with that induced by the presence of others to produce an arousal level above the optimum for performance.

Social influence and conformity

When we turn to the effects of others on a person's behaviour in a qualitative sense, we find that studies have mostly examined such influences in terms of conformity with the group's *social norms*. We have already considered (in Chapter 3) the notion of norms within a society as an important sociological concept. Here we should note that the term may be used in two ways: on the one hand to describe observable regularities of behaviour shared by members of a group, and which may therefore be called a *behavioural* or *descriptive* norm; and on the other hand to denote shared expectations of how group members should behave, and therefore termed an *expectational* or *prescriptive* norm (cf. the statistical and ideal concepts of normality). Another distinction may be drawn between *external* norms operating on the wider scale of a society and its culture, and *internal* norms that are developed by the members of a group as a consequence of their social interaction. It is these internal norms that have been the concern of social psychologists studying social influences in small groups.

One of the most convenient behaviours to observe in relation to its modification by social influences is perceptual judgement, and we shall consider two classic examples of such research. The first by Sherif (1935) depended upon a phenomenon known as the 'autokinetic effect' – the optical illusion that a spot of light on a screen in a dark room is moving when in fact it is stationary. If an individual is asked to judge the amount of this apparent movement over a number of trials, he will eventually settle to a fairly constant estimate. When, however, a group of subjects were tested together and announced their judgements in turn, Sherif found that their initially divergent estimates began to converge despite the fact that there was no overt pressure to do so; each group thus arrived at an internal norm to which its members were apparently under some social influence to conform. Alexander *et al*. (1970) later showed that this effect was, however, dependent upon the ambiguous and indeed misleading nature of the task. If the subjects had the situation explained to them – that the light was stationary and the movement illusory – neither the stability of individual judgement nor the convergence on a norm was obtained.

That social influence processes can operate even in quite unambiguous situations was, however, demonstrated by the similarly classic studies of Asch (1951). These were concerned with the effectiveness of a group's social influence to distort an individual member's judgement. The task involved selecting which of three lines of unequal length matched a standard line, and when subjects attempted this on their own they achieved a high rate of success. When, however, the judgement had to be made in a group of which (as the reader will probably have guessed) the other members were confederates of the experimenter who on certain trials would unanimously choose the wrong line, the experimental subject would often (on almost one occasion in three) agree with the manifestly incorrect answer. Here again we have a tendency (though less so than in the Sherif situation) to conform to a group norm, but did this mean that those subjects who were so influenced actually disbelieved the evidence of their eyes? At debriefing after the experiment some at least said they were sure that they were right and the rest of the group wrong, but just 'went along with the majority', or agreed so as 'not to spoil your (the experimenter's) results'. The importance of not wanting to be seen as going against the majority was illustrated by further studies by Asch in which conformity was shown to be decreased if just one (confederate) in the group supported the subject's judgement, or if the subject was not physically within the group (by being placed in a separate cubicle).

Studies of real-life groups (e.g. Festinger *et al.*, 1968) have also shown that conformity is likely to be greater in groups that have a high degree of cohesiveness (as indicated by friendship patterns). On the other hand it must not be assumed that social influence consists simply of the submission of the minority to the pressure of the majority. Moscovici and Faucheux (1972) showed that a minority (1 or 2) of experimental confederates were able, by maintaining a particular position over many trials, to influence the judgements of some members of the larger number of genuine subjects. An analogy may be drawn here with the introduction and spread of new ideas by an individual or a minority which at first are rejected by most of society (e.g. those of Darwin and Freud).

To return to the social influences leading to conformity, it is possible to distinguish between those that depend upon the effect of information in an ambiguous situation (the Sherif type) and termed *informational* social influences, and those that are concerned with the wish of the individual to be accepted by the group (the Asch situation) and called *normative* social influences. Of course the two will often be present together, but their distinction can be useful at times and may also be related to the difference mentioned earlier between informational power (similar to informational influence) and the five source-dependent bases of social power (probably significant for normative social influence).

Interpersonal relationships

Here we are concerned with the ways in which individuals relate to each other on a one-to-one basis (dyadic relationships) or in small groups, and encompassing interpersonal attraction – what draws people together both initially and subsequently, competitiveness and cooperation in relationships, including helping behavior.

Attraction

Peoples' attitudes towards others are seldom completely neutral – more often there will be positive or negative feelings of attraction or of dislike respectively. The subject of interpersonal attraction was an early interest of social psychology using a technique called *sociometry*, which was here concerned with determining the popularity of individual members of a group. All children within a school class, for example, might be asked to choose three other members whom they most liked. It was then easy to see which children were most and which least often chosen, and in fact the whole pattern of choices could be represented graphically in the form of a *sociogram* such as in Fig 18.1. The choices and their direction are indicated by the arrows joining members, and it is clear that E is the most and J the least popular member of the class.

In general, sociometric studies have confirmed the expectation that choices are not distributed equally within a group – usually there are a few who receive disproportionately more and a few disproportionately fewer choices. This led to research into the characteristics of those who are most popular and, not surprisingly, they tend to be more healthy, good looking, intelligent, outgoing and less selfish and neurotic than those who are rejected. Clearly, however,

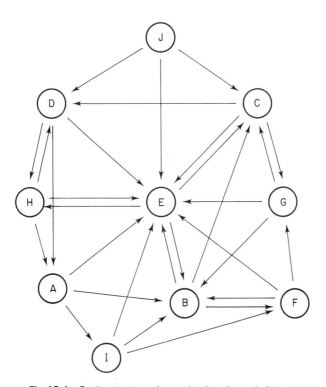

Fig.18.1 Sociogram – each member has three choices

such a combination of socially desirable qualities in one individual must be relatively rare, and as far as friendships are concerned, most have to be realistic choices of partners who fall somewhat short of the ideal. It then becomes a matter of some interest to consider what factors may lead to attraction between two individuals – perhaps a particular combination of qualities, for example. We have touched briefly on this subject (in Chapter 11) in relation to choice of marriage partners, but social psychologists have studied interpersonal attraction in a variety of situations. Although the evidence is not entirely consistent, it appears that *similarities* of attitudes and personality are important at least initially, though *complementarity of needs* may be more significant later. It is also perhaps not surprising in terms of learning theory that those who are liked tend to be those who provide rewards, or at least pleasant experiences, while punishment and unpleasant experiences evoke dislike! Finally, the physical proximity of a couple, or more correctly the opportunity for them to interact, increases the likelihood of attraction though it may also exaggerate a dislike between them.

The notion that the final pairings of individuals must represent a compromise, such that most end up with the best available to them in the circumstances, is consistent with a model of social behaviour known as *exchange theory* – so called because it sees behaviour as a 'commodity' which can be 'exchanged' in a 'social market'; thus the individual can choose to 'invest' behaviour with another person in the hope of a 'return' in terms of their behaviour. Such a choice between alternatives depends upon an evaluation of the other's behaviour and a weighing up of the estimated 'costs' and 'rewards' of the exchange – the aim being to maximize the outcome for the individual; if the rewards are high it may be worth the extra cost (e.g. to travel a long distance for someone who is particularly liked).

Implicit in exchange theory is, of course, the assumption of a relatively free choice in social relationships. It therefore has limitations in terms, for example, of marriage in a society where this is arranged. It may also be criticized on other grounds, and especially because of the difficulty of definition and measurement of rewards; for this reason it may be considered more useful as an explanatory model than as a predictive theory. We noted earlier (in Chapter 6) in relation to operant conditioning that positively reinforcing rewards can be identified with satisfaction of a primary biological drive, and here we can see that within a relationship, behaviour of a partner that satisfies a social drive can similarly be rewarding (e.g. warm, friendly behaviour meeting the need for affiliation).

Competition and cooperation

We now turn to an aspect of social interaction that has also been of great interest to social psychologists, not least because of its potential application to understanding and possibly preventing human conflict. The basic assumption tended to be that interpersonal competition and cooperation in an encounter can most easily be seen as a function of the 'payoff' to each individual – in other words whether it is in his best interest. It has further been claimed that real-life interactions can be simulated in the psychological laboratory in the form of two-person experimental games which enable theoretical predictions to be put to the test, though initial enthusiasm for such studies has been somewhat tempered by later criticism of their artificial and restricted conditions.

The best known of the experimental games was called the prisoner's dilemma since it was based on a hypothetical problem facing two men accused of a crime and each offered separately the most lenient sentence in return for a confession. If neither confesses they will be convicted on a minor charge carrying a moderate punishment; confession by only one man would, however, result in the most severe punishment for the other; if both confess they will each receive a harsh but less than the severest sentence. The choices for the prisoners can be shown in a matrix of possible punishments (Fig. 18.2). The problem for the prisoners is that they have no communication and therefore cannot plan a strategy, nor can they guess what the other will do; if they could both be sure that the other would not confess then this would be their best joint strategy. However, without that assurance the rational choice for each of them should be to confess, since this would not only avoid the worst punishment (from not confessing while the other does confess), it might also give them the best outcome (confessing while the other does not). The risk is that if they both confess they will each have a worse punishment than if neither of them had confessed. The essence of the problem is, of course, that the outcome for each prisoner depends not only on his own behaviour, but also on that of the other, and the dilemma lies in not knowing whether the latter can be trusted not to confess.

Translated to the laboratory the dilemma is represented by each of two players having to choose between two alternative responses for each of a number of trials to achieve the best payoff, as set out in a similar matrix (but with different scores instead of punishments). The responses equivalent to non-confession and confession are here cooperation and competition respectively. Now from the point of view of the individual it can be seen from the matrix that on any trial he will get a higher score for himself if he chooses to compete, whatever the other player chooses (i.e. one or five). However, if the

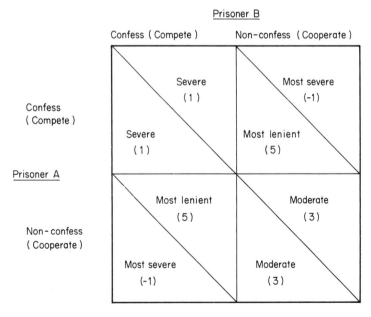

Fig. 18.2 The prisoner's dilemma matrix of punishment outcome and equivalent scores in the experimental game

other player takes the same view and they both choose competition, they will receive only the low score of one, whereas if they consistently choose cooperation they will both score three for each trial. Thus for the maximum joint score they should choose cooperation, but they each run the risk of exploitation if the other switches to competition. For a player to choose competition may therefore represent either an attempt at exploitation to get the highest payoff, or of self-defence to avoid the lowest.

What then is the usual outcome of such an experimental game? Sadly, perhaps, the level of cooperation is generally low, and there has therefore been much interest in attempting to define factors associated with decreased competitiveness. These have included (1) making the rewards more financially attractive, but this appears to increase motivation not only to cooperate but also to compete, with inconsistent effects on the level of cooperation; (2) varying the players' strategy by using a confederate of the experimenter who may, for example, either always cooperate or always compete – the former resulting in higher levels of cooperation from the experimental subject apart from a few individuals who will exploit the situation by consistently competing; and (3) introducing increasing degrees of visual and/or auditory contact between the players which results in increasing levels of cooperation (Wichman, 1970). In fact the opportunity to communicate seems to be the most effective way to increase cooperation, though it does not ensure it and this suggests the importance for the individual of being able to perceive or attribute the intentions of the other. The evidence here suggests that his own intentions affect the process of attribution in such a way that the competitive individual will tend to see only a competitive intention in the other, whereas the cooperative individual may anticipate either cooperation or competition.

Finally, the way in which the subject thinks his own behaviour will appear to others, including the experimenter and any spectators, may also influence behaviour as much as the actual payoffs produced. This effect may also be seen when the format of the payoff matrix is changed for each individual so that, for example, the choices are worded as 'give him three' and 'give me one', or when a 'decomposed' prisoner's dilemma game (Pruitt, 1967) is used with choices as 'your behaviour' and outcomes as 'your game' and 'other's game'. In all these circumstances the level of cooperation is raised, suggesting that the psychological significance of cooperation and competition may be as important as their resulting economic payoffs.

Helping behaviour

Cooperation as illustrated by the studies we have just considered consists of joint behaviour undertaken for mutual benefit. Sometimes, however, individuals provide assistance to another without evident benefit or even at some cost to themselves, though this is matched by other occasions when people display great reluctance to go to the aid of someone in obvious distress. Indeed, development of research in the field of so-called 'helping behaviour' was largely the consequence of an infamous event in New York City in 1964 when a woman, Kitty Genovese, was murdered during a half-hour-long assault witnessed by thirty-eight occupants of neighbouring apartments, none of whom went to her assistance or even called the police. On the face of it, it seems all the more incredible that so many observers were involved in this reluctance to help, yet the studies of simulated emergencies soon showed that bystanders are less likely to intervene in the presence of others than if they are on their own. Two possible explanations were advanced. Darley and Latané (1968) suggested that with a number of people present there is a *diffusion of responsibility*, so that each individual expects someone else to take action. An alternative theory is that of *conformity* with the reactions of other members of the group, which is then seen as setting the appropriate behaviour – no-one wants to go against the group and possibly make a fool of themselves. Evidence on the relative importance of these two factors is conflicting and probably both are relevant, but there are other influences on helping behaviour that have also been demonstrated; these include the inhibiting effect of ambiguity of the event in terms of both what is happening and what should be done, and of degrees of 'hurry' on the part of the bystander. On the other hand, in a situation when the bystander cannot escape by 'walking by on the other side', such as in an underground carriage (Piliavin *et al.*, 1969) help is much more likely to be given (and uninfluenced by numbers present) to a simulated 'collapse' of a fellow passenger. Apparent illness as a cause of the collapse attracts more help, however, than apparent drunkenness!

Responses to non-emergencies have also been studied. Requests from a passer-by for assistance (such as for a very small amount of money) are, not surprisingly, more likely to succeed if a reasonable explanation is given or a 'legitimate' request. Darley and Latané (1970) argue that whether help is offered in such situations depends upon *cost analysis*, i.e. how much it will 'cost' the potential helper. Clearly a high cost financially or in terms of danger to the individual will be inhibitory, but an additional influence is likely to be the *social norm* of justifiability for such behaviour. This view of helping behaviour sees it as guided by notions of fairness and justice – does the person deserve to be helped, or would others help him in these circumstances? Such a frame of reference will also permit behaviour motivated by *justified self-interest*, provided it is seen as fair. Such a gain at the expense of another may still, however, as Lerner and Lichtman (1968) have pointed out, be inhibited if the other makes an appeal for help putting himself in a dependent position, or if he refrains from taking advantage of an unexpected opportunity at the expense of his partner.

What may we conclude about what it is that determines whether a person will decide to help another or, within a relationship, to compete or cooperate with his partner? The evidence does not appear to support a simple cost–analysis approach as a sufficient explanation – instead it seems that psychosocial factors play a more significant part, and particularly conformity with normative ideas of fairness and justice. The extent to which *altruism* or the entirely disinterested desire to help others plays a part in helping behaviour is difficult to say. Some may take the view that there is always some reward for such behaviour, even if it is only internal as a feeling of being 'good', and as we saw earlier the sociobiological view is that it may be genetically determined.

Communication

This is a term that has become very fashionable with the enormous technological developments of means of mass communication – especially the so-called media (newspapers, radio, television). It implies an active process of imparting or transmitting information which is intentional on the part of the sender. We shall see that information can also sometimes be learned by an observer of another's so-called *non-verbal behaviour*, even when this was not so intended. It is obvious that social interaction is dependent on communication between people, and it is interesting in this respect that the word happens to be applied also to means of access between structured spaces, rooms, etc.

When we consider direct communication with another person, we obviously think first of language – that form of communication unique to the human race. In fact it is not as simple as that, and at least four systems of human communication can be distinguished (the second, third and fourth being collectively described as non-verbal in contrast to the first). Thus:

(1) *Verbal* – that aspect of speech that depends on the meaning of words and could equally be expressed in written form.

(2) *Intonation* – those patterns of pitch and stress in speech that contribute to its understanding by the listener (consider the differences of meaning of the sentence 'what have you done?' conveyed by placing the stress on each word in turn).

(3) *Paralinguistics* – those vocalizations outside the language, often culturally determined, such as hesitations, unfilled (silent) pauses and filled pauses (um, er, ah, etc.), coughs, giggles, loudness, tone of voice, etc.

(4) *Kinesics* – movements of the face or body that are clearly communicative.

In the course of conversation all four systems are likely to be operative, with their elements constantly changing as *dynamic features* of the interaction. At the same time there will be other, more constant, *standing features* such as the appearance, the position and distance apart of the participants which, though not strictly 'behaviour', can also be said to be part of the communication.

We shall consider shortly the roles and relative importance of verbal and non-verbal communication, but before doing so we may distinguish three purposes of communication within a social interaction.

The first of these, *interaction regulation*, is concerned with maintaining and controlling the conversation and includes various cues – particularly direction of gaze – which help to regulate the flow of talk between the participants. Thus an averted gaze by a speaker, if he stumbles or pauses, inhibits the other from interrupting, while a longer look directed at the listener signals that it will shortly be his turn to speak. Duncan (1972) has demonstrated turn-taking signals in all communication systems, linguistic, paralinguistic and kinesic. But since such feedback is mostly visual, it is not surprising that when deprived of it (e.g. talking on the telephone, or to a blind person for the first time) conversation becomes more difficult (Argyle *et al.*, 1968), though some compensatory feedback can be obtained through the auditory channel.

The second aspect, *interpersonal communication*, has to do with conveying from speaker to listener information concerning his social background and personal characteristics, his emotional state, and current attitudes (expressed particularly by non-verbal systems) towards both the other person and the topics of their conversation, and finally their relationship – its degree of intensity, for example, or their relative status.

The third characteristic of conversational communication is termed *representational* and is applied to the actual meaning of the dialogue. This may at first sight seem a simple matter; but closer examination shows it to be highly complex, involving such considerations as semantics (the meanings of particular words which may differ between individuals or cultures), and presuppositions concerning information already possessed by each speaker, or even shared assumptions (e.g. by husband and wife) which may make some conversations quite meaningless to an outsider. Speech of the latter type which depends upon shared meanings within particular groups has been described by Bernstein (1971, 1972 and 1975) as having a 'restricted code' and to have a strong social function, in contrast to an 'elaborated code' which is concerned more with the communication of ideas. We saw in Chapter 11 that Bernstein has demonstrated social class differences in the use of these codes. We should, however, also note that in new encounters appropriate suppositions concerning the other person which may be important for representational communication have to be acquired by interpersonal communication – indicating the close interrelationship of these two forms of communication.

Verbal and non-verbal communication

We have seen that communication depends upon both verbal and non-verbal systems, and we can also recognize that the former is highly structured and relatively unambiguous in comparison with the latter.

To be able to use these different forms of communication in any effective way depends upon the individual being able to select and control his own verbal and non-verbal behaviour (though the latter may be difficult to control and may communicate feelings, attitudes, etc., which a person might wish to conceal from an observer), and to be sensitive to that of the other as a form of feedback – it is, in fact, a social skill which has to be learned.

Why are there these two forms of communication? Various reasons have been advanced. The simplest would be that the quantity and complexity of human social interaction requires more than one channel of communication. Non-verbal communication, for example, by largely taking care of interaction regulation and interpersonal communication, leaves language freer for coping with ideas, things not actually present, etc.

Argyle (1969) has suggested that the ambiguity of non-verbal communication is a vital element in the process of regulating interpersonal attitudes and the nature of a relationship (e.g. its degree of intimacy). It allows each member in an encounter to accept or reject the ambiguous non-verbal signals of the other, using similar vague symbols himself, without embarrassment on either side. This is all the more important in societies where there is not a rigid social code to prescribe relationships between individuals – attitudes and relationships have to develop within each new encounter, and this could be difficult if restricted to entirely unambiguous verbal exchange.

Barriers to communication

Certain ways in which human communication may be impaired have been identified by Parry (1967), and though we cannot consider them in detail here, they will be listed because of their possible clinical significance:

(1) Limitation of receiver's capacity – too much or too complex information for the age or intelligence of the listener.

(2) Distraction – by (a) a competing stimulus (as in the 'cocktail party problem' discussed in Chapter 4), (b) environmental stress (heat, noise, etc.), (c) internal stress (anxiety, etc.), (d) ignorance of the communicating medium (e.g. of the language used).

(3) An unstated assumption – by the speaker (e.g. of the listener's understanding of a particular word).

(4) Incompatibility of schemas (schemas defined by Vernon as 'persistent, deep-rooted and well-organized classifications of ways of perceiving, thinking and behaving') – the same data interpreted in contradictory ways because of the incompatible schemas of the individuals concerned (e.g. socialist and tory, atheist and Christian).

(5) Influence of unconscious and partly conscious mechanisms – distortions caused by expectations, prejudices, dislikes, taboos, etc., on the part of the speaker or listener.

(6) Confused presentation – poor presentation of the message.

(7) Absence of communication channels – often quite obvious but sometimes not immediately recognizable (e.g. the apparent rather than real offer of a communication channel when a Commanding Officer says 'any complaints?').

Social roles

We have in previous chapters had occasion to refer to the concept of social role. In Chapter 16 we considered social role theory in relation to personality, and we concluded that there is an interactional relationship between 'role' and 'personality', with some longstanding roles contributing to some aspects of an individual's personality while the latter may colour performance of particular roles. In this sense a social role was seen as determining the way in which a person is expected habitually to act in appropriate circumstances by virtue of his holding a particular social position – such behaviour representing a so-called *role performance*. In Chapter 11 we noted that any individual will have *multiple roles* – some of which will be *ascribed* (i.e. over which he has no control) such as those associated with age and sex, while others are *achieved* (e.g. marital and occupation).

In this chapter we are more concerned with the social interactions occurring between holders of different roles. Most roles, in fact, exist in complementary or reciprocal pairs, where the nature of one role cannot be described without reference to the other. The male–female gender roles are a good example of such a reciprocal role relationship, and we considered this in the context of marriage and the family within our own society in Chapter 11 and within other societies in Chapter 15.

However, just as one person may have a number of roles, so in each of these he may relate to several different 'role others', either individuals or collections of individuals – a *role set* (e.g. doctor to patient, nurse, occupational therapist, hospital porter). This last example exemplifies the fact that occupational roles usually exist within a complex system or *organization* which has a specific aim or set of aims. Indeed, such organizations are commonly defined in terms of their interlocking and complementary social positions; these will include those associated with particular kinds of work and with different levels of responsibility or status. Ideally, of course, the relationships between the holders of these various positions within the organization will be such that it is optimally effective in achieving its stated aims. Not surprisingly, perhaps, this is not always the case. There may, for example, be various manifestations of *role conflict* such as were described in Chapter 16. In some positions the individual may not be at all content with his role; while the professional worker with high 'job satisfaction' is likely to be strongly attached to his occupational role, those in an uninteresting, tedious job may develop a detachment or even a resentment towards it, characterized by Goffman (1969) as *role distance*, and an 'alienated' or 'calculated' attitude to authority as described, for example, by Goldthorpe *et al.* in the study of Luton car workers referred to in Chapter 11.

When we are dealing with an organization whose aim is to produce an end-product or to provide a service (e.g. the health service) we have an additional and reciprocal role to consider – that of the consumer. Not only is there a relationship between the consumer and the organization as a whole, but there will of course, also be individual relationships with particular members of the organization.

In most organizations there is for their members a clear distinction between their occupation and the rest of their activities. There are, however, some – such as prisons, monastic institutions and mental hospitals – in which members live and work on the premises, so that they are in part formal organizations and in part residential communities. Goffman (1968) has described these organizations as *total institutions*, and he has claimed that they share an essentially similar social structure in which life is governed by a system of privileges so as to ensure conformity of behaviour and the general smooth running of the organization. In prisons and mental hospitals the inmates are placed in a quite separate category from the staff, and Goffman describes how they may become humiliated and 'depersonalized'. Various ways of coping with this situation may be displayed. Some may *withdraw* into a state of social apathy, while others, at least in the early stages, adopt an *intransigent* attitude with disobedience to the rules and appeals for release. Another adaptational role is that of the *colonizer*, who makes the best use of the available facilities and refuses to accept an inferior status. In contrast, the *convert* identifies with the institution and acts out the role of the perfect inmate. Before leaving this rather gloomy description of what could in some sense be seen as another example of 'man's inhumanity to man', it must be said that Goffman was writing of the situation in the USA a quarter of a century ago, and as we shall see there have been – certainly as far as mental hospitals are concerned – considerable changes since then.

Finally, in addition to the traditional or formal roles within an organization or within society itself, and which may be occupied by a number of persons, there are others which are personal to particular individuals. These *informal* roles are created out of social interaction and are most evident within small groups. Thus, for example, a pupil may acquire, within a school class, the role of clown or scapegoat or dunce, and as we have seen in relation to social perception, this may affect both the individual's behaviour and those in a reciprocal role such as the teacher – an example of the self-fulfilling characteristic of interpersonal attributions.

Other examples of informal roles are those associated with *leadership*. These have been the subject of social psychological study both in experimental, initially leaderless, discussion groups and in real-life functioning groups. In the former, Bales and Slater (1955), using a system for recording the amount of participation of each member – and categorizing such remarks into emotionally positive and negative responses and problem-solving responses in the form of questions and of answers – came to some conclusions concerning the development of leadership within the group. Taken together with group members' responses to questions after each session, the evidence suggested that leadership becomes organized around two roles. In the early sessions of the group an individual was identified who scored high on problem-solving answers and was seen as a popular leader. In later sessions a second person became preferred by the group – one who scored high on positive responses. In terms of stability it seemed that the first leader – a *task specialist* – was gradually felt to be dominating the group at the expense of others' contributions, causing tension and resentment. The second less active leader then assumed the responsibility of keeping the group together with greater skills in the interpersonal area as a *social-emotional specialist*.

Such dual leadership may have been in part a reflection of the artificial nature of the laboratory group. In real-life groups there is frequently a leader with legitimate power who may be able to combine both task and social-emotional leadership (Verba, 1961). At any rate it seems likely that these two components of leadership, whether combined in one person or represented by two, are important in the smooth running of the group. A comparison may perhaps be drawn with the family and the traditional roles of father and mother.

Further reading

Aronson, E. (1984) *The Social Animal*, 4th ed. San Francisco: Freeman.

Benn, D. (1970) *Beliefs, Attitudes and Human Affairs*. Belmont, California: Brooks-Cole.

Bersheid, E. and Walster, E. (1978) *Interpersonal Attraction*, 2nd ed. Reading, Mass: Addison-Wesley.

Cook, M. (1971) *Interpersonal Perception*. Harmondsworth: Penguin.

Danziger, K. (1976) *Interpersonal Communication*. New York: Academic Press.

Gahagan, J. (1975) *Interpersonal and Group Behaviour* (Essential Psychology Series). London: Methuen.

Orford, J. (1976) *The Social Psychology of Mental Disorder*. Harmondsworth: Penguin.

Tajfel, H. and Fraser, C. (eds.) (1978) *Introductory Social Psychology*. Harmondsworth: Penguin.

Wheldall, K. (1975) *Social Behaviour, Key Problems and Social Relevance* (Essential Psychology Series). London: Methuen.

19
Social interaction
II – Clinical aspects

There are many aspects of social interaction that are of relevance to the practice of medicine and of the health professions generally. We shall meet a number of them in the final chapter, but here we shall concentrate on social relationships in two situations. First we shall take a look at problems that can arise in social relationships within those major social institutions, marriage and the family, and which can cause such distress and perhaps even illness as to lead to help being sought from the health service. Second, we shall examine some relationships existing in the clinical context – especially those between patients and health professionals, between the latter themselves and more generally within the hospital as an organization.

Marriage and its breakdown

In Chapter 11 we considered marriage as a social institution which could be seen as fulfilling certain traditional social functions. At the same time it was noted that in recent times there has developed a much greater emphasis on marriage as a relationship concerned with satisfaction of the personal needs of its two members. We may at the same time observe that there has been another and perhaps related social trend towards the establishment of stable heterosexual relationships outside the legal/religious contract of marriage, and for all practical purposes the term 'marriage' will be taken here to include such dyadic relationships. Other stable two-person sexual relationships may, of course, exist between individuals of the same sex, but as these have been less studied from a social psychological standpoint they will not be considered further. If an important function of marriage is a mutual satisfaction of individual needs, then to the extent that this does not occur, there may be a state of *disharmony* which may ultimately lead to the complete breakdown of the relationship, with separation and/or divorce.

Before we examine some of the interpersonal factors that may contribute to such difficulties and possible breakdown, there is one obvious feature of the marital relationship which requires special consideration – namely the degree to which it succeeds or fails in fulfilling the sexual needs of the partners.

Sexual behaviour and problems

Our knowledge of human sexual behaviour, including its variations and disorders, has been increased greatly in the latter half of this century, stemming largely from the pioneering epidemiological surveys of Kinsey *et al.* (1948, 1953) and physiological studies of Masters and Johnson (1966, 1970). Sexual pleasure can be obtained from various activities, but for most couples the goal is orgasm reached through sexual intercourse.

Four stages of sexual response can be identified:

(1) *Excitement*, which in the man involves erection of the penis and in the woman lubrication of the vagina and engorgement of the clitoris, results from a wide range of stimuli. These may include thoughts and fantasies of a sexual nature, and visual, olfactory or tactile stimulation (in the latter case of particularly sensitive areas of the skin, the so-called erogenous zones).

(2) *Plateau*, a briefer period of more intense arousal which occurs with continuing stimulation and is accompanied by further swelling of the penis, vasodilatation in the outer third of the vagina and finally retraction of the clitoris.

(3) *Orgasm*, the height of sexual pleasure during which ejaculation of semen occurs in the man (lasting a few seconds), and spasmodic vaginal contractions in the woman (of more variable duration). In the man orgasm is followed by a refractory period, but women can, with effective stimulation, be capable of multiple orgasms; they are however, more likely to fail on occasions to achieve orgasm.

(4) *Resolution*, a gradual return to the sexually non-aroused state.

It is important to recognize that, while this sequence of events depends upon particular physiological mechanisms, it is also much influenced by emotional factors, as we shall see when we consider the ways in which sexual performance can be impaired in the various types of sexual dysfunction.

We shall now note, though without more detailed consideration, the occurrence of a wide range of sexual behaviours most of which, if regularly preferred to heterosexual intercourse, are generally regarded as abnormal or *sexual deviations*. These include:

(1) Variations of the sexual 'object' or stimulus (e.g. *fetishism* – an inanimate object or non-sexual part of the body; *transvestism* – sexual arousal associated with dressing in the clothes of the opposite sex).

(2) Variations of the sexual act (e.g. *exhibitionism* – exposure of the genitals to unprepared strangers to achieve sexual excitement; *voyeurism* – observing the sexual activity of others as a preferred means of sexual arousal; *sadomasochism* – sexual arousal achieved by either inflicting pain on another person or experiencing pain or suffering.

(3) Disorders of the gender role, particularly *transsexualism* – the wish to live as a person of the opposite sex. Social attitudes to *homosexuality* have changed; while hitherto classified as a form of sexual deviation (i.e. with an abnormal 'object'), there is now a widely held view that it should be regarded not as abnormal but as an alternative form of sexual behaviour.

It will be apparent that any of these forms of sexual behaviour within a marriage is likely to cause difficulties for the relationship. However, much more frequent are problems related to the sexual act itself and manifested as various types of *sexual dysfunction*; indeed so common are they that special clinics have been set up to deal with them. It is not the intention here to detail all the types of problem or their treatments, but to stress the important reciprocal relationship existing between the sexual dysfunction and the marital relationship.

Briefly, sexual problems can be classified according to the stages of the sexual response in which they occur. Thus there may, first, be an impairment of sexual desire; second, an impairment of sexual arousal, more obviously manifested in the male as a failure of erection or *impotence*; or third, a disturbance of orgasm. In the male the last problem may occur as *premature ejaculation* (if ejaculation occurs before penetration it is obviously premature, but even during coitus it may be too rapid for the partner's satisfaction). This is a problem which is very common among young and inexperienced males. *Retarded ejaculation* (failure to ejaculate) also may occur but is relatively uncommon. In the female the problem is described as *orgasmic dysfunction* (failure to achieve orgasm). The extent to which this is regarded as a disorder depends in part on social attitudes, since for many women failure to achieve orgasm regularly during intercourse is not uncommon, and at one time complete absence of orgasm in women was not considered abnormal.

An important clinical distinction is made between those cases in which a dysfunction occurs after a period of adequate sexual performance, when it is described as *secondary*, and those cases of *primary* dysfunction in which it has always been present.

In considering the causes of such sexual difficulties it is necessary to take account of possible physical factors, which may include medical and surgical conditions or their treatment. These may sometimes result in a direct interference with the physiological mechanisms involved, or it may be that the psychological response to illness leads indirectly to an impairment of sexual function. More often, however, there is no question of organic disease and the problem is essentially a psychological one.

Early environmental influences may be important (family attitudes, unpleasant sexual experiences, etc.), especially in the case of a primary dysfunction; but events occurring just prior to the onset of a secondary sexual problem may be significant (childbirth, infidelity, etc.). Once the difficulties are present, however, it is the maintaining factors that may be crucial and which are mostly dealt with in sex therapy. Of these anxiety is the most common – especially anxiety over sexual performance. Since this emotion is itself sexually inhibiting it is easy to see how a 'vicious circle' of anxiety and poor performance can be set up.

Emotional difficulties and poor communication in the relationship are also important, and the presence of sexual problems in both partners is frequent. Again it is obvious that sexual and interpersonal difficulties can be mutually reinforcing – and it is to the interpersonal relationship aspects of marriage as well as of the family that we shall now turn our attention.

Interpersonal aspects of marriage

We have discussed the nature of the attraction which is obviously important in relation to the coming together of men and women in marriage, and we have noted that complementarity of needs may be significant for maintaining the union. The whole question of marital stability or happiness and factors of relevance to this are of social psychological interest.

An early study by Terman (1938) of American marriages emphasized the importance of individual personality and described the typical features of happily and unhappily married members of each sex. This was consistent with a notion of *marital aptitude*. Later, Burgess and Wallin (1953), on the basis of several 'prediction' studies (i.e. correlating measures of personality before marriage with later marital success), listed a number of characteristics distinguishing happily from unhappily married individuals. These were: emotionally stable, self-confident, considerate as opposed to critical of others, yielding as opposed to dominating, companionable as opposed to isolated, emotionally dependent as opposed to emotionally self-sufficient.

Conversely, a psychiatric study by Slater and Woodside (1951) compared the marriages of neurotic soldiers with those of a control group. The study showed that certain personality features contributed to marital unhappiness. What they termed 'marriage-wrecking traits' included moodiness and irritability together with depression and hysterical characteristics. However, it has to be recognized that a difficulty of research in this area is that there is clearly a possibility of marital happiness or unhappiness affecting the perception of the spouses and therefore of assessment of their personalities, a reversal of the postulated cause and effect relationship.

Similar reservations apply to studies of interpersonal perception in marriages. Here, not surprisingly perhaps, satisfaction in marriage is found to be associated with favourable perceptions – both of self and of spouse (e.g. 'makes a good impression', 'self-respecting', in contrast to 'dominating', 'selfish', etc.). Again it is possible that such evaluative perception might be biased within an unhappy relationship. Other distortions of social perceptions which may contribute to a disturbed marital relationship are those associated, according to psychoanalytic theory, with the defence mechanism of projection. As we saw in Chapter 14, this involves the attribution to another person (in this case the spouse) of socially objectionable and denied aspects of the self.

Another aspect of the husband – wife relationship which may be important to the stability of the marriage concerns the extent of cooperation and competition. We have already looked at the idea of exchange theory in interpersonal relationships, and specifically the 'prisoners' dilemma' as a 'game' analogy for cooperation – competition generally. This notion of 'cost', 'payoff', 'risks', etc., and of 'disordered interpersonal contracts' in which couples attempt to achieve certain self-rewards at the expense of costs to the relationship from the deviant behaviour involved, is a feature of the well-known book by Eric Berne, *Games People Play* (1969).

These and other models of interpersonal disturbance form the theoretical basis for attempts to help couples with marital problems. The commonest arrangement, the conjoint approach, is for both partners to be seen together, sometimes by one and sometimes by two therapists. To take one example, an eclectic model based in part on psychoanalytic theory has been described by Dominion (1979). This takes account of five types of relationship between a couple (physical, emotional, social, intellectual and spiritual), and three stages in the marital life cycle. The first phase covers the first five years; the middle phase covers the time during which the children are growing up until the youngest leaves home and the couple are in their forties or early fifties; and the third phase starts when they once more become a couple on their own, and ends in the death of one of the partners.

The emphasis of the therapy is on improving patterns of communication, resolving issues of power, and providing a model for learning new ways of behaving (e.g. expressing more tenderness and affection). Another popular technique in marital therapy is based on behavioural principles and concentrates on areas of interpersonal conflict and the needs of each partner. A 'contract' is established in which husband and wife agree to begin to meet some of each other's needs - a process which once started can be self-reinforcing from the mutual rewards received by each of the partners.

The family

When we turn to social relationships within the family it is obvious that we are dealing with an even more complex situation. Not only are there a number of dyadic relationships in addition to the marital one, but there is also the relationship of each individual to the family as a whole. Clearly much of the work on the structure of small groups in terms of liking, communication, power, leadership, etc., and of the processes of social influence within them will be of relevance to the family.

However, when it comes to methods of trying to help families with interpersonal problems - often reflected in emotional distress or even overt illness in one or more members - it has been found useful to look to *general systems theory* (von Bertalanffy, 1968) for a conceptual basis for therapy. We considered something of the concept of systems in Chapter 1, when man and society were placed within a hierarchy of systems with emphasis on their interdependence. Each system is itself part of and influenced by a larger system. Thus the family is a system composed of individuals but is also a subsystem of a community or society. Each system is separate and defined by boundaries but is set within a hierarchy such that the smaller systems are to some degree subject to the greater. At each level there has to be a balance between freedom and authority - the individual member, though autonomous, is subject to the rules of his family and the family to those of its society. These ideas have led to emphasis in family therapy on achieving a balance between, on the one hand, open communication and sharing, and on the other hand separateness or autonomy for the individual members. An important issue is therefore that of authority and control in the family, so that the therapist often has to question its existing structure and hierarchy and put the parents firmly in charge of the children - usually with the emphasis on the father. This is not to deny a reasonable degree of freedom for the children, but it faces them with the reality of their membership of a family of interdependent individuals and of a wider community outside.

Professional relationships

Here we are looking at relationships between individuals within the context of the health service, though we shall place emphasis on a topic that has been the subject of much discussion in recent years - the doctor-patient relationship.

The doctor-patient relationship

We have referred to the reciprocal roles of doctor and patient, and in Chapter 16 some possible conflicts associated with them were mentioned.

Tuckett (1976) lists eight role conflicts which a doctor may face in relation to his patient and his practice. The specifically medical conflicts concerned: (1) the interests of the individual patient versus patients as a group; (2) the allocation of resources between patients; (3) the interests of the individual patient at any point in time versus the same patient's interests in the future; (4) the welfare of the patient against concern for the patient's family; (5) the doctor's inability to help the patient and his self-image as a curer, and (6) the doctor's obligation to the patient against his duties as an agent of the state or some other agency. The last two role conflicts mentioned by Tuckett are not confined to medicine and could apply equally to other occupations: namely (7) the potential conflict of interests between the responsibilities of a particular appointment (including, in medicine, towards patients) and career needs (e.g. research, postgraduate study), and (8) the even more frequent problem of conflict between any occupation and other social roles (e.g. of husband, father), but highlighted in those providing a 24-hour service.

The patient, too, may have conflicts over his 'sick-role'. While this involves certain 'rights', such as exemption from some social responsibilities, and recognition of his need for care for an illness for which he himself is not held responsible, it also carries with it the 'duty' to want to get well and therefore to seek and cooperate with medical treatment. The dependency that this may involve and the limitations that it may impose can conflict with the patient's personality and life style.

If we turn now to the nature of the interaction between doctor and patient, we can see that as a professional relationship it is in large part determined by the respective roles that society recognizes, though clearly their interpretation will vary from patient to patient and from doctor to doctor. There are also likely to be attitudes and perceptions of both participants which will affect the relationship, and especially the patient's judgement of the consultation. Thus the doctor is likely to see his main functions as twofold: first, to diagnose and treat the patient's disease, and second, to provide emotional support. However, it may be the latter which is of greater significance in terms of the patient's evaluation of the interaction – namely the degree to which the doctor shows himself to be 'a kindly, thoughtful, warm person, deeply interested in and committed to, the welfare of the individual' (Mechanic, 1968).

Studies of patients' satisfaction with their consultation with the doctor and whether they express a wish to see him again have shown that this is more likely to be positive when the doctor usually early in the consultation, discovers and deals with the patient's concerns and expectations, when he communicates warmth, interest and concern about the patient, and when usually in the latter part of the consultation, he gives a lot of information and manages to explain things to the patient in such a way that they are understood (Pendelton, 1983). The same author has also reviewed studies relating aspects of the consultation to immediate outcome, such as the degree of compliance with advice and treatment (a matter to which we shall return in more detail later). Again it appears that patients cope best if they feel that they are understood and well informed by their doctor. The final negative judgement by patients is, of course, when they decide to change their doctor. Mechanic (1964) found that such patients more frequently complained of lack of interest, care and motivation on the part of their doctor, than questioned his clinical ability.

Attempts have been made to classify different types of doctor–patient interaction, and perhaps the best known is the analysis by Szasz and Hollander (1956). This distinguishes three possible relationships each appropriate to a particular clinical situation. The first, called *activity–passivity*, applies to circumstances such as medical emergencies, surgery or ECT, in which the patient's role is a largely passive one. The second, described as *guidance-*

cooperation and typifying the traditional view of the doctor–patient relationship, applies to the majority of short-lasting medical conditions where the patient recognizes that he is ill and in need of medical help with which he is expected to cooperate. The third model of relationship is termed *mutual participation*, and this is becoming increasingly important as it is most appropriate for the management of chronic diseases such as diabetes in which the patient has to play a major role.

It is apparent that these three types of relationship represent different degrees of activity on the part of the patient while remaining a model of doctor–patient interaction acceptable to doctors themselves. Freidson (1972) has criticized this scheme on logical grounds since it ignores a possible extension to relationships where the doctor actually assumes a passive role. He therefore proposes two more models of doctor–patient relationship: another one of *guidance-cooperation* but in which it is the patient who guides and the doctor who cooperates, and another of *activity–passivity* but this time with the doctor in the passive role. There is certainly evidence that patients not infrequently make up their minds about their problem and present the doctor with their own solution (e.g. medical support for rehousing, referral to a specialist). Complete passivity on the part of a doctor is probably rare, though such a tendency might perhaps exist in a situation of financial dependence on the patient, or where the latter is particularly prestigious.

What these alternatives suggest, however, is that there is frequently a bargaining or negotiation between doctor and patient over their respective roles, rather than an easy acceptance of the doctor-orientated model. This could be seen in terms of exchange theory as a 'game' in which doctor and patient are each making 'moves' aimed ultimately at maximizing benefits at least 'cost', though it is perhaps unlikely that either will recognize that this is what they are doing! However, there is also evidence (Byrne and Long, 1976) of doctors maintaining particular styles of consultation with a variety of patients – styles that is, of diagnosis and prescription which were considered to be distributed along a continuum from patient-centred to doctor-centred. Perhaps not surprisingly, doctors who were rated as patient-centred displayed fewer 'negative' behaviours towards their patients.

It is, of course, important to recognize some special features of the professional relationship between doctors and patients. One of these is the very privileged nature of the access of the doctor to the patient – not only to his body for the purpose of physical examination and special investigation, but often to intimate and confidential information about his life. The justification for this invasion of privacy is the expectation of the patient that the doctor will do everything possible to help him to recover from his illness. At the same time there is for the doctor always the problem of uncertainty both of diagnosis and of treatment, and hence such questions as how far to pursue investigations, some of which may be unpleasant or even dangerous, and how active to be with treatments which likewise may have side-effects if not actually harmful consequences.

In order to be able to cope with these and other problems which can be emotionally disturbing for the doctor, he maintains according to Parsons (1951) certain professional attitudes towards the patient, though the extent to which these are always reflected in practice may be questioned. The first, described as *affective neutrality*, implies an emotional distancing from the patient – a degree of detachment so that emotions will not cloud objective clinical judgement. It is chiefly for this reason that doctors avoid clinical responsibility for anything but minor illness in members of their own family. There is, of course, a danger of being too impersonal, and ideally the doctor should steer a path between emotional over-involvement and unfeeling coldness. *Universalism* is used by Parsons to mean that all patients should be treated equally and according to widely recognized scientific standards, while *functional specificity* implies a limitation of the doctor's concern to those aspects of the patient that are of strictly medical relevance – i.e. to the particular disease itself. While this latter attitude is consistent with the trend to specialization in medicine, it does conflict with the notion of 'whole person' medicine, at least as practised by the general practitioner or physician.

Doctor–patient communication

This is clearly a most important aspect of the interaction between doctor and patient, reflected in the amount of research attention that it has received. Fig. 19.1 illustrates some of the variables that have been examined.

The first thing to note is that communication is a two-way process. The patient has to provide information about his symptoms and their development because this, together with the findings of physical examination, is required by the doctor in order to assess the clinical condition. The patient then has to be advised of the doctor's conclusions and their consequences. In both cases it is expected that the recipient of the communication will accept and act upon it – i.e. will exhibit compliance. We have already, in discussing communication generally, noted a number of possible barriers to the process, but we can now briefly consider some of the problems in the clinical setting.

Failure of the doctor to elicit significant information from the patient may be due to several factors. On the patient's part there may be a diffidence or embarrassment in speaking about certain complaints, while many authors have drawn attention to errors of interviewing technique (e.g. Fletcher, 1980). Suggestions for improvement by training in interviewing skills for medical students

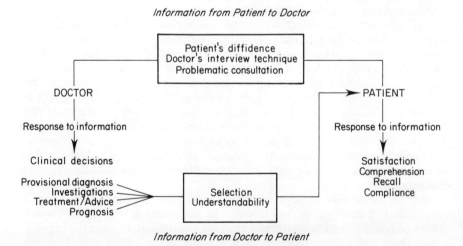

Fig. 19.1   A model of doctor–patient communication

(Maguire and Rutter, 1976) have received support from the increase of relevant information obtained by students who underwent such a programme of training (Rutter and Maguire, 1976). Difficulties in eliciting information may also be related to consultations perceived by the doctor as problematic in terms of the type of patient (e.g. young, lower social class, medically trained) or clinical situation (e.g. drug abuse, child abuse).

A clinical evaluation of a patient's problem having been made, it should then be the responsibility of the doctor to give the patient the relevant information. This is not as simple as it may appear. In the first place it is likely that the doctor will select which information he is going to give the patient, and the criteria for such selections may be varied and somewhat arbitrary. Looked at from the patient's point of view, it might be argued that the main determinant should be what he wants to know, and in many cases this will be everything. However, the doctor may not always be willing to accede to this on the grounds that some information may cause excessive anxiety, failure to comply with treatment, or some other undesirable outcome. Thus information may be withheld concerning such matters as a diagnosis of cancer, and risks of investigation and/or treatment.

However, empirical studies have generally failed to substantiate these fears of adverse reactions in patients; and against such restriction of information is the argument that the patient should be given the opportunity to make a rational decision as to whether or not to accept medical advice, and especially a particular treatment, by being given sufficient information to weigh up the probability of improvement against side-effects or adverse reactions.

Another possible factor that may affect the quality of information given to patients is the extent to which doctors themselves may fail to comply with what is considered to be the best available practice in relation, for example, to medication and advice to patients about this (Ley, 1981).

A third aspect of doctor's communication to the patient concerns understandability. Of course, whether a particular patient will understand what he is being told will in part depend on his level of intelligence or education, but doctors, too, may vary in their ability to present the information in an easily comprehensible form. This is difficult to assess, but attempts have been made to apply so-called readability measures to written information as provided in health leaflets (e.g. accompanying prescribed drugs), and the results have suggested likely understanding by a rather limited proportion of the general population.

What, then, of the recipient of the information from the doctor? How adequate is the communication for the patient and what effect does it have? There have been a number of studies of patient satisfaction with the communication they had received, and these have been summarized by Ley (1982a,b). A disappointingly large percentage of patients both in the UK and the USA expressed dissatisfaction with communications. It may be argued, of course, that such a subjective judgement by patients has limited relevance to their treatment and progress; but satisfaction with communication has been found to correlate with compliance with advice, as well as with understanding of what has been said and with retention of medical information.

If we look further at the question of patients' understanding of the information that has been given to them, here, too, we find that a high proportion report a failure to do so, and this subjective judgement is if anything exceeded by more direct measurements of patients' understanding of medical instructions (Ley, 1982a).

The extent to which patients are able to recall medical information has also been the subject of studies in a variety of settings, but methodological variations make for difficulties in interpretation of differences (Ley, 1982b). The amount of information that is forgotten is again disturbingly high, but as has also been found with patients' understanding, the position is much better with more prolonged disease and therefore longer medical contact.

Patients' compliance with medical advice has also been much investigated, particularly in terms of medication. A progressively higher rate of non-compliance is found when this is based on three increasingly reliable measures: self-report, pill count and urine and blood tests (Ley, 1979). In general the extent of non-compliance with medication is sufficient to be a cause for serious concern, even judged in purely financial terms within the health service.

A cognitive model (Fig. 19.2) relating communication and compliance via the intermediate variables of understanding, satisfaction and memory has been proposed by Ley (1982b). Attempts to improve compliance by increasing understanding have, however, produced conflicting results and have led to the suggestion that compliance is dependent on two factors – whether it is intentional or unintentional, and whether it is based on adequate or inadequate information. It is the inadequately informed, intentional non-complier who should benefit from the provision of more information. The adequately informed, unintentional non-complier is the patient who forgets to take his medicine and who may be helped by aids directed to reminding him of this. The inadequately informed, unintentional non-complier also requires correct information about medicine taking, since he believes he is complying with advice – it is the understanding of the latter which is at fault. Finally the adequately informed, intentional non-complier will not be influenced by information – a behavioural change here will require more persuasive techniques.

It would seem that in some patients at least, a greater degree of compliance could be achieved by improving communication, which would in turn increase the comprehensibility and memorability as well as satisfaction. Not surprisingly, then, there have been a number of attempts to bring about an improvement in communication. Most information is given to patients orally, and various memory-enhancing techniques such as simplification, making advice more specific, and repetition by doctor or patient, has been tried with some success in order to reduce the amount that is forgotten by the patient. The addition of written information, especially in the case of medication, has also proved successful, as have more unusual techniques such as providing the

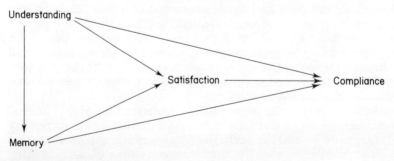

Fig. 19.2   The cognitive hypothesis (after Ley 1982b)

patient with a tape recording of the interview, or educational audio-visual materials at the surgery. Rather more controversial approaches to increasing patients' understanding have involved a more active participation by the patients, including full access to their case records and even a proposal for co-authorship with the doctor of the notes.

In addition to the effect of improved communication on patient compliance there is evidence that the provision of adequate information is helpful in post-operative recovery. We have already seen in Chapter 5 that Egbert *et al.* (1964) showed that postoperative pain could be reduced by encouragement and instruction of patients; but studies have also shown that not only may post-operative distress be reduced, but recovery can be speeded with a shortening of hospital stay. There is evidence, however, that using cognitive coping methods directed at patients' worries may be more effective than simply providing more information about procedures and likely sensations to be experienced by the patient (Ridgeway and Mathews, 1982).

Relationships between staff

The National Health Service is a complex organization whose ultimate aim is the promotion of health and prevention and treatment of disease. To achieve these objectives it depends upon the services of staff within a wide range of occupations, some directly and some only distantly concerned with the actual care of the individual patient. Members of each occupation not only fulfil specialized roles, but also share a particular subculture consisting of a common language (in the sense not only of certain technical words, but often of differences of meaning of everyday words) and a set of beliefs about themselves and their work. They do, however, have to interact with persons from other occupations who may have a different language and a different set of beliefs, and therein lies a potential for misunderstanding and conflict. The doctor and the nurse, the medical social worker and the hospital administrator – although they are in their various ways working together to provide a service to the patient – may nevertheless find it difficult at times to see eye to eye over particular policies and decisions.

This may then lead to a questioning of individual authority, Certainly in relation to clinical decisions the doctor has traditionally been seen as the legitimate holder of such authority, but this has increasingly come under challenge from others directly involved in patient care such as nurses, medical social workers, clinical psychologists and occupational therapists. This has accompanied a drive towards professionalization within these occupations, and with it a claim to a degree of autonomy in decision-making.

The doctor–nurse relationship

The profession most closely involved with medicine itself is nursing, and it is the relationship between doctors and nurses that has received most attention. Christman (1965) listed seven factors which in the USA at the time could be seen to distinguish between members of the two professions and which were liable to increase the social distance between them. These differences were in (1) education, (2) career pattern, (3) language, (4) social class, (5) sex, (6) authority, and (7) orientation to patients. The last of these factors may be related to the extent of interaction with patients. Hospital nurses are in close and pro-longed day-to-day contact with inpatients and they may thus acquire much information about them which extends beyond their immediate medical condition. The doctor, on the other hand, spends much less time with the patient and sees as his primary concern the latter's immediate medical needs and comfort. From these somewhat different perspectives the nurse and doctor may each believe that they are in the best position to decide what is most appropriate to the patient's needs. They may also have differing perceptions of their relative authority to take such decisions – nurses generally believing themselves to have a higher level of discretion in this matter than doctor's would recognize. This discrepancy is highlighted in the relationship between the nurse and the newly qualified doctor who, despite the possession of a medical degree has, by comparison, usually had little practical experience, yet is anxious to assume clinical authority.

It is hardly surprising, especially in view of the frequency of their interaction on the ward, that difficulties and frustrations may be experienced and complaints made on both sides. However, there may be some comfort to be derived from the finding of a comparative study by Glaser (1963) that, at least at that time, there was less evidence of conflicts between doctors and nurses in European than in US hospitals – though this might be less reassuring to the nurses since it was considered to be due to their greater subservience!

The multidisciplinary team

We have already seen that there are several professions directly involved in patient care, and there has therefore developed the concept of the multi-professional or multidisciplinary team – particularly in relation to the so-called 'long-stay' specialities such as geriatrics and psychiatry where patients may need prolonged care. Whereas at one time the social worker was seen as the person who dealt with the patient's family, obtained from them a history of his life and illness, and looked into the question of his future accommodation and employment; the clinical psychologist's role was to carry out various tests (of intelligence, personality, etc.) at the request, if not the order, of the psychiatrist; and the occupational therapist was concerned simply with providing diversional activity for the patient – all these professions are now much more often involved in direct care and treatment such as counselling, behaviour therapy, cognitive therapy, art therapy, or drama therapy. At the same time there has been a trend towards a blurring of the distinctions between the disciplines and an emphasis on what is common to them – reflected in some clinical settings, particularly those in the community such as day hospitals and mental health centres – in what is called the 'key worker' approach to treatment. This involves the allocation of the patient to a member of any one of the professions for their main care, rather than this always being the responsibility of the doctor.

Such developments have again led to conflicts over questions of responsibility, authority and leadership between the various professions involved. Generally speaking doctors have continued to claim ultimate clinical responsibility and authority for decision-making over individual patient's treatment, and to argue for leadership of the multidisciplinary team in clinical matters, though not necessarily in relation to administrative or management issues. An additional problem may arise from the fact that, compared with doctors who are relatively independent free agents, some disciplines such as nursing and social work are governed by a hierarchical structure with tiers of authority, so that theoretically a decision of the multidisciplinary team could be overridden by a more senior officer within one discipline. However, it must be said that in practice most multidisciplinary teams, especially at ward level, work quite smoothly and effectively in the interests of the patient. Furthermore, the notion of the multiprofessional team is not restricted to psychiatry; there are other clinical departments within the general hospital which depend upon close cooperation between a number of disciplines each bringing its own particular expertise to the care and treatment of the patient, and often under a considerable degree of pressure (a good example being the renal dialysis unit) (Pritchard, 1982).

If we move further from the hospital into the community, the role of the social worker becomes more evident, and there is once again a potential for misunderstanding and dispute. The social worker and community psychiatric nurse are both concerned with the patient in his own home, and their roles may therefore overlap with some uncertainty about individual responsibility. The social worker and the doctor stand in a particular relationship in dealing with the question of the compulsory admission of psychiatric patients to hospital – the former having a statutory responsibility in making an application for such admission, and the latter in providing the medical recommendation on which it is based – a situation in which a failure to agree on the need for admission is not unknown.

Other relationships

So far we have looked at interaction between members of professions directly involved with care of the patient. There are though, as we have said, other disciplines less directly, but no less importantly, involved in providing that care. One of these which has expanded in recent years is that of the hospital administrator, and to this has been added even more recently the manager (Regional, District and Unit) who may or may not be a doctor or nurse. At the same time there has been, owing to administrative and management developments, an increase in the day-to-day interaction between administrators and other personnel, including doctors and nurses. Misunderstandings and conflicts may here arise in part because of the extent to which the work situations of the administrators and the clinician differ in their degree of uncertainty. Administration, for example, depends upon the availability of sufficient accurate routine information (paperwork) about numbers of patients, investigative and treatment requirements, etc., in order to make adequate provision of these facilities. The clinician, on the other hand, is used to non-routine, unpredictable and often emergency situations dealing directly with the needs of patients, against which the recording of statistical information may seem an unnecessary inconvenience. Once again this highlights the need for good interdisciplinary communication and understanding if the best possible service is to be provided for patients.

The hospital as an institution

We have seen that Goffman (1968) described the mental hospital as an example of what he called a 'total institution' which, so he claimed, far from providing a therapeutic environment, actually dehumanized the patients and disabled them in terms of their return to a life outside hospital. Such a damning indictment of the mental asylums – which, when they were established mostly in the last century, had as their name implies the worthy aim of rescuing the mentally sick from the ill-treatment, neglect and inhumanity to which they had been exposed in the community – was actually based on very limited evidence from a small study of a single hospital. However, it was supported by a number of other studies of US psychiatric institutions, while in the UK similar ideas led to pioneering changes towards a more 'open' policy in the mental hospital to prevent what a British psychiatrist, Russell Barton (1965), called 'institutional neurosis' in the patients.

As well as literally opening up the institutions by removing the locked doors from most of the wards, there were changes in their social structure. This had been extremely hierarchical, with much power and authority exercised by those at the top of the medical and nursing divisions and with attitudes that characterized the role of staff towards patients as custodial, restricted, authoritarian, even if basically benevolent. The new changes in social structure were most evident in the idea of the *therapeutic community* (Jones, 1952) which, along with reduction in social distance between staff and patients, reflected for example in the abandonment of staff uniforms, regarded the community as a whole as having a therapeutic potential.

Rapoport (1960) described four aspects of this approach as 'democratization', 'permissiveness', 'communalism' and 'reality confrontation' – all aimed at helping the patient to understand, take responsibility for, and modify his behaviour by making use of the observations and insights of other members of the community, both patients and staff. In its most developed form the approach has had a rather limited application, mostly to patients with serious personality disorders rather than other forms of psychiatric illness. However, it has had a more widespread influence on ward practice in many psychiatric units – including, for example, such features as large group meetings of all the patients and some or all of the staff, whose aims range from the simple expression and discussion of problems of ward living to attempts to achieve greater understanding of individual disturbed behaviour. Such an approach can be seen as complementary to the use of drugs and other physical means of treatment for the patients.

Further reading

Dominion, J. (1968) *Marital Breakdown*. Harmondsworth: Penguin.

Enelow, A.J. and Swisher, S.N. (1979) *Interviewing and Patient Care*, 2nd ed. New York: Oxford University Press.

Fletcher, C.M. (1973) *Communication in Medicine*. London: Nuffield Provinicial Hospitals Trust.

McCary, J.L. and McCary, S.P. (1981) *Human Sexuality*, 4th ed. Belmont, California: Wadsworth.

Wilson-Barnett, J. (1979) *Stress in Hospitals: Psychological Reactions to Illness and Health Care*. Edinburgh: Churchill Livingstone.

Part 6
Conclusion

This last section takes a look at the contribution of the behavioural sciences specifically to the recognition, treatment and management generally of disease.

First, however, the concept of disease itself is examined, with recognition of its essentially social definition.

Possible social and psychological causes of disease are then considered, followed by Mechanic's concept of 'illness behaviour' and its pathological derivation 'abnormal illness behaviour'.

Finally, consideration of psychological responses to illness and their determinants looks back to the question of individual differences of patients' behaviour posed at the beginning of the book.

20
Psychosocial aspects of disease

The concept of disease

It may be supposed that at all times and in all societies there has been an awareness that people are liable to experience those unpleasant subjective symptoms, physical changes and behavioural disturbances that we today regard as evidence of disease. Our own ideas about the nature and manifestation of disease are of relatively recent origin and tend to reflect the generally haphazard and piecemeal way that they have developed over the centuries. It is important to recognize that they have represented man's attempt to understand and deal with the problems of sickness in the same way that he tries generally to make sense and meaning of the world, by organizing information about it in terms of classes and concepts. Thus our modern concept of disease is aimed at defining a class of phenomena which is then seen as properly the concern of the medical and related professions – though it is soon apparent that this is a more difficult task than might appear at first sight. Before we address this problem in more detail it may be helpful to consider something of the historical background of beliefs about the nature of disease and its causation.

The oldest explanation for the occurrence of the manifestations of disease, and which still exists (as we saw in Chapter 15) in some contemporary but less 'developed' societies, is based on *supernatural* beliefs – in spirits, demons, witches and spells. The first *naturalistic* forms of medicine that we know of were those of ancient Greece and Rome, according to which schools a disease was defined by a particular symptom or physical sign – a skin rash, a fever, a pain. Its causation was considered to be an imbalance of the four humours, which were also responsible for what we would now call the personality of the individual, and the whole approach concentrated on the physical – on treating the body itself. Interestingly enough, Greek philosophers were somewhat critical of this and complained of a lack of attention to the soul (equivalent to what we would call the mind), though Hippocrates (420 – 375 BC) spoke of the relationship between various emotions and organs of the body – anger contracting and good feelings dilating the heart, for example (Ackerknecht, 1982).

In Europe the idea of disease based on a symptom or physical sign persisted until the seventeenth century. A disease was considered to be an entity existing in its own right and created, like everything else, by God – and therefore referred to by the direct article: *the* ague, *the* dropsy, etc. However, in the seventeenth century the great English physician, Thomas Sydenham (1624–89), recorded the tendency for certain symptoms to cluster together in individual patients and for such symptom constellations, or *syndromes*, to be associated with a characteristic outcome or prognosis. His notion of such diseases was that they were parasitic entities existing in the body of the patient.

In the second half of the eighteenth century the findings from post mortem studies began to be correlated with the syndromes observed in life, each of which seemed to be associated with a characteristic morbid anatomy, i.e. with pathological changes in particular organs of the body. In the nineteenth century, with development of the microscope, it became possible to further relate diseases to changes in the cells of individual tissues. The German pathologist Rudolph Virchow (1821–1902) established the concept of a disease as an entity defined by an altered part of the body, and specifically a cellular derangement. Finally, the emergence of bacteriology associated with Robert Koch (1843–1910) and Louis Pasteur (1822–95) provided a causative explanation for many diseases in terms of a single invading microorganism.

Alongside this increasing emphasis on disease as a physical entity with an organic pathology, and a single aetiological agent, there had been an interest in the role of the *passions* (emotions) in causation and treatment. According to the Roman (but Greek-born) physician Galen (AD 131–200), not only could they produce disease, but passions could be fought with passions – a forerunner perhaps of the idea of psychosomatic medicine to which we shall return later. Another psychosomatic notion introduced by Renaissance physicians was that of *imagination* (equivalent to suggestion) which was considered to be a more likely explanation of causation (and to be of use in curing some diseases) than the contemporary supernatural beliefs like witchcraft. Even during the nineteenth century while great progress was being made in the knowledge of diseases and their pathological basis, there continued to be a recognition of the contribution of psychological factors (passions) to the causation of some of them, including such obvious organic disorders as tuberculosis and cancer.

If we return to the present century we find that technological advances such as electrophoresis, electron microscopy and chromosome analysis have broadened the concept of the pathological basis of disease to include abnormalities down to the molecular level.

All this has resulted in a classification (nosology) of diseases which depends upon a wide range of identifying characteristics. Thus there are still diseases described by a single symptom (e.g. proctalgia fugax); others that are clinical syndromes (e.g. migraine); while yet others are defined by morbid anatomy (e.g. mitral stenosis), histopathology (e.g. glioma), bacteriology (e.g. tuberculosis), biochemistry (e.g. porphyria), physiological dysfunction (e.g. myasthenia gravis), and chromosomes (e.g. Down's syndrome) (Kendell, 1975). We have left out so far the psychiatric disorders, the majority of which have no demonstrable underlying organic pathology, and whose status as diseases has been challenged, notably by the American psychiatrist Thomas Szasz in a famous book entitled *The Myth of Mental Illness* (1961).

This has led to renewed debate about the precise definition and nature of disease. Some have argued that since the concept of disease originally arose as a means of explaining suffering and incapacity in the absence of injury, these should be the defining criteria. This, however, raises problems since some individuals may complain of symptoms and disabilities which are without any evidence of organic pathology, while others with a recognizable serious condition may be symptom-free. A distinction is therefore sometimes made between an illness – referring to a patient's subjective feeling of ill-health – and any underlying disease which may or may not be responsible for the symptoms; but this still leaves the nature of disease unresolved.

Another way of looking at the problem is to equate sickness with the need for treatment. For example, Kraüpl Taylor (1976) suggests that patients can be distinguished from non-patients by the presence of 'abnormal attributes that arouse therapeutic concern'. This, however, is also open to the objection that disease is then dependent on recognition of that need. Thus any definition of disease in terms of what people complain of or what doctors treat will make it dependent on social and medical attitudes, and therefore likely to vary from time to time and from place to place.

We have seen that in the last century disease came to be identified with the presence of a demonstrable physical abnormality, and this came to include the structural, physiological or biochemical. One of the difficulties with this definition is that it implies a qualitative difference between health and sickness – there is either a pathological change or there is not – whereas in some conditions such as hypertension there is every gradation (e.g. of blood pressure) between the patient and the normal person.

Such a quantitative deviation in sickness from the norm or a normal range of values suggests a statistical approach to the concept of normality/abnormality and health/sickness. Two problems arise with such an approach. First, there are some conditions which though clearly pathological (e.g. dental caries) are so common as to be *statistically* 'normal'; this would suggest the need for a concept of an *ideal* normal – something which, though infrequent, is considered desirable. Second, a distinction has to be made between deviations from the statistical norms that are harmful and those which are not.

Scadding (1967) therefore proposed the idea of disease as a departure from the norm which places the individual at a biological disadvantage (Campbell *et al.*, 1979). In attempting to justify the application of this concept of disease to psychiatric illness, Kendell (1975) elaborated the meaning of 'biological disadvantage' to embrace both increased mortality and reduced fertility. He then concluded that the evidence supported such disadvantages for the major psychiatric disorders (the psychoses), and that it is therefore correct to regard them as forms of illness – though this could not necessarily be claimed for the milder neurotic illnesses and personality disorders.

The fact that the latter may thus fall outside this definition of illness/disease may argue for a wider concept. Some (e.g. Fabrega, 1975) have drawn attention to the fact that the prevailing Western 'biomedical' way of looking at disease, though it has proved extremely successful, should nevertheless be seen as part of our particular contemporary culture. A broader view might consider as more universal or 'generic' such characteristics of sickness as that it is person-centred, undesirable, harmful, a deviation, an impairment, produces discomfort, gives rise to the need for help, etc. This would, of course, take account of cultural variations within the definition, but in so doing would be more consistent with social anthropological evidence (e.g. Leach, 1978), showing how culture-bound and relativistic is the distinction between normal and abnormal beliefs and behaviour generally.

Perhaps we can summarize by proposing that when we speak of disease we are essentially employing a man-made or social concept which refers to a variety of ways in which the structure and/or functioning of an individual's body or parts of it, or his total behaviour and/or experience, may depart from a state or range that has, for him, been normal or is normal or considered as desirable for his social group, which is seen by him and/or others as adversely affecting the quality or quantity of his life, or likely to do so, for the origin of which he is not directly responsible and for which he is considered to need medical help.

In the context of the behavioural sciences we are, of course, primarily interested in psychosocial aspects of disease, and this will include the role of social and psychological factors in causation as well as social aspects of illness-recognition and treatment as well as the psychological response of patients to their illness. Before turning to these topics in more detail we should first introduce a concept which has received much attention in this area. The term *illness behaviour* was coined by the American sociologist David Mechanic (1962) to describe 'the ways in which given symptoms may be differentially perceived, evaluated and acted (or not acted) upon by different kinds of person'. In this sense it refers to the process by which an individual comes to the view that he may be ill and in need of medical attention, how he seeks that help from the doctor and thus passes from being a well person to an ill patient. Subsequently the concept of illness behaviour has come to be applied, particularly by clinicians, in a more restricted sense to the psychological responses (or behaviour) of patients to their (already recognized) illness.

Finally, the term *abnormal illness behaviour* has been applied by Issy Pilowsky (1969, 1978) to cover a number of conditions in which patients complain of physical symptoms for which no organic explanation can be found. We shall have need to refer again to these concepts, but we shall begin by considering something of the causation of disease both in general and in relation to social and psychological factors.

Causes of disease

In discussing the concept of disease, we have made some historical reference to notions of causation. Present-day Western orthodox medicine operates, of course, within a naturalistic frame of reference, and a 'scientific' explanation is sought for any disease. Whereas at one time this would generally have been considered to have been a single causative agent, it is now recognized that for most diseases it will be multifactorial (i.e. a number of aetiological factors), of which one may be *essential* in the sense that the disease cannot occur without it (e.g. a particular pathogenic organism, an abnormal gene) though not itself a *sufficient* cause for the actual occurrence of the disease for which *contributory* causes are required (e.g. environmental factors reducing resistance to infection).

One way of approaching the subject of aetiology is to look at the processes of adaptation between the individual and the environment, of which three aspects can be considered: the physical, the biological and the social. Thus the individual has to adjust to the *physicochemical* environment – to changes, for example, in temperature and oxygen content – by using physiological homeostatic mechanisms to maintain the constancy of the internal (body) environment despite variations in the exterior (in the examples just cited, the temperature of the body and oxygen content of the blood respectively). Deviation from a limited range of values can be damaging, as in the condition of abnormally low body temperature (hypothermia) which has received much attention in recent years. Exposure to certain chemicals can also be harmful both in the short term, sometimes even causing death (e.g. poisons) and in the longer term by producing diseases such as cancer (cigarette smoking, asbestos).

The *biological*, or more especially the *microbiological*, environment is of great importance in causing many diseases. A condition such as pneumonia is really the manifestation of a struggle between the body's immune defences and an invading micro-organism within a particular organ system, in this case the lung. In such a battle it is clear that whether it even becomes apparent as an illness, and if so what the outcome will be, depends in part upon factors relating to the individual – the strength of the body's defences against the particular bacterium, virus, etc. (A similar consideration may also apply to responses to chemicals – some people are prone to react in a harmful way to certain substances and are said to show an allergy to them.)

When we turn to the third aspect of the environment – the *social* – we can see that the nature of the interaction is even more recognizably dependent on aspects of the individual; as we saw in the last chapter we all have to respond and adapt to other people, but that process can be difficult and may lead in various ways to disease.

Not all diseases, however, can be accommodated so easily within this interactional model. Many are related to degenerative changes associated with the process of ageing, others have a major genetic determination such that they will appear whatever the environment, and yet others represent failures of normal development for various reasons. Nevertheless in each of these cases environmental factors may play a modifying role in the condition.

After this brief introduction to aetiological factors in disease, we shall consider in a little more detail those that can be considered as social and then those of a psychological nature.

Social structure

Here we shall consider those contributions to ill-health that arise from man's social existence, i.e. his membership of social groups of all sizes ranging from the nation to the family. If we accept the notion of multifactorial aetiology and of an interaction between the individual and the environment as basic to the causation of much if not all disease, then social factors are likely to play a role in influencing both sides of that interaction. Thus poor social conditions may, through inadequate nutrition, weaken resistance to infection from an organism, the risk of exposure to which could likewise be greater due to overcrowding and lack of sanitation.

We are, of course, dealing here primarily with *economic* factors; indeed, while in Britain the death rate from pulmonary tuberculosis, for example, was declining even before the introduction of antituberculous drugs, associated with an improved standard of living, the picture in contemporary less economically developed Third World countries is of high mortality rates from infectious diseases similar to those which prevailed here a century ago. The relationship between the health and the economy of different societies is not, however, restricted to the well-established effects of poverty on disease. The affluence of Western societies carries with it an increased risk of certain diseases resulting from such behaviours as cigarette smoking and excessive alcohol consumption. At the same time, within our own society, economic factors may in part at least be responsible for the differences of disease prevalence between social classes (a subject to which we shall be turning shortly).

When we look at differences in patterns of disease between different countries we must take account not only of their levels of economic development, but also of various *cultural* factors. Thus nations of roughly the same economic status may have quite marked differences in the incidence of particular diseases. This could reflect both genetic and environmental differences, but generally speaking the evidence is in favour of the latter since immigrants tend to show disease rates more closely resembling those of their host country than of their country of origin. This still leaves open the difficult question of whether environmental factors are cultural or geographical; or, if both, their relative significance.

Of more immediate importance and relevance to the health services of this country are *subcultural* factors in relation to disease – especially the role of differences of life style between social classes. Obviously the most objective evidence of a greater incidence of serious disease is increased mortality, and a measure that is used for this purpose is the *standardized mortality ratio* (SMR). This compares the actual with the expected death rate for a group, taking into account its age distribution. A figure of 100 means an average expectancy of death between certain ages (e.g. 20 and 64). Figures above and below this indicate a greater and a lesser risk than average respectively.

SMRs for males for each of the social classes classified according to the Registrar General's classification have shown consistent differences throughout this century, with increasingly higher rates across social classes I – V. Interestingly, there is a similar trend for married women (whose social class is determined by their husband's occupation), which suggests that the differences cannot be wholly attributed to occupational diseases (which would here, of course, be confined to the husband).

What, then, is the explanation for the higher mortality in the lower social classes? In the last century it was attributed to poor nutrition, inadequate housing, hard labour, and lack of care in childhood, and some of these factors may still be operative. However, behavioural differences such as the higher rates of smoking, and of heavy drinking among manual workers, probably also contribute to the higher mortality.

There is, in fact, a clear association between cigarette smoking and socioeconomic status, with a higher percentage of smokers (among both men and women) in the manual than in the non-manual groups. Although there has been a general decline in the numbers of smokers between 1972 and 1982, this has been most pronounced among professionals of both sexes, while for women in the unskilled manual group it has actually remained at a constant level since 1978. There has during this period been much publicity about the harmful effects of smoking, and since 1971 a health warning has been printed on cigarette packets. At the same time the price of cigarettes has risen steeply owing to heavy taxation.

It is only possible to speculate as to why there has been a differential class response to the anti-smoking campaign. One explanation might lie in the differences of social perspective and general life style referred to in Chapter 11, specifically between the working-class fatalistic present-orientated attitude compared with the more determinist and future-orientated middle-class perspective. Alternatively it may be supposed that the brunt of the economic recession in recent years has fallen mainly on the poorer social groups, whose stressful lives have therefore made it more difficult for them to give up smoking despite its increasing cost. Some support for this view may be found in the relationship of heavy drinking (as possibly another reflection of level of stress) to unemployment. Thus in 1982 there was a considerably higher proportion

(43 per cent) among unemployed men aged 25–44 than among employed men in this age range (28 per cent). However, a higher rate for the unemployed would in any case be expected since most of the men were in the manual socioeconomic groups which include relatively high proportions of heavier drinkers.

Not all disease shows a higher incidence among the poorer classes. In the 1930s and 1940s the mortality for coronary heart disease showed a declining gradient from upper to lower social classes, and various explanations were advanced to explain this, focussing particularly on diet, physical exercise and emotional stress. However, in the 1950s a change in the pattern occurred, especially among younger men, so that the gradient across social classes was reversed – attributable perhaps to social and occupational changes that had occurred in the interval.

There are other examples of medical conditions that show such relationships with social class and with gradients sloping in both directions, but our concern here is simply to note the aetiological importance of such social influences.

If we turn briefly to mental illness, there is another well-recognized association between social class and schizophrenia, with a preponderance among the lowest social class. This corresponds with ecological studies which have shown a concentration of schizophrenic patients living within the poorest run-down inner areas of cities (e.g. in Chicago (Faris and Dunham, 1939) and in Bristol (Hare, 1956). There was for a long time much argument as to the causal direction of these associations – did poor social conditions contribute to the development of the illness, or did sufferers from it 'drift' down the social scale owing to occupational failure resulting from the illness itself or pre-existing deficiencies of personality? Support for the latter view came from a study (Goldberg and Morrison, 1963) in which the social class of male schizophrenic patients was compared with that of their fathers at the time of their (the patient's) birth. Whereas the patients showed the expected high proportion of social class V, the fathers showed a social class distribution similar to the population at large. The sons had thus either never reached, or had declined from, the social class of their fathers (who were found to have maintained their position since the birth of the patient).

The smallest social group that we can consider is the family. Apart from looking at the effects of particular aspects of family life on certain conditions (such as we shall discuss shortly in relation to psychiatric illness), the most obvious social variable to investigate is marital status. In general it appears that the risk of many diseases is less for married people (though less so for women than men) compared with those that are single, widowed or divorced. It is, of course, dangerous to conclude that this is directly attributable to some protective factor of marriage, since the association between non-marriage and sickness might be explained in terms of a factor common to both. This could certainly be at least part of the explanation for the higher rates of suicide for the unmarried, where some personal attributes might predispose both to unmarried status and a predisposition to suicide. Rates for the divorced are even higher, but again this could be partly attributable to personality factors; this would be less plausible for the widowed who are similarly prone to suicide.

Social change

We have touched upon the possible effect of social change on the incidence of disease, and in Chapter 12 we considered in particular its role in contributing to suicide, and to the sometimes adverse effects of rehousing on the mental health of some people. We also referred then to some studies of the relationship of migration between societies to the incidence of mental illness, and to the concept of culture shock experienced by new immigrants to a foreign land. Such a shock may by lessened for those who on arrival join a community of fellow immigrants and maintain some of their traditional customs, while it is often the first generation to be born in the host country (described as second-generation immigrants) who face the greatest problem of adaptation to the latter's culture – a process known as *acculturation*. This is consistent with the finding (Wardwell *et al.*, 1964) of low rates of heart disease among foreign-born (first-generation) immigrants in the USA compared with high rates among first- and subsequent-generations Americans (second- and later-generation immigrants), and even more so with the demonstration (Medalie and Kahn, 1973) of the high incidence of heart attacks among first-generation Israelis (second-generation immigrants) compared with lowest rates for second- and subsequent-generation Israelis and intermediate rates in immigrants themselves.

When looking at the relationship of immigration to organic disease indices it is of course, necessary to consider, as with comparisons between different countries, the effects of factors other than psychosocial stress (e.g. diet, weather, immunities to infection acquired early in life); but this is not our primary concern here. One way of excluding or at least reducing the effects of such geographical factors is to study *migration within a society* (e.g. between urban and rural areas of the same country). In Chapter 12 we considered the process of urbanization from a historical perspective and noted some of the social changes that are involved. Here we are concerned with the immediate effects of movement of individuals from a rural area to the town and city environment. The fact that studies of both industrial and developing countries have shown rates of sickness higher in first- than in second-generation urban dwellers suggests that here the acculturation process is more important than urban life itself. In relation to hypertension there is additional support for the hypothesis from the fact that a higher prevalence of the condition is found among those town dwellers who continue to show manifestations of their traditional cultural attitudes and ways of life which are out of harmony with the rest of the urban population (Gampel *et al.*, 1962; Scotch, 1963).

In Chapter 11 we discussed the concept of *social mobility* – meaning the movement of individuals from one social class to another. Clearly such movement both between generations and within an individual's lifetime is likely to be associated with social changes, and again there has been interest in their possible effects on health. Thus in Connecticut (Wardwell *et al.*, 1968) the risk of coronary heart disease was found to be modestly raised with upward social mobility, but only in Protestants – a change which, bearing in mind the so-called protestant ethic (see Chapter 12), would be expected to be rewarding rather than stressful. However, downward mobility was associated with a markedly raised risk for Protestants and a slightly raised risk for Catholics. In a similar study in California (Syme *et al.*, 1965, 1966) upward mobility appeared to be significant. Thus the risk of coronary heart disease was found to be higher in such a group, comprising college graduate sons of foreign-born fathers, compared with two less mobile groups, namely non-graduate sons of foreign-born fathers and graduate sons of native-born fathers.

Not all the evidence has supported these associations, and it seems likely

(Jenkins, 1976) that a number of factors are involved in any relationship between social mobility and disease (or at any rate coronary heart disease); so that it may be valid only in certain places and at certain times, only for certain presentations of the disease, and only when other variables are present.

Psychological factors

The influence on disease patterns of the social factors we have been considering, although detectable by statistical comparisons of groups comprising many people, is mediated at the level of individuals by the effects of membership or change of membership of those groups. Such influences are likely to affect both personality and life experiences, and it is these two psychological variables and their interaction that we shall examine in relation to health and disease.

First, however, we shall consider the concept of *psychosomatic medicine*. As we have seen, there is a long history of concern with psychological factors (the passions) in the causation of disease, and in the last century there were *psychogenic* theories for many conditions. Unfortunately, these included some such as typhus, rabies and cholera which proved later to have an infective origin. Against this and other advances in organic medicine, however, the expansion of knowledge of endocrinology and the autonomic nervous system, together with the use of hypnosis, and later experiments in psychophysiology, provided some notions of mechanisms that could link the emotions with the bodily changes of disease, and encouraged the development of psychosomatic medicine.

In the early part of this century, particularly in the years leading up to and following the Second World War, psychoanalytic concepts came to be applied to the field. Especially influential were the views of H. Flanders Dunbar (1954) on personality and disease, and the specificity theory of Franz Alexander (1950) which held that certain constellations of intrapsychic conflicts, with their associated emotions, could specifically affect particular organs of the body. Although Alexander himself supported the idea of multicausality, others applied his hypothesis in such a way that certain diseases (namely bronchial asthma, rheumatoid arthritis, ulcerative colitis, essential hypertension, neurodermatitis, thyrotoxicosis and peptic ulcer) came to be identified as 'psychosomatic' with a 'psychogenic' basis in a way that was analogous to the class of infectious diseases with their essential aetiological micro-organisms – they thus fell into the same trap of looking for a specific psychological causation for a group of so-called psychosomatic diseases.

The evidence to support such a view proved generally to be lacking, and gradually a new concept developed, which, while it acknowledged that in some diseases (those originally described as psychosomatic) psychological factors might play a major or even predominant role in causing the condition, affecting its course or influencing its response to treatment, at the same time claimed that such factors could have a wider significance in relation to all diseases. When applied to the whole of medicine such a view was described as the *psychosomatic approach* and took account of all possible influences – biological, psychological and social – on patients and their diseases. An alternative term applied to this approach was *whole-person* medicine to distinguish it from what was seen to have been an over-emphasis on biological sciences and technology and a too specialized concern with particular organs or systems of the body. The most recent manifestation is perhaps the development of what is called *holistic medicine* – again seen as alternative, or perhaps complementary, to the basic philosophical and scientific assumptions of traditional medicine (dualistic, mechanistic and reductionist – replacing them by a monistic, humanistic, and holistic approach (Pietroni, 1984)).

Such developments within medicine probably in part reflect wider changes of social attitudes towards health and sickness among the general public. Interest in such activities as jogging and aerobics, in so-called natural health foods and 'alternative' medicine, may all suggest some disillusionment with what is seen as 'scientific' medicine's orientation towards the treatment of disease rather than its prevention.

This does not mean that a more comprehensive approach to medicine should eschew the contribution of the scientific method to establishing the role of psychosocial factors in disease and to testing the value of particular kinds of treatment. What then is the evidence?

There have been two main areas of research reflecting the two sides of the patient–environment interaction: psychological factors within the individual (especially personality), and life experiences. Clearly what is required is some demonstration of a greater than chance association between certain psychological variables, individual or environmental, and the occurrence of disease. Such an association could be shown by retrospective or (preferably) prospective studies of groups of patients – i.e. either starting with the disease (the dependent variable) and looking for antecedent factors (the independent variables), or starting with the latter and looking for consequent disease. The psychological factors, as with those of a social nature relating to social structure and social change, may be relatively long-lasting (e.g. personality or family structure), or episodic (e.g. bereavement and life events generally).

Individual factors

The idea of certain diseases being associated with particular personality types was a feature of psychoanalytically based theories, such as those of Dunbar and Alexander to which we have already referred. However, the evidence for such associations has generally been disappointing, and apart from two exceptions there is little interest now in such an approach. The first exception concerns a particular type of behaviour which is said to occur in patients with coronary heart disease – i.e. a *coronary prone personality* associated with a so-called *type-A behaviour pattern* (Friedman and Rosenman, 1959). The characteristics of the latter (relating primarily to work) include: intense striving for achievement, competitiveness, over-commitment to vocation or profession, a sense of time urgency and excesses of drive and hostility (in contrast to a relaxed easygoing pattern described as type-B).

Many studies (reviewed by Jenkins, 1976), both prospective and retrospective, have found evidence supporting the association of at least some part of the type-A behaviour pattern with incidence or prevalence of coronary heart disease. However, other studies have found that coronary prone patients show obsessional perfectionistic attitudes in other areas of their lives as well as in relation to work, while such personality characteristics and even behaviours resembling type-A have been demonstrated in some non-coronary diseases. This would suggest that the personality/behaviour characteristics of this type may be less specifically related to coronary artery disease than was at first thought; they might perhaps represent a more general predisposition towards several forms of disease.

The second but somewhat related personality characteristic that has frequently been considered to predispose towards disease – especially cancer – is *emotional inhibition*, particularly the suppression of anger. However, most of the evidence comes from retrospective studies while the results of prospective investigations to date (though not specifically designed to test the anger-suppression hypothesis) do not allow firm conclusions regarding a cancer-prone personality (Greer, 1983).

Thus, while the early psychoanalytic concept of specific intrapsychic conflict associated with a limited number of psychosomatic diseases has been abandoned, there is sufficient evidence to suggest a role for some personality traits in predisposing to at least some diseases.

Other but less persisting psychological aspects of the individual have also been considered in relation to disease – in particular the presence of certain *emotions* and feelings. These, of course, are likely to be aroused by social and other situations and events, so that they may be seen as an intervening variable or mediating process between the latter and any consequent disease. Thus Engel (1962) and his colleagues in Rochester, USA (based on their studies of a number of diseases), described a 'giving-up/given-up' complex which may occur in response to actual or threatened loss of a significant 'object' (material or abstract) and which provides a permissive setting for the occurrence of disease, though not of itself being a necessary or sufficient cause. The complex comprises a mood of *depression* associated with feelings of helplessness and/or hopelessness. The *giving-up* part of the complex involves the inability to give up either (a) a desired gratification which has been lost but for which the individual does not accept responsibility and feels the need of outside help – giving rise to a feeling of *helplessness*, or (b) a self-selected goal or ambition which is no longer obtainable, responsibility for which is accepted by the individual, resulting in a feeling of *hopelessness*. It is, of course, these painful feelings that are considered harmful, but the *given-up* part of the complex represents its healthy resolution – by the individual's recognition and tolerance of the loss of gratification and goals which brings relief.

There has been much anecdotal description of depressive states (whatever their cause) preceding the clinical onset of cancers, but interpretation exemplifies the difficulties inherent in this kind of retrospective evidence – in particular the inability to date the actual onset of the disease. Thus it could be that the depression is a manifestation of early, as yet undetected, malignant disease; and in fact a suggested mechanism for this in terms of immunological interference with the activity of the neurotransmitter 5-hydroxy-tryptamine (5HT) has been proposed (Brown and Paraskevas, 1982). More convincing evidence of an association between depression and subsequent cancers comes from prospective studies. The largest of these (Shekelle *et al.*, 1981) used the depressive subscale of the MMPI (see Chapter 16) administered to over 2000 middle-aged American men, and found at follow-up 17 years later a significant association between death from cancer and earlier depressive scores.

Environmental factors

It is now time to turn to the other side of the individual–environment interaction and look at the kinds of life experience which might in a predisposed person result in a disease process. It has become common to speak of events (usually seen as unpleasant) that may have an adverse effect on the individual as stressful. The notion of *stress* has in fact been much used in the field of psychosomatic medicine (Kimball, 1982), though its precise definition has been problematic. A major advocate of the relationship of stress to illness was Hans Selye (1956), who applied the term *stressor* to an external stimulus which provoked a stress response of physiological arousal involving the adrenal cortical–pituitary axis and the secretion of corticosteroid hormones – the so-called *general adaptation syndrome*. If the individual is unable to respond behaviourally in an adaptive way to the stressful situation, then a state of prolonged arousal results which may become irreversible. Selye claimed that this was responsible for certain *diseases of adaptation*. Here the concept of stress is seen in terms of its response in the individual, and this is in keeping with the views of Alexander and Engel to which have already referred – the extent of the personal response to any stimulus being the important measure rather than the stimulus itself.

Other investigators have (as we shall see) been more concerned with the provoking events, but in the end it is clear the property of stress lies within and not outside the individual. Ursin *et al.* (1978) suggested that what is stressful depends upon the ability of the person to respond at an optimal level (i.e. not too much and not too little) to the provoking situation. This, of course, will in turn be influenced by many individual variables such as the perception and evaluation of the stimulus, past experience of coping with stress, intelligence, motivation etc.

Let us, then, turn to studies of life events and their possible effects on health, bearing in mind two particular methodological problems: first, the danger in retrospective studies of ill persons of their being more aware of preceding life events than if they were well; and second, in prospective investigations, the sometimes impossibility of concluding whether a disease has been actually caused by an event or whether it was already present and has only been exacerbated.

One of the earliest retrospective studies was carried out by Hinkle and Wolff (1958) using the longitudinal health records of a large group of male and female employees. A major finding was that instead of periods of illness being randomly distributed over a number of years, they in fact tended to occur in clusters. Furthermore, those clusters of illness were more likely to arise at times when the individual felt under stress from having to adapt to conflicting and threatening demands.

There have been two principal approaches to prospective studies. The first and perhaps the most obvious has involved monitoring the physical and mental health of people who have experienced a particular life event – the two commonest being major, often large-scale man-made or natural disasters, and the death of a spouse. In considering the former (e.g. imprisonment in a concentration camp or other type of prison, wartime combat duty, peacetime floods) it is usually necessary to separate, if possible, physical from mental stress. In general, psychological stress has been shown to result in increased psychiatric but not physical illness. Where greater incidence of physical morbidity has been found it has been attributable to earlier death from already existing disease rather than the occurrence of new disease (Bennett, 1970).

We referred earlier to the higher morbidity among the widowed compared with the married, but here we are concerned with the short-term effects of bereavement. Several studies have shown an increased mortality for widowers in the first six months after bereavement, but that by the second year the mortality rate returns to the level of the still married. Other studies have failed to confirm this, but in any case there is still the problem of whether the deaths are due to a worsening of already existing disease. As far as morbidity generally is concerned, while there is increased medical consultation in the early months after bereavement especially for symptoms of a psychological nature or origin, there is little evidence of an increased risk of physical disease (Clayton, 1973). The changes of life style that have been found (Parkes and Brown, 1972), with increased consumption of alcohol or tobacco, may contribute to the generally higher mortality of the widowed already mentioned.

The second type of prospective study has proliferated in the last twenty years, has been of interest to both sociologists and psychologists as well as psychiatrists, and is generally described as *life events research*. Instead of concentrating on a particular life experience, the approach attempts to measure a number of life changes that may be experienced by an individual within a defined period of time. Thus Thomas Holmes and Richard Rahe (1967) were the first to draw up a checklist of life events – the 'schedule of recent experiences' – which when completed by patients suffering from a variety of conditions showed a greater incidence of events requiring major social readjustment prior to the onset of the illness compared with a group of 'normals'.

The next development was a *social readjustment rating scale* (SRRS) in which a number of life events (42 – most but not all unpleasant) were given values by a standardizing population of 400 people in terms of the amount of (re)adjustment considered to be required in each case to handle the event; to guide the raters the highest score of 100 was already allotted to death of a spouse and 50 to marriage. By taking the mean of all the scores for each item and then ranking them, a scale was produced which could be used as a research tool. Individuals could be given a score measured in *life change units* by noting their recent life events and summing the values. The scores could then be compared with those of others as well as with their own earlier or later scores. It is important to note that what is being measured here is not a stress response within the individual, but the amount of readjustment a certain event is considered likely to require were it to occur. It is open to question whether in a particular individual it would in fact result in that degree of readjustment.

A large number of studies have been carried out using this technique for measuring life change events in an attempt to relate them to illness – the hypothesis being that an accumulation of events may evoke faulty processes of adaptation which will lower the resistance of the body and thus increase the probability of disease occurring. The general conclusion (e.g. Birley and Connolly, 1976) seems to be that only a modest association can be found between disease and stress as measured in this way.

One of the weaknesses of the SRRS – namely the likely individual variation in degree of stressfulness of the same life event – has been met in an alternative technique of assessment devised by George Brown (1974). This is based on a structured interview in which the subject is asked about a number of possible life events and then encouraged to give a detailed account of preceding and surrounding circumstances of any that have occurred recently. These details are then given to independent trained research personnel who rate the degree of 'contextual threat' of the event for that individual. Assessment is also made of the degree to which life events could be a consequence of the person's

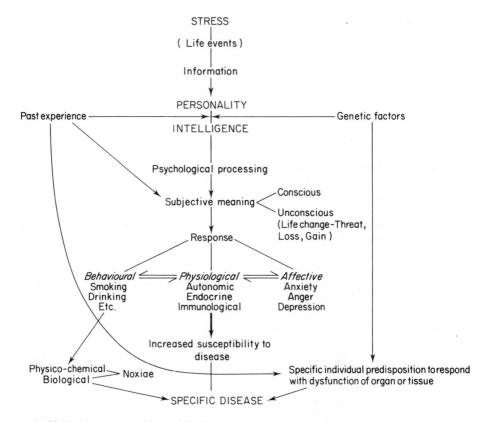

Fig.20.1   A 'psychosomatic model' with theoretical pathways between external events and organic disease

own behaviour rather than an independent happening. Further methodological refinements by Paykel (1974) have included the classification of events into subcategories depending on their meaning: desirable versus undesirable (in terms of generally shared values) and 'exit' versus 'entrance' (exits involving departure of a person, entrances the introduction of a new person).

Most of the studies using these instruments have been concerned with psychiatric (we shall return to this later) rather than physical illness, and the evidence for an association between the latter and life events has been inconclusive. It may be, of course, that the techniques for measuring psychological stress are still too crude for the purpose, but the conclusion for the moment (Andrews and Tennant, 1978) has to be that life event stress has not been shown to lead directly to physical illness but may exacerbate existing but unrecognized disease and can lead to changes of behaviour which may in turn damage physical health. Fig. 20.1 summarizes some of the processes involved in this psychosomatic interaction.

The idea that psychological factors may influence the course of an established disease is clearly of great importance clinically, and we shall return to this when we consider the psychological response to illness.

Psychiatric illness

It would perhaps be expected that evidence for an association between psychological factors and psychiatric illness is greater than that found in relation to physical disease. Attention has been directed prinicipally to family influences and to recent and remote life events.

The methodological problems faced by researchers in this field are formidable, particularly in retrospective studies. More than the physically ill, the psychiatric patient is likely to search for an explanation for the onset of the illness in some life experience, or to misperceive events owing to the distorting effects of mood disturbance, paranoid feelings, etc. At the same time psychiatric illness itself may bring about life changes (loss of a job, marital disturbance), which may then be mistakenly seen as causative. The accurate dating of events and illness is thus crucial.

Care has been taken to try to avoid these pitfalls in a number of retrospective studies and associations demonstrated between *depression* and life events – especially 'exits' and 'undesirable' events (e.g. Paykel *et al.*, 1969). However, in a review of eight controlled prospective studies of life events and neuroses and depression, Tennant (1983) concluded that there is little evidence to show they have any substantial causal role, so the position remains uncertain. Even if life events do increase the risk of depressive illness it does not appear to be overwhelming and should be seen as part of a multifactorial causation.

Brown, from the viewpoint of the sociologist, has looked at the role of social modifying factors in a study of women living in the borough of Camberwell in London (Brown and Harris, 1978). He found that certain *provoking agents* (severe life events, mainly losses or disappointments, or major difficulties) appeared to determine when depression would occur. However, whether it occurred was related to four so-called *vulnerability factors*; lack of an intimate relationship with a husband or boyfriend, the presence of three or more children under 14 at home, absence of a job outside the home, and loss of mother before the age of 11. The fact that working-class women were at greater risk of depression could be attributed mostly to the more frequent presence of vulnerability factors. In a later study of *anxiety states* in women attending a London general practitioner, serious events involving 'danger' rather than 'loss' were found to have preceded the onset, while for mixed states of depression and anxiety, events of both kinds had occurred.

The importance of life stresses as precipitants of *schizophrenia* was clearly demonstrated in a study by Brown and Birley (1968) comparing 50 patients admitted with a first onset or relapse of the condition against a control group. The number of independent life events (which appeared to be non-specific) was found to be significantly higher for the schizophrenics in the three weeks prior to the onset of symptoms. Similar results have been obtained in subsequent studies.

Another important area of research in relation to schizophrenia has been concerned with the effects of certain aspects of family life on the risk of relapse after patients have been discharged from hospital. In studies carried out at the MRC Social Psychiatry Unit at the Maudsley Hospital in London (Brown *et al.*, 1962) it has been shown that relapse rates are greater in families in which there is high expressed emotion (relatives making critical comments, showing hostility and emotional over-involvement with the patient) and face-to-face contact between patient and relatives for more than 35 hours a week (less contact reducing the relapse rate in high-expressed-emotion families, presumably as a protective device against the relatives' hostility). The high expressed emotion in a relative appears to be associated with autonomic arousal in the patient (Sturgeon *et al.*, 1981). Clearly there is likely to be a complex set of interactions between these various psychosocial factors. Thus Leff and Vaughn (1981) showed that relapse could be associated with either a high level of expressed emotion or an independent life event in the preceding three months before the onset. If antipsychotic medication is also taken into account it has been possible (Vaughn and Leff, 1976) to determine various relapse rates depending on the presence or absence of three variables: with high expressed emotion, more than 35 hours per week contact and no medication the relapse rate is 92 per cent; with medication and low contact it is as low as 15 per cent. Finally, it has been demonstrated (Leff *et al.*, 1982) that the relapse rate can also be reduced by family intervention to reduce relatives' expressed emotion.

Recognition and treatment of disease

Here we shall first be concerned with the process of becoming ill and seeking treatment – described by David Mechanic as illness behaviour.

Illness behaviour

The significance of this choice of words is that we are not here concerned with disease or illness itself but with its behavioural consequences; i.e. how the individual perceives the symptoms and acts or does not act upon them. As Mechanic pointed out, his concept of illness behaviour falls in medicine between aetiology and treatment: the causative processes that we have just been considering have already occurred, but whether a diagnosis is made and treatment given is determined by illness behaviour.

The importance of this intervening step between illness and medical consultation may be seen when we consider the so-called *clinical iceberg* – the fact that much of the sickness in the community remains hidden from medical attention. Epidemiological surveys over the last three decades have shown that, while distressing symptoms are very common, only a proportion (ranging from a quarter to less than a half) of members of the community who experience them will visit a doctor (e.g. Wadsworth *et al.*, 1971). Obviously many symptoms could be short-lasting and not indicative of any significant disease, but evidence from other studies (e.g. screening a random population with a medical history, physical examination and some routine tests (Epson, 1969)) has revealed the even more disturbing fact that as many as half the members may be in need of more specialized investigation and possible treatment for unrecognized disease.

Clearly it is important to try to understand the reasons why one person seeks help and another does not for the same symptom and even the same disease – i.e. the factors responsible for individual differences of illness behaviour. A conceptual scheme developed by Kasl and Cobb (1966) for this purpose proposed two major determinants of the decision to seek medical help: first, the perception of the symptom as a *threat* of disease, and second, a belief in the *value* of a visit to the doctor in reducing that threat. Each of these factors is in turn influenced by a number of sociocultural variables. Thus in relation to symptom evaluation, for example, we have seen earlier (in Chapter 5) that the experience of pain, the ability to tolerate it and the significance attached to it, show ethnic and cultural variations, while what is considered to be the value of seeking medical help will depend upon membership of particular social groups – those within the working class, for example, are less likely to make full use of health care facilities such as antenatal clinics, welfare clinics for the children, etc. In addition to the socioculture influences, Kasl and Cobb include more individual variables such as past experience of medical care, degree of psychological distress and the presence of particularly threatening symptoms. A similar scheme for interpreting illness behaviour has been proposed by Rosenstock (1967) but includes the notion of a 'cue' leading to action – a 'trigger' – often a stressful event.

However, Tuckett (1976), while recognizing the value of these schemes in providing a conceptual framework for considering illness behaviour, has pointed out that most of the related evidence has been concerned with the influence of sociocultural factors on the perceived threat of symptoms and the perceived value of visiting a doctor, and that these group factors, important though they are, are not large enough to account for much of the variation of medical care utilization that exists between individuals. This is perhaps because the schemes are based on an underlying rational assumption that the reason why people go to a doctor is because they have threatening symptoms for which they want relief. While this is obviously true in part, it leaves out of consideration a number of other reasons for seeking help from a doctor – not all related directly to treatment for a particular illness.

Another criticism by Tuckett is of the assumption that symptoms are isolated incidents in a normally healthy individual, whereas in fact as we have seen earlier, symptoms are a common feature of peoples' lives. Finally the nature of the on-going relationship between an individual and his doctor (certainly in the UK at any rate where most people are registered with an NHS general practitioner) is another factor to be taken into account.

The picture that emerges is of people experiencing many symptoms but in most cases dealing with them in ways other than going to the doctor – the most common being with self-medication with various patent remedies. There is, in fact, an on-going *accommodation* to symptoms and generally a reluctance to accept the presence of illness and a need for medical attention. It appears that a visit to the doctor is made when a breakdown has occurred in the accommodation to symptoms owing to some trigger – often a domestic crisis (Zola, 1973); or when the doctor is seen as someone who can solve other than purely medical problems – those of a social, interpersonal or emotional kind to do with family, housing, job, etc. (Balint, 1957).

What, then, are some of the implications of these considerations of illness behaviour? If we take the Kasl and Cobb and Rosenstock approach it would seem important to concentrate efforts on health education of patients to improve their understanding of the 'perceived threat' of disease or the 'perceived value' of visiting a doctor. On the other hand, Tuckett's view suggests a need for change in medical practice so that the doctor may become more sensitive to, and concerned with, the triggers to consultation as well as the patient's symptoms. It seems likely, in fact, that these two approaches are complementary and that there would be an advantage in further education of both patients and doctors!

Abnormal illness behaviour

This concept has been developed by Pilowsky (1969) in an attempt to increase understanding in an area of medical and psychiatric diagnosis that has always presented difficulties. It concerns patients who complain of physical symptoms, and especially pain, for which no organic basis can be found, and who may receive any one of a number of diagnoses – the two commonest of which are hysteria and hypochondriasis.

We are not concerned here with the details of these various conditions, but rather with the notion of illness behaviour as a unifying concept. This derived, of course, from Mechanic's illness behaviour, but also from Parson's idea of the sick role to which we have referred earlier on several occasions. The assumption is that the kind of patient we are considering here displays illness behaviour aimed at achieving the sick role but without the presence of objective pathology which would justify this to the doctor; he is thus manifesting 'abnormal' illness behaviour. The most important question then concerns the patient's motivation for this behaviour and the extent to which he is conscious of it – ranging from a totally unconscious desire for the social and other benefits associated with the sick role, to an entirely conscious attempt (i.e. malingering) to obtain financial compensation (e.g. from an accident).

Pilowsky has developed this concept further (1978) to include a classification of abnormal illness behaviour covering both physical and psychological presentations and both the affirmation of non-existent disease and the denial of existent disease. His expanded definition of the concept is 'the persistence of an inappropriate or maladaptive mode of perceiving, evaluating and acting in relation to one's state of health, despite the fact that a doctor (or other appropriate agent) has offered a reasonably lucid explanation of the nature of the illness and the appropriate course of management to be followed, based on a thorough examination and assessment of all parameters of functioning (including the use of special investigations where necessary) and taking into account the individual's age, educational and sociocultural background'.

Apart from an obvious discrepancy between the patient's illness behaviour and the objective evidence of a recognized disease, there may be other signs of abnormal illness behaviour, including a persistence of complaints and demands in contrast to the more usual reaction of relief or resignation displayed by other patients to the physician's explanations. It is hoped that using these insights into abnormal illness behaviour will improve the physician's ability to help a group of patients who often pose considerable diagnostic and treatment problems.

Psychological response to illness

We now come to the last psychosocial aspect of disease – namely the different ways in which patients (e.g. Mr Smith and Mr Jones to whom we referred at the beginning of the first chapter) behave once its presence is recognized and treatment has commenced – and which may also sometimes be referred to as illness behaviour. In recent years there has been increasing interest (Lipowski, 1969, 1970) in this side of the 'psychosomatic coin' – the ways in which patients perceive and respond to their illness and try to cope with it. One reason for this stems from a shift of the major concerns in the practice of medicine from acute to chronic disease which requires long-time care. Technological developments such as transplant surgery and long-term haemodialysis for renal failure have resulted in psychological problems which in some cases outweigh the physical.

An important concept here is that of *coping*. From a psychological stand-point Lazarus (1966) sees it as 'strategies for dealing with threat', while as a sociologist Mechanic (1968) defines it as 'instrumental behaviour and problem solving capacities of persons in meeting life demands and goals'. The emphasis in the former approach is on danger, conflict and defences and in the latter on challenge and adaptation. Both aspects are obviously involved in coping with physical illness and disability, which Lipowski (1970) defined as 'cognitive and motor activities which a sick person employs to preserve his bodily and psychic integrity, to recover reversibly impaired function and compensate to the limit for any irreversible impairment'.

Thus consideration of the response of a patient to an illness will include some idea of the coping mechanisms being employed. It may also be subdivided into behavioural and subjective aspects, the latter including perceptual, cognitive and emotional components. Different patients will, of course, respond in different ways to their illness, and the possible factors determining this may also be categorized as intrapersonal (i.e. related to the individual), the disease itself and the environment. To complete the picture (represented by Fig. 20.2) we may consider as an intervening variable between these determinants of the response to illness and the response itself, certain 'meanings' that the illness may have for the individual. We shall now examine in a little more detail each of these aspects.

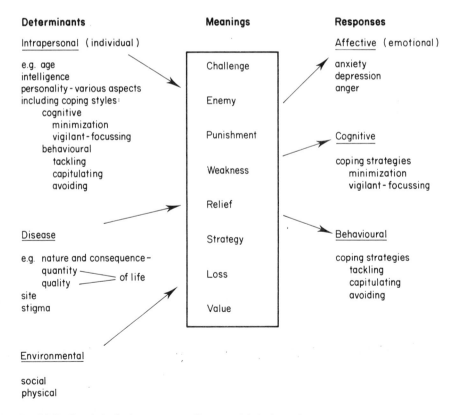

Fig. 20.2 Psychological responses to illness and their determinants

Determinants of the illness response

Intrapersonal determinants will include such factors as age, intelligence and personality. A serious life-threatening disease will usually be more disturbing to a young patient than to one who is already well into old age, while psychological immaturity in an adult will also create difficulties in coping with the demands of illness. Level of intelligence may be of some importance for patients who are involved in high-technology treatments such as haemodialysis, but it is clearly personality that is the main consideration. We have already (in Chapter 16) referred to several aspects of personality in relation to patients' reactions to illness – position on the introversion/extraversion dimension, habitual use of particular defence mechanisms such as projection, presence of a poor self-image, strength of achievement motivation, degree of sensation seeking, locus of control, field dependence, etc. Another aspect concerns the individual's characteristic and enduring ways of dealing with stress, and two cognitive and three behavioural *coping styles* can be recognized clinically.

Cognitive coping styles are obviously concerned with cognitive functioning, including perceptual and intellectual activities. *Minimization* is the term applied to a tendency to ignore, deny or rationalize the significance of a threat – in this case that posed by illness when it may range from complete delusional denial of its existence to misinterpretation of some fact in order to reduce anxiety. *Vigilant focussing* describes a contrasting cognitive style which attempts to reduce uncertainty and ambiguity by seeking all relevant information; it ranges from an exaggerated hypochondriacal preoccupation with anything to do with the illness to a more realistic appraisal of the threat and what can be done to cope with it.

Behavioural coping styles are the habitual ways individuals act in the face of a threat or challenge. *Tackling* describes an active approach to coping with the challenge of illness – advantageous if moderate, but in extreme form leading to a dangerous unwillingness to accept necessary restrictions imposed by the illness. *Capitulating* is applied to a style of coping which involves a passive surrender to the illness with no attempt to combat it, and leading to a withdrawal from, or undue dependence on, others. Such a form of behaviour may be appropriate in the acute stage of a serious illness when it may be necessary to accept a period of inactivity and passive dependence on others, but the tendency to behave in this way in other situations may result in little attempt to achieve the maximum possible recovery from illness. *Avoiding* behaviour is an attempt to escape from illness and its consequences – sometimes described as a 'flight into health' – and tends to occur in patients for whom acceptance of illness and the sick role represents a serious threat to their self image – a role conflict to which we referred in Chapter 16. Clearly this type of behaviour is likely to accompany minimization or denial of illness.

Disease-related factors are also important determinants of the psychological response of the patient. These will include such variables as the nature and consequences of the disease for both the quantity (life expectancy) and quality (distressing symptoms, loss of function, etc.) of the patient's life; the site of the pathology (whether it is visible and possibly disfiguring, the value and psychological significance of the part or organ – e.g. the heart, the head, the breast); the existence of any degree of social stigma attached to a particular disease; etc. It is important to recognize that such variables will themselves have different meanings to different individuals; some of the varieties may not be fully conscious to the sufferer, in which case the psychological response is likely to be more irrational and less predictable than if full awareness is present.

Environmental factors, both social and physical, are likely to influence the patient's experience of illness and ability to cope with it. The amount of psychological support or otherwise within the family or other interpersonal relationships may be crucial to maximum recovery, while the physical quality of the surroundings may affect not only the patient's mood but may even disorganize cognitive function (e.g. with sensory deprivation in intensive care units, as we saw in Chapter 4).

Psychological responses

These will include *affective* (emotional), *cognitive* and *behavioural* components. The latter two aspects will, as coping *strategies*, to a greater or lesser extent reflect the habitual cognitive and behavioural coping styles, respectively, that we have already discussed, but influenced by the other determinants and by the meanings of the illness which we shall be considering shortly. The affective response may include anxiety, depression and anger, either singly or in combination. Again these will depend upon both the meanings which the patient attaches to the illness, modes of coping which are employed and their success or failure.

Meanings of the illness

These may be seen as providing the link between the major determinants of the illness response and that response, since they will be influenced by the former and in turn exert an influence on the latter. Lipowski (1970) has listed eight meanings of illness which appear to be most prevalent in our Western culture.

Illness as a challenge

This meaning of illness leads generally to active and adaptive coping strategies with little affective disturbance. The illness is seen as a problem to be tackled with whatever resources are available. The patient seeks advice where necessary, cooperates with treatment, appropriately modifies his activities and finds substitute satisfactions for those that are lost through the illness.

Illness as an enemy

This view of illness as an invasion by hostile forces is, of course, a very common one within our culture and is reflected in everyday speech when we talk of an 'attack' of illness and of patients 'fighting' for their lives (even if they are unconscious in an intensive care unit). The affective response to this perception of illness is likely to be a negative one of anger and anxiety. The behavioural response, as to an enemy, will be to fight, flee or surrender, depending upon the patient's view of the likelihood of defeating the disease. If anger is extreme it may be displaced on to other people, such as medical and nursing staff. Blame for the illness may also be placed on others. This combination obviously makes for the 'difficult' patient.

Other responses may include denial as a way of dealing with anxiety, and a regressive dependency and passivity reflecting a sense of helplessness in the face of the illness. A fighting attitude, if not too extreme, may however be beneficial in terms of outcome of the illness, as we shall see shortly.

Illness as a punishment

This is also a common meaning attached by patients to their illness. It may, however, be felt to be just or unjust – with consequent feelings of depression (but if allowing attonement and redemption, with feelings of hope and elation) or anger respectively. Behaviourally, seeing the illness as a just punishment may result in an accepting, passive response, while if it is considered unjust there may be a more paranoid reaction.

Illness as a weakness

Some patients see any form of illness as evidence of failure and morally reprehensible. Feelings of shame may therefore lead them to try to deny or conceal its existence.

Illness as relief

Illness may provide for some patients a welcome relief from responsibilities of family or work, or other more intrapsychic conflicts. The risk is, of course, that this may lead to a clinging to the sick role – either conscious or unconscious – the situation which we have already considered as abnormal illness behaviour.

Illness as strategy

This is related to the last meaning but is applied to the use of illness as a means of securing attention, support or compliance from others. Again this is not necessarily at a fully conscious level; but it may be seen, for example, in parents who prevent their children from leaving home by exaggerating or even simulating illness, and in other patients who derive great satisfaction from having 'interesting' diseases which attract much medical attention.

Illness as irreparable loss or damage

Illness may, of course, result in irreversible loss in a literal sense (e.g. amputation). Some patients, however, feel that even a minor disability represents an overwhelming loss, while for others the inability to carry on with a particular interest, hobby or sport may be seen in the same way. The emotional response to such loss will include depression and anger, with resistance to rehabilitation and possibly even suicide.

Illness as a value

For some patients illness has a positive value when they see it as enhancing their spiritual, aesthetic or intellectual values.

The above eight meanings of illness are not mutually exclusive but are likely to occur in various combinations. It is unlikely that patients are initially aware of them and they are mostly to be inferred from behaviour. Patients can, however, usually recognize their existence once they are pointed out as possible explanations of their ways of responding to the illness. This can then lead to attempts to help the patient to cope more effectively, to the advantage of both patient and staff – including their relationship.

Attempts have been made (e.g. Pritchard, 1974) to quantify some of these aspects of illness behaviour (in the sense of the response to existing illness) so that they may be measured and related to clinical problems such as adjustment to illness, compliance with treatment and outcome of particular diseases.

Relationship of psychological factors to outcome of disease

Obviously psychological factors can affect the course and outcome of a disease indirectly through their influence on the degree of compliance with effective medical treatment. However, it may be that they can have a more direct influence, and we shall take a brief look at the evidence for this in relation to cancer (Greer, 1983).

Clinical observations (Stoll, 1979) have noted that reactivation of cancer, after it has been quiescent for some years, often seems to follow an episode of severe emotional stress, while a few patients with great faith or fighting spirit seem to remain alive longer than expected. Growth rates of cancers certainly vary over time so that they may regress or become dormant for long periods. Such changes probably involve immunological and hormonal mechanisms which could in turn be influenced by psychological factors.

Early retrospective studies had methodological weaknesses, but more recent prospective studies have suggested an association between survival time and certain psychological, variables. Thus Greer *et al.* (1979) obtained patients' psychological responses three months after mastectomy for early breast cancer. These were classified into four broad categories: 'stoic acceptance', 'denial', 'fighting spirit' and 'helplessness/hopelessness'. Outcome at five years and again at eight years (Greer *et al.*, 1981) was found to be significantly related to these responses, recurrence-free survival being associated with fighting spirit or denial. The results could not be explained on the basis that the psychological responses and outcome were both a reflection of the stage of cancer development at the time of operation, since the psychological responses were not related to measures of the tumours. Significant correlations were, however, discovered between psychological responses and serum levels of immunoglobulins (Pettingale *et al.*, 1977), so that this might indicate the mechanism by which the psychological responses affected outcome.

It would seem, then, that the type of psychological response made by patients to their illness may be of significance not only for the quality of their lives, but also in some instances even their survival. It is, therefore, also conceivable that the latter might be beneficially influenced by some form of psychological intervention – a final optimistic note on which to end our examination of the behavioural sciences and their contribution to medicine.

Further reading

Balint, M. (1963) *The Doctor, his Patient and the Illness*, 3rd ed. New York: International Universities Press.

Dohrenwend, B.S. and Dohrenwend, B.P. (eds.) (1974) *Stressful Life Events: their Nature and Effects*. New York: Wiley.

Moos, R.H. (ed.) (1977) *Coping with Physical Illness*. New York: Plenum.

Nichols, K. (1984) *Psychological Care in Physical Illness*. London: Croom Helm.

Robinson, D. (1971) *The Process of Becoming Ill*. London: Routledge & Kegan Paul.

Susser, M.W., Watson, W. and Hopper, K. (1985) *Sociology in Medicine*, 3rd ed. Oxford: Oxford University Press.

Tuckett, D. (ed.) (1976) *An Introduction to Medical Sociology*. London: Tavistock.

References

Ackerknecht, E.H. (1982). The history of psychosomatic medicine. *Psychological Medicine* **12**, 17.

Adorno, T.W., Frenkel-Brunswick, E., Levinson, D.J. and Sanford, R.N. (1950). *The Authoritarian Personality*. Harper and Row, New York.

Ainsworth, M.D. (1962). The effects of maternal deprivation: a review of findings and controversy in the context of research strategy. In *Deprivation of Maternal Care. A Reassessment of its Effects*. WHO, Geneva.

Alexander, C.N.Jr., Zucker, L.G. and Brady, C.L. (1970). Experimental expectations and autokinetic experiences: consistency theories and judgemental convergence. *Sociometry* **33**, 108.

Alexander, F. (1950). *Psychosomatic Medicine*. Norton, New York.

Andrews, G. and Tennant, C. (1978). Being upset and becoming ill: an appraisal of the relation between life events and physical illness. *Medical Journal of Australia* **1**, 324.

Apley, J. (1975). *The Child with Abdominal Pains*. Blackwell Scientific Publications, Oxford.

Argyle, M., Lalljee, M. and Cook, M. (1968). The effects of visibility on interaction in a dyad. *Human Relations* **21**, 3.

Argyle, M. (1969). *Social Interaction*. Methuen, Atherton.

Argyle, M. (1972). *The Psychology of Interpersonal Behaviour*. (2nd Edition). Penguin, Harmondsworth.

Asch, S.E. (1951). Effects of group pressure upon the modification and distortion of judgements. In *Groups, Leadership and Men*. Edited by Guetzkow, H. Carnegie Press, Pittsburgh.

Aserinsky, E. and Kleitman, N. (1953). Regularly occurring periods of eye motility and concomitant phenomena during sleep. *Science* **118**, 273.

Astrup, C. and Ødegaard, Ø. (1960). Internal migration and mental disease in Norway. *Psychiatric Quarterly*. Supplement **34**, 116.

Atkinson, R.C. and Shiffrin, R.M. (1971). The control of short-term memory. *Scientific American* **225**, 82.

Ax, A. (1953). The physiological differentiation between fear and anger in humans. *Psychosomatic Medicine* **15**, 433.

Baddeley, A.D. and Hitch, G.J. (1974). Working memory. In *Recent Advances in Learning and Motivation*. Vol 8. Edited by Bower, G.H. Academic Press, New York.

Baddeley, A.D. (1982). Amnesia: a minimal model and an interpretation. In *Human Memory and Amnesia*. Edited by Cermak, L.S. Erlbaum, Hillsdale, N.J.

Baddeley, A.D. (1984). The fractionation of human memory. *Psychological Medicine* **14**, 259.

Bales, R.F. and Slater, P.E. (1955). Role differentiation in small decision making groups. In *Family, Socialisation and Interaction Process*. Edited by Parsons, T. and Bales, R.F. Free Press, New York.

Balint, M. (1957). *The Doctor, His Patient and the Illness.* Tavistock, London.

Bandura, A. (1962). Social learning through imitation. In *Nebraska Symposium on Motivation.* Edited by Jones, M.R. University of Nebraska Press, Lincoln.

Bandura, A. (1969). Social learning theory of identificatory processes. In *Handbook of Socialisation Theory and Research.* Edited by Goslin, D.A. Rand McNally, Chicago.

Banfield, E. (1970). *The Heavenly City. The Nature and Future of our Urban Crisis.* Little Brown, Boston.

Bannister, D. (1963). The genesis of schizophrenic thought disorder: a serial invalidation hypothesis. *British Journal of Psychiatry* **109**, 680.

Bannister, D. and Fransella, F. (1967). A grid test of schizophrenic thought disorder. *British Journal of Social and Clinical Psychology* **5**, 95.

Bartlett, F.C. (1932). *Remembering: A Study in Experimental and Social Psychology.* Cambridge University Press, Cambridge.

Bartlett, F.C. (1953). The nature and place of thinking in medicine. *British Medical Journal* **1**, 795.

Barton, R. (1965). *Institutional Neurosis.* (2nd Edition). Wright, Bristol.

Beck, A.T. (1967). *Depression: Clinical, Experimental and Theoretical Aspects.* Harper and Row, New York.

Beck, A.T. (1974). The development of depression: a cognitive model. In *The Psychology of Depression: Contemporary Theory and Research.* Edited by Friedman, R.J. and Katz, M.M. Wiley, New York.

Beck, A.T., Rush, A.J., Shaw, B.F. and Emery, G. (1979). *Cognitive Theory of Depression.* Guildford Press, New York.

Beecher, H.K. (1956). Relationship of significance of wound to the pain experienced. *Journal of the American Medical Association* **161**, 1609.

Beecher, H.K. (1959). *Measurement of Subjective Responses.* Oxford University Press, London.

Bell, R.Q. (1968). A reinterpretation of the direction of effect in studies of socialisation. *Psychological Reviews* **75**, 81.

Bem, D.J. (1968). Attitudes and self-description: another look at the attitude-behaviour link. In *Psychological Foundations of Attitudes.* Edited by Greenwald, A.G., Brock, T.C. and Ostrom, T.M. Academic Press, New York.

Bennett, G. (1970). Bristol floods 1968: controlled survey of effect on health of local community disaster. *British Medical Journal* **3**, 454.

Berger, R.J. (1963). Experimental modification of dream content by meaningful verbal stimuli. *British Journal of Psychiatry* **109**, 722.

Berlyne, D.E. (1966). Curiosity and exploration. *Science* **153**, 25.

Berne, E. (1969). *Games People Play.* Penguin, Harmondsworth.

Bernstein, B. (Editor). (1971, 1972, 1975). *Class, Codes and Control.* (3 Vols.). Routledge and Kegan Paul, London.

Bertelanffy, L. von. (1968). *General Symptoms Theory.* Braziller, New York.

Bettelheim, B. (1971). *The Children of the Dream: Communal Child-rearing and its Implications for Society.* Paladin, London.

Birley, J.L.T. and Connolly, J. (1976). Life events and physical illness. In *Modern Trends in Psychosomatic Medicine 3.* Edited by Hill, O.W. Butterworths, London.

Blackburn, I.M., Bishop, S., Glen, A.I.M., Whalley, L.J. and Christie, J.E. (1981). The efficacy of cognitive therapy on depression: a treatment trial using cognitive therapy and pharmacotherapy, each alone and in combination. *British Journal of Psychiatry* **139**, 181.

Blakemore, C. and Cooper, J.F. (1970). Development of the brain depends on the visual environment. *Nature* **228**, 477.

Bower, G.H., Clark, M.C., Lesgold, A.M. and Winzenz, D. (1969). Hierarchical retrieval schemes in recall of categorised word lists. *Journal of Verbal Learning and Verbal Behaviour* **8**, 323.

Bower, T.G.R. (1977). *A Primer of Infant Development*. Freeman, San Francisco.

Bowlby, J. (1944). Forty-four juvenile thieves: their characters and home life. *International Journal of Psychoanalysis* **25**, 19.

Bowlby, J. (1969). *Attachment and Loss. I Attachment*. Hogarth, London.

Braine, M.D.S. (1963). The ontogeny of the English phrase structure: the first phase. *Language* **39**, 1.

Brehm, J.W, (1962). Motivational effect of cognitive dissonance. In *Nebraska Symposium on Motivation*. Edited by Jones, M.R. University of Nebraska Press, Lincoln.

Bremer, F. (1935). Cerveau isolé et physiologie du sommeil. *Compte Rendu de la Société de Biologie* (Paris) **118**, 1235.

Brickman, P. (1980). A social psychology of human concerns. In *The Development of Social Psychology*. Edited by Gilmour, R. and Duck, S. Academic Press, London.

Broadbent, D.E. (1958). *Perception and Communication*. Pergamon Press, London.

Broadbent, D.E. (1977). The hidden preattentive process. *American Psychologist* **32**, 109.

Bromley, D.B. (1963). Age differences in conceptual abilities. In *Processes of Aging: Social and Psychological Perspectives I*. Edited by Williams, R.H., Tibbitts, C. and Donahue, W. Atherton Press, New York.

Brown, G.W. (1974). Meaning, measurement and stress of life events. In *Stressful Life Events: Their Nature and Effects*. Edited by Dohrenwend, B.S. and Dohrenwend, B.P. Wiley, New York.

Brown, G.W. and Birley, J.L.T. (1968). Crisis and life changes at onset of schizophrenia. *Journal of Health and Social Behaviour* **9**, 203.

Brown, G.W. and Harris, T. (1978). *Social Origins of Depression: A Study of Psychiatric Disorders in Women*. Tavistock, London.

Brown, G.W., Monck, E.M., Carstairs, G.M. and Wing, J.K. (1962). Influence of family life on the course of schizophrenic illness. *British Journal of Preventive and Social Medicine* **16**, 55.

Brown, J.H. and Paraskevas, F. (1982). Cancer and depression: cancer presenting with depressive illness: an autoimmune disease. *British Journal of Psychiatry* **141**, 227.

Brown, R. (1973). *A First Language: the Early Stages*. Allen and Unwin, London.

Brown, R.W. (1965). *Social Psychology*. The Free Press, New York.

Bruner, J.S. (1973). *Beyond the Information Given*. Norton, New York.

Bruner, J.S., Goodnow, J.S. and Austin, G.A. (1956). *A Study of Thinking*. Wiley, New York.

Burgess, E.W. and Wallin, P. (1953). *Engagement and Marriage*. Lippincott, Philadelphia.

Burt, C. (1966). The genetic determination of differences in intelligence: a study of monozygotic twins raised together and apart. *British Journal of Educational Psychology* **57**, 137.

Byrne, P.S. and Long, B.E.L. (1976). *Doctors Talking to Patients*. HMSO, London.

Campbell, D.T. (1964). Distinguishing differences of perception from failures of communication in crosscultural studies. In *Crosscultural Understanding*. Edited by Northrop, F.S.C. and Livingstone, M.H. Harper and Row, New York and London.

Campbell, E.J.M., Scadding, J.G. and Roberts, R.S. (1979). The concept of disease. *British Medical Journal* **2**, 757.

Campbell, H.J. (1973). *The Pleasure Areas*. Eyre Methuen, London.

Cannon, W.B. (1927). The James–Lange theory of emotion: a critical examination and an alternative theory. *American Journal of Psychology* **39**, 106.

Cannon, W.B. (1932). *The Wisdom of the Body*. Norton, New York.

Card, W.I. and Good, I.J. (1971). Logical foundations of medicine. *British Medical Journal* **1**, 718.

Carpenter, G.C. (1974). Mother's face and the newborn. *New Scientist* **61**, 742.

Cattell, R.B. (1963). Theory of fluid and crystallised intelligence: a critical experiment. *Journal of Educational Psychology* **54**, 1.

Cattell, R.B. (1965). *The Scientific Analysis of Personality*. Penguin, Harmondsworth.

Cattell, R.B. (1971). *Abilities: Their Structure, Growth and Action*. Houghton Mifflin, Boston.

Cattell, R.B. and Warburton, F.W. (1961). A cross-cultural comparison of patterns of extraversion and anxiety. *British Journal of Psychology* **52**, 3.

Cherry, C. (1953). Some experiments on the recognition of speech with one and two ears. *Journal of the Acoustical Society of America* **25**, 975.

Chomsky, N. (1957). *Syntactic Structures*. Mouton, The Hague.

Christman, L.P. (1965). Nurse–physician communications in the hospital. *Journal of the American Medical Association* **194**, 541.

Clayton, P.J. (1973). The clinical morbidity of the first year of bereavement: a review. *Comprehensive Psychiatry* **14**, 151.

Collins, B.E. and Raven, B.H. (1969). Group structure: attraction, coalitions, communication and power. In *The Handbook of Social Psychology*. Vol 4. (2nd Edition). Edited by Lindsey, G. and Aronson, E. Addison-Wesley, Reading, Mass.

Cooley, C.H. (1909). *Social Organisations*. Scribner's, New York.

Craig, K.D. (1978). Social modelling influences on pain. In *The Psychology of Pain*. Edited by Sternbach, R.A. Raven Press, New York.

Craik, F.I.M. and Lockhart, R.S. (1972). Five levels of processing: a framework for memory research. *Journal of Verbal Learning and Verbal Behaviour* **11**, 671.

Dahrendorf, R. (1959). *Class and Class Conflict in Industrial Society*. Routledge and Kegan Paul, London.

Darley, J.M. and Latané, B. (1968). Bystander intervention in emergencies: diffusion of responsibility. *Journal of Personality and Social Psychology* **8**, 377.

Darley, J.M. and Latané, B. (1970). Norms and normative behaviour: field studies of social interdependence. In *Altruism and Helping Behaviour*. Edited by Macaulay, J. and Berkowitz, L. Academic Press, New York.

Davis, K. and Moore, W.E. (1945). Some principles of stratification. *American Sociological Review* **10**, 242.

Davis, R.C. (1957). Response patterns. *Transactions of the New York Academy of Sciences* **19**, 731.

Dement, W. (1960). The effect of dream deprivation. *Science* **131**, 1705.

Dement, W. and Kleitman, N. (1957). Cyclic variations in EEG during sleep and their relation to eye movements, body motility and dreaming. *Electroencephalography and Clinical Neurophysiology* **9**, 673.

Dollard, J., Miller, N.E., Doob, L., Mowrer, O.H. and Sears, R.R. (1939). *Frustration and Aggression*. Yale University Press, New Haven.

Dominion, J. (1968). *Marital Breakdown*. Penguin, Harmondsworth.

Dominion, J. (1979). Marital therapy. In *An Introduction to the Psychotherapies*. Edited by Bloch, S. Oxford University Press, London.

Dunbar, H.F. (1954). *Emotions and Bodily Changes: a Survey of Literature on Psychosomatic Interrelationships*. Columbia University Press, New York.

Duncan, S.Jr. (1972). Some signals and rules for taking speaking turns in conversations. *Journal of Personality and Social Psychology* **23**, 283.

Duncker, K. (1945). On problem solving. (Translated from the 1935 original by Lees, L.S.). *Psychological Monographs* **58**, (5), no 270.

Durkheim, E. (1964). *The Division of Labor in Society*. (First published in French 1893). Free Press, New York.

Durkheim, E. (1970). *Suicide: a Study in Sociology*. (First published in French 1897). Routledge and Kegan Paul, London.

Egbert, L.D., Battit, G.E., Welch, C.E. and Bartlett, M.K. (1964). Reduction of post operative pain by encouragement and instruction of patients. *New England Journal of Medicine* **270**, 825.

Elliott, C.D., Murray, D.J. and Pearson, L.S. (1978). *British Ability Scales.* N.F.E.R. Publishing Company.

Elmadjian, F., Hope, J.M. and Lamson, E.T. (1957). Excretion of epinephrine and nor epinephrine in various emotional states. *Journal of Clinical Endocrinology and Metabolism* **17**, 608.

Engel, B. and Bickford, A.F. (1961). Response specificity: stimulus-response and individual-response specificity in essential hypertensives. *Archives of General Psychiatry* **5**, 478.

Engel, G.L. (1962). *Psychological Development in Health and Disease.* Saunders, Philadelphia.

Epson, J.E. (1969). The mobile health clinic: an interim report on a preliminary analysis of the first 1000 patients to attend. London Borough of Southwark Health Department (Mimeo) London. Quoted by Tuckett, D. (1976). Becoming a patient. In *An Introduction to Medical Sociology.* Edited by Tuckett, D. Tavistock, London.

Evans, C.R. and Newman, E.A. (1964). Dreaming analogy from computers. *New Scientist* **24**, 577.

Evans-Pritchard, E.E. (1937). *The Azande.* Oxford University Press, London.

Evans-Pritchard, E.E. (1940). *The Nuer.* Oxford University Press, London.

Eysenck, H.J. (1953). *The Structure of Human Personality.* Methuen, London.

Eysenck, H.J. (1972). Experimental study of Freudian concepts. *Bulletin of the British Psychological Society* **25**, 261.

Eysenck, H.J. (Editor). (1973). *The Measurement of Intelligence.* Medical and Technical Press, Lancaster.

Eysenck, H.J. and Rachman, S. (1965). *The Causes and Cures of Neurosis.* Routledge and Kegan Paul, London.

Eysenck, H.J. and Wilson, G.D. (1973). *The Experimental Study of Freudian Theories.* Methuen, London.

Fabrega, H.Jr. (1975). The position of psychiatry in the understanding of human disease. *Archives of General Psychiatry* **32**, 1500.

Fantz, R.L. (1961). The origin of form perception. *Scientific American* **204**, 66.

Faris, R.E.L. and Dunham, H.W. (1939). *Mental Disorders in Urban Areas.* Chicago University Press, Chicago.

Festinger, L. (1957). *A Theory of Cognitive Dissonance.* Row-Peterson, New York.

Festinger, L., Schachter, S. and Back, K. (1968). Operation of group standards. In *Group Dynamics, Research and Theory.* Edited by Cartwright, D. and Zander, A. Harper and Row, New York.

Flannery, R.B., Sos, J. and McGovern, P. (1981). Ethnicity factor in the expression of pain. *Psychosomatics* **22**, 39.

Flavell, J.H. (1977). *Cognitive Development.* Prentice-Hall, Englewood Cliffs, N.J.

Fletcher, C. (1980). Listening and talking to patients. I The problem. *British Medical Journal* **281**, 845.

Fletcher, R. (1966). *The Family and Marriage in Britain.* Penguin, Harmondsworth.

Fonagy, P. (1986). Research on psychoanalytic concepts. In *Personality: Theory, Measurement and Research.* (2nd Edition). Edited by Fransella, F. Methuen, London.

Fordyce, W.E. (1978). Learning processes in pain. In *The Psychology of Pain.* Edited by Sternbach, R.A. Raven Press, New York.

Freedman, D.G. and Keller, B. (1963). Inheritance of behaviour in infants. *Science* **140**, 196.

Freidson, E. (1972). *Profession of Medicine: a Study of the Sociology of Applied Knowledge.* Dodd Mead, New York.

Freud, A. (1937). *The Ego and the Mechanisms of Defence.* Hogarth Press, London.

Freud, S. (1905). *Three Essays on the Theory of Sexuality.* Standard Edition, Vol. 7. Hogarth Press, London.

Freud, S. (1917). *Mourning and Melancholia.* Standard Edition, Vol. 14. Hogarth Press, London.

Freud, S. (1933). *New Introductory Lectures on Psychoanalysis*. Standard Edition, Vol. 22. Hogarth Press, London.

Freud, S. (1976). *Two Short Accounts of Psychoanalysis*. Penguin, Harmondsworth.

Friedman, M. and Rosenman, R.K. (1959). Association of specific behaviour patterns with blood cholesterol. *Journal of the American Medical Association* **169**, 1286.

Fuster, J.M. (1958). Effects of stimulation of brain stem on tachistoscopic perception. *Science* **127**, 150.

Gampel, B., Slome, C., Scotch, N.A. and Abramson, J. (1962). Urbanisation and hypertension among zulu adults. *Journal of Chronic Diseases* **15**, 67.

Gavron, H. (1968). *The Captive Wife: Conflicts of Housebound Mothers*. Penguin, Harmondsworth.

Gerth, H.H. and Mills, C.W. (1954). *Character and Social Structure*. Routledge and Kegan Paul, London.

Gesell, A. (1954). The ontogenesis of infant behaviour. In *Handbook of Child Psychology*. (2nd Edition). Edited by Carmichael, L. Wiley, New York.

Gesell, A. and Thompson, H. (1929). Learning and growth in identical twins. *Genetic Psychology Monographs* **6**, 1.

Gesell, A. and Thompson, H. (1941). Twins T and C from infancy to adolescence: a biogenetic study of individual differences by the method of co-twin control. *Genetic Psychology Monographs* **24**, 3.

Glaser, W.A. (1963). American and foreign hospitals: some sociological comparisons. In *The Hospital in Modern Society*. Edited by Freidson, E. Free Press, New York.

Glass, D.V. (Editor). (1954). *Social Mobility in Britain*. Routledge and Kegan Paul, London.

Goffman, E. (1968). *Asylums*. Penguin, Harmondsworth.

Goffman, E. (1969). *Where the action is*. Allen Lane, London.

Goldberg, E.M. and Morrison, S.L. (1963). Schizophrenia and social class. *British Journal of Psychiatry* **109**, 785.

Goldfarb, W. (1943). Effects of institutional care on adolescent personality. *Journal of Experimental Education* **12**, 106.

Goldthorpe, J.H., Lockwood, D., Bechhofer, F. and Platt, J. (1969). *The Affluent Worker in the Class Structure*. Cambridge University Press, Cambridge.

Goldthorpe, J.H. and Hope, K. (1972). Occupational grading and occupational prestige. In *The Study of Social Mobility: methods and approaches*. Edited by Hope, K. Oxford University Press, London.

Goldthorpe, J.H. and Llewellyn, C. (1977). Class mobility in modern Britain: three theses reexamined. *Sociology* **11**, No. 2, 257.

Gorer, G. (1965). *Death, Grief and Mourning*. Crescent Press, London.

Gray, J. (1971). *The Psychology of Fear and Stress*. World University Library, London.

Greer, S. (1983). Cancer and the mind. *British Journal of Psychiatry* **143**, 535.

Greer, S., Morris, T. and Pettingale, K.W. (1979). Psychological response to breast cancer: effect on outcome. *Lancet* **ii**, 785.

Greer, S., Morris, T. and Pettingale, K.W. (1981). Psychological response to breast cancer and eight year outcome. Paper presented at *American Psychological Association Convention Symposium*. August 1981.

Guilford, J.P. (1956). The structure of intellect. *Psychological Bulletin* **53**, 267.

Guilford, J.P. (1967). *The Nature of Human Intelligence*. McGraw Hill, New York.

Hadfield, J.A. (1954). *Dreams and Nightmares*. Penguin, Harmondsworth.

Hall, C.S. (1953). A cognitive theory of dream symbols. *Journal of General Psychology* **48**, 169.

Hall, C.S. and Lindzey, G. (1957). *Theories of Personality*. Wiley, New York.

Hall, J. and Jones, D.C. (1950). Social grading of occupations. *British Journal of Sociology* **1**, 31.

Hare, E.H. (1956). Mental illness and social conditions in Bristol. *Journal of Mental Science* **102**, 349.

Hare, E.H. and Shaw, G.K.M. (1965). Mental health on a new housing estate. *Maudsley Monograph No. 12*. Oxford University Press, London.

Hargreaves, D. (1972). *Interpersonal Relations and Education*. Routledge and Kegan Paul, London.

Harlow, H.F. (1949). The formation of learning sets. *Psychological Reviews* **56**, 51.

Harlow, H.F. (1959). Love in infant monkeys. *Scientific American* **200**, 68.

Harlow, H.F., Blazer, N.C. and McClearn, G.E. (1956). Manipulatory motivation in the infant rhesus monkey. *Journal of Comparative and Physiological Psychology* **49**, 444.

Harlow, H.F., Harlow, M.K., Dodsworth, R.O. and Arling, G.L. (1966). Maternal behaviour of rhesus monkeys deprived of mothering and peer associations in infancy. *Proceedings of the American Philosphical Society* **110**, 58.

Harris, A. and Clausen, R. (1966). *Labour Mobility in Britain 1953–63*. HMSO, London.

Hastrup, J.L. and Katkin, E.S. (1976). Electrodermal lability: an attempt to measure its physiological correlates. *Psychophysiology* **13**, 296.

Hathaway, S.R. and McKinley, J.C. (1943). *The Minnesota Multiphasic Personality Inventory*. University of Minnesota, Minneapolis.

Hebb, D.O. (1949). *The Organisation of Behaviour*. Wiley, New York.

Hebb, D.O. (1959). A neuropsychological theory. In *Psychology: a Study of Science*. Vol 1. Edited by Koch, S. McGraw-Hill, New York.

Hebb, D.O. (1966). *Textbook of Psychology*. Saunders, Philadelphia.

Heider, F. (1958). *The Psychology of Interpersonal Relations*. Wiley, New York.

Hernandez-Peón, R., Scherrer, H. and Jouvet, M. (1956). Modification of electric activity in cochlear nucleus during 'attention' in unanaesthetized cats. *Science* **123**, 331.

Hess, W.R. (1954). *Diencephalon: Anatomic and Extrapyramidal Functions*. Grune and Stratton, New York.

Hetherington, E.M. and Frankie, G. (1967). Effects of parental dominance, warmth and conflict on imitation in children. *Journal of Personality and Social Psychology* **6**, 119.

Hill, H.E., Kornetsky, C.H., Flanary, H.G. and Wikler, A. (1952). Effects of anxiety and morphine on discrimination of intensities of painful stimuli. *Journal of Clinical Investigation* **31**, 473.

Hinkle, L.E. and Wolff, H.G. (1958). Ecological investigations of the relationship between illness, life experiences and the social environment. *Annals of Internal Medicine* **49**, 1373.

Hinton, J.M. (1963). The physical and mental distress of the dying. *Quarterly Journal of Medicine* **32**, 1.

Hinton, J.M. (1967). *Dying*. Penguin, Harmondsworth.

Holmes, T.H. and Rahe, R.H. (1967). The social readjustment rating scale. *Journal of Psychosomatic Research* **11**, 217.

Hubel, D.H. and Wiesel, T.N. (1962) Receptive fields, binocular interaction and functional architecture in the cat's visual cortex. *Journal of Physiology* **160**, 106.

Hudson, L. (1966). *Contrary Imaginations*. Methuen, London.

Hull, C.L. (1943). *Principles of Behaviour*. Appleton-Century-Crofts, New York.

Hunt, E.B. (1962). *Concept Learning: an Information Processing Problem*. Wiley, New York.

James, W. (1884). What is emotion? *Mind* **9**, 188.

Jenkins, C.D. (1976). Recent evidence supporting psychologic and social risk factors for coronary disease. *New England Journal of Medicine* **294**, 987.

Jensen, A.R. (1969). How much can we boost IQ and scholastic achievement? *Harvard Educational Revue* **39**, 1.

Jephcott, P., Seear, N. and Smith, J.H. (1962). *Married Women Working*. Allen and Unwin, London.

Jersild, A.T. and Holmes, F.B. (1935). *Children's Fears*. Teachers College Bureau of Publications, New York.

Jevons, W.S. (1871). The power numerical discrimination. *Nature* 3, 281.

Johnson, M.L. (1953). Seeing's believing. *New Biology*. No. 15.

Jones, E.E. and Davis, K.E. (1965). From acts to dispositions: the attribution process in person perception. In *Advances in Experimental Social Psychology*. Vol 2. Edited by Berkowitz, L. Academic Press, New York.

Jones, E.E. and Nisbett, R.E. (1971). The actor and observer: divergent perceptions of the causes of behaviour. In *Attribution: perceiving the causes of behaviour*. Edited by Jones, E.E., Kanouse, D.E., Kelley, H.H., Nisbett, R.E., Valins, S. and Weiner, B. General Learning Press, Morristown.

Jones, M. (1952). *Social Psychiatry: a Study of Therapeutic Communications*. Tavistock, London.

Kahneman, D. (1973). *Attention and Effort*. Prentice-Hall, New York.

Kamin, L.J. (1974). *The Science and Politics of IQ*. Lawrence Erlbaum Associates, Potomac, Md.

Kardiner, A. (1945). *Psychological Frontiers of Society*. Columbia University Press, New York.

Kasl, S.V. and Cobb, S. (1966). Health behaviour, illness behaviour and sick role behaviour. *Archives of Environmental Health* 12, 246.

Kay, W. (1969). *Moral Development: a Psychological Study of Moral Growth from Childhood to Adolescence*. Allen and Unwin, London.

Keele, S.W. and Neill, W.T. (1978). Mechanisms of attention. In *Handbook of Perception*. Vol 9. Edited by Carterette, E.C. and Friedman, M.P. Academic Press, New York.

Kelly, G.A. (1955). *The Psychology of Personal Constructs*. Norton, New York.

Kendell, R.E. (1975). The concept of disease and its implication for psychiatry. *British Journal of Psychiatry* 127, 305.

Kimball, C.P. (1982). Stress and psychosomatic illness. *Journal of Psychosomatic Research* 26, 63.

Kinsey, A.C., Pomeroy, W.B. and Martin, C.E. (1948). *Sexual Behaviour in the Human Male*. Saunders, Philadelphia.

Kinsey, A.C., Pomeroy, W.B., Martin, C.E. and Gebhard, P.H. (1953). *Sexual Behaviour in the Human Female*. Saunders, Philadelphia.

Kline, P. (1981). *Fact and Fantasy in Freudian Theory*. (2nd Edition). Methuen, London.

Klüver, H. and Bucy, P.C. (1939). Preliminary analysis of functions of the temporal lobes in monkeys. *Archives of Neurology and Psychiatry* 42, 979.

Koffka, K. (1935). *Principles of Gestalt Psychology*. Routledge and Kegan-Paul, London.

Köhler, W. (1925). *The Mentality of Apes*. Harcourt, Brace, New York.

Kretschmer, E. (1925). *Physique and Character*. Harcourt, Brace, New York.

Kübler-Ross, E. (1969). *On Death and Dying*. MacMillan, New York.

Lacey, J.I. (1950). Individual differences in somatic response patterns. *Journal of Comparative and Physiological Psychology* 43, 338.

Lange, C. (1885). Om sindsbevaegelser et psyko-fysiolog-studie, Krønar. English translation in *The Emotions*. Edited by Dunlop, K. (1967). Hafner, New York.

Lashley, K.S. (1929). *Brain Mechanisms and Intelligence*. University of Chicago Press, Chicago.

Lazarus, R.S. (1966). *Psychological Stress and the Coping Process*. McGraw-Hill, New York.

Leach, E. (1978). Culture and reality. *Psychological Medicine* 8, 555.

Leff, J. and Vaughn, C.E. (1981). The role of maintenance therapy and relatives' expressed emotion in relapse of schizophrenia: a two-year follow-up. *British Journal of Psychiatry* 139, 102.

Leff, J., Kuipers, L., Berkowitz, R., Eberlein-Vries, R. and Sturgeon, D.A. (1982). A controlled trial of social intervention in the families of schizophrenic patients. *British Journal of Psychiatry* **141**, 121.

Lehman, H.C. (1953). *Age and Achievement*. Oxford University Press, London.

Lerner, M.J. and Lichtman, R.R. (1968). Effects of perceived norms on attitudes and altruistic behaviour towards a dependent other. *Journal of Personality and Social Psychology* **9**, 226.

Lesser, G.S., Fifer, G. and Clarke, D.H. (1965). Mental abilities of children from different social-class and cultural groups. *Monographs of the Society for Research on Child Development* 30, No. 4.

Levi, L. (1965). The urinary output of adrenalin and noradrenalin during pleasant and unpleasant emotional states: a preliminary report. *Psychosomatic Medicine* **27**, 80.

Le Vine, R.A. (1966). *Dreams and Deeds: achievement motivation in nigeria*. Chicago University Press, Illinois.

Ley, P. (1979). The psychology of compliance. In *Research in Psychology and Medicine*. Vol 2. Edited by Osborne, D.J., Gruneberg, M.M. and Eiser, J.R. Academic Press, London.

Ley, P. (1981). Professional non-compliance: a neglected problem. *British Journal of Clinical Psychology* **20**, 151.

Ley, P. (1982a). Giving information to patients. In *Social Psychology and Behavioural Medicine*. Edited by Eiser, J.R. Wiley, New York.

Ley, P. (1982b). Satisfaction, compliance and communication. *British Journal of Clinical Psychology* **21**, 241.

Likert, R.A. (1932). A technique for the measurement of attitudes. *Archives of Psychology*. No. 140.

Lindemann, E. (1944). The symptomatology and management of acute grief. *American Journal of Psychiatry* **101**, 141.

Lindsley, D.B., Schreiner, L.H., Knowles, W.B. and Magoun, H.W. (1950). Behavioural and EEG changes following chronic brain stem lesions in the cat. *Electroencephalography and Clinical Neurophysiology* **2**, 483.

Lindsley, D.B. (1957). The reticular system and perceptual discrimination. In *Reticular Formation of the Brain*. Edited by Jasper, H.H., Proctor, L.D., Knighton, R.S., Noshay, W.C. and Costello, R.T. Churchill, London.

Lipowski, Z.J. (1969). Psychosocial aspects of disease. *Annals of Internal Medicine* **71**, 1197.

Lipowski, Z.J. (1970). Physical illness, the individual and the coping process. *Psychiatry in Medicine* **1**, 91.

Loevinger, J. (1959). Patterns of parenthood and theories of learning. *Journal of Abnormal Social Psychology* **59**, 148.

Lorenz, K. (1937). The companion in the bird's world. *Auk* **54**, 245.

Lorenz, K. (1966). *On Aggression*. Methuen, London.

Luchins, A.S. (1942). Mechanization in problem-solving. *Psychological Monographs* **54**, 1.

Luria, A.R. (1973). The frontal lobes and the regulation of behaviour. In *Psychophysiology of the Frontal Lobes*. Edited by Pibram, K.H. and Luria, A.R. Academic Press, New York.

Lynch, J.J. (1973). Biofeedback: some reflections in modern behavioural science. In *Biofeedback: Behavioural Medicine*. Edited by Birk, L. Grune and Stratton, New York.

MacIver, R.M. (1937). *Society*. Macmillan, London.

Mackay, D. (1975). *Clinical Psychology: Theory and Therapy*. Essential Psychology Series. Methuen, London.

Maguire, G.P. and Rutter, D.R. (1976b). Training medical students to communicate. In *Communication Between Doctors and Patients*. Edited by Bennett, A.E. Oxford University Press for the Nuffield Provincial Hospitals Trust, London.

Maguire, G.P. and Rutter, D.R. (1976a) History taking for medical students. *Lancet* ii, 556.

Mallick, S.K. and McCandless, B.R. (1966). A study of catharsis of aggression. *Journal of Personality and Social Psychology* 4, 591.

Maltzman, I. (1955). Thinking from a behaviouristic point of view. *Psychology Review* 62, 275.

Mandler, G. (1967). Organisation and memory. In *The Psychology of Learning and Motivation*. Vol. 1. Edited by Spence, K.W. and Spence, J.T. Academic Press, New York.

Mandler, G., Mandler, J.M. and Uviller, E.T. (1958). Autonomic feedback: the perception of autonomic activity. *Journal of Abnormal and Social Psychology* 56, 367.

Marks, I.M. (1969). *Fears and Phobias*. Heinemann, London.

Martin, F.M., Brotherston, J.H.F. and Chave, S.P.W. (1957). Incidence of neurosis in a new housing estate. *British Journal of Preventive and Social Medicine* 11, 196.

Masters, W.H. and Johnson, V.E. (1966). *Human Sexual Response*. Churchill-Livingstone, London.

Masters, W.H. and Johnson, V.E. (1970). *Human Sexual Inadequacy*. Little Brown, Boston.

McArthur, L.A. (1972). The how and what of why: some determinants and consequences of causal attribution. *Journal of Personality and Social Psychology* 22, 171.

McCarthy, D. (1954). Language development in children. In *Manual of Child Psychology*. (2nd Edition). Edited by Carmichael, L. Wiley, New York.

McClelland, D.C. (1961). *The Achieving Society*. Van Nostrand, Princeton, N.J.

McClelland, D.C., Atkinson, J.W., Clark, R.A. and Cowell, E.L. (1953). *The Achievement Motive*. Appleton-Century-Crofts, New York.

McGinnies, E. (1949). Emotionality and perceptual defence. *Psychological Reviews* 56, 244.

McGuire, W.J. (1969). The nature of attitudes and attitude change. In *Handbook of Social Psychology*. Vol. 3. (2nd Edition). Edited by Lindzey, G. and Aronson, E. Addison-Wesley, Reading, Mass.

McKellar, P. (1949). The emotion of anger in the expression of human aggression. *British Journal of Psychology* 39, 3.

McKellar, P. (1950). Provocation to anger in the development of attitudes of hostility. *British Journal of Psychology* 40, 3.

McKellar, P. (1957). *Imagination and Thinking*. Cohen and West, London.

Mead, M. (1958). Adolescence in primitive and modern society. In *Readings in Social Psychology*. Edited by Macoby, E.E., Newcomb, T.M. and Harty, E.L. Henry Holt, New York.

Mead, M. (1962). *Male and Female: A Study of the Sexes in a Changing World*. Penguin, Harmondsworth.

Mechanic, D. (1962). The concept of illness behaviour. *Journal of Chronic Diseases* 15, 189.

Mechanic, D. (1964). The influence of mothers on their children's health behaviour. *Pediatrics* 38, 444.

Mechanic, D. (1968). *Medical Sociology*. Free Press, New York.

Medalie, J.H. and Kahn, H.A. (1973). Myocardial infarction over a five year period. I Prevalence, incidence and mortality experience. *Journal of Chronic Diseases* 26, 63.

Meichenbaum, D.H. and Smart, I. (1971). Use of direct expectancy to modify academic performance and attitudes of college students. *Journal of Counselling Psychology* 18, 531.

Meltzoff, J. and Kornreich, M. (1970). *Research in Psychotherapy*. Atherton, New York.

Melzack, R. and Scott, T.H. (1957). The effects of early experience on the response to pain. *Journal of Comparative Psysiology and Psychology* 50, 155.

Melzack, R. and Wall, P.D. (1965). Pain mechanisms: a new theory. *Science* **150**, 971.
Merskey, H. and Spear, F.H. (1967). *Pain: Psychological and Psychiatric Aspects.* Ballière, Tindall and Cassell, London.
Meyersburg, H.A. and Post, R.M. (1979). An holistic developmental view of neural and psychological processes; a neurobiologic-psychoanalytic integration. *British Journal of Psychiatry* **135**, 139.
Milgram, S. (1974) *Obedience to Authority.* Harper and Row, New York.
Miller, N.E. (1944). Experimental studies of conflict. In *Personality and the Behaviour Disorders.* Edited by Hunt, J. McV. Ronald Press, New York.
Miller, N.E. (1969). Learning of visceral and glandular responses. *Science* **163**, 434.
Miller, W.R., Seligman, M.E.P. and Kurlander, H.M. (1975). Learned helplessness, depression and anxiety. *Journal of Nervous and Mental Disease* **161**, 347.
Mills, C. Wright. (1959). *The Sociological Imagination.* Oxford University Press, London.
Milner, B. (1963). Effects of different brain lesions on card sorting. *Archives of Neurology* **9**, 90.
Moray, N. (1959). Attention in dichotic listening: affective cues and the influence of instructions. *Quarterly Journal of Experimental Psychology* **11**, 56.
Moray, N. (1967). Where is capacity limited? a survey and a model. *Acta Psychologica* **27**, 84.
Moray, N. (1969). *Attention: Selective Processes in Vision and Hearing.* Hutchinson, London.
Moruzzi, G. and Magoun, H.W. (1949). Brain stem reticular formation and activation of the EEG. *Electroencephalography and Clinical Neurophysiology* **1**, 455.
Moscovici, S. and Faucheux, C. (1972). Social influence, conformity bias, and the study of active minorities. In *Advances in Experimental Social Psychology.* Vol. 6. Edited by Berkowitz, L. Academic Press, New York.
Mowrer, O.H. (1950). *Learning Theory and Personality Dynamics.* Ronald, New York.
Murdock, G.P. (1949). *Social Structure.* Macmillan, New York.
Murphy, H.B.M. (1977). Migration, culture and mental health. *Psychological Medicine* **7**, 677.
Murray, H.A. (1943). *Thematic Apperception Test.* Harvard University Press, Cambridge, Mass.
Naitoh, P. (1975). Sleep deprivation in humans. In *Research in Psychophysiology.* Edited by Venables, P.H. and Christie, M.J. Wiley, New York.
Newell, A. and Simon, H.A. (1963). GPS, a program that simulates human thought. In *Computers and Thought.* Edited by Feigenbaum, E.A. and Feldman, J. McGraw-Hill, New York.
Notturno, M.A. (1984). The Popper/Kuhn debate: truth and two faces of relativism. *Psychological Medicine* **14**, 273.
Ødegard, Ø. (1932). Emigration and insanity. *Acta Psychiatrica Scandinavica.* Supp. 4.
Olds, J. and Milner, P.M. (1954). Positive reinforcement produced by electrical stimulation of the septal area and other regions of the rat brain. *Journal of Comparative and Physiological Psychology* **47**, 419.
Orne, M.T. (1962). On the social psychology of the psychological experiment: with particular reference to demand characteristics and their implications. *American Psychologist* **17**, 776.
Oswald, I. (1980). *Sleep.* (4th Edition). Penguin, Harmondsworth.
Oswald, I., Taylor, A.M. and Treisman, M. (1960). Discriminative responses to stimulation during human sleep. *Brain* **83**, 440.
Papez, J.W. (1937). A proposed mechanism of emotion. *Archives of Neurology and Psychiatry* **38**, 725.
Parkes, C.M. (1965). Bereavement and mental illness. Part II A classification of bereavement reactions. *British Journal of Medical Psychology* **38**, 1.
Parkes, C.M. (1975). *Bereavement: Studies of Grief in Adult Life.* Penguin, Harmondsworth.

Parkes, C.M. and Brown, R.J. (1972). Health after bereavement: a controlled study of young Boston widows and widowers. *Psychosomatic Medicine* **34**, 449.

Parloff, M.B., Waskow, I.E. and Wolfe, B.E. (1978). Research on therapist variables in relation to process and outcome. In *Handbook of Psychotherapy and Behaviour Change: an Emprical Analysis*. (2nd Edition). Edited by Garfield, S.L. and Bergin, A.E. Wiley, New York.

Parry, J. (1967). *The Psychology of Human Communication*. University of London Press, London.

Parsons, T. (1951). *The Social System*. The Free Press, New York.

Paykel, E.S. (1974). Recent life events and clinical depression. In *Life Stress and Illness*. Edited by Gunderson, E.K. and Rahe, R.H. Charles C. Thomas, Springfield, Illinois.

Paykel, E.S., Myers, J.K., Dienelt, M.N., Klerman, G.L., Lindenthal, J.J. and Pepper, M.P. (1969). Life events and depression: a controlled study. *Archives of General Psychiatry* **21**, 753.

Peck, D. and Whitlow, D. (1975). *Approaches to Personality Theory*. Essential Psychology Series. Methuen, London.

Pendleton, D. (1983). Doctor–patient communication: a revue. In *Doctor–Patient Communication*. Edited by Pendleton, D. and Haslar, J. Academic Press, London.

Peterson, C.R. and Peterson, M.J. (1959). Short-term retention of individual verbal items. *Journal of Experimental Psychology* **58**, 193.

Pettingale, K.W., Merrett, T.G. and Tee, D.E.H. (1977). Prognostic value of serum levels of immunoglobulins (IgG, IgA, IgM and IgE) in breast cancer: a preliminary study. *British Journal of Cancer* **36**, 550.

Piaget, J. (1932). *The Moral Judgement of the Child*. Routledge and Kegan Paul, London.

Piaget, J. (1966). *The Origins of Intelligence in the Child*. Routledge and Kegan Paul, London.

Pietroni, P.C. (1984). Holistic medicine: new map, old territory. *British Journal of Holistic Medicine* **1**, 3.

Piliavin, I., Rodin, J. and Piliavin, J. (1969). Good samaritanism: an underground phenomenon? *Journal of Personality and Social Psychology* **13**, 289.

Pilowsky, I. (1969). Abnormal illness behaviour. *British Journal of Medical Psychology* **42**, 347.

Pilowsky, I. (1978). A general classification of abnormal illness behaviours. *British Journal of Medical Psychology* **51**, 131.

Popper, K.R. (1959). *The Logic of Scientific Discovery*. Hutchinson, London.

Pritchard, M.J. (1974). Meaning of illness and patients' response to long-term haemodialysis. *Journal of Psychosomatic Research* **18**, 457.

Pritchard, M.J. (1982). Psychological pressure in a renal unit. *British Journal of Hospital Medicine* **27**, 512.

Pruitt, D.G. (1967). Reward structure and cooperation: the decomposed Prisoner's Dilemma game. *Journal of Personality and Social Psychology* **7**, 21.

Rapoport, R.N. (1960). *Community as Doctor*. Tavistock, London.

Resnick, L.B. (Editor). (1976). *The Nature of Intelligence*. Lawrence Erlbaum Associates, Hillsdale, New Jersey.

Richardson, P.H. and Vincent, C.A. (1986). Acupuncture for the treatment of pain: a review of evaluative research. *Pain* **24**, 15.

Ridgeway, V. and Mathews, A. (1982). Psychological preparation for surgery: a comparison of methods. *British Journal of Clinical Psychology* **21**, 271.

Rivers, W.H.R. (1901). Visual spatial perception. Part I, Vol. II of *Reports of the Cambridge Anthropological Expedition to Torres Straits*. Edited by Haddon, A.C. Cambridge University Press, Cambridge.

Roethlisberger, F.J. and Dickson, W.J. (1939). *Management and the Worker: an Account of a Research Program Conducted by the Western Electric Company, Hawthorne Works, Chicago*. Harvard University Press, Cambridge, Mass.

Rogers, C.R. (1951). *Client Centred Therapy*. Houghton, Boston, Mass.

Rogers, C.R. (1959). A theory of therapy, personality and interpersonal relationships as developed in a client-centred framework. In *Psychology: a Study of a Science. Study I: Conceptual and Systematic. Vol. 3. Formulations of the Persons and the Social Context*. Edited by Koch, S. McGraw-Hill, New York.

Rogers, C.R. (1970). *Encounter Groups*. Penguin, Harmondsworth.

Rokeach, M. (1960). *The Open and Closed Mind: Investigations into the Nature of Belief Systems and Personality*. Basic Books, New York.

Rosenhan, D.L. (1973). On being sane in insane places. *Science* **179**, 250.

Rosenstock, I.M. (1967). Why people use health services. In *Health Services Research*. Edited by Mainland, D. Millbank Fund, New York. (Reprinted from Millbank Memorial Fund Quarterly. 1966. **44**. Part 2.)

Rosenthal, R. (1966). *Experimenter effects in behavioural research*. Appleton-Century-Crofts, New York.

Rosenthal, R, and Jacobson, L. (1968). *Pygmalion in the Classroom: Teacher Expectations and Pupils' Intellectual Development*. Holt, Rinehart and Winston, New York.

Rotter, J.B. (1966). Generalised expectancies for internal versus external control of reinforcement. *Psychological Monographs* **80**, No. 1.

Routtenberg, A. (1968). The two arousal hypotheses: reticular formation and limbic system. *Psychological Reviews* **75**, 51.

Rutter, M. (1972). *Maternal Deprivation Reassessed*. Penguin, Harmondsworth.

Rutter, M. (1979). *Changing Youth in a Changing Society: Patterns of Adolescent Development and Disorder*. The Nuffield Provincial Hospitals Trust, London.

Rutter, D.R. and Maguire, G.P. (1976). History taking for medical students. II Evaluation of a training programme. *Lancet* **ii**, 558.

Saunders, C. (1959). *Care of the Dying*. Macmillian, London.

Scadding, J.G. (1967). Diagnosis: the clinician and the computer. *Lancet* **ii**, 877.

Schachter, S. and Singer, J.E. (1962). Cognitive, social and physiological determinants of emotional states. *Psychological Reviews* **69**, 379.

Schnore, M.M. (1959). Individual patterns of psysiological activity as a function of task differences and degree of arousal. *Journal of Experimental Psychology* **58**, 117.

Schofield, M. (1965). *The Sexual Behaviour of Young People*. Longmans, London.

Scotch, N.A. (1963). Sociocultural factors in the epidemiology of Zulu hypertension. *American Journal of Public Health* **53**, 125.

Sears, R.R. (1936). Experimental studies of projection: I Attribution of traits. *Journal of Social Psychology* **7**, 151.

Seligman, M.E.P. (1975). *Helplessness: on Depression, Development and Death*. W.H. Freeman, San Francisco.

Selye, H. (1956). *The Stress of Life*. McGraw-Hill, New York.

Shekelle, R.B., Raynor, W.J., Ostfeld, A.M., Garron, D.C., Bieliauskas, L. A., Liu, S.C., Maliza, C. and Oglesby, P. (1981). Psychological depression and 17 year risk of death from cancer. *Psychosomatic Research* **43**, 117.

Sheldon, W.H. and Stevens, S.S. (1942). *The Varieties of Temperament*. Harper, New York.

Sherif, M. (1935). A study of some social factors in perception. *Archives of Psychology* **27**, No. 187.

Sherrington, C.G. (1906). *The Integrative Action of the Nervous System*. Yale University Press.

Shields, J. (1962). *Monozygotic Twins*. Oxford University Press, London.

Skinner, B.F. (1948). *Walden Two*. Macmillan, New York.

Skinner, B.F. (1957). *Verbal Behaviour*. Appleton-Century-Crofts, New York.

Slater, E. and Woodside, M. (1951). *Patterns of Marriage: a Study of Marriage Relationships in the Urban Working Classes*. Cassell, London.

Sokolov, E.N. (1960). Neuronal models and the orienting reflex. In *The Central*

Nervous System and Behaviour. Edited by Brazier, M.A.B. Josiah Macey Jr. Foundation, New York.

Sorokin, P.A. (1937). *Social and Cultural Dynamics*. 4 Vol. Badminster Press, Englewood Cliffs, N.J.

Spearman, C. (1904). 'General Intelligence' objectively determined and measured. *American Journal of Psychology* 15, 201.

Sperling, G. (1960). The information available in brief visual presentations. *Psychological Monographs* 74, No. 11.

Sperry, R.W. (1964). The great cerebral commissure. *Scientific American* 210, 42.

Sperry, R.W. (1974). Lateral specialisation in the surgically separated hemispheres. In *The Neurosciences: Third Study Program*. Edited by Schmitt, F.O. and Warden, F.G. M.I.T. Press, Cambridge, Mass.

Spitz, R.A. (1945). Hospitalism: an inquiry into the genesis of psychiatric conditions in early childhood. *Psychoanalytical Studies of the Child* 1, 53.

Sternbach, R.A. and Tursky, B. (1965). Ethnic differences among housewives in psychological and skin potential responses to electric shock. *Psychophysiology* 1, 241.

Sternberg, S. (1966). High-speed scanning in human memory. *Science* 153, 652.

Stoll, B.A. (1979). Restraint of growth and spontaneous regression of cancer. In *Mind and Cancer Prognosis*. Edited by Stoll, B.A. Wiley, Chichester.

Storms, M.D. (1973). Videotape and the attribution process: reversing actors' and observers' points of view. *Journal of Personality and Social Psychology* 27, 165.

Storr, A. (1968). *Human Agression*. Penguin, Harmondsworth.

Sturgeon, D., Kuipers, L., Berkowitz, R., Turpin, G. and Leff, J. (1981). Psychophysiological responses of schizophrenic patients to high and low expressed emotion relatives. *British Journal of Psychiatry* 138, 40.

Syme, S.L., Human, M.M. and Enterline, P.E. (1965). Cultural mobility and the occurence of coronary heart disease. *Journal of Health and Human Behaviours* 6, 178.

Syme, S.L., Berhani, N.O. and Buechley, R.W. (1966). Cultural mobility and coronary heart disease in an urban area. *American Journal of Epidemiology* 82, 334.

Szasz, T.S. (1961). *The Myth of Mental Illness*. Hoeber, New York.

Szasz, T.S. and Hollander, M.H. (1956). A contribution to the philosophy of medicine: the basic models of the doctor–patient relationship. *A.M.A. Archives of Internal Medicine* 97, 585.

Taylor, F. Kräupl. (1976). The medical model of the disease concept. *British Journal of Psychiatry* 128, 588.

Taylor, S. (1938). Surburban neurosis. *Lancet* i, 759.

Taylor, S. and Chave, S.P.W. (1964). *Mental Health and Environment*. Longmans, London.

Taylor, T.R., Mitcheson, J. and McGirr, E.M. (1971). Doctors as decision-makers: a computer-assisted study of diagnosis as a cognitive skill. *British Medical Journal* 3, 35.

Tennant, C. (1983). Editorial. Life events and psychological morbidity: the evidence from prospective studies. *Psychological Medicine* 13, 483.

Terman, L.M. (1938). *Psychological Factors in Marital Happiness*. McGraw-Hill, New York.

Thomas, G. (1949). *Labour Mobility in Great Britain 1945–49*. HMSO, London.

Thorndike, E.L. (1911). *Animal Intelligence*. Macmillan, New York.

Thurstone, L.L. (1938). Primary mental abilities. *Psychometric Monograph*. No. 4.

Thurstone, L.L. and Chave, E.J. (1929). *The Measurement of Attitudes*. University of Chicago Press, Chicago.

Tinbergen, N. (1951). *The Study of Instinct*. Clarenden Press, Oxford.

Tolman, E.C. and Honzik, C.H. (1930). Introduction and removal of reward and maze performance of rats. *University of California Publications in Psychology* 4, 257.

Tönnies, F. (1955). *Community and Association*. Routledge and Kegan Paul, London. (First published in German 1887).

Torda, C. (1968). Observations on a physiological process related to dreams. *Communications in Behavioural Biology* 2, 39.

Torgerson, W.S. (1958). *Theory and Methods of Scaling*. Wiley, New York.

Treisman, A.M. (1960). Contextual cues in selective listening. *Quartely Journal of Experimental Psychology* 12, 242.

Treisman, A.M. (1964). Verbal cues, language and meaning in selective attention. *American Journal of Psychology* 77, 206.

Trethowan, W.H. and Conlon, M.F. (1965). The 'couvade' syndrome. *British Journal of Psychiatry* 111, 16.

Truax, C.B. and Carkhuff, R.R. (1967). *Towards Effective Counselling and Psychotherapy*. Aldine, Chicago.

Tuckett, D. (1976). (Editor). *An Introduction to Medical Sociology*. Tavistock, London.

Tulving, E. (1972). Episodic and semantic memory. In *Organisation and Memory*. Edited by Tulving, E. and Donaldson, W. Academic Press, New York.

Tyrer, P. (1976). Towards rational therapy with mono-amine oxidase inhibitors. *British Journal of Psychiatry* 128, 354.

Tyrer, S.P. (1986). Learned pain behaviour. *British Medical Journal* 292, 1.

Underwood, G. (1976). *Attention and Memory*. Pergamon Press, Oxford.

Ursin, H., Boade, E. and Levine, S. (1978). *Psychobiology of Stress: a Study of Coping in Man*. Academic Press, New York.

Valentine, C. (1930). The innate causes of fear. *Journal of Genetic Psychology* 37, 394.

Valins, S. (1970). The perception and labelling of bodily changes as determinants of emotional behaviour. In *Physiological Correlates of Emotion*. Edited by Black, P. Academic Press, New York.

Vaughn, C.E. and Leff, J. (1976). The influence of family and social factors on the course of psychiatric illness. *British Journal of Psychiatry* 129, 125.

Verba, S. (1961). *Small Groups and Political Behaviour: a Study of Leadership*. Princeton University Press, Princeton.

Vernon, P.E. (1950). *The Structure of Human Abilities*. Methuen, London.

Vernon, P.E. (1969). *Intelligence and Cultural Environment*. Methuen, London.

Vogel, G.W. (1975). A review of REM sleep deprivation. *Archives of General Psychiatry* 32, 749.

Wadsworth, M., Butterfield, W.J.H. and Blaney, R. (1971). *Health and Sickness: The Choice of Treatment*. Tavistock, London.

Walk, R.D. and Gibson, E.J. (1961). A comparative and analytical study of visual depth perception. *Psychological Monographs*. Vol. 75, No. 519.

Wardwell, W.I., Hyman, M.M. and Bahnson, C.B. (1964). Stress and coronary disease in three field studies. *Journal of Chronic Diseases* 17, 73.

Wardwell, W.I. Hyman, M.M. and Bahnson, C.B. (1968). Socio-environmental antecedents to coronary heart disease in 87 white males. *Social Science and Medicine* 2, 165.

Wason, P.C. and Johnson-Laird, P.N. (1972). *Psychology of Reasoning: Structure and Content*. B.T. Batsford, London.

Watson, J.B. (1924). *Behaviourism*. Norton, New York.

Watson, J.B. and Rayner, R. (1920). Conditional emotional reactions. *Journal of Experimental Psychology* 3, 1.

Waugh, N.C. and Norman, D.A. (1965). Primary memory. *Psychological Revues* 72, 89.

Weber, M. (1952). *The Protestant Ethic and the Spirit of Capitalism*. Allen and Unwin, London. (First published in German in 1904/5).

Weber, M. (1964). *The Theory of Social and Economic Organization*. Free Press, New York. (First published in German 1925).

Wenger, M.A., Clemens, T.L., Darsie, M.L., Engel, B.T., Estess, F.M. and Sonnenschein, R.R. (1960). Autonomic response patterns during intravenous infusion of epinephrine and norepinephrine. *Psychosomatic Medicine* 22, 294.

Whiting, B.B. (1963). *Six Cultures: Studies of Child Rearing*. Wiley, New York.

Wichman, H. (1970). Effects of isolation and communication on cooperating in a two-person game. *Journal of Personality and Social Psychology* **16**, 114.

Wicker, A.W. (1969). Attitudes versus actions: the relationship of verbal and overt behavioural responses to attitude objects. *Journal of Social Issues* **25**, 41.

Wilkinson, R.T. (1965). Sleep deprivation. In *Sleep Deprivation*. Edited by Bacharach, A.L. and Edholm, O.G. Academic Press, London.

Wilson, E.O. (1975). *Sociobiology*. Harvard University Press, Cambridge, Mass.

Wirth, L. (1963). *Urbanism as a Way of Life in Cities in Society*. Edited by Hatt, P.K. and Reiss, A.J. Free Press New York. (First published in *American Journal of Sociology* 1938, **44**.)

Witkin, H.A., Dyk, R.B., Faterson, H.F., Goodenough, D.R. and Karp, S.A. (1962). *Psychological Differentiation*. Wiley, New York.

Wolf. S. and Wolff, H.G. (1943). *Human Gastric Function*. Oxford University Press, London.

Wolpe, J. (1958). *Psychotherapy by Reciprocal Inhibition*. Stanford University Press, Stanford, California.

Wynne, L.C. and Solomon, R.L. (1955). Traumatic avoidance learning: acquisition and extinction in dogs deprived of normal peripheral autonomic functions. *Genetic Psychology Monographs* **52**, 241.

Yerkes, R.M. and Dodson, J.D. (1908). The relation of strength of stimulus to rapidity of habit formation. *Journal of Comparative and Physiological Psychology* **18**, 458.

Young, M. (1965). *The Rise of the Meritocracy*. Penguin, Harmondsworth.

Young, M. and Willmott, P. (1956). Social gradings by manual workers. *British Journal of Sociology* **7**, 337.

Young, M. and Willmott, P. (1957). *The Family and Kinship in East London*. Routledge and Kegan Paul, London.

Young, M. and Willmott, P. (1960). *Family and Class in a London Suburb*. Routledge and Kegan Paul, London.

Young, M. and Willmott. P. (1973). *The Symmetrical Family*. Routledge and Kegan Paul, London.

Yudkin, S. and Holme, A. (1963). *Working Mothers and Their Children*. Michael Joseph, London.

Zajonc, R.B. (1966). *Social Psychology: an Experimental Approach*. Wadsworth, Belmont.

Zborowski, M. (1952). Cultural components in responses to pain. *Journal of Social Sciences* **8**, 16.

Zola, I.K. (1973). Pathways to the doctor: from person to patient. *Social Science and Medicine* **7**, 677.

Zuckerman, M., Kolin, E.A., Price. L., and Zoob, I. (1964). Development of a sensation-seeking scale. *Journal of Consulting and Clinical Psychology* **28**, 477.

Zuckerman, M., Bone. R.N., Neary, R., Mangelsdorff, D., and Brustman, B. (1972). What is the sensation-seeker? Personality trait and experience correlates of the sensation-seeking scales. *Journal of Consulting and Clinical Psychology* **39**, 308.

Name index

In the case of co-authorship only the first named author has been included.

Subject index